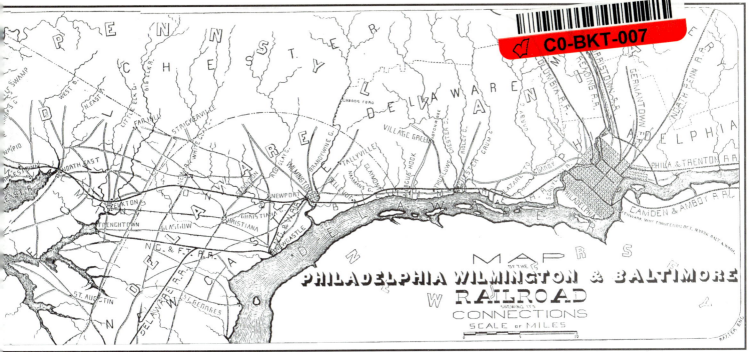

PW&B 1856 Guide/Ted Xaras Collection

into the heart of B&O territory, and the pioneering Baltimore & Ohio RR itself, always a challenger to PRR. Not yet in existence is the Baltimore & Potomac RR, which would become critical to Thomson's triumphant success in the struggle to access the nation's capital and assemble a New York-Washington route despite B&O's repeated obstructions.

This map predates B&O's own line constructed in 1886 between Baltimore and Philadelphia, born of necessity out of John Garrett's abysmal 1881 failure in the hotly contested PW&B sweepstakes. Note the four wide rivers (three of them primarily tidal inlets) that the lower end of the PW&B line had to cross to reach Baltimore.

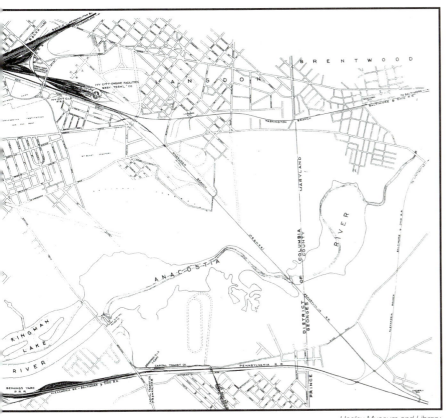

Hagley Museum and Library

Washington DC, PRR's southern destination, is shown in this overview of the area dated 17 March 1943. The PB&W passenger main, known as the Magruder Branch, extends from Landover MD at lower right to the junction with the B&O Washington (upper right) and Metropolitan (top) Branches. Here were located the B&O Washington yards and New York Avenue freight station. Alongside the PB&W main is the Ivy City engine terminal, and to the southwest Washington Union Station, both operated by the Washington Terminal RR.

The PRR freight branch leaves the passenger main at Landover and runs past Bennings Yard before crossing the Anacostia River and through the Virginia Avenue Tunnel, where it joins with the passenger connection through the 1st Street Tunnel. It then passes several small freight yards and the 7th Street station before crossing the Long Bridge and entering Potomac Yard, owned by the Richmond, Fredericksburg & Potomac RR.

Triumph VI

**PHILADELPHIA, COLUMBIA,
HARRISBURG TO BALTIMORE
AND WASHINGTON DC**

1827 - 2003

by Charles S. Roberts
and
David W. Messer

"Books that make a Difference"

COPYRIGHT © 2003 BARNARD, ROBERTS AND CO., INC.
Manufactured in the United States of America

FIRST EDITION September 2003

Published by
BARNARD, ROBERTS AND CO., INC.
2606 Willow Avenue
P. O. Box 7344
Baltimore MD 21227
(410) 247-2242

ISBN 0-934118-28-0

FRONTISPIECE: Although PRR had made implementation of its vaunted "four-track system" a priority on the east-west main and between Philadelphia and New York City as early as the mid-1870s (for the Centennial Exposition), installation on the line between Philadelphia and Washington took place piecemeal over several decades, extending into the World War II era. However, the track just south of Philadelphia received four tracks in the early 1890s, as this stunning early morning view looking southward near Norwood shows. A northbound "flyer" speeding toward the City in 1892 meets a general merchandise freight headed south. In the distance we can just make out the fourth track in the process of being laid. *Ted Xaras Collection.*

COVER: Penn Station in Baltimore was a grand symbol of PRR's incursion into B&O's home turf and the various victories achieved. It is seen here in a 1998 night scene under the Amtrak flag. Sadly, it is also a monument to PRR's flawed strategy of reliance on passenger business, a bottomless pit of capital expenditure and operating losses which would play a major role in the demise of PRR. By the way, this photo is the second to grace a Triumph cover by the talented *Thomas Fuchs.*

A NOTE ABOUT CREDITS: Lack of credits indicate that the subject came from the camera or collection of the authors, the library of the publisher or from untraceable sources. Some material obviously originated with the railroad (e.g. track charts) so credits were not used in these cases.

Dedication

Thomas Swann 1809 – 1883

Thomas Swann was unanimously elected president of the Baltimore and Ohio Rail Road on 11 October 1848. The railroad had reached Cumberland MD in 1842 and had been stalled there for six years. Meanwhile, PRR had been chartered in 1846 and beginning to get their act together.

Swann was a politician. In a long career marked by rough and tumble infighting, he was Attorney General of the United States, 37th Governor of Maryland and Mayor of Baltimore. Numerous historians have, with disdain and distaste, derided his practice of the "art of politics" as violent and brutal.

But in 1848, stiffed by the States of Pennsylvania and Virginia, B&O desperately needed just such a man to lead the railroad to its goal of the Ohio River at Wheeling.

With his brilliant chief-engineer Benjamin H. Latrobe, Swann took just four years to complete the railroad via the notorious West End and create the largest trunkline of the times. His accomplishment was a great victory.

Yet this was just the *first* battle in the B&O/PRR war and, as this book will detail, proved to be the *last* major conflict won by B&O. By 1873 B&O was in third place, never to recover.

We visited his grave in Greenmount Cemetery in Baltimore a few years ago and noted that we were both born on the third of February. Mother, an accomplished artist, has painted his mansion Morven Park in Leesburg VA. We alone in the family have yet to visit his home.

That Swann was our great-grandmother's brother has nothing to do with our decision to dedicate this book to him. It just doesn't seem fair that this conqueror, a hero of the times, has never received the accolades due him.

This book seemed like an appropriate place to acknowledge his triumph.

Charles Swann Roberts
30 August 2003

Table of Contents_____

Chapter A

Genesis

The Quest for the Golden Grain

Digital shaded-relief portrayal of landforms of the conterminous United States by Gail P. Thelin and Richard J . Pike 1991. U.S. Geological Survey, vertical exaggeration 2x.

THIS IS THE STAGE on which the titanic struggle for the Ohio River and Maryland was fought between pioneer Baltimore and Ohio Railroad and challenger Pennsylvania Railroad. The result was a contest that kindled the creation of a vast agricultural and industrial Superpower that remains beyond comparison in the history of the planet.

The roots of the story took hold in Europe as continuous wars between Great Britain, France, Spain and the Netherlands. These empires had been at each other's throats for thousands of years. The discovery of a New World broadened the field of battle.

The Spanish thirsted for gold and conquered South and Central America. The other three powers decided to vie for furs, the French and British in Canada and the British and Dutch along the Atlantic coast. The fur trade was the principal economic activity north of the Gulf Coast for many, many years as odd as this seems today.

In the event, the British reigned supreme along the East Coast and ultimately in Canada. Colonization in this arena was mostly, but not entirely, British. These Europeans occupied the coastal regions and began to farm the Coastal Plains and rolling Piedmont areas. The topsoil was one or two feet deep and while it ultimately would be tagged as "tired soil" it was nonetheless reasonably fertile and close to water transportation, both tidal and inland.

After providing for local consumption, food and fibre were exported and exchanged for manufactured goods, principally from Britain where the Industrial Revolution was born. A considerable trade went to Central and South America. Imports from the latter areas were primarily sugar, rum and guano.

Three principal ports handled most of this trade – New York, Philadelphia and Baltimore. In short order, New York became the commercial capital of the nation for several very good reasons.

First, she boasted the finest natural port in the world with easy ingress and egress from tidewater no matter which way the wind was blowing, a vital advantage in the days of sail.

Second, the Hudson River provided a splendid pathway from the interior directly to the port and served a large and productive agricultural area.

Third, New York was much closer to Europe than the other two ports and quickly dominated the nation's trade, exporting furs and then grain and importing manufactured goods.

Philadelphia was not as well placed, being farther from Europe and able only to draw on the Delaware and Schuykill River valleys, in relative size much smaller than the Hudson Valley and environs. As this map clearly shows, the Piedmont hills press rather closely to the port, complicating overland transportation from inner farming valleys.

Baltimore was a mixed bag vis-á-vis her two rivals. She was most distant from Europe and burdened with the two-hundred mile long Chesapeake Bay which obviously ran in the wrong direction. Worse, in the era of sail northerly or southerly winds would stall trade for days on end. Baltimore was blessed with a large and fertile agricultural area, much of it served by water and the balance by short roads.

Also, Baltimore was better placed in regard to Central and South America. But above all, those lush valleys in central Pennsylvania led to Baltimore – not Philadelphia. Thus, Baltimore became the "flour capital of the world" and during the first third of the 19th Century vied with Philadelphia as the nation's "second major port."

All this, however, is just the beginning of the saga. Look to the west, past the mountains and notice what is the *most fertile and vast granary on Earth*. It stretches 1200 miles west and 1200 miles north into Canada and down to the Gulf of Mexico. Here the topsoil is *fifteen feet deep* and corn literally grows as high as an elephant's eye.

There are five *billion* acres in this incredible region which stretches from the Great Mountain Barrier in the East to the Rocky Mountains in the West. Plus another huge and abundant crescent southeast and south of the Barrier.

Then *and now* this mindboggling granary is capable of providing food and fibre for the *entire planet*.

There are only three basic human activities . . . growing things, making things and carrying things. Now Mother Nature has been very generous in creating resources for all of these needs, but with a perversity quite reasonably associated with the female gender, She rarely puts her gifts where mankind wants to use them. Thus *carrying things* at reasonable cost is an essential element in the equation. She says, with a charming smirk, I'll give you what you need but you are going to have to work for it.

And, indeed, she laced her granary with equally vast river systems and giant lakes on which to carry her bounty. But most of these rivers ran south to the Gulf of Mexico and New Orleans, *not* to the eastern seaports. And in the wrong direction in relation to Europe.

She also neatly placed a thousand-mile long chain of mountains between the granary and eastern seaports and made this chain about 150 miles wide. To be sure, she gave our forefathers one through valley – the Hudson – and then a few rivers west through New York State, all of which ran in the wrong direction. On top of all that, She made sure that the distances would be as vast as the prize. They are measured by *thousands* of miles.

Well, the fledgling United States had "married" this granary via the Louisiana Purchase in 1803 but the honeymoon was over in short order. To bed this bride, our forefathers had to get to the bedroom over this mountain barrier with an overland transportation system that made economic sense.

There was no such system in existence.

The brilliant philosopher/historian Will Durant averred that the history of mankind has been characterized by two eternal wars . . . the wars between men and the wars between the sexes. In this story, we must add the struggle against *gravity* and *distance*.

Durant also said that "when genius stands in our presence we can only bow down before it as an act of God, a continuance of creation. Such men are the very life-blood of history, to which politics and industry are but frame and bones."

In February of 1827 the genesis of the solution began in an unremarkable city in a small State. Baltimore, Maryland. The Baltimore and Ohio Rail Road Company was chartered in this city in that month.

The stirring and stunning adventure story that ensued is told in this book.

The aged Charles Carroll of Carrollton, the last surviving signer of the Declaration of Independence, was the principal feature at the laying of the first stone of the Baltimore and Ohio Rail Road near Mt. Clare in Baltimore on 4 July 1828.

> "This is among the most important acts of my life, second only to my signing of the Declaration, even if it be second to that."

So spoke Charles Carroll, or so it is said. As an equally-aged historian of some experience, we have learned to become suspicious of prophetic statements that gain wide currency many years after the event.

Yet Alfred, Lord Tennyson "dipt into the future" and saw a vision of "heavens filled with commerce, argosies of magic sails" so perhaps Carroll was on to something. This 1828 ceremony, by the way, was a full Masonic function and Carroll was Roman Catholic – in fact, the only Roman Catholic signer of the Declaration. Catholicism and Freemasonry were not exactly bedfellows then and now, so this act of unity is refreshing. As in Love and Marriage, Business and Religion are two separate subjects.

Was Carroll prescient? Well, just 41 years later the nation was laced with rails that reached as far as the Pacific Coast and just 72 years later the United States was the largest agricultural and industrial Superpower on the planet exceeding that of Great Britain and Germany *combined*. Without the railroad, such dominance would not have been possible. So let us anoint him as a seer. But more on Carroll later in this book. Now let us go back to 27 February 1827 when B&O was chartered, just fourteen months prior to this ceremony. Now we *know* this act has been shrouded in myth.

Two words. Rail Road. The founders of B&O were determined to build a super *highway* to Ohio. A road on rails, with the load pulled by *horses*. Because a horse could pull *twelve times* the weight of a horse pulling a wagon on a road so long as the load is suspended on rails and the grade kept to a minimum.

This was a quantum leap in overland transportation efficiency and, in the eyes of Baltimore Cavaliers, at least a partial answer to the New Orleans and Canal threats because Baltimore lay an average of 200 miles *closer* to Ohio than her northern rivals.

Was it possible to build a low-grade highway over the mountains and into Ohio? Certainly it was. Men had been building roads for thousands of years but without any regard to the grade. Straight-line was the theme, to keep down capital investment. The shorter the road, the less the investment. Up hill and down dale. But the price was low operating efficiency. To go *around* the hill involved a longer route but gained from far lower operating costs. And suspending the load on rails, as we have seen, gives a twelvefold improvement in operating efficiency. The investment cost was higher, but the *return* on investment was enormous.

It took just *nine days* for a band of Baltimore merchant Cavaliers to conclude that a super highway was the way to go and to form a corporation to give effect to their conclusions. And they put up their own money!

We have reported this and other aspects of railroad history in great detail in a number of books, principally *Triumph I, East End, West End* and *Sand Patch*.

The myth that we wish to put to rest is that the founders were a bunch of starry-eyed dreamers betting on future technological progress to bail them out. The "technology" was in existence. Their genius was in applying known facts to solve their problem.

"Even if it be second to that." Charles Carroll began his career as a merchant out of the port of Liverpool in England, so it is reasonable to conclude that he and his fellow Baltimore merchants understood arithmetic. All of them understood that opportunity must be seized when presented. Or, put less elegantly, the dice must not stick to your fingers at moments of decision.

Prescient? Well, let us study what followed the fateful years 1827-28.

In 1842 B&O reached Cumberland MD (and found coal). By 1852 B&O reached Ohio at Wheeling albeit with a far longer and brutal route than originally envisioned. Canal mileage peaked in 1859 and then began a slow decline.

B&O followed the National Road and local turnpikes to leach traffic in the quest for Ohio and soon found that a railroad could produce gross profits of 50% (revenues less the cost of transportation), a staggering return on investment almost equal to counterfeiting without the risk of jail.

By 1835 B&O concluded that steam power was far more efficient than horse power and thus established an urgent need for a manufacturing base of massive proportions.

By 1853 the price of moving a ton one mile on a railroad (ton/miles) ranged between one and two dollars. On a turnpike the price was fifteen dollars! On a waterway/canal the price was only 50 cents, but water movement was far slower, serpentine and, above all, not all-weather. Water freezes. Speed is an important element in overall costing i.e. time and turnover and railroads were far faster than rival forms.

In 1870 ten *billion* ton/miles moved on American railroads. In 1910 the figure was 150 *billion* ton/miles.

Ten million tons of coal were mined in 1850. By 1910 it was 500 million tons. In 1850 just 100 *thousand* tons of steel were produced. In 1910 the figure was 25 *million* tons.

The rates for freight in the period 1866-1873 were 5.2¢ per ton/mile for freight and 2.1¢ per passenger mile. By 1880 it was .8¢ for freight and .7¢ for passenger.

The astronomical increase in industrial capacity that was required to service this growth was incredible.

And it was accompanied by eye-popping agricultural growth in the Great Granary fed by burgeoning mechanization which in turn added to the industrial explosion.

Railroad mileage reached 256 thousand miles in 1914 and a peak of 260 thousand in 1930. While now down to about 230 thousand miles, these figures dwarf the mileage in all other nations and, indeed, continents on the planet.

Not only did the railroad trigger vast industrial and agricultural growth, it also fostered the largest human immigration in human history. All this growth required farmers, miners, artisans, strong backs and brains in numbers far beyond the existing population no matter how fecund.

The population of Europe (including Russia, by the way) in 1780 was about 110 million souls. In 1790 in the United States the total was a mere four million and 20% of those were slaves, victims of a warped system.

Our borders were flung open and people flooded in, creating a diverse population basking in the "pursuit of happiness." There is no American race, but there is an American nation. To become American, all one has to do is to take an oath to defend the Constitution against all of its enemies, foreign and domestic, and *ipso facto* you are an American citizen entitled to all the benefits, protections and responsibilities of that blessed Constitution.

That there are warts in the United States is apparent, but a free society is versatile enough to correct inequities. In a discussion of this subject a few years ago, we posed this question – If tomorrow morning the headlines blared that a cure for cancer had been found, would anyone care about the color, religion, ethnicity, sex or national origin of the discoverer? The answer is obviously negative. We replied that if one doesn't care about the end result, one shouldn't care about entry.

"From each according to his abilities – to each according to his need" was the battlecry of Communism. The United States was practicing this philosophy long before Marx burst upon the scene with his vile vision.

All of the fantastic growth in the 19th Century required money. Capital by name. Now there are only three sources of capital. Equity, debt and earnings. *By far the most abundant source of capital is earnings.* And study after study confirms that about 70% of earnings, or profits if you will, *never leave the enterprise.* While some dividends are paid as recompense for the rent of money, earnings stay in the enterprise to provide capital for growth and improvements.

Debt is borrowing against the assets of the enterprise and interest is paid in compensation. Debt is the second largest source of capital.

Now we come to equity. Ownership represented by shares in the enterprise, of divers forms.

Equity is really seed money, to be passed in importance by debt and earnings. But equity is also the source of a great gambling casino that has little to do with the production of real capital. It has everything to do with enriching traders. And it does that big time.

"Where are the customers' yachts?" There are none. One of the more telling indictments of this system is the Greater Fool Theory. "I am a fool to pay this price for these shares, but there is a greater fool out there who will pay me more."

But none, or little, of this trading produces real capital for real investment. It does, however, produce "panics" when everyone heads for the doors at the same time and these panics, in turn, impede real productive growth.

In the 19th Century the United States was short of capital to support the explosive growth of railroads. During that century most of the securities traded were those of railroads. Only late in that century did industrial securities begin to blossom, or wilt as you will.

B&O was the leader in raising money for growth and set the pattern for the future. The founders evolved a system of issuing equity, selling debt and producing earnings in reasonable balance that produced a sound railroad, helped, to be fair, by State and foreign investment. This method worked quite well until the panic of 1857 and John Work Garrett became president in 1858. He was a banker and trader and he, allied with Johns Hopkins, increased dividends to puff the stock, capitalized expenses to boost borrowing power and goosed earnings by not reinvesting them in the railroad.

At rival PRR, however, John Edgar Thomson was smarter. He emulated the original B&O approach and prospered, building PRR into a monolith by 1873. For B&O, the net result was receivership in 1896 and permanent third-place trunkline status. Worse, PRR controlled B&O from 1901 to 1906. Bean counters can count beans, but they do not create them.

As we have pointed out in *Sand Patch*, Garrett's depredations were not the sole cause of B&O's defeat. Thomas Swann and Benjamin Latrobe outwitted Pennsylvania and PRR by bypassing that State in B&O's lunge to Ohio, but the price was a very high-cost railroad. In 1854 the average cost per mile run on B&O was 8.97 cents. On PRR it was 7.05 cents. (On Erie it was 10.30 cents.) The low-cost producer always wins.

This book is about what we have characterized as the *first* "War Between the States" that encompassed Maryland, Virginia and Pennsylvania as B&O and PRR battled for supremacy in the railroad wars. It is a high adventure story complete with Giants, Geniuses, Knaves and Blunderers.

It is a story of conflict sufficient to warrant Durant's assertion of the wars between men. (We will amuse you with the sexual aspect in a later chapter.) And our prediction of the war against gravity and distance.

What roads were to the Roman Empire, what the seas were to the British Empire, the railroad was to the United States.

The B&O Railroad Museum in Baltimore avows that it is the Birthplace of American Railroading.

We feel that it is the Birthplace of American Hegemony. Perhaps Charles Carroll was indeed prescient.

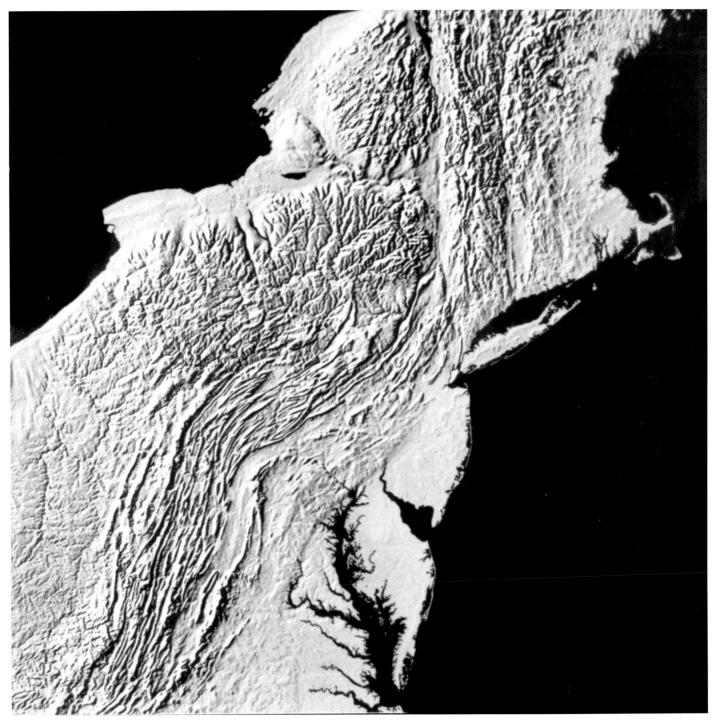

(caption for art on previous page)

WE HAVE ENLARGED the preceding map to bring more clarity to the situation facing the cities of the eastern seaboard at the beginning of the 19th century. From an overland transportation standpoint, the visage was forbidding to say the least. It is easy to follow the trace of the Erie Canal west from the Hudson River valley, the completion of which confirmed New York City's status as the premier port of the nation. To the others, however, the challenge was daunting.

Following are excerpts from an editorial that appeared in the American Railroad Journal *for 1835:*

"We . . . cannot refrain from here expressing our own, and we believe the thanks of the entire Rail Road community, as well in Europe as in America, for the candid, business-like liberal manner in which they annually lay before the world the result of their experience."

"We . . . nominate them the Rail Road University of the United States . . . they have published annually the results of their experiments, and distributed their reports with a liberal hand that the world might be *cautioned by their errors and instructed by their discoveries.*"

"This country owes to the enterprise, public spirit and perseverance of the citizens of Baltimore a debt of gratitude of no ordinary magnitude . . ."

✳ ✳ ✳

WE CONCLUDED long ago that the greatest gift that B&O presented to Society as a whole, national and international, was the liberality saluted above. Courtliness as well as conviviality tinged with generosity are hallmarks of Cavalierism and gentle conduct. PRR, among many others, drank from the B&O well but very, very few put anything back.

Chapter 1

The Battleground
Cavaliers and Quakers

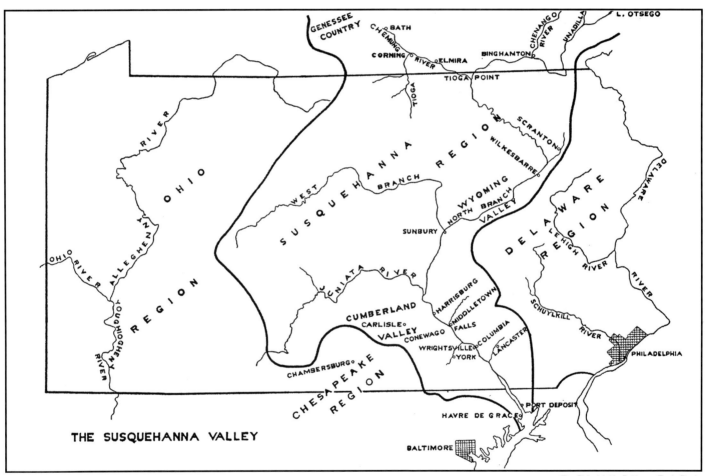

The Philadelphia-Baltimore Trade Rivalry

THE SUSQUEHANNA VALLEY extended from Chesapeake Bay northward through the central portion of Pennsylvania and even reached into the southern tier of New York State. The river's multiple branches embraced a wide range of terrain, from lush piedmont ideal for growing wheat – to the rugged foothills of the Allegheny Mountains, covered with stands of hardwood and holding rich deposits of coal and iron ore. All of this bounty – and the potential value that it represented to the two major centers of commerce, Philadelphia and Baltimore, would prove to be a driving force that would strongly influence the actions of both and create a fierce rivalry that began in the late 18th Century and continued unabated for nearly a century.

13

In the beginning of European settlement of the North American continent several colonial seaports situated on the eastern coast of what was to become the United States gradually emerged as major commercial centers. Chief among these as the colonies developed were the bustling ports of Boston, New York, Philadelphia and Baltimore. Boston is out of our purview and we have already covered the dramatic interaction between Philadelphia and New York City in earlier volumes in the *Triumph* series – now we turn our attention to the equally dramatic Philadelphia-Baltimore rivalry, and particularly the critical role the Baltimore area was to play in the development of early commerce and transportation systems in the young nation.

As settlers from these centers pushed farther and farther westward, the importance of communication and trade interaction not only among them along the East Coast but also with the interior gradually increased. As their spheres of trade influence expanded they eventually overlapped, resulting in growing competition and subsequently struggles for commercial supremacy among the major port cities. In particular, as frontier migration from Philadelphia gradually moved out of its initial Delaware Valley sphere and spread westward across Pennsylvania, it of necessity encountered the wide region in the interior of the state embraced by the broad Susquehanna River.

The Susquehanna and its three main branches fill the entire central portion of Pennsylvania – the main North Branch even extends into New York State – and flows 448 miles southward through Maryland to its outlet into Chesapeake Bay, north of Baltimore. The Susquehanna watershed is enormous, covering 27,500 sq. miles across the Appalachian and Piedmont plateaus – larger than the area drained by any other river on the Eastern seaboard south of the St. Lawrence. The upper reaches of the Susquehanna cut through several mountainous ridges – the largest of these is the Blue Mountain range, extending in a huge arc southwestward to just west of Harrisburg, which the timeless waters were unable to completely wear down, resulting in the Conewago Falls near Middletown, the first major obstacle to navigation on the river's course.

Above the falls, although the river branches were winding, they were generally deep enough to allow navigation in keel (also known as Durham) boats, resulting in the movement of lumber, wheat and later pig and bar iron from the Juniata Valley (see *Triumph*

IV). All of this traffic ended up in Middletown, which was laid out in 1755 and rapidly became the early center of river commerce in central Pennsylvania.

Below the falls the river was swift all the way to tidewater at Chesapeake Bay, with rocky ridges below the surface making navigation treacherous. Thus traffic destined to either Philadelphia or Baltimore had to move primarily overland, a costly and time-consuming passage by lumbering wagons over poor roads.

This lush area benefited from its closeness to older settlements that could assist the new colonists until their farms were established. The relatively mild climate (compared to New York and New England) and the rich, fertile soil in this region proved ideal for farming and the family farms were soon producing bumper crops. The most important crop, particularly for export to the West Indies, was wheat and wheat production in the Susquehanna Valley fortuitously increased at a time when it suffered from a disastrous blight in New England, whose stony slopes did not provide ideal growing conditions in any event.

The Quaker capitalists of Philadelphia looked to this fertile area for commerce in grain, flour and lumber, and later coal and iron. Ever cautious, even reluctant at first, they were eventually willing to invest in internal improvements to the interior of Pennsylvania – turnpikes, canals and subsequently railroads – to facilitate transport of these goods to tidewater at Philadelphia.

What the conservative Philadelphia merchants were slow to understand, however, was that the Susquehanna River Valley, by far the largest natural waterway into the region, was geographically oriented more towards Baltimore than to Philadelphia and that the local settlers – increasingly of German origin – were quite willing to put personal profit and convenience ahead of provincial loyalty. Baltimore interests soon recognized this trend and began to implement internal improvements of their own, viewing access to the interior of Pennsylvania as a key to success in developing their city as *the* premier mid-Atlantic seaport.

Another major factor in the evolution of this story was social, an aspect little commented upon but nonetheless real.

A major portion of Pennsylvania's population, and almost half of Maryland's, consisted of people of British and German extraction. By British we mean, of course, English, Welsh and Scots. While the first colonists were British, German immigration began quite early. For example, George Washington as a young surveyor venturing into the mountains and valleys of western Virginia was surprised to find settlers who spoke "Dutch". If he had visited Pennsylvania, he would have found a lot more. If he had been a student of this subject, he would have learned that English is regarded as a Germanic language and that both are Anglo-Saxon in origin. While the Welsh and Scots are Celtic, in this new nation all of these races shared a common attitude … in short, they got along just fine. Forget the travails of Europe. All of their ancestors came to this country to get away from that nonsense.

They shared many similar attributes … industrious, creative, vigorous, family-oriented, orderly and adventuresome.

So many Pennsylvanians were quite comfortable dealing with cavalier Marylanders. Neither were comfortable with the dour Quaker attitude, particularly having to do with libation.

Philadelphia, which was in the process of losing its lofty position of commercial dominance that it had held during the colonial period to New York City as the 18th Century neared its end, understandably resisted these efforts, thus setting the stage for a titanic 100-year long struggle for commercial supremacy in the mid-Atlantic region. This would manifest itself in many ways, sometimes in bitter sectional rivalries, sometimes in bizarre twists of legislative action – and relevant to this volume, heated and prolonged conflict between the newly-formed canal companies and later railroads representing their respective centers of commerce that would persist for generations. Out of this seething cauldron would emerge two railroad titans that would repeatedly clash for regional supremacy.

The northern regions of the valley were sparsely populated, and the hardy pioneers who settled there were relatively isolated. But the settlers in central Pennsylvania gradually became politically more akin to the inhabitants of colonial Baltimore, rather than those in Philadelphia (as discussed in *Triumph IV*, the Scots and Scotch-Irish Presbyterian settlers tended to settle farther west into the mountainous areas and down the Cumberland Valley, beyond the lush agricultural lands and benign climate – ideal for growing bumper crops of grain – in the valley areas sought by those of primarily German origin). The steep prices and monopolistic business climate also turned the settlers away from the Quaker City – because the farms were primarily family-owned and operated, the economic prosperity was fairly broad-based, with less concentration of wealth in the hands of a few individuals.

Gradually leading Pennsylvania citizens became aware of this growing threat to their own lines of commerce to Philadelphia, which suffered from notoriously poor roads and the seemingly endless obstructions to river navigation. Many earnest pleas and proposals for internal improvements were made until "A Society for Promoting the Improvement of Roads and Inland Navigation in the State of Pennsylvania" was organized on 31 January 1789, with Revolutionary War financier Robert Morris as its first president. More discussions and proposals ensued during the early 1790s, and some improvements were actually undertaken – the most successful was the 66-mile Lancaster Turnpike, connecting that city with Philadelphia in the middle part of the decade.

This stone and gravel road, costing nearly a half-million dollars, was desperately needed – and reasonably successful, leading to the construction of several other improved roadways in the state – but it failed to divert the movement of the produce of the Susquehanna Valley to Philadelphia as much as was envisioned and desired. By the time a 10-mile extension reached Columbia on the Susquehanna in 1803, commerce was already moving downriver in makeshift rafts and crude but sturdy flat-bottomed boats (known as "arks") and through the treacherous rocky lower portions of the river that the Pennsylvania Legislature had intentionally left unimproved. They reached tidewater just north of the growing port of Baltimore, where – unable to ascend the river again – they were broken down and sold for lumber.

By 1796, when New York City actually moved ahead of Philadelphia commercially, Baltimore had grown to become an energetic and ambitious rival of the Quaker City. Founded in 1729 and thus the youngest of the three port cities, Baltimore Town was laid out on an inlet of the Patapsco River 200 miles up the Chesapeake Bay from the open ocean. The town was named for Cecilius Calvert, the second Lord Baltimore, who was granted 12 million acres at the head of Chesapeake Bay in 1632 to establish a proprietary colony named Maryland (after Mary, queen to Charles I). Its location was not convenient for European or northern coastal shipping – although that commerce gradually evolved – but it was ideally situated for West Indian and southern coastal trade.

Baltimore experienced only slow growth for a number of years after its founding – it was surrounded by older rivals for the limited commerce within the Chesapeake Bay area itself – but gradually conditions changed in its favor. First, wheat replaced tobacco as the primary crop along the shores of the Bay and in the Piedmont, and exports increased rapidly after 1750. Secondly, the Revolutionary War provided a strong stimulus to the local industry and commerce of Baltimore because, unlike its coastal rivals, it was outside of the British blockade and its fast sailing ships were able to operate freely.

Before the war Baltimore merchants were generally agents for Philadelphia interests – afterwards increasing commerce generated large supplies of local capital and resulted in the establishment of a local banking business, enabling the city to lose its dependency on outside funds. Prior to 1832 Philadelphia could lay claim to being the center of banking in the U. S. However in that year Andrew Jackson's heavy-handed veto of the Second National Bank's charter forever ended that exalted position and, as political/economic commentator Kevin Phillips has so succinctly put it, "iced the cake of New York's financial preeminence."

After the death of Philadelphia financier Stephen Girard in 1831 (estimated worth in 1830 – $6 million), Philadelphia never again was home to one of the country's wealthiest individuals. Even so, Baltimore was never able to come close to Philadelphia in terms of serious individual wealth, achieving less than half of the number of millionaires by the mid-19th Century – notwithstanding Johns Hopkins and Alex. Brown and his family.

Baltimore became a port of entry after the Revolution, a critical step in its development, and by the end of the 18th Century it had become the preeminent port on Chesapeake Bay, largely on the basis of its lucrative wheat and flour trade. There were several reasons for the city's rapid rise from a relatively minor port to become a major center of international commerce. First, the city was favorably located to carry on trade with the West Indies (particularly after the French alliance of 1778) and later even to Europe and South America. Second, the wheat grown in the temperate Piedmont areas of Maryland and Pennsylvania produced a premium grade of flour that could withstand tropical temperatures. Thirdly, the city was the home port for a growing fleet of fast sailing clippers that could outrun threatening Royal Navy warships during the Revolution and after the war allow the trade to grow, "from absolute insignificance, to a degree of commercial importance, which brought down upon it, the envy and jealousy of all the great cities of the union."

Fourth, Baltimore rapidly developed into a ready market for grain and its by-products. Flour could be shipped into the city by wagon and find buyers quickly at premium prices, which in turn increased the demand for more. This strong demand was the primary driving force for farmers in the Susquehanna Valley to plant and harvest larger and larger acreage of wheat. In return Baltimore merchants and educators helped the farmers to become more efficient by improving their agricultural practices and increasing yields.

Roads to transport flour into the city were constructed as early as the 1730s and often made use of those originally built for tobacco rolling. A road extending from Baltimore up the Susquehanna Valley as far as Peach Bottom, PA, was opened in 1740. Unmilled wheat was also brought into the city and the surrounding area, where multiple streams flowing rapidly into the Bay provided excellent sites for the construction of water-powered flour mills – by 1802 there were 50 major mills within an 18-mile radius of the city. The enterprising owners quickly made use of the inventions of Oliver Evans that improved the quality and productivity of their milling operations.

For all of these reasons, the Port of Baltimore developed into the foremost flour processing and exporting center in the U. S. – an exalted title it held well into the second decade of the 19th Century. At that time some 450,000 barrels of flour and 200,000 bu. of grain entered the city from the Valley environs.

Looking for a way to facilitate this commerce, several Baltimore citizens led the effort for internal improvements in the Susquehanna Valley after the Revolution. This included improved turnpikes extending up the valley as well as the short Susquehanna Canal extending 8-1/2 miles from Port Deposit at the mouth of the river to Love Island at the Pennsylvania border. This crude waterway, one of the first of its kind in the U. S., was completed in late 1802 and opened for regular service the following year.

Cooperation from the Pennsylvania Legislature for road improvements in the Valley was minimal at best, and for removing obstructions from the river was decidedly nonexistent except for completion of another short canal around Conewago Falls and in the immediate area of the terminus of the Union Canal opened in 1827 by Philadelphia investors to link the Susquehanna and Schuylkill Rivers.

Pennsylvania's deliberate policy of keeping the lower Susquehanna unimproved between Columbia and the Maryland line was intended to force the traffic to move eastward to Philadelphia (as was the Union Canal), rather than southward to Baltimore. This self-serving strategy originated as early as 1701, but was strengthened in 1799 in an Act that unequivocally stated, "Any individual or company, who shall without proper authority from the governor of the commonwealth, remove or attempt to remove, the obstructions in the river Susquehanna, between Wright's ferry and the Maryland line, shall be fined in a sum not less than two hundred dollars, nor more than two thousand dollars, with such imprisonment as the court . . . may direct, not exceeding six months."

This decidedly harsh policy was based on a deeply-entrenched belief – some might say obsession – in the Pennsylvania Legislature for many years that the state borders were sacrosanct and that the very proximity of the "foreign" state of Maryland somehow defiled the border regions. This intransigence on the part of Pennsylvania severely reduced the value of Baltimore's own short stretch of canal at the lower end – as a result of this and other less than successful endeavors, Baltimore's early enthusiasm for canals was short-lived – at least for a while.

The 1799 law blocked improvements in the lower portion of the river until 1801 when new legislation declared it a public highway – in return for the concession that Philadelphia interests be allowed to construct the Chesapeake & Delaware Canal connecting the upper end of the Bay with the Delaware River, thus allowing the Quaker merchants to dip their hand into the growing Susquehanna trade. Again Baltimore's efforts were thwarted.

Although interest in building a waterway across the narrow isthmus of land separating the waters of Delaware and Chesapeake Bays dated back to the late 17th Century and later had the backing of George Washington, Benjamin Franklin and James Madison, nothing substantive was done until after the Revolutionary War, 100 years later. Pennsylvania obtained agreement from the Maryland Legislature for such an endeavor in 1799, but the citizens of Baltimore strenuously objected, claiming that it would divert the potential trade of the Susquehanna River and even Chesapeake Bay towards Philadelphia.

These protests notwithstanding, the three states agreed to proceed – Delaware granted a charter on 29 January 1801 and Pennsylvania quickly followed on February 19 – and a company was organized on 1 May 1803 to construct the canal. Work was finally begun on a feeder in 1804, but was discontinued the following year because the funds, most of which had come from Philadelphia, ran out – the stubborn Baltimore investors refused to purchase a single share of stock in this venture!

The canal project languished for years – appeals to the federal government got nowhere, despite a favorable report supporting the project from Treasury Secretary Albert Gallatin. The War of 1812 and the Panic of 1819 came and went – each time efforts to get the project moving again came to no avail.

Both Philadelphia and Baltimore continued to sponsor the building of more turnpikes into the Susquehanna Valley – the former in the northern and eastern portions, the latter in the southern and western areas. Because there was no adequate provision to traverse the Susquehanna upstream the river trade to Baltimore was predominately eastward. Return traffic including merchandise, manufactured goods and imported products such as sugar, coffee and tea moved westward from Philadelphia (and to a much lesser extent from Baltimore) via the turnpikes to the Valley, resulting in an odd triangular trade pattern and increasing the enmity between the two cities.

Dangerous conditions for coastal shipping during the War of 1812 underlined the need for additional internal improvements, but the business downturn after the war seriously affected the spirit and availability of working capital in both cities. It took a grand project to the north – New York's landmark and ambitious Erie Canal – (see *Triumph I*) – to galvanize both Pennsylvania and Maryland (as well as New Jersey, discussed in *Triumph V*) to undertake major improvements themselves. Pennsylvania launched the Main Line of Public Works, an equally ambitious but politically and economically ill-conceived amalgam of railroads and canals (see *Triumph I-IV*) to reclaim traffic from the West and bolster Philadelphia's lagging export business.

Baltimore developed equally grand plans to strengthen its claim on the potentially lucrative traffic from the West through the Susquehanna Valley.

After an on-site survey by a group of appointed commissioners and promises of access to the vast Susquehanna Valley and beyond, plans were made to dig a canal from Baltimore to Havre de Grace at the mouth of the river and from there upriver to Conewago Falls. If Pennsylvania citizens suffered from episodes of acute canal fever during this turbulent period, Baltimore residents were afflicted with recurrent bouts of "canal rage."

But the canal projects were again thwarted at the border by Pennsylvania's adamant refusal to grant a charter in that state. In conjunction with construction of branches to the Pennsylvania Canal system, a series of dams 8-10 ft. high were built across the river at several locations including Duncan's Island, Nanticoke and Sunbury, ostensibly to provide water for the canal feeders. Although the dams had sluiceways through them to allow rafts to pass, navigation was extremely difficult. Pennsylvanians claimed the dams were necessary to improved interior commerce – Baltimore citizens saw them as obstructions to river navigation and a blatant violation of the 1801 agreement, unfairly forcing traffic to use the Pennsylvania State Works to Philadelphia.

In 1822 the C&D Canal company was again revived, the services of New York's experienced canal engineers were obtained and new surveys were made. Funds were secured from the states of Pennsylvania, Delaware and Maryland in the following year – as well as the federal government. By the end of the following year the company had raised $1 million, almost enough to complete the project, at least according to the prevailing estimates. Philadelphia investors were reluctantly agreeable to Baltimore's proposal for a canal on the lower Susquehanna but were opposed to a waterway all the way to Conewago Falls. The threat of a continuous canal along the river spurred them onward to finally complete the C&D project.

Construction began in 1824, following a slightly different route – there were many disputes on just where the canal should go. Working first under John Randel, Jr., who ran the first surveys, and later Benjamin Wright, who was an engineer for the Erie Canal across upstate New York, some 2600 Irish immigrant workers used picks and shovels to dig their way through the hostile terrain. They immediately encountered a whole host of problems, including mosquito-infested swamps, peat bogs, clay and even quicksand, all of which dramatically slowed progress – and increased the cost. The greatest obstacle was the long ridge that runs down the middle of the peninsula, requiring a mile-long cut through solid rock. Landslides were a frequent problem in that section, causing critics to point out the folly of the effort. Nevertheless the cut, 90 feet deep at its deepest point, was hailed as "one of the greatest works of human skill and ingenuity in the world."

But the work continued – the eastern portion was completed in 1828 and immediately saw considerable traffic in produce from Port Deposit northward to Philadelphia. Finally on 17 October 1829 a festive celebration with gun salutes and the requisite lengthy orations heralded the formal opening of the entire canal. The 13-1/2 mile waterway – its final costs had risen to $2.25 million – extended from Chesapeake City, Maryland, located on Back Creek (a branch of the Elk River) to Delaware City, 46 miles south of Philadelphia on Delaware Bay. It was 60 ft. wide and 10 ft. deep (enlarged in 1854 to 66 ft. in width), allowing it to accommodate sloops used in coastal and Bay traffic.

Shortening the sea route between Philadelphia and Baltimore by some 300 miles, the canal carried considerable traffic – mostly eastward – in its early years, although it took 15 years before toll revenue was enough to pay the interest on the huge debt. The company suffered through many lean years, but after 1847 the debt was refinanced and it was able to survive a while longer. Boats loaded with grain products (wheat, flour and whiskey), along with lumber, fish, oysters and iron were hauled through the canal by mules, destined for – as it was claimed by Philadelphia merchants – "its legitimate market." Eventually swift steam-powered packet boats carrying both freight and passengers replaced the sluggish process of towing.

Frustrated by the failure of the efforts to construct a continuous canal waterway in the Susquehanna Valley, New York's dramatically successful opening of the landmark Erie Canal and the imminent threat of the C&D Canal, Baltimore businessmen, faced with being "still in the wilderness," turned to railroads as an innovative means of survival in their increasingly bitter rivalry with Philadelphia and New Orleans. Early in 1827 two major events occurred that would have profound consequences for the city. A charter was granted to the pioneering Baltimore & Ohio Rail Road to tap the commerce of the West, and a meeting of delegates from four turnpike companies was convened to consider the prospect of building a railroad up the Susquehanna Valley.

At the time of its charter on 28 February 1827 the idea of a "rail road" to reach the Ohio River, gateway to the vast and potentially lucrative Midwestern breadbasket, was an unknown mixture of folly and stalwart vision. In the fall of 1826 Evan Thomas, brother of Baltimore financier Philip E. Thomas, had returned home with glowing reports on the successful 25-mile Stockton & Darlington RR in England, which hauled coal from the mines to colliers and the docks. Joined by his brother, George Brown and William Patterson, the group bravely set about to organize a railroad of their own.

The first line of the historic charter set the tone – and clearly stated the objective: "Resolved, That immediate application be made to the Legislature of Maryland for an act incorporating a joint stock company to be styled, the 'Baltimore and Ohio Rail Road' and clothing such company with all the powers necessary to the construction of a railroad, with two or more sets of rails, from the City of Baltimore to the Ohio River."

Needless to say, the charter was quickly approved.

After over a year of planning and fundraising – some 20,000 investors including the City of Baltimore, came forth with $5 million – on 4 July 1828 the fledgling Baltimore and Ohio Railroad was launched on its way westward with a festive celebration the likes of which the city had never witnessed before – or arguably given relative populations – since. A grand procession with bands and floats representing all of the city's major enterprises – plus the requisite politicians – marched westward from the Merchants Exchange building to the point where the planned right of way crossed the city line. There venerable 90-year old Charles Carroll or Carrolton, the last surviving signer of the Declaration of Independence, turned a symbolic silver shovel of red earth and dedicated the road's First Stone in a full Masonic ceremony.

The symbolism was fitting to the momentous significance of the occasion – a new adventure that would subsequently help the Union's cause in holding the warring nation together (for which it was to pay a grievous price) and then supporting a burgeoning industrial revolution. It was also a journey of trepidation into the unknown – from the familiar to the decidedly unfamiliar. As noted author/historian Herbert H. Harwood, Jr. has pointed out in *Impossible Challenge II*, "many of the institutions represented in the celebration would be irrevocably altered or even destroyed by the creature whose birth they were celebrating."

Building the B&O was a daunting physical challenge, laid out across 300 miles of rugged mountainous terrain intersected by narrow, twisting streams and making use of new and unproven construction methods, often improvising as it went. In the process it became the proving ground for new railway engineering methods – and in fact helped create and expand the field itself.

Lacking engineering expertise in building a railroad – there simply wasn't any to be had at the time – the B&O directors secured the services of a group of Army engineers with the next best thing, surveying and road building experience. Led by Lt. Colonel Stephen H. Long and Captain William Gibbs McNeill plus civilian turnpike engineer Jonathan Knight, this group surveyed several alternate routes westward.

There were a multitude of questions to be answered, including motive power to be utilized, grades and curvature. The engineers settled on the Potomac River Valley – generally the same route used by the Chesapeake & Ohio Canal – that provided a relatively level route west to the base of the Alleghenies. But how to reach the Potomac? Here they chose to follow the Patapsco River, which they traversed for 40 miles to Bush Creek, and then to the Monocacy River, which was the final link to the Potomac.

Just getting to the Patapsco was a challenge unto itself: Baltimore is situated in a "bowl" surrounded by hills and streams cascading from the fall line – the geologic line separating the Coastal Plain from the Piedmont Plateau – that would profoundly influence the course of railroad building in and out of the city. The engineers decided to follow a "level" line, 7.5 miles at an elevation 66 ft. above Baltimore harbor to present-day Relay MD. This required extensive – and expensive – grading through deep cuts, along long fills and across elaborate bridge structures.

The grand plan was to reach the Ohio at Wheeling, West Virginia, in 10 years at an estimated cost of $10 million. The first short section to Ellicott's Mills (now Ellicott City) was opened on 24 May 1830, but progress beyond that point – through the rugged Piedmont topography – was painfully slow. Finally, after a Herculean effort B&O finally reached the Ohio in December 1852, 379 miles, $30 million and nearly 26 years after its charter was granted. In the process it became a lightning rod for the conflict between Baltimore and Philadelphia and the growing strength of its surrogate railroad, PRR.

The origins of the titanic PRR-B&O clash are worth exploring because their influence is so pervasive in what was to transpire later. In addition to receiving its charter from the State of Maryland, the B&O also obtained charter approval from the Pennsylvania Legislature, with vague wording allowing it "to construct a railroad through Pennsylvania in a direction from Baltimore to the Ohio River," presumably at either Pittsburgh or Wheeling, West Virginia. The charter also stipulated that the line must be completed within 15 years, by 27 February 1843 (in 1839 because of construction delays this was extended to 27 February 1847).

With completion of the line to Cumberland in 1842 the citizens of Pittsburgh woke up to the imminent possibility of a rail connection to Baltimore. Hoping to head off a line to rival Wheeling, public meetings held in the Pittsburgh area produced mixed feelings on the subject, but generally favored the B&O connection. However, sentiment east of the mountains preferred a rail line across Pennsylvania to Philadelphia, but the conservative Quaker merchants were dragging their well-buckled heels (or was it well-heeled buckles?) on financing such an endeavor.

In November 1845 a convention of concerned citizens was held in Philadelphia. The outcome was a series of resolutions favoring construction of a railroad from Harrisburg to Pittsburgh, with connections via the Philadelphia & Columbia line to Philadelphia, opposing the "strenuous and persevering efforts" of rival cities and states (read Baltimore, Maryland) to lay claim to the western traffic. The Pennsylvania Legislature was urgently requested to charter such a line to supplement the State Canal.

Within a month, on 6 January 1846, the Legislature duly convened in Harrisburg and was shortly asked to consider two bills: The first was "An Act to authorize the Baltimore and Ohio Rail Road Company to construct a railroad through Pennsylvania in a direction from Baltimore to the Ohio river, [and more precisely this time] at the city of Pittsburgh," and the second was "An Act to incorporate the Pennsylvania Rail Road Company."

Sentiment in the Legislature actually was evenly divided on the two bills, primarily along sectional lines. The pressure was enormous, with lobbyists often outnumbering the beleaguered legislators. Finally after over two months of intense – and often rancorous – deliberation (including the bizarre passage and then dramatic reversal of the B&O measure) the PRR bill was approved by the House on 19 March and the Senate on 10 April and signed by Governor Shunk on the 13th.

Thus PRR was born out of a simmering cauldron of both sectional and interstate rivalries – eastern vs. western Pennsylvania, Pittsburgh vs. Wheeling and of course, Baltimore vs. Philadelphia.

Eight days later the B&O Act was also signed, but its unrelenting opponents had added a critical – and ultimately fatal – amendment. This provision postponed implementation of the Act until 30 July 1847, and providing that PRR met certain requirements of stock subscription and letting of contracts for construction of 30 miles of road was completed by that date, B&O's charter to build a line to Pittsburgh "shall be null and void."

John Edgar Thomson, the enterprising and politically astute Chief Engineer hired by PRR to actually build the line, met the deadline – barely – and B&O had to go the long way around, through difficult terrain, to meet the Ohio at Wheeling, adding many brutal grades and miles to its route.

PRR had its first of many triumphs to come at the expense of the B&O, and Philadelphia added another to its collection to the detriment of its neighbor to the south. Increasingly disgruntled Pittsburgh shippers, however, were not entirely pleased with the outcome, and lingering resentment against PRR and its practices would continue to plague the line for decades, leading to more conflict (see *Triumph IV*). This was the first of many clashes in which these corporate titans would engage – in many areas of endeavor – both during their formative years as each attempted to invade the other's territory and later as both sought to gain advantages in traffic volume.

But B&O survived this engagement, and went on to become a major east-west trunk line carrier to the Midwest, substantially increasing Baltimore's commerce in grain products as well as other bulk cargo. It would also prove to be a constant threat to PRR's desire to be *the* major east-west carrier – and to capture the critical New York City-Washington route (see Chapter 2).

The lagging spirit of Baltimore citizens had been energized by the initial success of the B&O, and it turned to a second railroad project a year later. After several surveys it was determined that a line from Baltimore via York to York Haven would be the most advantageous route (York Haven was a milling town on the river opposite Middletown ideally situated for transshipment of river traffic headed for Baltimore).

On 13 February 1828 the Maryland Legislature chartered the Baltimore & Susquehanna RR. George Winchester, who had worked on the route of both the C&O and B&S Canals, was named President of Baltimore's second railroad venture on 5 May. Stock subscriptions for the new line were oversubscribed within a few days, reflecting the growing public enthusiasm for such an endeavor.

Philadelphia citizens, however, were anything but enthusiastic at this latest threat to their lines of commerce – in fact petitions presented to the Pennsylvania Legislature for a charter allowing the line to proceed from the state line below York to Conewago Falls were greeted with intense alarm in the City. It was passionately asserted that no measure had ever been put forth in the Commonwealth that was "so immediately and expressly designed" to harm their welfare, asserting that it would, "prove a funeral knell to our city." The project was also viewed as a direct threat to the State Works, claiming, "it would be a paltry return to our State for her immense expenditure to become the mere thoroughfare of wealth passing to Baltimore." In case anyone missed the point, Baltimore's petitions were attacked as "barefaced, exorbitant and unreasonable."

But reaction in the towns and rural areas of central Pennsylvania was considerably more favorable. Since the lower Susquehanna Valley was closer to Baltimore than to Philadelphia, its commerce had always been primarily with the former. Furthermore the Pennsylvania State Works had resulted in increased taxes and improvements that did not particularly benefit them. Accordingly, these citizens became vocal advocates for Baltimore's cause in the Pennsylvania Legislature. However, Philadelphia interests marshaled their forces and the bill was defeated early in 1828 – but the invective continued.

In December, prior to the next session of the Legislature, public meetings were held in York and Carlisle. A resolution from the York meeting made their position pointedly clear:

> "That it is the interest of the interior to contribute its support, as it is the wish of this meeting to cherish friendly feelings toward the metropolis of our state, but we cannot extend a servile friendship for an ungenerous return, and shall never carry along with our own interests and those of the community at large."

The measure was reintroduced to the Legislature on 20 December 1828, but instead of a request to charter an extension of the B&S into Pennsylvania, the petition called upon the legislators to "confer the privileges and immunities of a Pennsylvania corporation" on the Maryland-incorporated B&S company. But despite strong protests from *The York Gazette*,

which bitterly characterized the citizens of southern Pennsylvania as worse off than southern slaves, the bill was again defeated.

In the 1829 session the bill was introduced again, this time for a railroad from the Maryland line only as far as York. It passed the House of Representatives because of a split within the Philadelphia delegation, but failed in the Senate.

The bill came up again the following year. Each time the invective and heat of battle became more intense – public meetings in York and Philadelphia hurled charges and countercharges – creating an internal rivalry within Pennsylvania. However, in the 1831-2 session the success of the B&O operation strengthened the cause of the B&S project, and Pennsylvania Governor Wolf announced his support of two compromise measures – if Maryland would agree to allow construction of the proposed Tidewater canal along the Susquehanna, and the portion of the line in Pennsylvania would be owned and financed by a separate Pennsylvania-chartered company. Accordingly, on 14 March 1832, after seemingly endless amendments, the bill to charter the York & Maryland Line RR finally became law.

On learning the news, York erupted in celebration, captured by *The York Gazette* in breathless prose:

> "Men, women and children seemed to have but one wish, the wish of testimony to one another how deep, sincere and heartfelt was their joy. Words were inadequate to the purpose . . . The national flag was unfurled . . . bells rang merrily and long . . . cannon growled in the distance. At night there was an illumination [fireworks], not partial, but general. A procession was formed, composed of the people, and set in motion by our excellent band of musicians. In a word, the town was literally alive in spite of wind and weather."

One cannot help but wonder if the local York residents were reacting to the scathing criticism aimed at them when members of the Continental Congress fled to the remote village in September 1777 to escape British troops advancing on Philadelphia. At that time many of the Founding Fathers expressed disdain for their hosts, labeling them with such epithets as, "an inactive, lifeless, unwieldy mass" and charging that, "in politics, they are a breed of mongrels or neutrals, and benumbed with general torpor." Perhaps being able to claim itself as "the first U. S. Capital" after the Articles of Confederation were signed there in 1778 made the difference – whatever the reasons the good citizens of York had taken a stand regarding *their* railroad, and they had been rewarded with their own triumph.

Work had actually begun on the B&S during the long charter battle in Pennsylvania under the able guidance of Long and McNeill fresh from their initial successes on the B&O. (Actually the two had been relieved of their duties by the B&O Board in favor of Caspar Werner, a local engineer. They subsequently published a long diatribe against B&O management). The 7-mile first division was begun on 8 August 1829 with appropriate Masonic ceremonies in Baltimore and the inevitable grand procession. The date was chosen because it was the centennial of the Act laying out Baltimore-Town. This time the celebration took place without the presence of venerable Charles Carroll, who was too feeble to attend, but his portrait was prominently displayed at the courthouse.

It was completed on 4 July 1831 and faced with a possible change in the route, the line made a sudden turn to the west at Relay through the Green Spring Valley toward Westminster. After the charter issue was resolved, the line resumed its way northward, but construction proceeded slowly through the bad weather and difficult terrain, which consists of narrow valleys winding between many steep rocky hills. The line was opened to Timonium on 12 September 1832, which was the northern limit of service for several years. As the track approached the Pennsylvania border the right of way left the Gunpowder Falls Valley and encountered another obstacle to crossing the Mason Dixon line – this time a natural one. New Freedom Hill, with its 1.5 per cent grade, would prove to be the road's greatest operating challenge. South of York, it was necessary to dig a 300-ft. long tunnel through a rocky ridge that took two years to complete.

In addition to the difficult construction the company also faced labor problems and the usual lack of funds. A plea to the Maryland Legislature resulted in a loan of $1 million in early 1835, alleviating the latter problem temporarily, but it would return for more funds from both Baltimore and the state. The company continued to be plagued by labor shortages, resulting in demands for higher wages and at least one strike by the brawny Irish immigrant workers.

During the construction of the road huge gangs of these laborers performed the heavy pick and shovel work while local farmers provided dump carts to haul the fill to level the right of way. At night the farmers brought gallons of whiskey from their distilleries to sell to the thirsty workers, who organized raucous parties around huge bonfires, singing and dancing to the lively tunes of the fiddlers among their midst. Large numbers of female camp followers added to the revelry and gave new meaning to "fiddling." One wonders where they found the energy to work.

The original intent of the planners of the B&S was to construct a through line to the Susquehanna River, but the so-called York plan called for slack water navigation from there to the mouth of Codorus Creek. However, with completion of the Pennsylvania Canal to Columbia, the center of navigation on the river shifted from Middletown downstream to that terminus. The York plan was defeated in the Pennsylvania Legislature, leaving the B&S free to construct its line to Wrightsville, opposite Columbia.

Following the old adage, "if you can't beat them, join them," the York & Wrightsville RR was chartered by the Pennsylvania Legislature on 15 April 1835 to connect the B&S with the Pennsylvania State Works. However as soon as construction began the local residents objected, petitioning the Legislature to rescind the charter. Instead the legislators in their wisdom chartered a second railroad on 21 March 1836 to extend from Wrightsville southwestward to Gettysburg. This created the prospect of two lines between York and Wrightsville, predictably setting off political battles between the staunch supporters of each. Finally reason prevailed and the two were consolidated into one road, the Wrightsville, York & Gettysburg RR Co., on 28 February 1837, with the B&S to provide financing equivalent to that given to the original line, plus additional funds to quickly complete that section of the line.

The B&S was completed and opened to York on 23 August 1838, and the first train – consisting of a locomotive and tender (constructed in York) plus four cars loaded with 14 tons of freight – traversed the line in September, resulting in that enterprising town becoming a "vast hive, the receptacle of the wealth of the surrounding country." The 13-mile line from York to Wrightsville was opened on 24 May 1840, ironically about the same time as the Susquehanna & Tide Water Canal was finally completed up the valley.

Flushed with the progress of the B&S RR and faced with increased demands from lumber, coal and iron merchants, Baltimore interests again tried to construct a canal up the Susquehanna, this time to a junction with the Pennsylvania State Canal at Columbia. This struggle for charter rights in Pennsylvania was shorter but no less intense than that for the railroad. Philadelphia supporters proclaimed it as "completely subversive to the principles" of their own State Works and "inimical to the interest of their city," which it clearly was. Despite organized public protests and intense lobbying by Philadelphia interests, this outcome was likewise successful for Baltimore.

After much deliberation and lobbying, an Act was passed on 15 April 1835 by the Pennsylvania Legislature authorizing the Susquehanna Canal Co. to construct a 26-mile water way along the eastern shore of the river from Columbia to the Maryland border, where it was to connect with a 20-mile section to be built by the Tide Water Canal Co., a Maryland corporation.

Characteristically, the two rival cities reacted quickly to the passage of the Act. Baltimore citizens, emulating their newfound colleagues in York, reportedly were "almost ready to illuminate" and gleefully felt that they were now in a position to utilize Pennsylvania's entire internal improvements system to their own advantage. Philadelphians, who had footed a good portion of the cost, were correspondingly disgusted at this prospect, railing (sorry) that the Act "strikes a deadly blow at the prosperity" of their city. Their only consolation was that freight charges on lumber, coal and iron had to be the same as on the Pennsylvania State Works, and the fees charged for other items could not be less.

Baltimore's seemingly unbounded enthusiasm immediately ran into a problem. The charter stipulated that the canal was to be routed along the eastern shore of the river, and the incorporators planned to utilize the old Susquehanna Canal bed for the lower portion of the new one. However the owners of the old waterway made demands far beyond what the new sponsors were willing to pay.

After lengthy negotiations – that ultimately failed – it was decided to ask for an amendment to the charter, changing the routing of the canal to the *western* shore and crossing the river at Wrightsville across a dam and towing bridge. This change was granted in 1836, providing that Maryland authorize a branch of the B&O from Hagerstown or Williamsport to the Pennsylvania border. Maryland in turn secured agreement that the proprietors of the old Susquehanna Canal receive $2000 worth of stock in the new company for each share of the old one, which was much less than they had initially demanded.

Construction began immediately, again using hundreds of hearty Irish immigrants. But labor and financial problems soon arose, caused by the prevailing high wages of the period, exacerbated by a scarcity of workers as a result of construction and repairs to the chronically trouble-prone Pennsylvania Canal system. In addition, the State of Maryland had to loan $1 million to the undercapitalized Tide Water company to construct its section of the route.

Late in the fall of 1839 water was allowed to flow into the $3.5 million waterway, an event marked by another festive celebration, this time at Havre de Grace, which had become in effect the focus of competition between Philadelphia and Baltimore. Philadelphia financier Nicholas Biddle, former president of the controversial Second Bank of the United States, addressed the assembled crowd on the stem-winding subject of "Internal Improvements." In a moment of beneficence, he acknowledged that like other Philadelphians he had feared the development of this project, but predicted that it would reap (ah) great benefit to both cities. Philadelphia was hailed in a toast to the city's "public spirit [that] so largely aided in the completion of the work we meet to celebrate," indicating that old rivalries had been set aside, at least for the day.

However, the seemingly warm enthusiasm was dampened by cold torrential rains and consequent flooding that inflicted heavy damage on the embankments and even sections of the masonry. After extensive – and costly – repairs the canal was reopened in the spring of 1840.

In its first year of through operations the B&S RR carried nearly 20 thousand tons of freight and generated almost $100 thousand in earnings. With the completion of the York & Wrightsville line earnings increased by $40 thousand. Several of the enterprising Main Line Transporters, independent partnerships that operated their own fleets of equipment, opened depots in Baltimore on the Howard Street connecting track (see Chapter 5) and operated through freight service between Baltimore and western points utilizing the B&S and then the Pennsylvania Canal system westward. This was the best route for two years until the B&O reached Cumberland and established a stage/wagon connection to Brownsville PA via the National Road (See *Sand Patch*).

However, the revenue was not as much as anticipated – there simply was not enough business to allow both the railroad and the S&T Canal to prosper. In

1843 the B&S resorted to a rate war against the canal, lowering revenues for the next several years. By 1846 the company had to request the Maryland Legislature for the right to secure capital for badly needed additional rolling stock, which had been blocked by the governor.

But that year a momentous event would have a more profound effect on the struggling line – as we have noted on 13 April the Pennsylvania Legislature chartered the Pennsylvania Railroad to build a line from Harrisburg across the mountains to Pittsburgh. With eastward connections via the Harrisburg, Portsmouth Mt. Joy & Lancaster and the Philadelphia & Columbia (see *Triumph I* and *II*), Philadelphia investors and merchants would have the decided advantage of a through rail route all the way across the state.

Baltimore responded to this formidable challenge by seeking to extend the B&S farther up the Susquehanna Valley. Scarcely a week after PRR was granted its charter the Pennsylvania Legislature authorized a company to build a railroad from York to Bridgeport, a tiny hamlet on the west bank of the Susquehanna, opposite Harrisburg.

But the B&S was in no position financially to extend itself. All of its earnings were needed to complete the existing line and its branches and pay off its accumulated debts – thus far no dividends had been paid to its investors. However, Baltimore merchants had gained valuable commerce from their railroad up the valley and saw the potential value of extending it to connect with the proposed new line to the West. Putting their money in the right place, Baltimore citizens subscribed to over $500 thousand in stock and $200 in bonds.

This substantial level of support allowed the B&S to restructure its debts and proceed with the new section, known as the York & Cumberland RR. Work began in 1849, and the new line was completed and opened for business on 10 February 1851, immediately generating income for its parent, which actually operated the road under an agreement signed the previous year.

In its 1851 Annual Report the B&S waxed optimistically on the future: "Strong in the natural advantage of her geographical position, sustained by the operation of liberal and enlightened legislation on the part of sister states, our city has it now within the limits of her own will, to solve the problem of her future prosperity."

Not satisfied with just connecting with PRR, the B&S now planned to cross the river and extend farther northward up the Susquehanna Valley, penetrating into the anthracite coal regions and even into New York State, in response to Baltimore's dream of being a center of the potentially lucrative coal trade – in addition to its established grain franchise. Again an intense battle ensued with Philadelphia interests, who strongly objected to their PRR tracks being crossed by a foreign road in another "Baltimore-financed scheme." The new line, known as the Susquehanna Railroad Company, was finally chartered on 14 April 1851 and construction began in February 1853 but was suspended a year later because of financial difficulties – the B&S, faced with the need to both rebuild its main and improve its terminal facilities in Baltimore, had simply overextended itself in its zeal to reach farther north.

As a result, on 4 December 1854 the B&S was consolidated with the other lines extending from it and emerged as a new entity, to be known as the Northern Central Railway Company. This new company would subsequently complete the lines extending northward and form an important line of commerce for Baltimore deep into the Susquehanna Valley, particularly for coal traffic (We will discuss the later history of the Northern Central from Baltimore to Harrisburg in more detail in Chapter 5, and the northward extensions in a subsequent volume in the *Triumph* series).

Thus by mid-century the citizens of Baltimore could take great pride – their great plan of internal improvements into the Susquehanna Valley had been completed, although it often seemed that their efforts to take full advantage of them were repeatedly thwarted by rival Philadelphia – a pattern of fierce clashes that would continue between PRR and rival B&O. The lines of commerce, both rail and water, tapped the rich resources of wheat, flour, whiskey and other agricultural products, plus lumber, coal and iron.

But Biddle proved to be correct, at least initially – a report issued during the first year of S&T Canal operation indicated that commerce was about equally divided between Baltimore and Philadelphia. To exploit this further, Philadelphia interests soon established a steam tow-boat operation to seize a larger share of the S&T canal business – from 1846 to 1856 more than half of the boats towed from Havre de Grace via the C&D Canal terminated in Philadelphia, not Baltimore.

But by 1857 the balance had shifted in Baltimore's favor. Although Philadelphia continued to receive a portion of the wheat and lumber business, Baltimore actively sought and was successful in obtaining an increasing share of the coal trade – so much so that Virginia ports grew nervous at the prospect of losing dominance of their lucrative bituminous coal export business. Coal traffic through the canal increased from 70,000 tons in 1845 to almost 230,000 tons in 1860, a good portion of it headed for Baltimore.

In its early years the S&T Canal was reasonably successful. Toll revenues rose from a little over $41,000 in its first year of operation to nearly four times that amount 10 years later. Both the Union Canal and the struggling Philadelphia & Columbia RR suffered reduced business as a result. However when the Union Canal was enlarged in 1855 to accommodate larger boats, annual revenues on the S&T peaked at a little over $211,000 and then declined markedly. Another factor in the decline of shipping through the canal was PRR, which by this time had absorbed – or driven out of business – most of the Main Line Transporters that had previously used the waterway.

In retrospect, one wonders how the S&T Canal survived as long as it did. Like all canal waterways it was subject to the vagaries of weather – freezing in the winter, flooding in the spring as water (often carrying massive ice jams) surged down the Susquehanna, and suffering from low water in Summer and Fall droughts. Maintenance was expensive, and the undercapitalized S&T company had difficulty paying its debts, causing Pennsylvania (which was having similar problems with its own system) to threaten to close the outlet lock to the State Works, which would have completely isolated Baltimore's venture.

As long as we are discussing rivalries in this region, we should not fail to mention that Philadelphia and Baltimore from very early days had engaged in what might be termed the Mother of all boundary disputes. As unlikely as it seems today, under the vaguely-worded charters of Pennsylvania and Maryland, the proprietary colonies couldn't even determine which city belonged to which. Finally the two agreed to petition the royal astronomer in Greenwich, England to settle the long-standing dispute. A contract with the august body was signed, and two distinguished astronomers, Charles Mason and Jeremiah Dixon, arrived in November 1763 to assist beleaguered local survey-

ing parties. Working diligently it still took the duo nearly five years to set the borders of Pennsylvania and Maryland (as well as Delaware and Virginia). Establishment of the Mason-Dixon line ended the bitter border struggle between the Penns and the Calverts, but it set the stage for a new conflict by establishing the dividing line between slavery and free soil, forever setting it in stone – the markers had the heralds of the Penns on one side and the Calverts on the other, not surprisingly facing in opposite directions. The upheaval would tear the nation apart. This subject is thoroughly covered in *Triumph I*.

As the gathering storm of the Civil War approached, both cities could boast some advantages. Although Baltimore still had its enterprising spirit and now not only a geographical connection but also both canal and railroad links to the Susquehanna Valley, Philadelphia had over twice the population and still maintained rigid political control over the projects within Pennsylvania's borders. The two retained their intense rivalry, but both gradually came to realize that neither could surpass the other, and that both would continue to be dominated by New York City.

The S&T struggled through the war, and in 1872 was leased to the Philadelphia & Reading RR, which also took over the faltering Union and Schuylkill Canals (PRR had taken over the Pennsylvania Canal as part of its purchase of the Main Line of Public Works in 1857). Portions of the Northern Central were ravaged during the war (which we will cover in detail in Chapter 5), but the road survived to provide a vital link to the north and west, itself becoming a formidable weapon brandished in the epic PRR-B&O clash. The C&D Canal proved of strategic importance, carrying both troops and supplies for the Union Army during the Civil War.

Baltimore continued as a major flour milling, marketing and export center until the early years of the 20th Century. After the halcyon years of the late 1820s, however, it relinquished its top ranking to New York, Buffalo, Rochester and subsequently Minneapolis. New industries, such as textiles, iron and steelmaking and shipbuilding, then arose to dominate Baltimore's manufacturing economy.

Meanwhile, the PRR and B&O conflict would not only not subside – the sound of clashing swords would continue to shatter the silence in a whole array of arenas across the land . . . with the most intense battles taking place right in Baltimore.

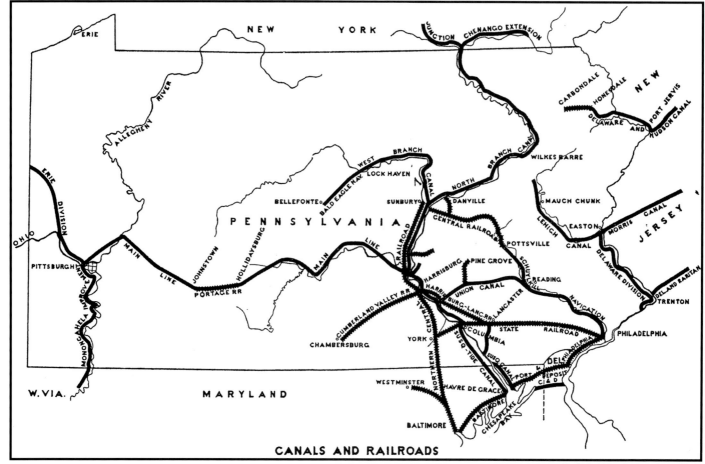

CANALS AND RAILROADS

The Philadelphia-Baltimore Trade Rivalry

AS A RESULT of the potential riches of the Susquehanna Valley the two cities both set about building their own transportation infrastructure to move the products of this region eastward into their domain as well as connecting with the West to tap its riches as well. Reflecting their respective geographic locations, Philadelphia would place emphasis on east-west routes across the Commonwealth while Baltimore would focus on the Susquehanna Valley, each leading to their own center.

First were the roads – the early turnpikes of the late 18th-early 19th Century were a welcome improvement over the generally poor (or nonexistent) roads, but hauling goods by wagon was painfully slow and expensive under the best of conditions – and nearly impossible in bad weather.

Then came the canals – Philadelphia interests afflicted with acute bouts of canal fever supported construction of the Schuylkill and Union Canals as well as the ambitious Main Line of Public Works, an amalgam of canals and railroads extending across the Commonwealth. Meanwhile Baltimore citizens suf-

fering episodes of chronic canal rage responded with the Susquehanna and Susquehanna & Tide Water Canals to move goods down that valley, although these endeavors were undermined by the Chesapeake & Delaware Canal, which diverted some of this traffic to Philadelphia.

And finally the railroads. Philadelphia investors financed the Pennsylvania Railroad to lay tracks west of Harrisburg – the road subsequently took over the lines east of the state capital to extend into the Quaker City. Disenchanted with canals – and being continually thwarted by their rival – Baltimore supported the shaky Baltimore & Susquehanna RR up the Susquehanna Valley (and of course the pioneering B&O line to the West). The lines that eventually came together as the Philadelphia, Wilmington & Baltimore RR connecting the two rivals represented a begrudging realization that cooperation made more sense than confrontation, albeit not without continuing conflict, setting the stage for the clash of titans as PRR thrust into Baltimore – the B&O's own sacrosanct arena.

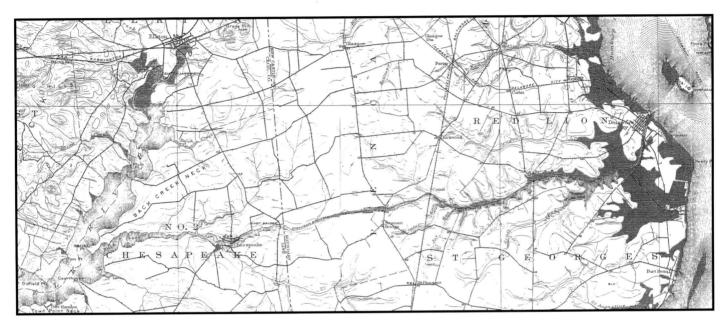

THE Chesapeake & Delaware Canal, one of the earliest pawns in the rivalry between Philadelphia and Baltimore to tap the commerce of the Susquehanna Valley, was formally opened on 17 October 1829. It was 60 ft. wide and 10 ft. deep, and extended 13.6 miles across the neck of the Delmarva Peninsula from Delaware City (on the namesake river) to Chesapeake City MD, where it emptied into Back Creek, a tributary of the Elk River which in turn flowed into the head of Chesapeake Bay. The canal was enlarged in 1854, widening it to 66 ft. As built it had two lift locks and two tide locks for a total rise and fall of 32 ft. When rebuilt the locks were reduced to three – one lift lock, one combined lift and tide lock and one tide lock.

The canal is shown here in a 1900 USGS map, after undergoing additional improvements. It is crossed by the Delaware Branch of the PB&W – the main cuts across the diagram through Elkton at the upper left. Note also the Newark & Delaware City Branch at the upper right.

In 1919 the Army Corps of Engineers took over ownership and operation of the canal from its private owners and implemented a major program of improvements. This involved widening it to 90 ft. to allow oceangoing ships to navigate the waterway. The locks were removed, making it a sea-level operation, and the eastern entrance was moved southward to Reedy Point. The improved canal was opened remotely by President Calvin Coolidge on 15 May 1927, with the yacht *Memoosha* (owned by Alfred I. du Pont) leading a ceremonial flotilla under the new Reedy Point lift bridge. The canal was again deepened during the 1930s and once again played a valuable wartime role when Nazi U-boats threatened maritime shipping. Now some 450 ft. wide and 35 ft. deep, it carries 40% of all ship traffic (some 22,000 vessels) in and out of Baltimore Harbor. It's the busiest canal in the nation and third busiest in the world.

Hagley Museum & Library

HERE WE HAVE a very early view of the canal looking eastward at the "High Bridge" at Chesapeake City MD. This structure was subsequently replaced with a much higher steel lift structure worthy of the designation. The pump house at the right was de-stroyed by fire in 1856. A similar one at Summit housed a steam-driven water wheel that lifted 200 thousand cu. ft. of water per hour a distance of 16 ft. – it continued in operation until the 1920s.

THE DEVELOPMENT of what is now the Port of Baltimore is a triumphant saga in its own right. It was once five separate small entities located on the outlet of the Patapsco River within the present port area – Baltimore Town, Fells Point, Humphreys Creek, Jones Town and Whetstone Point. In the early 18th Century these points of entry competed not only with each other but also with the established ports of Annapolis, on the Severn River, and Joppa, on the winding Bush River.

Initially the commerce of all of these small colonial ports was based entirely on trade with England, with the primary export being tobacco from surrounding plantations. Interestingly, although Baltimore Town in the early years did less trade than the others because of its then very shallow harbor area, it would go on to absorb its four close rivals and become one of the major eastern seaports.

Although the settlement of Baltimore actually began in 1607 with Captain John Smith – the first white man to disembark on the pleasant shores of the Patapsco – considerable credit for de-velopment of the harbor area should be given to David Jones, an entrepreneur who constructed what became known as Jones Town. Humphreys Point and Joppa Town became ports of entry in 1683, but the natural harbor at the outlet of the Patapsco proved to offer better potential than the silt-laden Bush River, and commerce migrated to this area. Whetstone Point, later Locust Point, became a port in 1706.

After two earlier attempts to name a town after Lord Baltimore failed, when the General Assembly appropriated $600 in 1729 to purchase 60 acres on the north side of the Patapsco, the area was designated Baltimore Town – this site initially developed as a manufacturing center rather than a port. Finally, in 1730 William Fell established a shipyard at a location that became known as Fells Point.

The earliest known depiction of Baltimore is this lithograph based on the historic 1752 map by John Moale.

BALTIMORE TOWN nearly doubled in size by absorbing Jones Town in 1745. In that same year two Irish physicians, brothers John and Henry Stevenson, settled in the rapidly growing town. While Henry went on to establish the nation's first hospital for the treatment of smallpox, his brother John decided to forego medicine and concentrate on development of the port facilities.

He was the first to establish trade in grain export – in 1750 he succeeded in persuading some of his Irish associates to send a ship, which he then loaded up with bulk grain. The venture netted a substantial profit, and Baltimore was on its way to becoming a major grain processing and exporting center.

In the succeeding years trade was established with the West

Indies and other East Coast colonial ports. During this period Baltimore expanded again, absorbing Fells Point just before the onset of the Revolutionary War. During the war the port remained open and Baltimore secured a major portion of the trade from Annapolis, which suffered under the British blockade. After the war port wardens were appointed to manage the harbor – they proceeded to plot out the course and depth of the river channel, greatly facilitating safe navigation in and out of the harbor.

Finally, in 1797 Baltimore was incorporated as a city, and development of the port was encouraged. This engraving by W. Wellstood depicts the bustling city port at about the time of its incorporation.

DURING the Revolutionary war local shipyards produced many fast ships that not only maintained commerce but also helped fight the war – these craft were refined into what became known as the famous Baltimore clippers. Shortly after this the young nation again went to war with Great Britain. These ships – and their skilled captains – played a large role in the eventual defeat of the vaunted Royal Navy in American waters and on the high seas. Over half of the American ships used during this bloody conflict were constructed in Baltimore shipyards, resulting in further expansion of the port facilities.

These ships were really privateers and enriched themselves preying upon British merchantmen to the extent that Britain regarded Baltimore as a "nest of pirates," which was certainly true. In *Triumph I* we relate this story, pointing out that we suspect many private Baltimore fortunes had provenance to those days and perhaps were used in part to finance B&O.

In the summer of 1814 the British had enough and arrived in Maryland with a large fleet and accompanying army to put paid to these depredations. They first went to Washington DC, burning the White House among many other public buildings and also, by the way, the Library of Congress, in an orgy of vandalism. They then reembarked and sailed up Chesapeake Bay to lay waste to the city and its shipyards.

The British, of course, have many positive attributes but sometimes they are slow learners. It didn't work in the Revolutionary War and it didn't work now. Their proud army landed at North Point, just southeast of the city, and marched forth to give battle to a corps of citizen soldiers consisting of many Maryland regiments (and several companies from York and Hanover PA). By the way, this corps included the 5th Maryland Regiment in which we had the honor to serve many years later as the renumbered 175th Regiment.

Some 4,000 British troops with an additional 1,000 marines and sailors landed at 7am and pushed forward to sweep away these ragged colonials. By 10am their advance was repulsed and their commander, General Robert Ross, was killed. They tried again the next day and again were savagely beaten. Having decided that this nest of pirates was also a nest of vipers, they retreated to their ships in an early rehearsal for Dunkirk.

They then used their fleet to bombard Fort McHenry and that didn't work either, but did give rise to "The Star Spangled Banner" which, of course, became our national anthem in 1931. Originally a poem written by Francis Scott Key (who was aboard a British ship as an emissary), it was later put to the music of a British drinking song thus adding more insult to injury.

They tried one more time in New Orleans and Andrew Jackson sent them reeling back to their ships.

Finally they learned and never tried again. Not in the United States, anyway.

This woodcut depicts a typical scene on Frederick Street in 1819 along the waterfont. There is no evidence of burning.

AS FAST as they were, however, the Baltimore clippers lacked adequate cargo space for lengthy ocean voyages. Enlargement and modifications to the design resulted in the *Ann McKim*, which combined speed and cargo space, enabling it to compete economically in the expanding China trade. Clipper ships of this design spanned the globe, allowing the Port of Baltimore to rival Boston, Philadelphia, New York and New Orleans for the amount of tonnage handled.

But there was a new development underway – while the War of 1812 was still raging the steamboat *Chesapeake* began service up the Bay to Frenchtown, forming a link in a developing Philadelphia-Baltimore route of commerce (see Chapter 2). Ships began to combine a steam boiler connected to large side-wheel paddles with sails – such a vessel has made its appearance among the straight sailing ships in this 1837 view of the harbor from Federal Hill. Note the ship signal station in the foreground.

STEAMBOATS continued to grow in size and numbers. In 1840 the Baltimore Steam Packet Line (commonly known as the Old Bay Line) inaugurated operations in the Bay, and in 1854 the Merchants & Miners Transportation Company began operations along the coast. (Father, by the way, worked for those two venerable lines during the 1930s after having been furloughed by B&O.)

With the development of larger draft ships, channel width and depth became a serious consideration. Although dredging around the wharf areas had been carried out for many years, and a 12-ft. main channel had been dug from the inner harbor out to Fort McHenry, deep draft vessels were not allowed into the harbor until 1858. In 1866 work finally began on the 24-ft. deep Craighill Channel under Federal authorization.

This 1852 daguerreotype shows the increasing number of steam-powered sidewheelers in the harbor.

UNLIKE the War of 1812, the Civil War paralyzed Baltimore, and trade through the port came to a near standstill, although the armor plates for the revolutionary Union ironclad *Monitor* were forged at the Abbott Iron Works in Canton. It took the port several years after the war ended to regain its former level of trade.

Access to the port by rail was difficult because of the cumbersome passage through the city streets, but this was greatly improved when the B&O established its line to a terminal at Locust Point before the war, and afterwards the Union RR finally completed its line to Canton in 1873.

Here a Union battery threatens the harbor from Federal Hill in 1865. Note the large number of steamboats.

Abraham Lincoln also regarded Baltimore as a nest of pro-Southern vipers, centered in the Maryland Club which at that time was located on the far shore of the harbor in this scene.

Lincoln dispatched Federal artillery to this hill and the commander informed the club members that any more secession talk would result in the club being bombarded with the members inside. For good measure, Lincoln also suspended habeas corpus in Baltimore and jailed any hotheads who weren't getting the message. After all, Maryland lay between Washington DC and the rest of the Union with vital rail lines running through Baltimore. He had to have Maryland and also, by the way, Kentucky. Both states stayed in the Union, but to this day Lincoln's birthday is not a holiday in Maryland.

The Civil War was a great tragedy for a border state like Maryland. The typical Marylander's heart may have been South in cavalier spirit, but his head was North. We are rather distantly related to Ulysses S. Grant so there is no question where our sympathies lie. And indeed there was little Southern sympathy in Maryland outside Baltimore and the Eastern Shore. When General Robert E. Lee invaded Central Maryland to "liberate the State" he found no sympathy and much resistance. They did not want to be "liberated" by a bunch of Virginians.

And of course it was a great tragedy for B&O, related in this and many other of our books, and resulted in PRR's invasion, if you will, of Maryland.

That regiment to which we referred earlier in this chapter split, part North and part South. They met at Culps Hill on the first day at Gettysburg and fought each other to a bloody draw. In very recent years a Baltimore sculptor produced a statue (the first new one at Gettysburg in a long time) depicting two wounded soldiers – one Rebel and one Union – helping each other off the battlefield. That fight was so ferocious that it is said that no trees grew there for many years.

And that same regiment was only one of a handful authorized by the Army to carry the Stars and Bars on parade, behind of course the Stars and Stripes.

Over what? This savage calamity has no rational explanation. And, while writing these words, genuine tears formed in our eyes, unbidden.

RECOVERY after the war was spurred when both the B&O and the Union Grain Elevator Company constructed large grain elevators, allowing the port to regain its position as a premier center of grain and flour exporting. However, the sugar trade was dealt a severe blow when four local refineries went bankrupt in the late 1870s – it was not a major commodity here until the 1920s.

In the latter years of the 19th Century the port wardens were replaced by a Harbor Board, and the channel was deepened to 30 ft., setting the stage for the larger steel ships, both foreign and domestic.

This view shows the predominance of steamboats at the Inner Harbor in the early 1870s.

ANOTHER FIRST STONE records the start of construction of Baltimore's second railroad, the Baltimore & Susquehanna, up that historic valley on 8 August 1829. Made of Port Deposit granite, it was originally set at trackside near North Avenue. It was moved from this location on 28 November 1870 when fill dirt was needed for the B&P Tunnel project and mounted on the fence wall of Calvert Street Station, where it was eventually forgotten. It was rediscovered 21 years later by Baltimore General Agent George C. Wilkins, who had it restored and on 4 December 1891 placed on the wall of the Northern Central office building at Calvert and Center Street as shown here in a 1931 photo. When that building was razed the historic marker was given to the Maryland Historical Society.

Gunnarsson Collection/Railroad Museum of Pennsylvania (PHMC)

Chapter 2

Moving South

Philadelphia to Baltimore

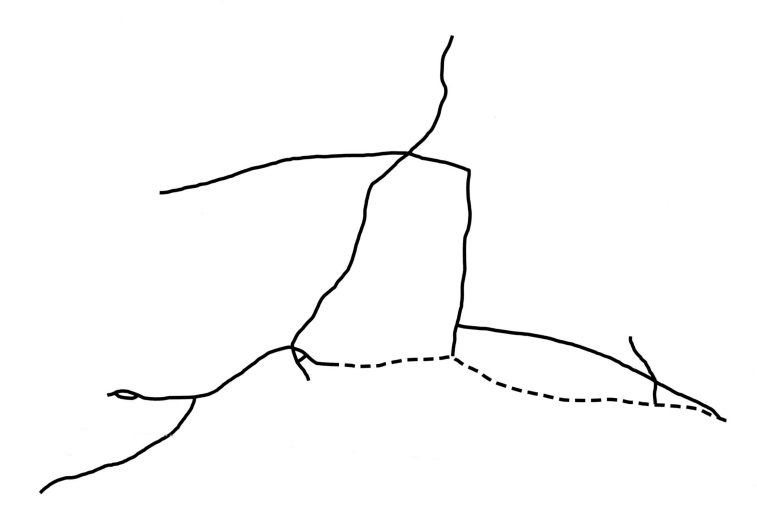

(Caption for artwork on next page)

THE PW&B published a version of this map in its Annual Report for many years, updating it as the system grew. This one shows the complete system as of 1897, when it was operated under lease to PRR. At this time the suburban lines to Newtown Square, West Chester and Octoraro Junction (with the Columbia & Port Deposit RR) were operated as part of the Philadelphia & Baltimore Central RR, and the lines to Washington and Pope's Creek as the Baltimore & Potomac RR. This chapter will deal with the main line to Baltimore, Chapter 3 will cover the P&BC (later known as the Octoraro and West Chester Branches of PRR) and Chapter 7 will deal with the line from Baltimore to Washington. We will address the lines on the Delmarva Peninsula in a future volume in the *Triumph* series.

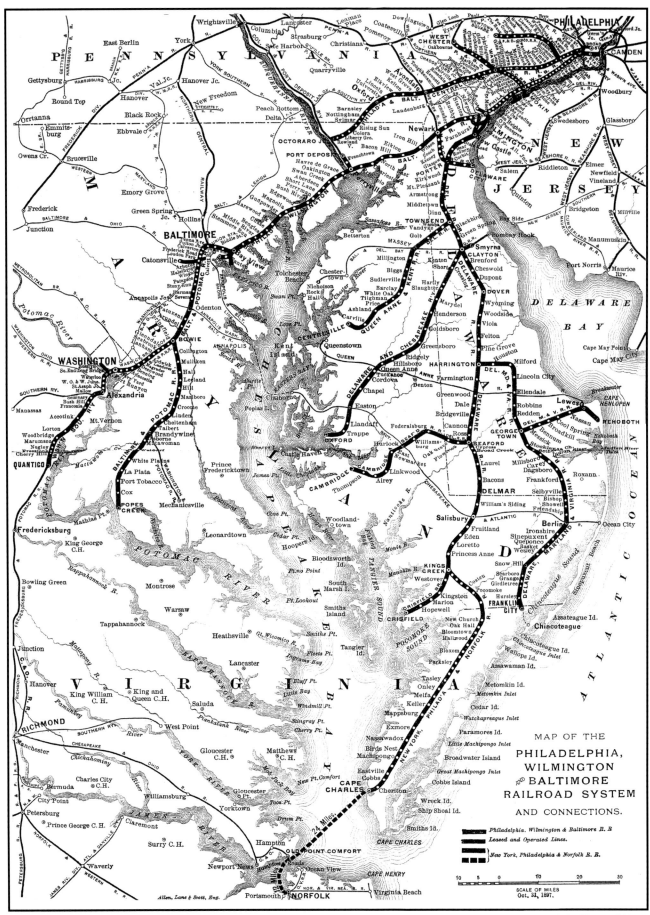

MAP OF THE
PHILADELPHIA,
WILMINGTON
AND BALTIMORE
RAILROAD SYSTEM
AND CONNECTIONS.

Philadelphia, Wilmington & Baltimore R. R
Leased and Operated Lines.
New York, Philadelphia & Norfolk R. R.

SCALE OF MILES
Oct. 31, 1897.

Allen, Lane & Scott, Eng.

Long before Thomas Jefferson brokered the remarkable political deal in 1790 allowing the permanent federal capital to be located on the Potomac River, the corridor connecting Philadelphia, Baltimore and what would be designated Washington DC – in honor of the revered Revolutionary War leader and first President – was an important avenue of commerce. For eons the route had been used by Native American tribes moving between seasonal hunting and fishing grounds and when white settlers established towns in the early 17th Century it became the primary link between the developing Northern and Southern colonies.

The area south of Philadelphia along the Delaware River and Chesapeake Bay played a pivotal role in the development of the United States during the Colonial and Revolutionary War period. Gray's Ferry (as it was originally spelled) was a critical point where the Schuylkill River could be readily crossed, affording a route through Philadelphia and connecting the northern and southern areas.

South of Gray's Ferry to Elkton (midway between Wilmington and the Susquehanna River) was an area heavily settled by Swedish immigrants and later Quakers led by William Penn. Elkton was the scene of an encounter between the Continental Army and the British during the Revolution and later during the War of 1812. North Point, north of Baltimore, was also the scene of military action in 1814 during the 1812 conflict as noted earlier.

Because of the surprisingly difficult overland passage, initially the route utilized a combination of land and water modes. The land portion, the "Queen's Road," was begun in 1706 between Gray's Ferry and Chester and then extended to New Castle DE in 1748 and from there it continued to the shores of Chesapeake Bay for the 45-mile journey to Baltimore by boat. This was the primary route used by both civilians and military forces during the Revolutionary War period. After the war, however, the condition of the road deteriorated and the passage from Philadelphia to New Castle was almost entirely by water, leaving the 20-mile "waggon" trip from there to Charlestown on the Bay as the only land portion. A stagecoach run was inaugurated between Philadelphia, Wilmington and Dover as early as 1794, but it must have been a bumpy ride as little or no improvements were made to the roads.

To remedy the problem of the "wretched" roads in this region, The New Castle & French-town Turnpike Company was incorporated in Delaware on 24 January 1809 and in Maryland on 6 January 1810 to build an improved turnpike between Clark's Corner DE and Frenchtown Landing on the Elk River in Maryland. The following year the New Castle Turnpike Company was chartered by the Delaware Legislature to build an improved road from that town to Clark's Corner. These two turnpikes extending 16 miles across the narrow neck of the Delmarva Peninsula, from the Delaware River to Chesapeake Bay, replaced the previous unimproved road and reduced travel time to two days.

The always enterprising Colonel John Stevens (see *Triumph V*) introduced steamboats on the Delaware River in 1809, and the steamer *Chesapeake* began its run between Frenchtown and Baltimore on 21 June 1813 even as British warships roamed the Bay waters during the War of 1812. This arrangement decreased the travel time to 30 hours including a night's layover – this was later reduced further to less than 24 hours, without lodging. Still later one could take a through steamboat for the entire journey between Philadelphia and Baltimore, departing in the morning and arriving that evening, with no change in accommodations. An advertisement in the *United States Gazette* dated 3 March 1834 proudly proclaimed that the steamboat *William Penn* "will leave the Railroad Line Wharf at Chestnut Street for Baltimore every morning at 7 o'clock."

Responding to this competition, the two turnpike companies took the bold step of transforming themselves into railroads, which were just beginning to make their appearance on the transportation scene. The same year the C&D Canal was opened the two companies resolved to construct a railroad along their right of way – if the capital could be secured – and on 31 March 1830 they were consolidated as the Newcastle & Frenchtown Turnpike & Railroad Company, notably the first railroad in Delaware.

But we are getting ahead of ourselves. Under the able engineering direction of John Randel, Jr., the newly-named company completed a 16-mile single-track rail line between its two termini in February 1832, using strap iron rails laid either on granite blocks or oak stringers. The road initially used horse-drawn cars in revenue service, although there were early experiments with steam locomotives on the track. The first steam locomotive in regular service, the *Delaware*, (believed to be one designed by pioneer English builder Robert Stephenson), was assembled in New Castle and after two months of testing put into operation on 10 September, thus ending the use of horses on the line (this assembly operation later led to a locomotive works in that town).

But this railroad was still part of a rail-water route and consideration soon shifted to building a through rail line. A public meeting had been held in Wilmington on 26 January 1828 to advocate building such a railroad between Philadelphia and Baltimore. In response to growing public pressure the "Philadelphia & Delaware county rail-road company" was chartered by the Pennsylvania Legislature on 2 April 1831 to construct a line from Gray's Ferry to Wilmington (although its Pennsylvania charter only authorized construction to the Delaware border). The Wilmington & Susquehanna Rail Road Company was chartered in Delaware on 18 January 1832 and the Delaware & Maryland Rail Road Company was chartered in Maryland on 14 March to build to Port Deposit on the Susquehanna, and the "Baltimore & Port Deposite" Rail Road was incorporated in Maryland on 5 March 1832 for the line from the Susquehanna southward – thus completing a continuous rail line between Philadelphia and Baltimore, at least on paper (except for a means to cross the river).

We apologize for this recitation of corporate entities, especially because their charters languished initially for lack of funding, but the important thing is that there was now the potential for an all-rail route from Philadelphia to Baltimore (well, almost). To simplify things a bit, the Delaware & Maryland RR was subsequently consolidated with the Wilmington & Susquehanna.

To gain access to Philadelphia, the Philadelphia & Delaware County obtained rights to the Gray's Ferry line and the bridge across the Schuylkill for $50 thousand, but had difficulty raising funds to complete the line. Fortunately new investors including Nicholas Biddle, James Canby, Roswell Colt and Matthew

Newkirk came forward (Newkirk was named President on 18 January 1836) and on 14 March the name of this road was changed by the Pennsylvania Legislature to the "Philadelphia, Wilmington & Baltimore Railroad Company" and its capital stock increased to $400 thousand, fortunately closer to the actual cost of construction.

The final piece of the rail link between Philadelphia and Baltimore and allowing access within Philadelphia itself was the "Southwark rail-road company," incorporated on 2 April 1831. The engineer was none other than a young John Edgar Thomson, later PRR's first Chief Engineer and subsequently rising to become its first truly visionary President (see *Triumph I* and *II*). Completed in 1835, this line ran along the streets, connecting with the City railroad tracks at Broad and Cedar (later South) Streets and running south along Broad Street to Prime (later Washington) Avenue and later extending from there eastward to the docks on the Delaware River. This line, which was leased by the Philadelphia & Delaware County, provided access both to the riverfront and to the growing commercial district, where the PW&B subsequently located its first station at the corner of Eleventh and Market.

The line north of the Susquehanna was laid out by prominent engineers whom we have met in previous volumes, Samuel Kneass and William Strickland. Because of organizational difficulties and initial lack of adequate funding, construction did not actually commence until 1835. The portion from Wilmington to Perryville (which replaced Port Deposit as the terminus on the north bank of the Susquehanna) was completed in 1837. The rights to the section from the Pennsylvania state line south to Wilmington were sold to the Pennsylvania company, which began work in 1836 and completed and opened its line to Gray's Ferry on 15 January 1838.

After a preliminary survey from Baltimore as far north as the Gunpowder River was carried out in 1833, the line south of the Susquehanna was laid out in 1834 under the direction of the distinguished B&O engineer Benjamin H. Latrobe. It was originally planned to extend from Baltimore to opposite Port Deposit, but fortunately under joint agreement with the Delaware & Maryland RR in April 1836 Havre de Grace was established as the northern terminus, directly across from Perryville at the outlet of the river. Unable to raise sufficient funds, the line was re-organized under the auspices of Matthew Newkirk in May 1835 and work finally began in earnest. Construction was completed and a gala celebration held on 1 July 1837, with regular service between Havre de Grace and Baltimore beginning five days later.

Operation between Wilmington and Baltimore commenced on 14 July. This was marked by another festive celebration five days later, this time on board the ferry *Susquehanna*. The delegation from Baltimore, which included B&O officers and city officials, joined counterparts from Philadelphia and Wilmington in enjoying a dinner, "never seen surpassed for abundance, elegance, variety or excellence of preparation . . . to which peculiar zest was imparted by [toasts with] the generous juice of the grape . . . the drinking of which was accompanied by appropriate airs from two excellent bands of music, and speeches from several distinguished gentlemen." It was to be one of the rare times of accord between Philadelphia and Baltimore officialdom, railroad or otherwise. Through service between Grays Ferry and Baltimore began on 17 January 1838, and with the completion of the Schuylkill River bridge on Christmas Day late in that year, the two cities finally had their rail link.

To simplify the corporate structure somewhat and provide one operating management, the three companies were consolidated as the Philadelphia, Wilmington & Baltimore RR by Articles of Union dated 5 February 1838, with the enterprising Matthew Newkirk named as President (they were formally merged with the Southwark RR on 28 March 1877). On 15 March 1839 the PW&B also took control of the original New Castle & Frenchtown RR that started it all.

The broad river was crossed by the ferry appropriately named *Susquehanna*. Passengers were required to walk between the cars and the boat, but the cars themselves were moved onto a track on the upper deck of the vessel – thus inaugurating the first railroad car ferry service in the U. S. Rebuilt at least once, the *Susquehanna* operated successfully back and forth across the outlet of the river until December 1854, when it was retired and replaced with another suitably named boat, the larger and more commodious steamer *Maryland*, which could accommodate an en-tire passenger train on its twin-tracked top deck. This reduced both the transit time and the equipment required to cover the route.

Philadelphia and Baltimore now had a rail artery connecting them, but its condition, both physical and financial, left much to be desired. It was described thusly in 1838 by Charles P. Dare, in his *Railroad Guide*:

> "Although the Road was now in condition for travel, it was necessarily very incomplete. The foundation, newly-graded, lacked solidity; the track was laid with bar rail on continuous [wooden] string pieces, with but little ballast. There were but few depots and water-stations, and those few quite deficient in accommodations and supply. There were but few cars and engines; and the cost of the road and equipments was nearly four and a half millions, while the capital stock was but two and a quarter millions; or, in other words the Company found themselves with a new and incomplete road and burthened with a debt almost equal to their capital stock."

Efforts were made to obtain loans in both the U. S. and Europe, although the low regard held by the latter investors for American securities of the period made this nearly impossible. The company lurched to the brink of financial disaster by regularly issuing dividends in the misplaced hope of placating stockholders. In 1842 and again in July 1847 PW&B refinanced its debt, but this provided only temporary relief.

One of the expenses of the road was constant replacement of the thin strap iron rail, which wore out quickly – sometimes with disastrous results. Beginning in 1844 the section between Philadelphia and Wilmington was re-laid with 62-lb. T-section rail on wooden crossties, which proved to be superior to other types. Several smaller bridges were rebuilt during this period, new shops were established in Wilmington and several new locomotives were purchased and older ones rebuilt. On 18 February 1850 the PW&B took a significant step – opening its own station on President Street in Baltimore, replacing the rented space in the B&O depot on congested Pratt Street that had been a constant early source of friction.

On 2 December 1850 PW&B inaugurated a Day Express train on a trial basis between Philadelphia and Baltimore. Connecting with the morning express train from New York, the southbound train left Philadelphia at 3 p.m., making the run in an impressive 4-1/2 hours! The following year the schedule was revised and expanded as follows: connecting with the 9 a.m. express from New York, the southbound train left Philadelphia at 2 p.m., arriving in Baltimore at 6:30 in time to make the 7:30 train from Baltimore to Washington, for a total travel time of 12 hours – not bad for 1851, considering the cars had to be hauled by horses from the terminal in Philadelphia to Gray's Ferry and also transported by boat across the Susquehanna River! In 1859 two passenger cars were converted to sleepers and attached to the Night Express between Philadelphia and Washington, in order that "passengers may have a comfortable night's sleep and not be disturbed by any change of cars at the Susquehanna."

By 1862, with the Civil War raging, it was decided to attempt through service to New York, in large part because of pressure from the Union Army. Because there was no easy connection through Philadelphia northward, this involved either shunting cars by ferry to the Camden & Amboy (on 26 June 1854 the PW&B had begun running cars via the Southwark RR to the docks at the foot of Washington Street for this connection) or later over Philadelphia & Reading rails to the Philadelphia & Trenton depot in Kensington, but either routing was extremely cumbersome and time consuming. Accordingly, PW&B entered into a joint agreement with PRR and the Reading to construct the Junction RR in West Philadelphia, which had been chartered on 3 May 1860. This involved a still circuitous – but now at least all-rail – route through the City when the northern portion of this line was opened in November 1863. It was not until 1867, when the PRR opened the Connecting Railway directly to the P&T main, that efficient through service between New York City and Washington could take place (see *Triumph III* for more on these two critical links through Philadelphia).

On 28 February 1851 Samuel Morse Felton, who would become one of the foremost railroad officials of the time, was brought from the Fitchburg RR by the New England owners of the PW&B and elected President – from that point the affairs of the company began to turn around. A dedicated, industrious and resourceful leader, Felton set about making the

PW&B a first-class operation. Citing the imminent completion of the B&O to Wheeling, West Virginia, and connections to the West, he secured funding to re-lay additional sections of track with heavier T-section rail (a program completed over the entire line in 1858) and add new and heavier locomotives as well as new passenger equipment to carry the anticipated increase in traffic.

He replaced many of the old frame passenger stations along the line with new brick ones, and on 17 May 1852 opened a "commodious" new passenger and freight terminal at Broad and Prime Streets in Philadelphia, then the largest in the City. For the first time trains were hauled into this grand new terminal by steam locomotives, eliminating the need for cumbersome horse-drawn conveyance over City-owned trackage. Heavier rail was laid on this line to accommodate the traffic. A new freight station was also opened in Baltimore, and the Delaware RR extending southward into the central part of the state was completed and operated under lease.

The improvements were favorably received by Charles Dare:

> "All these changes, with the reduced time between the cities, had the effect of fitting the road for favorable comparison with any other first class lines in the country."

But one improvement that was still sorely needed was a bridge over the Susquehanna. In the early days passengers tolerated the time-consuming transfer from train to ferry and back again. However, complaints increased as rail travel improved and other lines constructed bridges over major waterways. In severe winters the river often froze to such a thickness that ferry passage was impossible. This occurred in the winter of 1848-9, when passengers had to walk across the ice or go the long way around by boat.

It happened again in the frigid winter of 1851-2, but this time the ice jam was so severe that the company initially used wagons – and then when that didn't work took the unusual step of laying tracks across it. Between 15 January and 24 February, when a winter thaw loosened its grip, some 1378 cars were hauled across the temporary "ice bridge," resulting in the trip between Philadelphia and Baltimore taking upwards of 48 hours on numerous occasions.

As a result of this bizarre incident, public agitation grew for construction of a permanent bridge, and authorization was requested from the Maryland Legislature in the late winter of 1852. However one person's remedy is another's threat, and river navigation interests located in Port Deposit blocked legislative action for a time. This group, led by influential State Senators Jacob Tome and Hiram McCullough (Tome curiously was a large PW&B stockholder), waged a series of "bridge fights" (reminiscent of earlier canal vs. railroad battles) opposing a railroad bridge across the river. Their objection was based on the fear that a bridge would restrict access to the schooners that transported large quantities of lumber and stone out of Port Deposit.

An amiable solution was eventually found – authority to build the bridge was granted on 12 May 1852, providing that the PW&B build a 3.8-mile branch to Port Deposit (the beginning of the Columbia & Port Deposit RR – see Chapter 4) and include two draws in the bridge to allow river navigation.

Initial construction work began in 1854 under the leadership of Chief Engineer George A. Parker and the esteemed Benjamin Latrobe as consultant, but was suspended shortly thereafter for engineering reasons – there was serious concern if a bridge would hold – and because of financial constraints associated with the Panic of 1857. Because of its potential role in transporting large numbers of Union troops during the Civil War, work was resumed in the fall of 1862 with construction of a test pier – in the deepest water ever attempted – to determine if it could withstand the ravages of winter ice conditions on the river. It actually held for three winters, but the remaining masonry piers and the wooden truss spans were not completed until mid-summer 1866, and the *Maryland* had to perform the heroic task instead.

On 22 July (some sources say 25 July) violence of a different sort struck – a disastrous tornado swept down-river and destroyed all the spans except one (This was eerily reminiscent of a similar blow by Mother Nature that destroyed the PRR bridge under construction upriver at Rockville in March 1849 – see *Triumph II*). The area is still susceptible to high winds, as duly noted on the approaches to the I-95 highway bridge farther upstream.). The 3269-ft. long arch reinforced truss bridge was quickly rebuilt and opened for regular traffic on 26 November 1866 – providing for the first time a truly all-rail route between Philadelphia and Baltimore. The achievement came at a huge price – nearly $2.3 million – which of course reflected the cost of nearly two wooden bridge structures.

In 1862-5 a large coal wharf was constructed at New Castle in conjunction with the Reading RR. This deep-water wharf allowed export of coal year-round and winter shipments whenever the ice obstructed the Delaware farther north.

The PW&B main suffered only relatively minor damage during the Civil War, when the Sixth Massachusetts Regiment being sent to relieve threatened Washington, DC was fired on by an unruly mob of Southern partisans in Baltimore on 19 April 1861. As a result officials of the State of Maryland and the City of Baltimore directed that several bridges between Baltimore and the Susquehanna River be destroyed to thwart use of the line by more Northern forces (see Chapter 5). By agreement between Felton and Thomson, Union troops were forwarded to Perryville where the steamer *Maryland* carried them to Annapolis for connection to the B&O's Washington Branch, thus saving the nation's capital. When the threat abated PW&B completed repair of the bridges, and service was restored on 13 May.

The mainline of the B&O was cut early in the war, essentially ending traffic interchange with that beleaguered road for some time. During the invasion of Maryland in the early summer of 1864, the PW&B bridge over the Gunpowder River was again burned, and a train was briefly captured by Confederate forces at Magnolia on 11 July. This was the last hostile act suffered by the road, and a year later the line handled the surge of weary but thankful Union troops returning northward at the war's conclusion.

Although the PW&B suffered considerably less damage than the B&O or even the Northern Central (see Chapter 5), Felton soon learned that heavy military traffic was both a blessing and a curse, and he invested considerable time and effort not only managing and maintaining the road, but also in staunchly defending his road's efforts in support of the Union Army. Foremost among these was preventing the government from constructing a parallel "Air Line" between New York and Washington (see *Triumph III*).

Largely in response to heavy wartime traffic the

road began double-tracking the line in 1863, continuing the program in sections until 1866 when all but 14 miles were completed. On 17 December of that year the branch was opened to Port Deposit, site of the original planned terminus of the main on the north bank of the Susquehanna.

Having successfully rebuilt the railroad and guided it through the worst of the difficult Civil War years, an exhausted and partially paralyzed (from a stroke) Samuel Felton retired as President, although he remained on the Board and was active in real estate developments along the new main line realignment south of Philadelphia (discussed below). In 1865 he was succeeded by Isaac Hinckley, who hailed from Lowell, Massachusetts. Under Hinckley's able direction steel rails were substituted for iron in several stretches and found to be decidedly superior. In 1869 it was decided to use steel rails thereafter, at least on the main, and by the late 1870s the PW&B could boast an all-steel right of way.

In 1870 PW&B decided to rebuild the main line between Grays Ferry and Chester on a new alignment away from the Delaware River, which frequently flooded and washed out sections of the line often rendering it impassable for days at a time. Known as the Darby Improvement, the new double-tracked line included several planned suburban communities envisioned by Hinckley to attract upscale clientele in competition with PRR's highly successful Main Line west of the City. No expense was spared in the construction of lakes, parks and resort hotels to attract both summer and year-round residents. Although it was delayed by labor strikes, the line was completed and the first passenger train passed over it on 18 November 1872. The new line was ballasted with broken stone, which was found to be so superior to gravel that Hinckley indicated that he "intended to continue the substitution over the whole line." The following year the old right of way was leased to the Reading for 999 years and became its Chester (freight) Branch.

This project was completed just in time, as flooding in 1873 resulted in the destruction of several bridges in Delaware including the stone arch structure at Christiana and several smaller bridges along the Delaware River. This caused considerable loss of traffic because it occurred during the height of that year's peach and oyster season, always a prime revenue source on the Delmarva Peninsula.

In anticipation of increased traffic to the grand Centennial Exposition in Philadelphia (see *Triumph III*), double-tracking of the entire line from Philadelphia to Baltimore was finally completed in 1875, and a new freight station was constructed in Philadelphia, allowing expansion of the adjacent passenger terminal at Broad and Prime Streets. It must have been worth it, as passenger receipts during 1876 increased by nearly 36 per cent.

The wooden bridge over the Susquehanna was rebuilt with iron trusses over the period 1873-9 and a new draw span was put in place in early 1880. Continuing its improvements to the right of way, the program of replacing gravel with stone ballast on the entire main line was implemented in 1878.

And thus by 1881 Messrs. Felton, Hinckley and associates had brought the PW&B to a state where it ranked among the finest roads in the U.S. A well-maintained double-tracked mainline extended from Philadelphia to Baltimore, with branches from Newark to Delaware City and Wilmington via New Castle to Porter DE. It controlled the West Chester & Philadelphia RR and the Philadelphia & Baltimore Central, running from Philadelphia to Octoraro Junction, where it connected with the Columbia & Port Deposit RR. It operated by lease the Delaware RR from Porter southward to Delmar, which in turn operated a host of branches to the rich agricultural areas on the Delmarva Peninsula.

It owned nearly 90 locomotives and a first-class passenger fleet consisting of almost 200 passenger, baggage and express cars along with nearly 1300 freight cars plus work equipment. The PW&B achieved a considerable measure of success in its own right, operating through trains to New York City that connected on the northern end with PRR via the Junction RR (and then with the New Jersey Railroads via the Connecting RR), and on the southern end to Washington, DC via the B&O, which also operated through trains on this route.

But this peaceful situation was not to last – in part because of its striking success and certainly because of its strategic location the PW&B was a prize highly sought after by the two titans with grand designs of their own. John Edgar Thomson made the first move in the titanic battle by quietly acquiring the Baltimore & Potomac RR in 1867 (see Chapter 5). This short but critical link gave PW&B direct access to the nation's capital, where B&O heretofore thought it had exclusive province. Thomson followed this shrewd move by another – constructing the Connecting RR across the northern reaches of Philadelphia and then leasing the United New Jersey's line to Jersey City, opposite New York City (see *Triumph III* and *V*).

Thus PW&B occupied the strategic route between these two to form a direct all-rail route from New York to Washington – and whoever gained the entire route could claim one of the most valuable stretches of railroad right of way in the nation.

Even after PRR's lease of the UNJ Joint Companies both PRR and PW&B remained neutral, at least outwardly, honoring the previous traffic agreements with B&O over the routing (relations between PRR and PW&B were competitive but generally cordial – PW&B wisely stayed out of the PRR-B&O conflict. However, John W. Garrett, B&O's bumbling and contentious president, always looking for an advantage in the struggle, decided to force the issue. In 1874 he launched an ill-advised but intense rate war, blatantly accusing PRR of refusing to sell New York-Washington tickets via B&O's Washington Branch – and worse – not accepting B&O freight traffic to industries located on PRR lines in the Philadelphia area. A general rate settlement the following year seemingly eased the conflict for a while, but the two corporate giants were merely biding their time, awaiting the next opportunity.

That opportunity came in 1879, when the Reading RR's ambitious president Franklin Gowen announced that he had put together his own route for the road's prize anthracite traffic to New York, utilizing a combination of short lines and trackage rights over the Central RR of New Jersey. As a result, on 1 December 1880 B&O abruptly withdrew its trains from PRR's leased New Jersey trackage and rerouted them over the Reading lines, known as the Bound Brook route.

However this revised routing still required the trains to traverse not only the PW&B to Philadelphia, but also the Junction RR, including a critical one-mile section through the West Philadelphia yards owned exclusively by PRR. In retaliation for Garrett's precipitous action PRR imposed an extra fee and enforced the court-authorized provision allowing it to use its own motive power in this section, resulting in untoward – and not unintended – traffic delays. B&O secured a Federal court order enjoining PRR from delaying their trains through the area, but conditions improved only marginally, with mysterious delays still occurring from time to time.

Fed up with PRR's backhanded tactics, Garrett went after outright control of the PW&B, and through a devious series of maneuvers finally reached agreement with the line's largest stockholder, Nathaniel P. Thayer of Boston, to deliver to the B&O a majority of the PW&B stock at $70 per share. On 17 February 1881 Garrett convinced a stellar group of investors to purchase 120,000 shares at the $70 price on his behalf, and publicly boasted on 23 February that the PB&W was in his expansive pocket.

Never one to keep his mouth shut, Garrett had spoken too soon. As it turned out, Thayer was having difficulty convincing PW&B stockholders to sell at $72, much less the agreed upon $70. With newly named First Vice President Alexander Cassatt pushing President George Roberts hard, PRR seized the opening, reaching agreement to purchase 92,000 shares at a premium $78, and the remainder by April 1 at that price.

Roberts and Cassatt triumphantly secured Board approval for the deal on 8 March, and on 7 June PRR delivered a check for exactly $14,949,052.30 to H. P Kidder and associates, giving it overwhelming stock control of the PW&B. It was the largest single corporate check written at that point in U.S. history. The purchase was completed on 1 July, and PRR began operating the line from 31 October 1881 (see *Triumph III* for more on this extraordinary – and exciting – corporate saga).

Garrett returned to Baltimore, once again thwarted by PRR. He then followed the only course of action left open to him – on 23 March he announced that B&O would construct its own parallel line into Philadelphia – regardless of the cost – connecting with the Reading for access into New York City. Making the best of the situation, and overcoming years of continued PRR harassment through the Philadelphia area, this became B&O's famed "Royal Blue Line" between Washington and New York, and survives today as a freight operation under CSX aegis.

Thus starting with no north-south presence along the East coast in the mid-19th Century, in just 14 years PRR emerged triumphant with the premium mainline route, today's Northeast Corridor, fulfilling Thomson's vision and setting the stage for Cassatt to complete the final entry into Manhattan in the first decade of the 20th Century (see Triumph V).

The PW&B was divided into three operating divisions: Maryland, from Philadelphia southward on the mainline to Baltimore (later extended to Washington DC – see Chapter 5) and branches – Delaware, consisting of the complex of lines south of Wilmington on the Delmarva Peninsula – and Central, the Philadelphia & Baltimore Central, including the West Chester and Newtown Square Branches (see Chapter 3).

An extensive program of right of way improvements was launched over the next several years to bring the line fully up to PRR standards and also to accommodate growing traffic. This consisted of new iron bridges at several locations, laying of heavier weight steel rail and installation of 40-car passing sidings for freight trains at several key locations along the main: Chester, Thurlow, Edge Moor, Newport, Newark, North East, Perryville and Aberdeen.

In October 1882 the PW&B Arsenal Extension was completed, connecting the Junction RR and the PRR Delaware Extension at Arsenal Bridge (see *Triumph III*), greatly reducing the need to use the Gray's Ferry bridge. This was extended farther northward along the banks of the Schuylkill River during the following years. In conjunction with this project, the freight yard at Gray's Ferry was expanded. On 1 March 1899 PRR purchased the share of the Junction RR previously owned by the Reading, and the short but critical link was leased to the PW&B.

On 28 March 1888 Isaac Hinckley, who had loyally served the PW&B as President for 23 years, died – the office being assumed by George Roberts, President of PRR, which would then be the subsequent pattern. This was followed less than a year later by the death of his predecessor, Samuel Felton, on 24 January 1889. Mr. Felton had served as President of the line for 14 years and a director for nearly 40.

It was the end of an era.

Although the PW&B had operated over the tracks of the Baltimore & Potomac RR (see Chapter 5) south of Baltimore since shortly after its takeover by PRR in 1867, access to the District of Columbia was difficult, requiring passage along city streets in some locations and crossing others at grade (a similar situation existed for the rival B&O line). In response to strong public pressure to solve the problem of dangerous grade crossings in the city the U. S. Congress passed legislation on 12 February 1901 directing both roads to build new stations and eliminate the grade crossings. The legislation also provided for formation of a terminal company to carry out this work, and the Washington Terminal Company was incorporated on 6 December.

In order to facilitate this formidable task plus rebuilding of the Long Bridge over the Potomac (even with partial federal compensation of $1.5 million), PRR took the step of consolidating the B&P with the PW&B, forming a new company, the Philadelphia, Baltimore & Washington RR, on 1 November 1902 (we will discuss the extensive changes in Washington, DC in Chapter 7). At this time PRR also undertook to acquire additional PW&B stock, but the new company continued to be operated as a separate unit like its predecessor.

Under PRR guidance the PB&W immediately began an extensive program to upgrade the line between Philadelphia and Baltimore, as part of Cassatt's massive 1902 Improvements program to increase the traffic-carrying capacity of the entire system. Central to this program on the Maryland Division was the elevation of the right of way through Chester and Wilmington, expansion of the Edge Moor freight yard just north of Wilmington and construction of a new double-track truss bridge on the new elevation crossing the Susquehanna between Perryville and Havre de Grace.

As with similar programs on the New York Division (see *Triumph V*) this involved track elevation through urban areas on large fills, supported in congested downtown sections on heavy masonry retaining walls with plate girder bridges over city streets. In many cases the track was realigned to reduce curvature and additional tracks were added, but unlike the program on the New York Division, third and fourth tracks were only added in stretches where traffic warranted.

This was a major effort for the Division, as always

receiving close personal scrutiny from Cassatt. In July 1905, upon receiving a favorable progress report from Chief Engineer William H. ("Stone") Brown on the Susquehanna bridge (except in this case it was a steel structure), he replied that he was "glad to know that everything is going along so well. If the American Bridge Company needs any further pushing on the erection of the bridge at Havre-de-Grace please let me know and I will telegraph Judge Gary [the chairman of U. S. Steel at that time]."

On 3 April 1916 the Philadelphia & Baltimore Central RR (see Chapter 3) and several other companies were merged into the PB&W, but operated as a separate unit within PRR. On 1 May the PB&W was reorganized to reflect the change – the Maryland Division now consisted of the following components – the PB&W main from 62nd Street in Philadelphia to Back River bridge, Baltimore – the C&PD Branch – the Newtown Square Branch – the Philadelphia & Baltimore Central to Octoraro Junction (Octoraro Branch) and Wawa to West Chester (Wawa Branch), plus short branches south of Philadelphia and Wilmington. On 1 January 1918, the PB&W and its branches became an integral part of the PRR system under a 999-year lease – becoming the Southern Grand (later General) Division.

The largest single capital improvement program in the division's history was electrification of the mainline. PRR had taken initial steps in 1905 on the Long Island and the West Jersey & Seashore, expanded it with electrification of the bold new line into Penn Station in New York City in 1910 (see *Triumph V*) and addressed another area of congested traffic with the Philadelphia suburban program out of Broad Street Station to Paoli and Chestnut Hill in 1915-18 (see *Triumph III*), but this massive program would ultimately take electrification well beyond the suburban areas.

In 1928 then President W. W. "General" Atterbury made the dramatic announcement that the Philadelphia suburban electrification would be extended to Wilmington, West Chester and Trenton as part of a comprehensive program to electrify the entire north-south mainline between New York City and Washington, DC. Both routes south of Philadelphia involved high-density suburban commuter traffic,

with stations located about one mile apart.

Work began almost immediately on the 27.5-mile line to Wilmington, using the same tubular catenary pole construction used on the Paoli project (although based on experience with that line, high-strength bronze cables and fittings were substituted for galvanized steel, thus providing a non-corrosive installation). However on the 25.5-mile West Chester Branch rolled H-columns were used, a successful design installed on the Norfolk & Western and the Virginian Railways and utilized subsequently on PRR.

Power was single-phase, 25-cycle 13,200 volts supplied by the Philadelphia Electric Company to a PRR substation at Lamokin, where it was stepped up to 132,000 volts for transmission to substations along the line and then stepped down to 11,000 volts for the trolley. Philadelphia Electric generated the power at its Chester plant and delivered it via underground cables to Lamokin, where three 15,000 kw frequency changers converted the 60-cycle current to 25-cycle for railroad use. PRR substations were constructed at Arsenal Bridge (Philadelphia), Glenolden, Lamokin, Bellevue and Wilmington (West Yard) for the main, and at Morton, Lenni, Cheyney, and West Chester for the Branch.

The expenditure, exclusive of the MU cars, was about $14.5 million. The MP54 fleet was augmented with 128 new cars, providing 50 trains daily to Wilmington and 46 to West Chester. Service to Wilmington began in September 1928 and on the Branch in December.

PRR resolutely continued work on the mainline electrification through the Depression, initially using its normal funding sources (In 1932 a $27.5 million loan was secured from the Reconstruction Finance Corporation, paid off the following year from internal funds). Service was inaugurated on the Philadelphia-New York City section of the mainline on 16 June 1933 (see *Triumph V*), but work south of Wilmington, which had begun in May 1931, was suspended in 1932 because of severe financial constraints, and trains had to change power at this point. Halting a program of this magnitude, with its resulting unemployment, was of serious concern to the Federal Government as well as to PRR. Finally on 30 December 1933 the Public Works Administration agreed to loan PRR the $70 million needed to complete the project over the next two years, and work resumed in January. All of the borrowed funds were subsequently repaid.

Although there were experienced pole-line construction workers available outside the railroad, PRR felt a strong loyalty to its own laid-off ("furloughed") employees. There ensued "one of the most unusual training programs in its history. At outdoor 'schools,' brakemen and firemen were turned into linemen, clerks and ticket sellers into carpenters, car repairmen and machinists into electricians."

It was a massive program that had a far-reaching effect at a critical time in the nation's economic history. Some 15,000 laid-off workers were recalled, retrained and put back to work. In addition the purchase of $41 million worth of equipment, materials, and supplies generated employment for an additional 10,000 workers in 35 states. Underscoring the impact of the program, the inaugural train from Washington to Philadelphia on 28 January 1935 carried Secretary of State Cordell Hull and Public Works Administrator Harold L. Ickes along with several senators, governors and PRR officials, including General Atterbury (who retired shortly thereafter) having seen at least part of his dream come to fruition. Regular service was initiated on 10 February 1935 when *The Congressional* was hauled by electric locomotives in both directions between New York and Washington.

Major freight yards between Harsimus Cove, Jersey City, and Potomac Yard, south of Washington, were also electrified and freight service under the wires between those two points began in May, allowing 24-hour utilization of the electric plant.

The magnitude of the 225-mile New York-Washington electrification program was impressive, only partially captured in the following statistics: 400-700 miles *each* of transmission, messenger, auxiliary, trolley, ground and signal wire on 4500 steel catenary poles, using some 8200 strings of transmission and 21,000 strings of catenary insulators, 83 large power transformers and nearly 3-1/2 tons of structural steel for substations spaced about every 10 miles on the main. Power for the main south of Wilmington was purchased from public utility companies at Perryville and Benning DC.

The program initially involved through passenger and freight trains only. Industrial switching continued to be handled by steam except in the mandated Baltimore Improvements area (see Chapter 6). South of Wilmington several improvements to the right of way were required – these included two additional tracks through Baltimore and enlargement of the existing tunnels and in Washington electrification of Union Station and approaches, as well as through the tunnel under the Capitol grounds leading to Potomac Yard (see Chapter 7). All of these areas involved extensive and exhaustive interaction with the B&O and the respective municipalities, generating endless public and private meetings, letters, telegrams, memos, plans and more plans – and at times considerable friction and even a series of city ordinances and lawsuits.

But it was finally completed – a triumph of major proportions – allowing PRR to enter the World War II period immensely better prepared to handle the huge wartime traffic surges. In conjunction with the electrification, a new automatic block signal system was completed in 1935, using new position light signals and corresponding cab signals. In addition, Centralized Traffic Control was installed in the area of the Susquehanna River bridge and approaches, controlled from Perryville Tower. The road also planned extensive right of way improvements, including additional sections of third and fourth tracks, but the financial constraints noted above required postponement of many of these projects until the wartime traffic made them mandatory.

What PRR had wrought was a triumph of spectacular proportions, allowing the New York-Washington route to become one of the nation's busiest traffic corridors, linking the national capital and the major eastern centers of commerce with a steel superhighway.

Watkins, History of the Pennsylvania Railroad/*Ted Xaras Collection*

THIS POSTER dated 1 June 1833 heavily promotes passenger service "propelled by a locomotive engine" on the Newcastle & Frenchtown Railroad, the earliest railroad in Delaware. It ran across the narrow neck of the Delmarva Peninsula, providing an early land link between steamboats running from both termini connecting to Philadelphia and Baltimore, respectively. It was the forerunner of the eventual all-rail route between these two rival cities and was later taken over by PW&B, thus becoming one of the earliest corporate entities in the PRR system. Note that the round-trip fare of 50 cents is the same as the one-way passage.

Watkins, History of the Pennsylvania Railroad/*Ted Xaras Collection*

ANOTHER POSTER advertising new direct mail service on PW&B between Philadelphia and Baltimore beginning 24 November 1845 notes that the former routing via steamboat and rail (on the New Castle & Frenchtown line) would be discontinued on the next day. Curiously, although mail contracts would eventually be very lucrative for the line, initially there was considerable disagreement between PW&B and the Postmaster General, each wanting jurisdiction over the schedule of mail runs. PW&B's refusal to run a night mail train caused them to lose the contract for 1839, with the bizarre result that the mails between Philadelphia and Baltimore were routed on the state-owned Philadelphia & Columbia westward to Columbia, by stage between Columbia and York and then down the Baltimore & Susquehanna to their final destination. Eventually, with compensation of $30 thousand annually for its trouble and expense, the road reluctantly agreed to run a midnight mail train beginning 1 April 1840.

Specially-equipped postal cars were introduced in 1864, and these led to further disagreements. In 1873 PW&B threatened to go back to the use of bulk mail transport in baggage cars unless the U. S. Senate allowed compensation to the road in line with the cost of the service. Agreement was eventually reached and mail handling became a valuable revenue source on PRR.

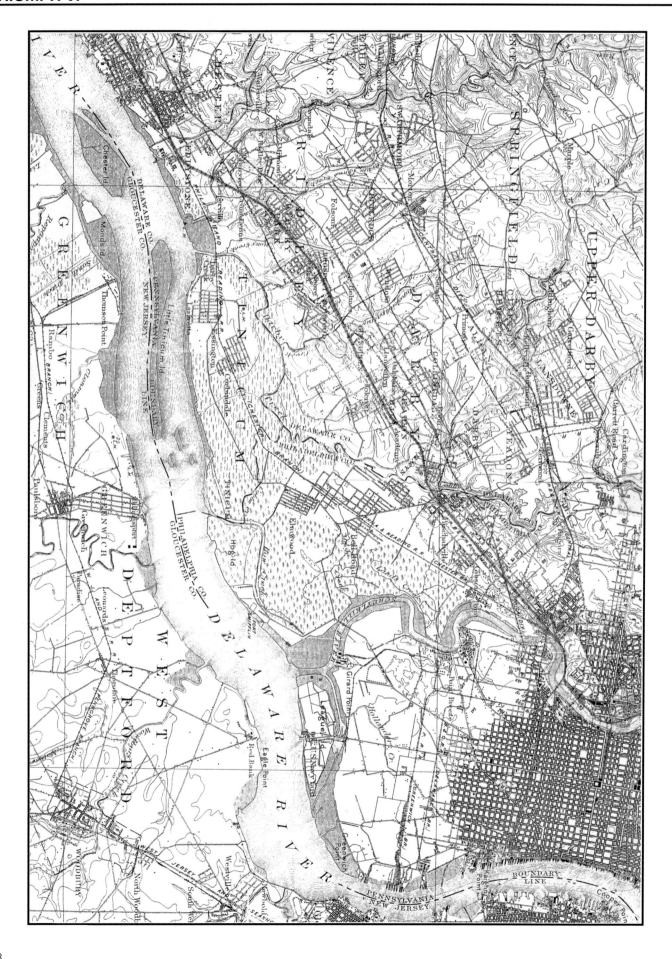

(Caption for artwork on previous page)

THE ORIGINAL ALIGNMENT of the PW&B from Grays Ferry opposite Philadelphia to Ridley Creek in Eddystone ran through the Tinicum marshlands along the Delaware River and was subject to frequent flooding and washouts. As a result PW&B engineers constructed a new line farther to the west. The project, known as the Darby Improvement, consisted not only of a new right of way but also 13 stations to serve planned suburban communities along the line. The project generated considerable excitement – land values along the new right of way more than doubled during construction. The new double-tracked route was built in 1870-2 using steel rails and the first train passed along it on 18 November 1872. The old right of way was leased to the Philadelphia & Reading on 1 July 1873 and became that road's Chester (freight) Branch. Both the new main (recently four-tracked) and the old line are shown here in a USGS map published in 1898.

Farther north, the tracks between Mill Creek and Grays Ferry connecting the PW&B main with the Junction RR (later the PRR Grays Ferry Branch) were finally completed in 1866,

providing direct access to the PRR system. The PRR Board approved the acquisition of PW&B in March 1881, and the purchase was completed on 1 July 1881. With the opening of Broad Street Station (upper right, opposite Philadelphia City Hall) in December 1881, PB&W trains were shifted to that terminal, immediately taxing its capacity (see *Triumph III*).

In 1881-3 PW&B constructed a line connecting the Junction RR with PRR's Delaware Extension, utilizing the Arsenal Bridge crossing instead of the Grays Ferry line, which was used for freight traffic after PW&B passenger trains were routed into the newly-opened Broad Street Station in 1881.

The map also shows the "back door" PW&B line into Philadelphia from the south – here designated the Central Division (originally the Philadelphia & Baltimore Central and later the Octoraro Branch), utilizing a portion of the old West Chester & Philadelphia right of way to enter West Philadelphia (see Chapter 3). And of course, we also have the B&O line (just above the PW&B main) that John Garrett – loser in the titanic battle to control the PW&B – was forced to build in 1886 to gain access to Philadelphia and connect with ally Reading to continue on to New York City..

E. P. Alexander Archive/Ted Xaras Collection

PW&B'S first station in Philadelphia (mostly just a ticket office) was located along the east-west tracks of the City RR, at the southeast corner of 3rd and Market Streets, which became the permanent axis of PRR stations in the City (see *Triumph III* for a full discussion of the evolution of PRR terminals in Philadelphia). Passengers were initially transported via coaches and later omnibus (and ferry across the Schuylkill River) to its Grays Ferry terminus. With completion of the bridge across the river in 1838, horse-drawn railcars could be moved via Prime Street (later Washington Avenue) and Broad Street to Market (City ordinance prohibited locomotives in the business district). In 1842 the station location was moved westward on Market to

the southeast corner of 11th Street, which can be considered the road's first depot in the City. To gain access to the City, PW&B was required to provide one-third of the cost of widening Prime Street to 100 ft. This allowed laying of a double-track line from Grays Ferry to Broad Street, enabling the cars to be hauled into the City. This in turn allowed discontinuation of the "annoying and expensive" omnibus system to Grays Ferry.

Here we have a rare view looking westward at the tracks along Washington Avenue ca. 1890. The two-track right of way now has long sidings on either side – note also the tracks serving local businesses and the switch tower in the background, behind the near signals.

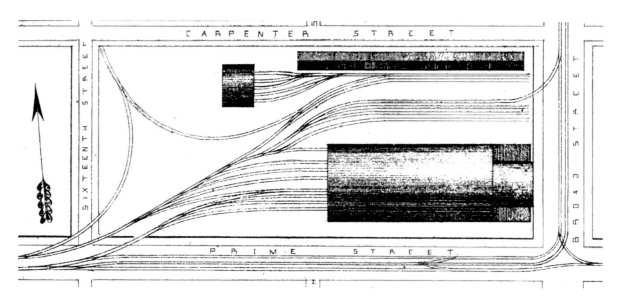

Ted Xaras Collection

ON 17 MAY 1852 PW&B took the bold step of opening a grand new terminal at the northwest corner of Broad and Prime, proudly boasting that the station contained "every convenience known or believed to be essential to a station of such prominence." The 150 x 400 ft. long structure – built for $65 thousand – included an enclosed train shed covering eight tracks and three platforms, handling both passenger and freight traffic. Amenities included Philadelphia's first station dining room, along with the waiting room, ladies and gentlemen's restrooms, baggage facilities and ticket office. The second floor contained a large meeting hall and Company offices. With completion of this terminal, trains were for the first time brought into the City by locomotives, over PW&B-owned trackage – a significant triumph in itself. This 1857 diagram shows the configuration of the station as expanded in 1856, with an iron freight shed and small engine house.

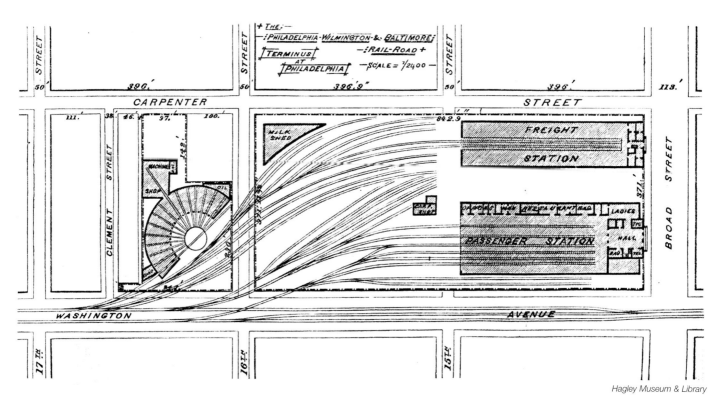

Hagley Museum & Library

THE GRAND Centennial Exposition brought massive crowds of passengers to Philadelphia to celebrate the nation's birthday and in particular to see the marvels of the age. Both PRR and PB&W heavily publicized the event and greatly enlarged their passenger facilities to handle the anticipated surge of traffic. PB&W expanded their terminal by rebuilding the front of the passenger station and constructing a separate freight station and roundhouse, as shown here in a diagram published in 1876.

THE BUSY STATION is shown in an 1876 engraving, along with the various means of transport of the period – carriage, omnibus and horse-drawn streetcar, plus freight wagon. Note the original name on the rebuilt façade, "Southern and Western Railroad Station." During the Civil War, thousands of Union troops passed through the terminal to Southern battlefields, making use of a large canteen located across the street.

Ted Xaras Collection

PASSENGERS traveling to the Centennial Exposition might have had their train headed by stylish PW&B 4-4-0 No. 64, here displaying its stunning – and abundant – polished brass finery in a photo from the mid-1870s. Up to the early 1860s PW&B locomotives were identified only by name, but by 31 October 1865 the roster included numbers in addition to names, and in the roster issued a year later names were discontinued. There were 76 locomotives listed in 1876, from a variety of builders including Baldwin, Norris, Taunton, and Schenectady. Units used on the Delmarva branches were primarily built by local builder New Castle.

Railroad Museum of Pennsylvania (PHMC)

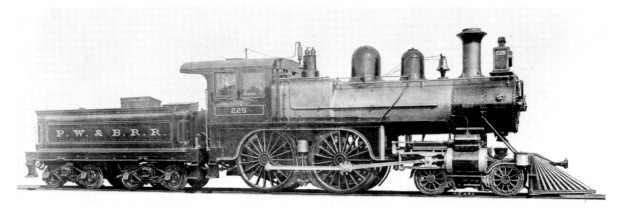

Ted Xaras Collection

IN THE 1890s the PW&B train might have been pulled by the 225. Most of the elegant brass-work is gone, but the gold-leaf striping is still very much in evidence. Note the Belpaire firebox.

WITH THE OPENING of PRR's grand Broad Street Station in 1881 PW&B passenger operations were moved into that terminal, which quickly taxed the capability of the new facility – the station at Broad and Washington then became freight only. The freight station was extended in 1904 and a carload delivery yard was constructed at 16th and Washington in 1905-7. This view looking north on Broad Street was taken on 5 October 1914. Note the tracks on Washington Avenue in the foreground and the classic X23 box car at left.

THIS VIEW of the back of the train shed in 1914 – now converted for freight use – shows the intricate window pattern. PW&B was justifiably proud of this station – an engraving depicting the delicately-styled windows from the inside graced the front cover of the company's Annual Report for several years.

Philadelphia City Hall Archive/Ted Xaras Collection

BY ACT of the Legislature approved 24 February 1837 PW&B constructed this remarkable 800-ft. long, five-span covered drawbridge over the Schuylkill River in 1837-8 to access Philadelphia. Replacing a pontoon bridge located nearby since at least 1740, it opened on Christmas Day 1838, allowing the road to operate service from Philadelphia to Baltimore. Known as the Newkirk Viaduct after President Matthew Newkirk, the $200 thousand structure consisted of a single-track wooden Towne Truss accommodating one lane for road traffic and one for the track. Tolls were initially imposed on vehicles, but these were lifted on 22 December 1847 in response to public agitation for a free crossing (and $55 thousand paid to PW&B by the County of Philadelphia).

To prevent fires from sparks the cars were initially hauled across the bridge by horses to and from the Grays Ferry station. This undated view looking westward clearly shows the telescoping draw span over the navigation channel. The bridge was damaged by flooding on 26 January 1839, destroyed by fire in 1863 and rebuilt in sections over the period 1882-91 before finally being replaced by a steel structure (Bridge No. 1) in 1901-2 (see *Triumph III*).

Ted Xaras Collection

MOVING ACROSS the river, we have a rare 1870 view along the original PW&B right of way near the estate and extensive gardens of John Bartram, Philadelphia's internationally renowned 18th Century horticulturalist called "the greatest natural botanist in the world." The early PW&B cars are lettered for stone service.

Ted Xaras Collection

TO COMMEMORATE the completion of the Newkirk Viaduct this monument was erected alongside the PW&B right of way just south of the bridge. Standing 30-ft. tall on a 10-ft. square base, the white marble column listed the officers and directors of the component lines making up the PW&B. It is shown here in an undated (but obviously post-electrification) photo with a southbound GG1-powered passenger train passing a freight at the junction of the Reading Chester Branch (the original PW&B alignment) southward to Chester.

THE FIRST STATION stop south of Grays Ferry on the original alignment was at Lazaretto (Essington), where a U. S. Government inspection and quarantine station was located for ships proceeding up the Delaware River. Situated on an island variously known as Tenako, Tenakonk, Mettinicum or simply Tinicum, it was the site of an early Swedish fort along the river known as New Gottenberg, built in 1643.

PW&B 1856 Guide/Ted Xaras Collection

Ted Xaras Collection

THE New York-Washington *Express* heads south past historic Woodland Cemetery c. 1898. No longer using the Broad and Washington terminal in South Philadelphia, this high-stepping train departed from PRR's Broad Street Station in the heart of the City and traveled on the new right of way, built for fast passenger service like this. The third track through this heavily traveled area was laid in 1889 and the fourth added in 1892.

Ted Xaras Collection

FORTY YEARS – and several generations of power – later, shiny PRR GG1 4861 moves a heavyweight passenger consist southward past a northbound freight and the junction with the Octoraro Branch in the left background. In the left foreground is the connection to Arsenal Bridge.

Ted Xaras Collection

BONNAFFON, shown here in a mid-1870s view, was one of the earliest stations established along the line by PW&B to promote suburban development (and thus railroad patronage) similar to that carried out by PRR to the west along The Main Line and northward to Chestnut Hill. The town was named after Albert Bonnaffon, a wealthy Philadelphia merchant whose mansion was located nearby. The station was tastefully landscaped with trees and shrubs from the nearby conservatories of Robert Buist, Jr., a successful Philadelphia seedsman.

THE STATION serving Sharon Hill (MP. 7.1) reflects the elegant ambience of one of the loveliest suburban towns on the PW&B mainline. In its early days the town was the home of many wealthy Philadelphia merchants, including Isaac H. Clothier, partner in the renowned dry goods firm (later department store chain) Strawbridge & Clothier. This ca. 1890 view (before four-tracking) shows the main stone station on the westbound side at upper left, with covered stairways leading down to the platforms. At track level are the "summer shelters" showing exquisite gingerbread detail matching the main building.

HERE'S a plan for a PB&W "Summer Station" similar in design to the ones at track level in Sharon Hill. The road clearly wanted to impress its largely upscale clientele with the latest in stylish Victorian architecture.

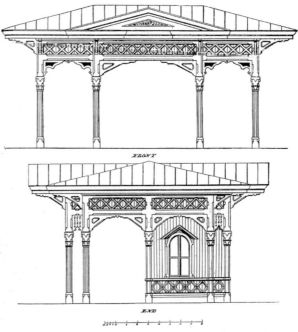

ANOTHER speeding train, this time headed southward through Folcroft (MP. 7.6) takes on water from the track pans as it passes under the Primos Avenue bridge. The right of way is now four-tracked through this area in an early 1900s view.

AMTRAK *Metroliner* No. 108 upholds the tradition, speeding past Folcroft station in July 1997. PRR identified the two center tracks through this area as "Northward Freight" and "Southward Freight." With very little freight traffic now on the Northeast Corridor, Amtrak normally routes their trains on the center tracks (Nos. 2 and 3) – hence the concrete ties and welded rail – and SEPTA locals on the outside tracks (1 and 4).

PW&B LAID OUT a 60-acre "pic-nic and excursion grounds" at Glenolden (MP. 8.2) that was a popular destination for Philadelphia residents to escape the heat of the city during the summer. The six-unit Penn Central Metroliner set shows no sign of stopping at the station as it zooms northward in October 1972. A freight station was added in 1887 – the replacement stone passenger station was built in the 1910-12 period along with several others on this section of the line.

Fred W. Schneider, III

Norwood (MP. 8.9) was another town established along the new right of way as a suburban development community. It was laid out by John Cochran of the Cochran Bros. real estate firm. Lots went for $800 and a "pretty, convenient cottage" could be purchased for about $3800. The station shown here, although smaller than some, was "fully as attractive and as highly finished as any of the other stations on the road." It was opened for business on 1 September 1875.

PW&B 1877 Guide Book/Ted Xaras Collection

HERE'S a later view of the attractive station looking eastward, with covered steps down to the now four-tracked right of way. The structure was demolished in September 1951, replaced by a one-story brick station.

Hagley Museum & Library

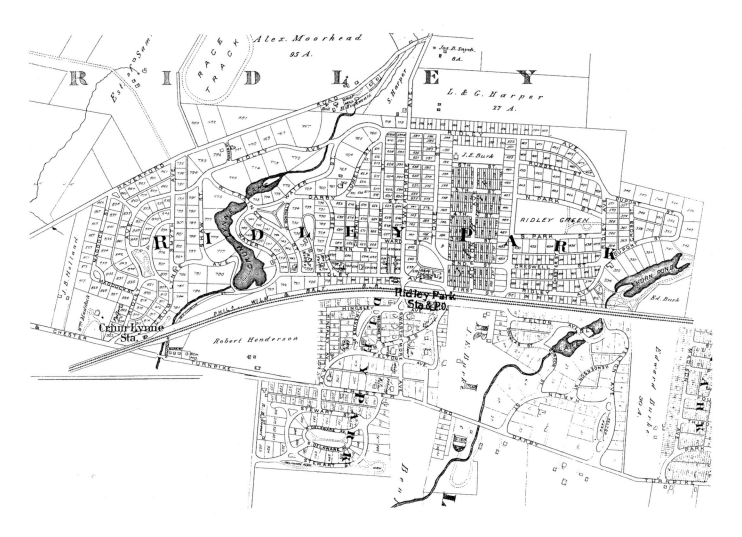

ON 26 May 1871 a distinguished committee including Isaac Hinckley, then President of the PW&B, and Samuel Felton, retired President, obtained a charter for the Ridley Park Association to establish an elegant residential community along the new line. Hinckley's vision was to actively promote development of a new "Main Line" southwest of Philadelphia, as PRR had done so successfully west of the City in the 1860s.

PW&B boasted, in true Victorian style, that "The plan of the Park is admirable, and no expense has been spared toward its ornamentation, grading, building of cottages, constructing artificial lakes, streams, rustic seats, arbors, bridges, etc. . . . The situation of the Park is high, giving pleasant views in all directions. From almost any point the eye is greeted with an endless variety of hills and valleys, copse and forest, cleft here and there with silver streams and shimmering lakes. Toward the east you can see the Delaware flecked with sails, and far in the distance, on the Jersey side, you look along over an extensive range of wood and meadow, while north and westward the beautiful country about Media and the city of Chester commands your gaze." Nice prose.

This map shows the Ridley Park plan as of 1886, the year before it was incorporated as a borough. We should note that even this peaceful community would suffer the results of the PRR-B&O conflict – the upper loop of Ridley Avenue would shortly be obliterated by the B&O mainline that Garrett was forced to build, cutting through the edge of town on its way to Philadelphia.

IN KEEPING WITH the PRR tradition on the Main Line, the Association constructed the large 50-room Ridley Park Hotel depicted here. The elegant Victorian structure, with piazzas on three sides, offered sweeping views of the Delaware River and Ridley Park. The PW&B Guide Book, leaving no stone unturned in its bid to rival the PRR Main Line, outdid itself in describing the hotel: "In truth the hotel partakes of that air of graceful dignity with which the loveliness of nature and the refined character of its lady guests surround it. . . . The tired, over-worked business man of the city, here finds the recuperation that his over-strained energies require. As each puff of the locomotive takes him farther and farther away from ledger, yard-stick, bonds, counting-room and warehouse, the load of cares gradually leaves him, and by the time Ridley Park is reached, the melody of singing birds and rustling leaves, the poetry of sighing breezes and murmuring brooks, have been so thoroughly mixed up with a sterner manhood, that he almost fancies that he is in some new-found paradise. . . . Their wives and children are also benefited by the summer's sojourn – the one receiving the necessary rest from a giddy winter's season of fashion and frivolity, the other the relaxation from study at school and college. The society which gathers here every season is of a character of which any establishment may be proud, as it embraces the very best families in Philadelphia." More nice prose.

THE STATION serving Ridley Park (MP. 10.3) reflected the planned elegance as well – Hinckley hired noted architect Theophilus P. Chandler, Jr. to design this fanciful edifice on delicate arched supporting trusses spanning the right of way. Chandler's design included four bays, two on each side topped with ornate steeples plus a central cupola and bell tower, also with an ornate steeple. Baggage elevators were located on either end and elaborate covered stairways descended the manicured banks to the platforms below. Sellen Avenue passed across on the north (eastward) side of the station on a similar truss structure and a 9-ft. walkway spanned the tracks on the south side.

Befitting its showcase role in the new community, the exterior of the station was covered in patterned slate of different colors, and the interior was lined with ash paneling. It featured an open timbered ceiling with stained glass in the four dormers. The *Delaware County Republican* of 21 June 1872, in a glowing article describing the features of the new station on its opening, boasted that the exposed wooden floor timbers "will be protected with iron, thus forming a fireproof structure."

WELL, evidently not fireproof enough – the original station burned to the ground in 1880, only eight years after it was built. The station was of course rebuilt and reopened in 1882, retaining the ornate arches, but the building itself was simplified, eliminating the bays, cupola and ornate steeples. The arch supporting structure was later replaced with the through girders shown here, to allow clearance for Tracks 1 and 4 added in 1892. Here D16sb 5105 pauses with a southbound train ca. 1906. Note the lawn on the embankments is still well maintained.

BY JULY 1981 all that was left at Ridley Park was a small station with its platform shelters. E60 955 leads an Amtrak train of solid Heritage equipment southbound. Note that the northbound through track (No. 2) has been re-laid with concrete ties as part of the NEC project.

RIDLEY PARK is also a stop for the Southeastern Pennsylvania Transportation Authority (SEPTA) Philadelphia-Wilmington local, as shown here in July 1981. Silverliner IV 383 was part of a 270-car order delivered to Penn Central by GE in 1974-5, displacing the venerable PRR MP54 units that had handled the run since Wilmington was made part of the Philadelphia suburban electrification in 1928.

CRUM LYNNE (MP. 11.0) station was located at the southern end of Ridley Park. Overlooking the station was the impressive three-story residence of Philadelphia businessman S. T. Fuller, with its "large and commanding observatory, from which an unobstructed view can be had of the surrounding country." In an attempt to elevate its communities into the big leagues of the day, the PW&B Guide noted that this mansion "will compare favorably with the most ornate villas at Newport [Rhode Island] or Saratoga [New York]." At the right is the two-story stable matching the house – all in an era of a more leisurely time when the elite escaped the cities for their summer house in the mountains or at the seashore, by taking the train of course.

IN A DIFFERENT FORM of escape, Amtrak *Acela Express* No. 2153 hurtles southward, seemingly free of gravity as it moves silently along the welded steel right of way in June 2001. The maximum speed for passenger trains on this portion of the main was 75 mph in 1965, but today it is 100 mph on Tracks 2 and 3 and 90 mph on Tracks 1 and 4.

William J. Coxey

Thomas M. Barnett / Ted Xaras Collection

EDDYSTONE station (MP.12.2) served the Chester suburb that was named after the nearby lighthouse. When it was built in the 1870s the station was considered to have a "truthful and faultless style of architecture," with walnut interior woodwork and furniture. It had suffered from the elements but still retained its dignity when this photo was taken in 1963, some 90 years later.

BALDWIN Tower, named after the near-legendary locomotive works located in Eddystone for many years, contained an electro-pneumatic machine that protected the mainline crossovers plus the industrial sidings leading to the Pittsburgh Mill Steel Co. and of course the source of countless steam and diesel locomotives for PW&B, PRR, B&O and many other U.S. and foreign railroads. The tower is shown here on 24 March 1962.

John F. Born

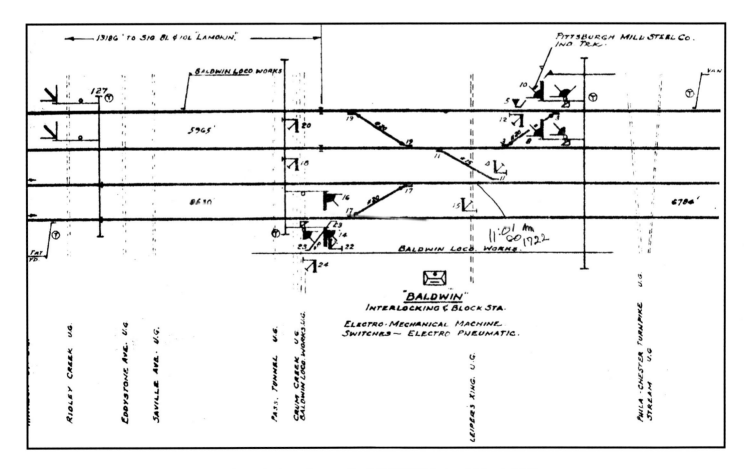

THE interlocking diagram for BALDWIN is dated March 1962.

Ted Xaras Collection

CHESTER (MP.13.3) carries the distinction of being the oldest city in Pennsylvania. Originally called Upland by the early settlers, it became the chief town of the Upper Delaware Settlements. William Penn took formal possession of his new proprietary colony in November 1682 and renamed the town, establishing it as the seat of government, an honor it soon lost when he established his "large Towne or Citty in the most Convenient place upon the river for health & Navigation" several miles upriver at Philadelphia.

The first railway station in Chester was this frame structure built in 1837 that also served as the residence for the ticket agent and his family. The first train arrived in 1838, and "a great crowd of gaping rustics and curious town people saw the wonder – a wood-burning locomotive drawing two coaches."

AFTER the arrival of the railroad Chester began to grow more rapidly. Industries including cotton and woolen mills, and later iron and steel works, developed along the creek and several shipbuilding yards were established on the waterfront. To serve the growing population, the PW&B constructed this larger building in 1854 which remained in service until it was demolished in 1903 to make way for a new elevated right of way.

PW&B 1856 Guide/Ted Xaras Collection

THE THIRD STATION in Chester was an attractive two-story brick structure with a tile roof, located on the northbound side between Market and Welsh Streets. The first floor (ground level) contained the ticket office and baggage room while the main waiting room was located on the second floor at track level shown here in a 1985 view. Note the date on the chimney.

SOUTHBOUND Train No. 403 pauses in a swirl of steam at the southbound shelter on 23 May 1967. Proof of the ancient jibe that B&O ran steam through its trains and PRR ran its trains through steam. Note the height of the track elevation at left, carried out in 1903-5. The platform on this side was extended 125 ft. in 1914.

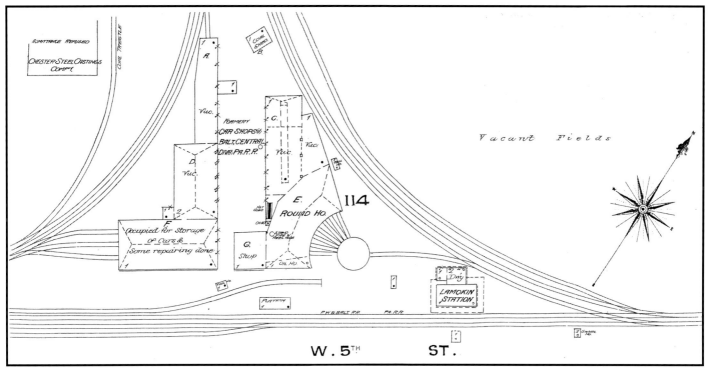

LAMOKIN station (MP. 14.2) served the borough of South Chester, at the junction of the Philadelphia & Baltimore Central RR (later PW&B Central Division) line that extended up the Chester Creek RR (later Branch) to West Chester Junction. This 1881 Sanborn map shows the location of the station and the former Baltimore Central shops within the wye.

HERE'S a view of the Lamokin station built in the 1870s with the P&BC roundhouse behind. As the drawing suggests, several steel works were established in South Chester, which was incorporated in 1866.

Railroad Museum of Pennsylvania (PHMC)

THAT STATION was replaced by a larger brick structure on the northbound side of the tracks in 1903, with a freight station added the following year. This photo taken on 23 November 1925 captures a train pausing at the southbound platform shelter. North of the shelter is LAMOKIN STREET Tower.

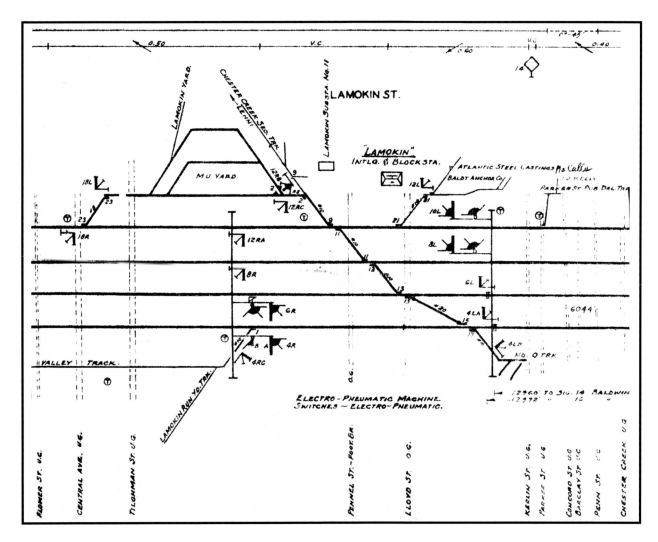

LAMOKIN STREET Tower protected the crossovers, yards and industrial sidings at the junction with the Chester Creek Branch – as well as the running tracks. It housed an electro-pneumatic machine.

ABOUT A MILE beyond the Chester borough line was the early station at Thurlow (MP.16.0), built to serve local travel from the area. Nearby was located a large summer resort offering a commanding view of the river and surrounding country. A replacement structure was constructed in 1904. A bit chilly for a summer resort.

PW&B 1856 Guide/ Ted Xaras Collection

NOT FAR from the Thurlow station was the residence of Samuel M. Felton, dynamic President of the PW&B and several subsidiary lines. The elegant house and grounds depicted here were "not surpassed by any on the line of the PW&B." Felton was a wealthy Philadelphia businessman who was also President of the Pennsylvania Steel Works and involved in extensive real estate dealings and ownership of several other industrial concerns.

PW&B 1856 Guide/ Ted Xaras Collection

THE STATION shown here situated in a shady grove in an 1870s view was named Linwood and handled a large volume of milk from the surrounding dairy farms. It also served the old river settlement of Marcus Hook, the second oldest town in Pennsylvania. Marcus Hook was named after the prominent Indian sachem Maarte, who lived on the point of land where the settlement was established. The station name was later changed to Marcus Hook (MP.17.0) to reflect the original settlement.

Ted Xaras Collection

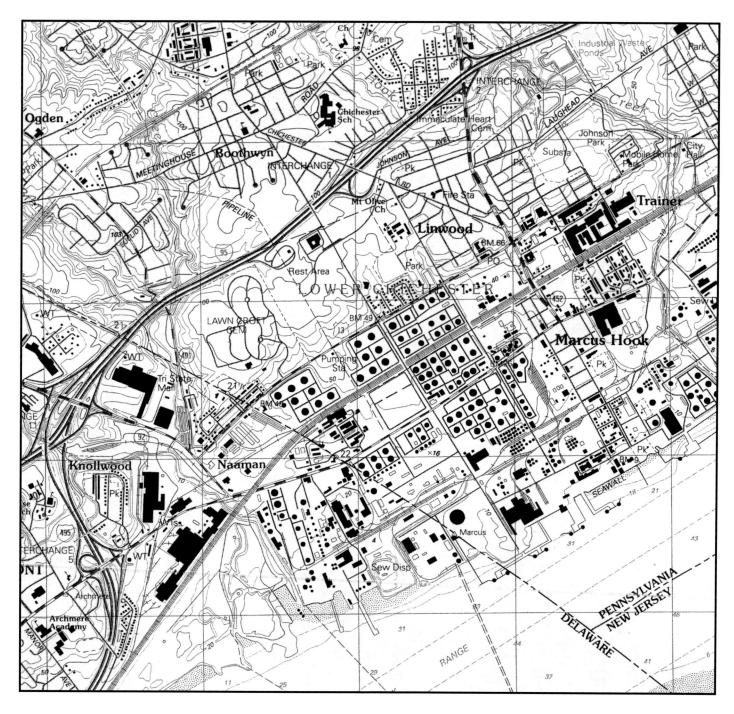

DURING World War I PRR developed a plan to construct an extensive series of branches and yards south of Grays Ferry to serve the growing heavy industrial complex along the Delaware Riverfront. This included the 60th Street Branch, the Chester & Philadelphia Branch and the South Chester Branch, along with yards and additional connections (including with the Reading Chester Branch – one wonders if PB&W later regretted selling off the old line). These branches formed a continuous freight line from Philadelphia through the Hogs Island Shipyard, the Westinghouse plant, Essington, Eddystone, Chester and Marcus

Hook to Claymont. Negotiations for these improvements, which were estimated to cost upwards of $6 million, began in April 1916 and much of the work was completed during 1918, but some areas were served using temporary connections during peak wartime activity and finally completed in the mid-1920s.

This 1995 USGS map shows how the Marcus Hook area looks in recent years, after some of the tracks had been removed. The area is dotted (literally) by large tank farms associated with the sprawling refinery and petrochemical complex.

THIS VIEW looking south along the riverfront in 1953 shows the Ford Motor Company plant in
Chester, which was accessed via the South Chester Branch to Stony Creek Yard at Marcus Hook.

MARCUS HOOK has a major cluster of oil refineries and associated tank farms, creating a unique pattern on the industrial landscape and lighting up the sky at night with flaming stack gasses. This 1953 view shows the sprawling Sunoco complex, served by both PRR and Reading tracks (center) at this time.

Tom Hollyman - Penn Central Railroad Collection/Pennsylvania State Archives

THE SINCLAIR REFINERY is shown in this view, with the PRR Stony Creek and Reading Yards in the foreground. This refinery has had a multitude of owners that over the years included Standard Oil of Ohio, British Petroleum, Phillips and Conoco as well as Sinclair.

Tom Hollyman - Penn Central Railroad Collection/Pennsylvania State Archives

MOVING SOUTH of the Marcus Hook refinery area along the river we come to the Worth Steel Company plant in Claymont, shown here in an aerial view looking to the northeast. A break in the clouds highlights the administration building across the road from the smoky mill. This photo is file-dated ca. 1925, but close inspection reveals catenary poles being installed along the main (upper left to lower right), which would place the date as 1928, when electrification of the line to Wilmington was initiated.

RETURNING TO THE MAIN, the first stop in Delaware is Claymont (MP. 19.4). The village was originally known as Naaman's Creek, after the nearby stream that flows into the Delaware. Claymont at one time handled the largest volume of milk on the PW&B system, shipping some 3,000 quarts daily to Philadelphia.

PW&B 1856 Guide/Ted Xaras Collection

THE ORIGINAL two-story frame station at Claymont was replaced with this single-story brick structure in 1903, shown in a 1916 Valuation photo. A freight station was added in 1906.

National Archives

SEPTA Train 9235, a local from North Broad Street (Philadelphia), enters the new Claymont station on its way to Wilmington in July 1991. Ending a long tradition, Wilmington local service was discontinued on 31 December 1982 when train operations on the Corridor were transferred from Conrail to SEPTA and Delaware DOT refused to pay for its portion of the service deficit. However, six years later service was restored on 15 January 1989 through the mutual cooperation of the Delaware Transportation Authority, SEPTA and Amtrak. The new station opened 28 October 1990.

William J. Coxey

Robert L. Davis

THROUGH RAIN OR SNOW the freight must go through – on a snowy New Year's day in 1971 E44s 4451 and 4433 haul Penn Central NE-2 with 126 cars through Claymont.

William J. Coxey

TWENTY YEARS LATER – but in much better weather – Conrail WPSC99 led by SD40-2 6441 approaches Claymont in July 1991. In the mid-1960s nearly a dozen freight trains in each direction passed here daily, but with a not inconsiderable touch of irony early in 1991 Conrail diverted its through freights off the Corridor to the CSX (ex-B&O) line between Park Junction (Philadelphia) and Benning (Washington) via trackage rights.

One exception was this local freight that ran weekdays between Stony Creek Yard in Marcus Hook and Edge Moor Yard in Wilmington, primarily to serve local industries but also to transfer traffic between yards. Note the cars carrying steel plate that were picked up at Citi Steel (which purchased the former Phoenix Steel – see *Triumph III*), located in Naaman, a mile north of Claymont.

Ernest L. Roberts, Jr.

SILK – Synonyms for smooth, please … silken, sleek, glabrous, slick … all fit the incomparable GG1. Now we see an unknown GG1 in classic multi-striped livery purring past Holly Oaks DE on 8 August 1954 with the southbound *Southerner* … as soft as a puppy's fur … as new as cashmere … as a maiden's fresh-washed hair in her lover's hands … humming to her destination through a latticework maze of catenary.

THIS TINY brick station named Bellevue (MP. 22.0) was built as an accommodation stop for the convenience of residents in the area, shown here enduring a mid-Atlantic blizzard. A freight station was added in 1887.

PW&B 1856 Guide/*Ted Xaras Collection*

THE ORIGINAL passenger station was replaced by another small one in 1904, this time of frame construction. It is shown here in better weather in 1916.

National Archives

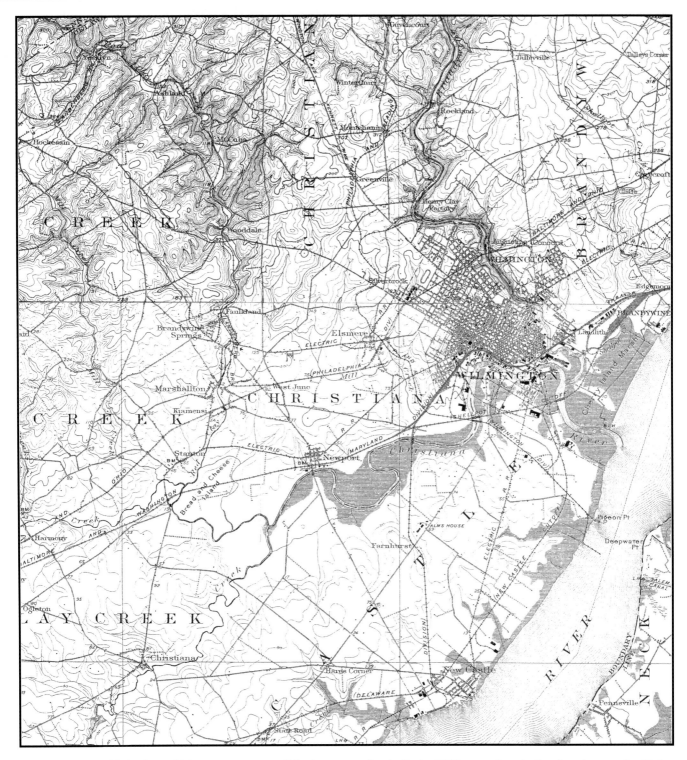

THIS USGS map published in 1904 gives us an overall look at the railroads serving the Wilmington area as of that time. The PW&B (PRR) line does a dramatic S-turn through the city, roughly following the banks of the winding Christiana River. The five-mile double-track Shellpot Cutoff (later Branch), which was built in 1888 to allow freight traffic to bypass the congested downtown area, swings east of the city and rejoins it at RAGAN Tower, immediately south of Delaware Junction, where the Delaware Division line extends to New Castle on the river. Construction of this line required erecting two draw bridges over the Christiana River. The larger northern one was 725 ft. long with a 242-ft. swing section over the river. The New Castle Cutoff (Branch),

also built in 1888, served a similar function to the Delmarva Peninsula, extending along the river to its namesake town.

The seemingly ubiquitous B&O main runs west of the city, with freight branches extending into it and cutting across the PRR tracks. Our old friend the Reading also cuts across these tracks, with its Wilmington Division (old Wilmington & Northern RR) line extending to the Delaware as well as several freight branches into the industrial areas.

This map also shows the early configuration of Edge Moor Yard and the relocated Wilmington Shops, between the yard and the main east of the downtown area.

77

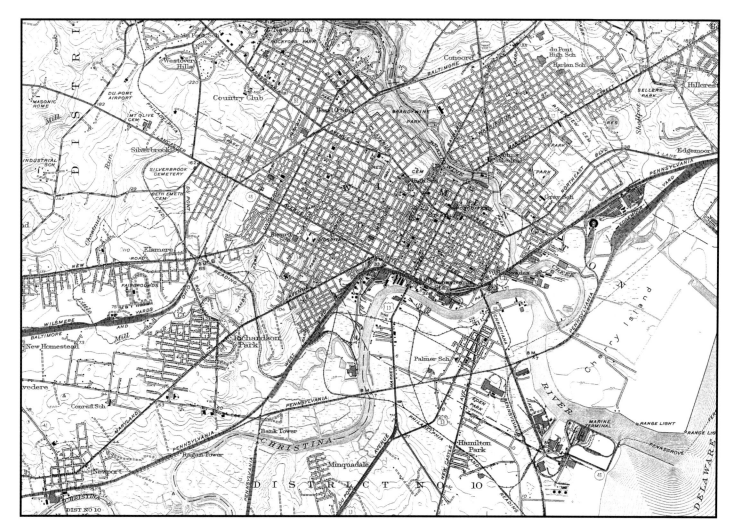

BY 1942 there have been several changes to the already complex trackage by the three major railroads serving the city and its industrial areas, notably that serving the marine terminal (lower right). B&O has constructed its Wilsmere Yard and the PRR Edge Moor Yard has been expanded (although not nearly as much as the extensive expansion proposed in 1929), as has the shop complex.

But before we enter the city itself we need to discuss an extensive track improvement program through the entire area. Shortly after the turn of the century PRR began a comprehensive grade crossing elimination program in several major urban areas between Philadelphia and New York City (see *Triumph V*) involving elevation of the right of way on large fills, supported within the downtown areas by heavy masonry retaining walls. In many areas the four-track system was completed in conjunction with this massive (and costly) undertaking. A similar program was carried out on the Maryland Division south of Philadelphia (although not uniformly four-tracked) that included track elevation and reductions in curvature through Chester and Wilmington, enlargement of the Edge Moor freight yard at Wilmington and construction of a new double-track truss bridge on the higher elevation across the Susquehanna between Perryville and Havre de Grace.

The track elevation began about 2 miles east of Chester station and extended for 4.6 miles through Chester, Lamokin, Thurlow and Trainer. At Lamokin the grade dropped down for about 1,000 ft. at the junction of the Central Division (later PRR Chester Creek Branch), which was not elevated. Two overhead and 27 undergrade road crossings were constructed in this section, replacing 14 crossings at grade. Most of the crossings over streets were built on steel plate girder structures similar to those used on the New York Division.

The $2 million track elevation through Wilmington began on 29 January 1902 at MP. 25, north of the city, and extended 3.5 miles to Delaware Junction, on a similar alignment but on a new grade about 15-20 ft. above the old. This section included a new draw bridge over the Brandywine River, plate girder bridges over 25 undergrade street crossings and a stretch of arched masonry viaduct on the southern end. It consisted of a four-track right of way from Fourth Street to Orange Street and three tracks from there to the B&O crossing near West Yard. The bridge over the B&O and Reading branches was double-tracked, and south of there the Maryland Division was double-tracked plus one for the Delaware Division.

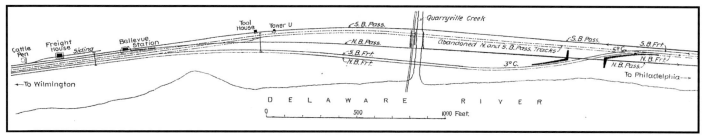

A KEY ELEMENT of the track elevation was a jumpover near Bellevue to allow freights to access Edge Moor Yard. Here the passenger tracks were realigned, with the northward track swung 110 ft. to the east, allowing the freight tracks to cross over them and then run alongside for 2 miles to the yard. The crossover bridge is 200 ft. long, supported on masonry abutments with long wing walls. The new Bellevue passenger and freight stations were located on the fill.

Fred W. Schneider, III

AN INTERESTING LASHUP powers a southbound freight through the interlocking at BELLVUE (BELL) Tower on 19 May 1956. Two odd experimental Baldwin-Westinghouse electrics, Class E3b (B-B-B configuration, built 1951) and E2c 4939 (C-C, built 1952) join with a pair of Class ERS15 (EMD GP7) units to move the mixed consist, probably into Edge Moor Yard. The Bellevue substation is visible in the background.

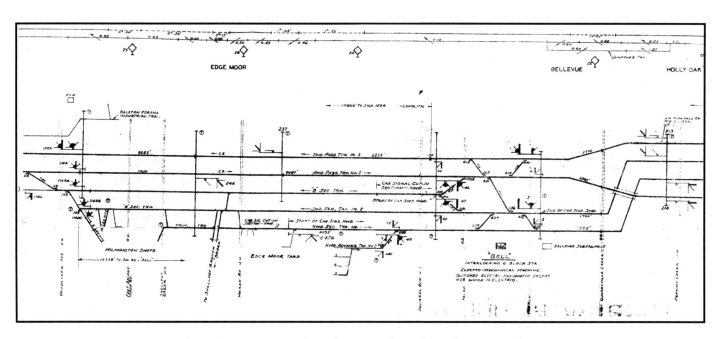

BELL Tower contained an electro-mechanical machine controlling the jumpover, the crossovers and the entrances to Edge Moor Yard and the Wilmington Shops, as shown here in a March 1962 diagram.

TWENTY-FOUR YEARS after the experimental electrics visited, a four-car Metroliner set crosses over to the southbound passenger track at the tower, now labeled BELL.

William D. Middleton/Fred W. Schneider, III Collection

TRAIN 109 continues southward on 26 January 1980. The tracks at left, in need of some work, run alongside the main and then extend into Edge Moor Yard. Shortly after this picture was taken the Amtrak police arrived to banish noted photographer and rail historian Bill Middleton and co-conspirator Fred Schneider from the scene.

Fred W. Schneider, III

GG1 4923 hustles a long passenger train, with a heavy head-end consist, past the tiny shelters at Edge Moor in 1956.

Fred W. Schneider, III

ANOTHER EXAMPLE of heavy industry in the Wilmington area served by PRR was the Edge Moor Iron Company, shown here on 9 May 1926. The PRR spur enters from the lower left, and above it note the two interesting sets of worker housing. This plant later became the Ludlow Sales & Manufacturing Company.

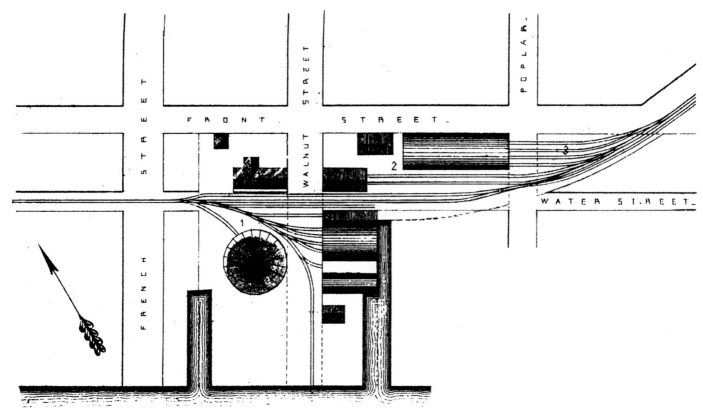

IN THE 1840s PW&B constructed a fairly extensive early shop complex in Wilmington alongside the river at Water Street, between French and Poplar as shown in this 1856 diagram. Here the road's growing fleet of locomotives were stored and maintained.

THE SHOPS included this 122-ft. diameter engine house constructed in 1847 with its marvelous iron "tent roof" (designed to funnel smoke upwards) and the arch roof blacksmith shop. The turntable was located inside the engine house, which could accommodate 18 locomotives. This view looks south toward the river, with a sailing ship visible in the background.

PW&B 1877 Guidebook/*Ted Xaras Collection*

ON 1 May 1871 the engine house and shops were destroyed by fire and subsequently rebuilt on the same location. In anticipation of traffic for the Centennial Exposition, PW&B constructed the 20-stall roundhouse shown here in early 1876, making it the largest on the system at the time. The shop buildings were expanded as well, allowing the road to build its own cars and locomotives as well as carrying out all the repair, rebuilding and painting operations.

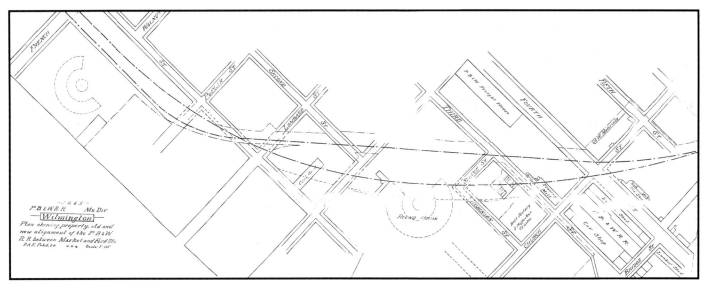

Hagley Museum & Library

THIS REMARKABLE DIAGRAM dated 5 February 1904 shows the location of the original engine house on French Street (left), the 1876 roundhouse and rebuilt shop buildings farther northward, and the realignment of the sharp curve between Ford and Market Streets as part of the track elevation project, necessitating moving the shops to a completely new location. Note also the location of the new Freight House on Fourth Street.

LONG CROSSING GATES frame the corrugated freight house in Wilmington, built in 1904 and shown here in a 1916 Valuation photo. The facility faced on Pine Street and extended along Fourth.

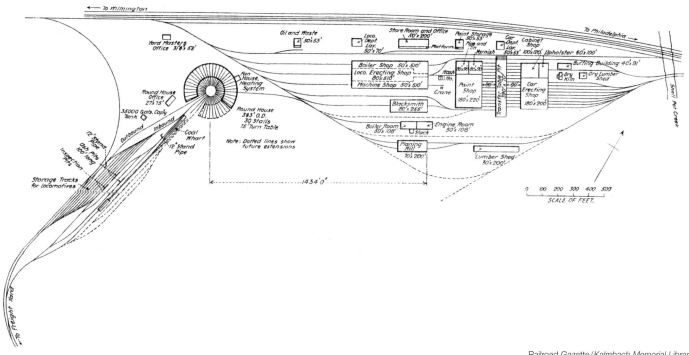

BY THE turn of the 19th century the road had completely outgrown the original shops which could no longer be expanded at that location. Instead it constructed an entirely new facility at a site on filled land alongside the main north of the city. In 1904, in conjunction with the track elevation project, a greatly expanded, state-of-the-art shop complex was opened. As shown here, it included the main locomotive shop, blacksmith shop and car erecting and paint shops connected by a 390-ft. long transfer table. Below that is located a power house, planning mill and lumber shed. At the west end of the shops is a 363-ft. diameter, 30-stall roundhouse (later expanded to 40 stalls), with 75-ft. turntable, plus engine service facilities including a 625-ft. trestle leading to a 96-ft. coal wharf and locomotive storage tracks.

National Archives

THE LOCOMOTIVE SHOP shown here in a 1916 view measured 180 X 510 ft. overall, with a center erecting bay 80 ft. wide. A 50-ft. bay on the east side contained a machine shop, with another 50-ft. bay on the west side for boiler and flue fabrication.

NEXT TO the Locomotive Shop was an 80 X 260-ft. Blacksmith Shop. Nearby was a Power House that generated steam, hot air and electrical power for the entire complex. The road took pride in the comfort and illumination level in the shops.

National Archives

National Archives

HERE we have a 1916 view of the east end of the Car Erecting Shop with the transfer table pit in the foreground. This 180 X 300-ft. structure contained a cabinet shop and upholstery shop for fitting out car interiors. Note the four-wheel cabin cars.

Tom Hollyman - Penn Central Railroad Collection/Pennsylvania State Archives

THE SHOPS continued to grow and evolve over the years, reflecting changes in motive power and cars. Here we see an aerial view of the complex looking southward in 1953, with the main behind it. The Car Shop is at the right with the Paint Shop beyond and the Locomotive shop behind that – the Roundhouse lies in the distance. In the foreground is the southbound hump of Edge Moor Yard.

CHANGE – A close-up view of the Roundhouse in 1953 reveals that quite a few stalls have been demolished. Steam locomotives wait out their days on the former stall tracks, but electric motors occupy the engine storage tracks and shiny diesels have invaded the area where the coal wharf once stood – and there would be more diesel facilities to come. Beyond is the former Erecting Shop, now the Electric Locomotive Shop. The main cuts across in the background.

Tom Hollyman - Penn Central Railroad Collection/Pennsylvania State Archives

A SOLID ARRAY of passenger equipment – coaches, combines, baggage cars and MU units – fills the tracks leading to the Car Shop in this 1953 view. A group of MP54 units were rebuilt here in the early 1950s to keep the aging fleet operating until new cars arrived. Edge Moor Yard is in the background.

IN AN EARLIER TIME the Wilmington local used the venerable MP54 units, shown here on 19 May 1956 passing the Car Shops where many of them were rebuilt in the early 1950s to extend their service life.

Fred W. Schneider, III

GRAVEYARD – With newer power coming into service, a group of PRR's remarkable GG1s await scrapping outside the Wilmington Shops on 18 February 1980. Photographer John Born compares this sad scene to "an old jungle movie in which the elephants went to a special place to die."

John F. Born

John F. Born

LAST LINEUP – Here the last 19 Conrail GG1s are stored at Edge Moor Yard – pants down and not even under the catenary – awaiting the scrapper's torch on 19 March 1980. Thankfully a few were preserved – never to run again – but at least we can imagine when they reigned supreme at the head of the Tuscan Red Fleet and performed yeoman service in freight duty as well.

LIKE DAYS OF OLD – Refurbished GG1 4935 reposes inside the shops on 15 April 1981. Sadly, it was a time to bid farewell to PRR's magnificent Queen of the Rails.

THIS AERIAL VIEW looks northeastward at an earlier time – on 10 July 1939. In the background are the shops, roundhouse (with the long coaling trestle still intact) and in the upper right Edge Moor Yard, completed 20 years before. At center right, in the bend of the Brandywine Creek, is the American Car & Foundry plant with several passenger cars in the yard and at bottom left in the trees is the historic Old Swedes Church. The three-track deck plate girder bridge was part of the massive track elevation project opened south of BELLEVUE Tower on 4 March 1906.

Tom Hollyman - Penn Central Railroad Collection/Pennsylvania State Archives

THIS VIEW looking northward gives us a superb overview of the expanse of Edge Moor Yard in 1953, with the Shellpot Branch running alongside the yard at right. The Wilmington Shops lie in the background with the Ralston Purina plant gleaming in the sun behind them.

Eric S. McKeown

MOVING SOUTHWARD for a quick look at the Shellpot Branch we come to the drawbridge that allowed the line to cross the Christiana River. Bridge 3, as it was once known, was more than a movable bridge – it was also an interlocking and block station. The interlocking included the junction to the New Castle Secondary which was the route of Delmarva Branch freights from

Edge Moor Yard. This photo was taken on 27 August 1993 about a year before the bridge constructed in 1907 was taken out of service. As of this writing it is being rebuilt to enable Norfolk Southern Delaware freights to avoid Amtrak's restrictions on the Corridor between BELL and DAVIS interlockings.

FARTHER SOUTH we come to the Pyrites Company plant (top center), and in the middle of this ca. 1929 photo, the new Wilmington Marine Terminal situated on the Christiana River. This facility was served by both PRR and the Reading W&N Branch with the loop tracks allowing direct access to ships at the pier.

Fred W. Schneider, III

WE MOVE back across the yards and shops in time to catch a GG1 highballing an interesting mix of four head end cars and two coaches past the Purina plant in May of 1956. Note the tubular catenary poles on this stretch.

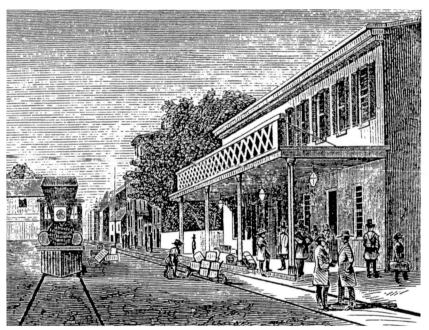

PW&B 1856 Guide/Ted Xaras Collection

WE NOW ENTER the City of Wilmington itself, which was originally settled in 1637-8 by a stalwart group of Swedish immigrants under the leadership of Peter Minuit in the service of the Dutch West India Company. With the colony subsequently taken over by the British, the town was granted a charter by King George II in 1739. It 1809 it was designated by the Delaware Legislature as a borough and incorporated as a city in 1832.

The coming of the PW&B in 1837 greatly increased Wilming-

ton's prosperity by developing its manufacturing establishments – notably ironmaking and shipbuilding – and providing additional outlets for the great agricultural bounty from the surrounding farms, making it readily accessible to the two great rival cities to the north and south – Philadelphia and Baltimore. PW&B located its first station (old MP. 28.0) on the west side of French Street, across from the roundhouse shown earlier.

Ted Xaras Collection

THE PW&B 1877 Guide Book promised, "to erect a Grand Union Depot here in a few years, as the present one has become inadequate for the business of the road at this point, and is not at all in keeping with the fine modern depot buildings at the other points." Making good on its promise, in 1881 PW&B hired noted architect Frank Furness to design this impressive Victorian cre-ation, certainly in keeping with the importance of the growing city. Opened on 2 August 1882, it was located on the east side of French Street (at MP.26.6). The 100-ft. wide train shed extended 525 ft. to the east in the area previously occupied by the old shops. Note the locomotive standpipe.

ELEVATION of the tracks through the city necessitated replacement of the grand structure and design of a new one. Work began late in 1905 with construction of a temporary frame station across the old surface tracks on Water Street and as soon as it was completed the old station was demolished and foundations laid for its replacement. The southern half of the station shown here in a 1916 view was built first, along with the four-track steel viaduct between French and Walnut Streets with the viaduct forming an integral part of the station. As soon as the rest of the viaduct was built the temporary station was torn down and the remainder of the new facility was completed and opened for service at 9 A.M. on 28 January 1907.

National Archives

The street level of the 167 X 193-ft. structure contained the baggage and express rooms, ticket office, newsstand and dining rooms. The north- and southbound men's and women's waiting rooms were located on the second floor at track level. The exterior of the building is finished in light-colored granite up to the first floor window sills – above the base the walls are red brick trimmed in red terra cotta, with a red tile roof. The interior has marble floors, with the main waiting rooms finished with a terra cotta base and light colored brick walls and plastered ceilings with heavy plastered beams and moldings. In this view a footbridge on the second floor connects to the four-story PRR Division office building at the far left, constructed in 1905.

National Archives

THIS VIEW looking east (northward) at track level shows the 600-ft. long northbound platform at the far right, with a 391-ft. shelter. The southbound platform at left extends 800 ft., with a 451-ft. shelter, and the center island platform for express trains is 750-ft. long with a 486-ft. shelter. As built there were two northbound and two southbound tracks through the station.

Eugene L. DiOrio

HERE'S a closer look at the clock tower in May 1962, rising above the main entrance at the corner of Front and French Streets. The tower is red brick with ornate red terra cotta trim and the clock has illuminated glass faces 3-1/2 ft. in diameter. Note the PRR keystone on the French Street bridge, which supports the tracks, platforms and shelters.

William J. Coxey

THE TRACKS through Wilmington were realigned in 1916 in conjunction with extension of the three-track system and again in 1940-41, resulting in the three-track configuration shown here in a southward view. In July 1991 SEPTA Train 0240 readies for de-parture to Philadelphia on Track 1, the normal arrival and departure track for MU locals. Wilmington locals that did not prompt-ly turn were stored in West Yard, 2 miles south of the station.

William J. Coxey

PENN CENTRAL Train 104, with one of the original Metroliner sets, pauses in Wilmington in June 1975. The high-level platforms for through trains have recently been installed on top of the old one, leading to an unusual platform configuration. Track 1 (far left) is served by a low-level platform only, while Track 2 (center) has just a high-level one. Track 3 (right) is served either by a high or low platform, depending on which side of the train the crew opens the doors – which could lead to some unexpected results! Track 1 served not only SEPTA locals but also northward through trains too long for Track 2's short high-level platform.

AMTRAK Train 19, the *Crescent*, arrives in Wilmington on Track 3 on the elevated right of way. A materials handling car brings up the rear of a lengthy Heritage Fleet consist in July 1991. Although the train is long, the small number of passengers board from the high-level platform.

William J. Coxey

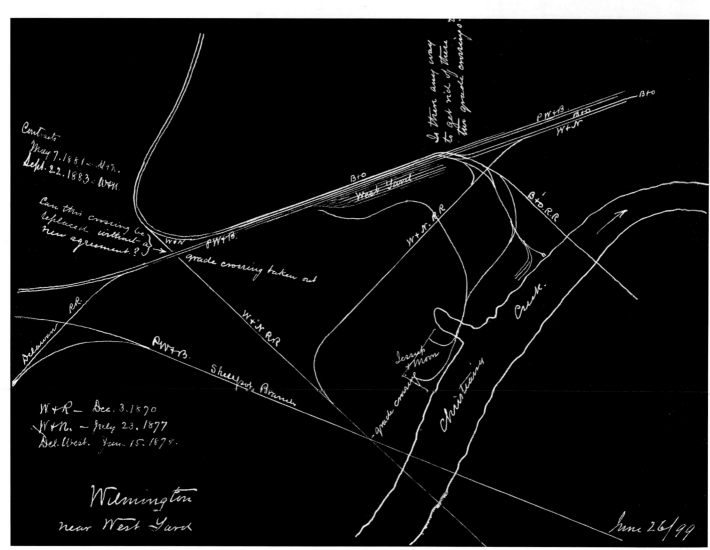

Hagley Museum & Library

SOUTH OF WILMINGTON, in the complex trackage area of West Yard, was where the B&O (former Delaware Western RR which B&O acquired to gain charter rights in Delaware and Pennsylvania) and Reading (former Wilmington & Northern RR) branch lines crossed the PW&B, still at grade in the 1899 PW&B diagram. Although the crossings were the subject of agreements with the predecessor railroads dating from the 1870s, they were the subject of constant disagreements with the two successor roads, mostly about poor maintenance, interfering with PW&B's high-speed operations.

Referring to the B&O crossing, this fascinating glimpse of corporate interaction pointedly asks, "Is there any way to get rid of these two grade crossings?" Well, yes there was – PRR would carry out an extensive track elevation project through the area after the turn of the century, crossing over them all on an arched masonry viaduct and plate girder bridges. But the problems would continue – only now over property rights and who was responsible for bridge maintenance. It was only one of several locations on the Maryland Division where PRR and the B&O would interact (read: clash) and contribute to the constant friction between the two roads.

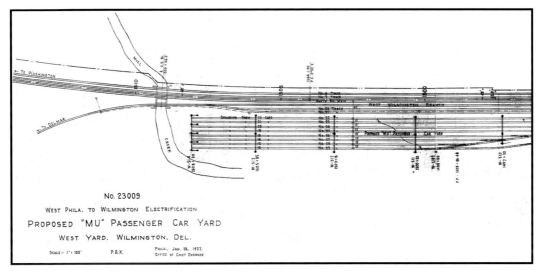

No. 23009

West Phila. to Wilmington Electrification

PROPOSED "MU" PASSENGER CAR YARD

West Yard, Wilmington, Del.

Scale:- 1" = 100'   P.B.K.   Phila., Jan. 10, 1927.
Office of Chief Engineer

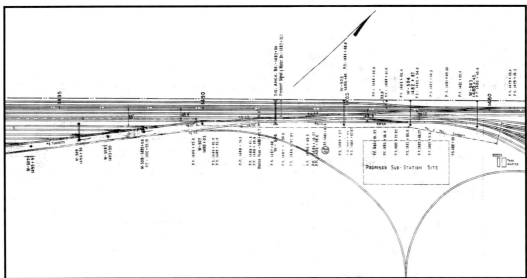

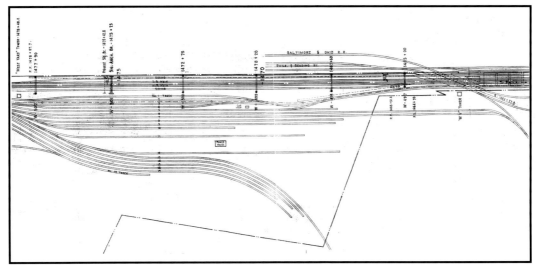

Hagley Museum & Library

ELECTRIFICATION would bring further changes to the West Yard area in the form of a new passenger car yard to handle MU equipment operating between Philadelphia and Wilmington, part of the initial Philadelphia Suburban Electrification Project. This 1927 PRR diagram shows the then proposed electrified facility extending southward from the existing freight yard. Note the location of W Tower at the north end of West Yard (Confused? PRR used north-south on the mainline of the Maryland Division, but the yard was located west of the old downtown area).

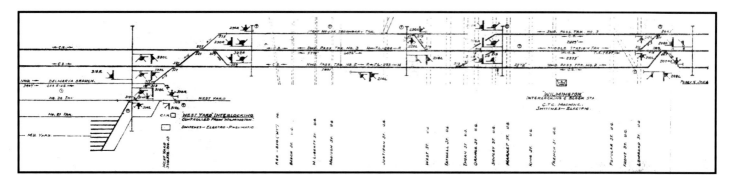

THIS DIAGRAM shows the interlockings under the control of WILMINGTON Tower (located in the station), which controlled train movements through the platform tracks as well as the

WEST YARD installation at the beginning of the Delmarva Branch (see the RAGAN diagram). Note the changes in track designations in this 1962 diagram after CTC had been installed.

DEAN OF CONDUCTORS – The interlocking located at the junction of the Shellpot Branch and the main three miles south of Wilmington was initially known as PJ. When PRR changed from telegraph call letters to names to designate block signal towers on the Maryland Division in 1924 this tower was named RAGAN in honor of Lewis W. Ragan, who had served the division for over 50 years, 43 of them as a passenger conductor. Looking every bit the part, Mr. Ragan is shown here standing on the stairway of the tower, where his train had stopped for an order.

Railway Age/Kalmbach Memorial Library

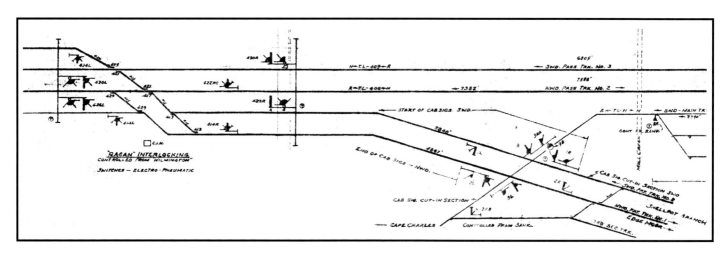

RAGAN controlled the junction of the Shellpot Branch where it rejoined the main south of Wilmington. Note the crossings where the Delmarva Branch cuts across the Shellpot Branch, shown here in a 1962 diagram.

PW&B 1856 Guide/Ted Xaras Collection

THE FIRST station stop south of Wilmington is at Newport (MP. 30.4), a community serving the surrounding agricultural areas. At one time long lines of heavy Conestoga wagons transferred their loads to waiting vessels on the riverfront, which is at the head of navigation on the Christiana River. This engraving depicts the early PW&B station.

THE TRIM replacement station and freight house built in 1903 are shown here as they appeared in a 1916 Valuation photo.

National Archives

AT LEAST TWO RAILFANS capture a northbound Amtrak train led by AEM7 914 as it passes the station at Newport in July 1981. Note the section of concrete ties beginning at this point as well as the interesting means of supporting the high-voltage lines.

Fred W. Schneider, III

STANTON (MP. 32.8) was another agricultural community and also the home of early woolen and flour mills. The two-story frame station is shown here in 1916.

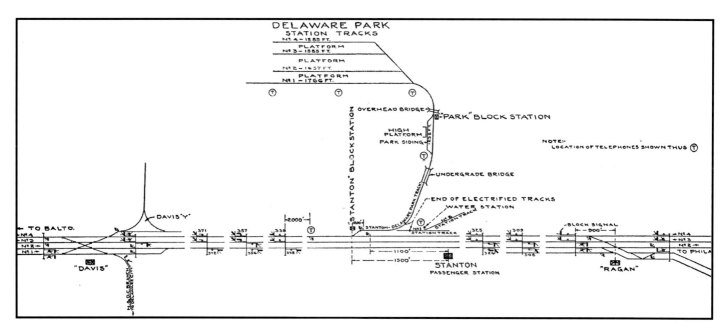

UNDER General Order No. 2605, dated 18 June 1937, PRR opened a spur connecting with Track No. 4 1500 ft. south of Stanton station and extending 1.1 miles to serve Delaware Park Racetrack. The order was to be in effect between 26 June and 24 July, during racing season. The order duly noted that, "On account of clearance, employees are prohibited from standing on top of box cars or other high equipment while passing under the overhead bridge located 5200 feet north of Stanton on the Stanton-Delaware Park Track." We trust that it was obeyed.

Construction of the spur and special service to the track from Philadelphia was authorized by the Board on 28 October, 1936 – service was discontinued on 11 August 1974.

SMOOTH RIDE – Passengers on the northbound Amtrak train enjoy the smooth ride provided by electric power and new Amfleet equipment on the welded rail and concrete ties of the Northeast Corridor on a balmy 7th of May 1988. The location is near Delaware Park Racetrack in Stanton.

William D. Middleton/Fred W. Schneider, III Collection

THIS TINY STATION served the village of Ruthby (MP. 35.8), only 0.3 miles from Stanton. It is shown here as it appeared in 1916.

National Archives

Ted Xaras Collection

PW&B OPENED this attractive station in 1878 to serve the thriving town of Newark (MP. 38.6). The substantial brick structure, shown here as it appeared in 1950, featured Gothic styling touches and a slate roof with elaborate wrought iron detailing – and like many larger stations of the period, separate men's and ladies' waiting rooms. Newark, strategically located at the head of the Delmarva Peninsula, was chosen as the site of Delaware College in 1834 (later becoming the University of Delaware).

Actually, the B&O main passed through Newark *Center* – the PW&B line passed to the south, connected via the old Newark & Delaware City RR (later Branch) and the rural Pomeroy & Newark RR (Branch) extending northward to the east-west main.

Herbert H. Harwood, Jr.

FLORIDA BOUND – On a chilly February 1968 day the *Florida Special* rolls past the station. The passengers are anxious to reach warmer climes and GG1 4915 will surely oblige. The design of the station is similar to those in Morton and Glen Mills on the Media-West Chester Branch (see Chapter 3).

William J. Coxey

CONRAIL freight JCWA (Jersey City-Washington), headed by two E44s, rumbles southward past DAVIS Tower in Newark in May 1979. The train (formerly MD3) departed Harsimus Cove about 8 a.m. for Potomac Yard. Track 1 in the foreground ends within the interlocking, about a quarter-mile to the north, with three main tracks northward to RAGAN interlocking in South Wilmington. The switch for the Delmarva Branch is just visible beyond the substation, with the track swinging sharply to the left.

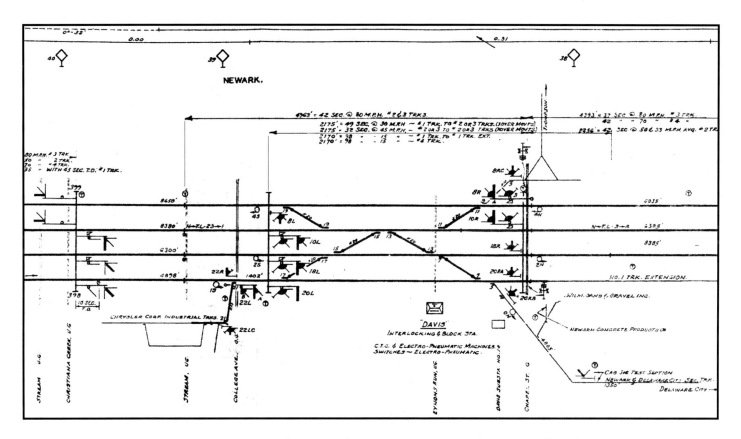

DAVIS Tower contained CTC and electro-pneumatic machines controlling the complete set of crossovers at Newark, along with the junctions of the Delmarva (Newark & Delaware City RR) and residual Pomeroy & Newark Branches, plus the Chrysler Corp. industrial track. The interlocking diagram is revised to March 1962.

William J. Coxey

FIVE LOCAL FREIGHTS were based in Newark in the early 1990s to drill area industries, principally Chrysler's auto assembly plant. Cabin cars were still being assigned to locals, especially if the train did much backing up. The locomotive on Train WPNK22 is a 1200 hp. SW1200, one of 48 still on Conrail's roster at the time.

ELKTON (MP. 44.7), the seat of government of Cecil County located at the head of navigation on Elk River, was the site of two early establishments curiously symbolic of the Philadelphia-Baltimore rivalry. A paper mill owned by one Harry Carter produced all the newsprint for the Philadelphia *Public Ledger*, while a mill owned by rival family member J. D. Carter provided the paper for the Baltimore *Sun*. Other paper and iron rolling mills were also located on the river.

The brick station shown here in an 1856 rendering was built at about the same time as the very similar one in Chester. The passengers awaiting the oncoming train are attired in the travel fashions of the day.

PW&B 1856 Guide/Ted Xaras Collection

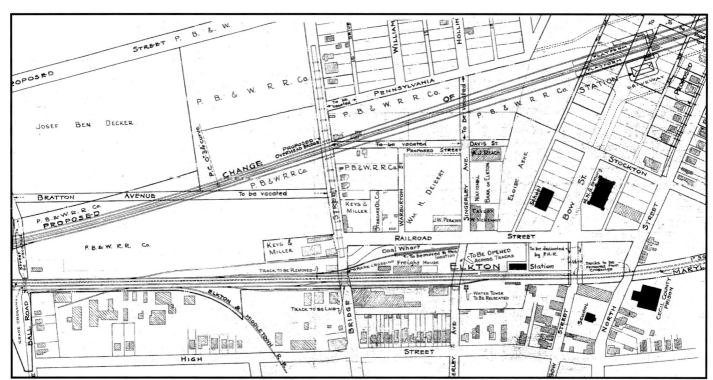

Hagley Museum & Library

ELIMINATION of grade crossings (and also reduction of curvature) through Elkton in 1932-4 was accomplished by keeping the new four-track line at ground level and carrying the main streets overhead, resulting in a savings of $900 thousand vs. the cost of track elevation. A replacement station was constructed on the new line, completed in 1935. Trackage on the old alignment north of the old station was removed, but access to the freight house from the south remained.

PW&B 1856 Guide / Ted Xaras Collection

NORTH EAST (MP. 49.9) was named after the river of the same name that empties into the head of Chesapeake Bay. Because of clay deposits suitable for making superior fire bricks, several concerns man-ufacturing the material for home use as well as for industry developed in the area. The extensive McCullough Iron Company plant was also located here, along with several early woolen and grist mills. The early passenger and freight stations are depicted ca. 1856.

Fred W. Schneider, III

ANOTHER FLORIDA-BOUND – Carrying on the PRR tradition GG1 927
in the early Amtrak scheme and an unidentified sister lead a Florida consist
of assorted Heritage equipment southward near North East on 22 May 1976.

CHARLESTOWN (MP. 53.5) was another of the "old towns" of Maryland, having been settled in 1742. Also located on the North East River, there were several early mills, causing it for a while to seriously challenge Baltimore as a grain and flour processing center. It was heavily damaged by the British during the War of 1812. When the early rail line was built southward from Wilmington, Charlestown was planned as the terminus with passengers to be conveyed to Baltimore by steamboat. Here was another early PW&B station doubling as the ticket agent's residence.

PW&B 1856 Guide/Ted Xaras Collection

CARS would do well to observe the flashing lights as GG1 4936 speeds a mixed consist northward at Charlestown crossing on a bleak December day in 1965.

Fred W. Schneider, III

THIS MANSARD-ROOFED STATION constructed by the PW&B at Principio (MP. 56.7) in 1876 contained a waiting room and ticket office, plus agent's quarters. It was destroyed by fire before being opened, but was immediately rebuilt. Principio was the location of many fisheries on the Bay.

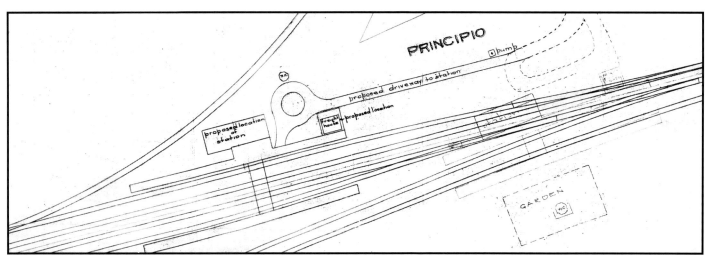

WITH FOUR-TRACKING through the area it was necessary to move both the passenger station and freight house. This 1906 PB&W diagram shows the new location – the tracks below the main are the Perryville Branch, those above are sidings. Note that the garden boasts a "W.C.", which we assume is a water closet. A thorn among roses.

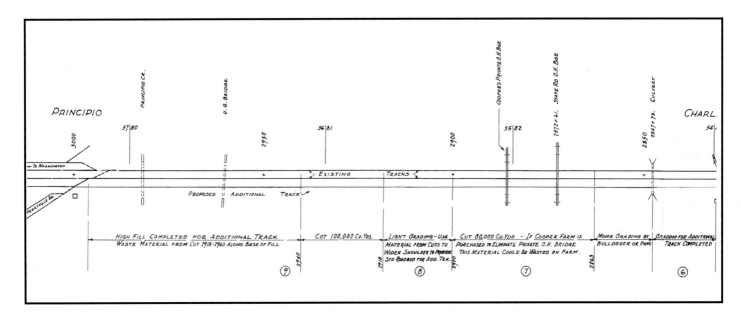

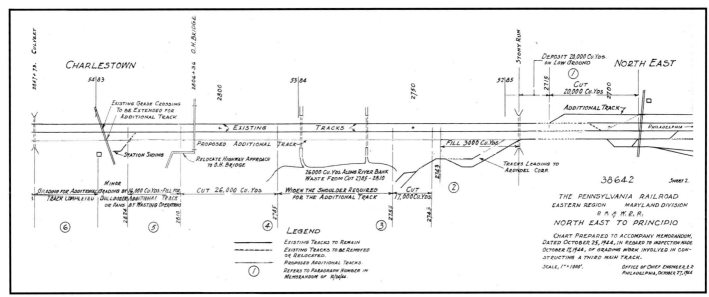

Hagley Museum & Library

AS WE HAVE NOTED, addition of a 3rd and 4th track south of Wilmington varied according to the traffic density in different areas, although track elevation projects after the turn of the century, electrification during the 1930s and the onslaught of World War II traffic all brought about periods of additional multiple tracking. In 1944 PRR developed this plan to construct a third track between North East and Principio. From North East the track extended a short distance through a cut on the southbound side and then ran the rest of the way on the northbound side. This was accomplished by cutting and filling, supplemented with wasting when needed. We will discuss additional multiple tracking projects farther south later in this chapter.

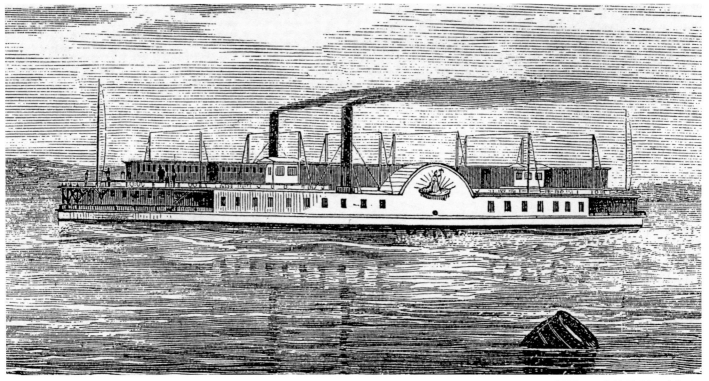

INITIAL CROSSINGS of the broad Susquehanna River to link the northern and southern sections of the PW&B were accomplished by the ferryboat *Susquehanna*. Rebuilt and lengthened in 1846, the elegant wooden boat operated successfully between Perryville and Havre de Grace until it was replaced by the 220-ft. long, iron-hulled steam ferry *Maryland*, shown here, in December 1854. Built in Wilmington at a cost of $110,000, she was a true car ferry with tracks on her top deck that could move an entire passenger train in one trip. Passengers were comfortably accommodated in a large hall extending the length of the vessel with saloons along each side.

In the early weeks of the Civil War in the spring of 1861, with hostile and unruly mobs of southern partisans preventing passage of Union troops through Baltimore, PW&B President Samuel Felton and his PRR counterpart John Edgar Thomson came up with an alternate solution to relieve Washington DC, then threat-ened by Confederate forces. For several months troops were moved on the PW&B to Perryville where they boarded the *Maryland*, cars and all, for the run via the Annapolis & Elk Ridge RR and the B&O's Washington Branch south of Baltimore to the nation's capital. Felton subsequently paid tribute to this operation, noting that, "the ferry-boat *Maryland* has performed an amount of work during the last year greater than any other boat of the kind in the world."

No longer needed with completion of a bridge, the *Maryland* made its final trip on 22 November 1866 and then laid up in Havre de Grace. She was moved to New York Harbor in October 1875, rebuilt and put back in service as a car transfer boat in June 1876. She was destroyed by fire on 7 December 1888, but her historic name lived on in a second steamer that began service on 28 February 1890.

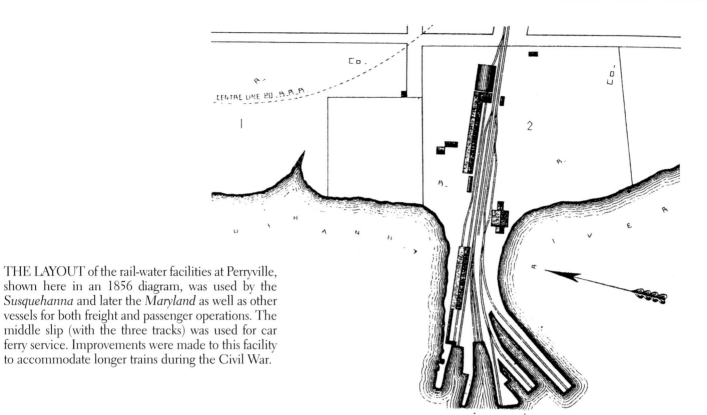

THE LAYOUT of the rail-water facilities at Perryville, shown here in an 1856 diagram, was used by the *Susquehanna* and later the *Maryland* as well as other vessels for both freight and passenger operations. The middle slip (with the three tracks) was used for car ferry service. Improvements were made to this facility to accommodate longer trains during the Civil War.

PW&B 1856 Annual Report/*Ted Xaras Collection*

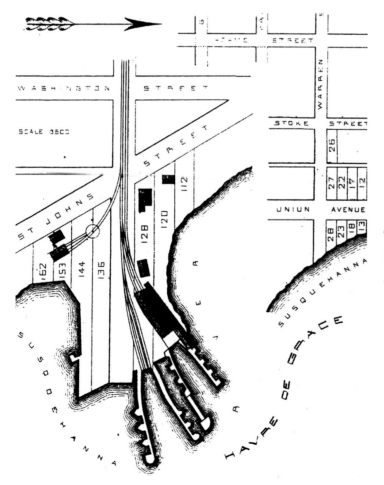

THE CORRESPONDING TERMINAL at Havre de Grace is depicted here, also in an 1856 diagram. Note the turntable and small engine house.

PW&B 1856 Annual Report/*Ted Xaras Collection*

THIS REMARKABLE PHOTO gives us a glimpse of the Havre de Grace facility in the early 1860s. A floating transfer bridge has been added and the track work rearranged accordingly. Note the early Union Tank Lines cars and the switch tower at left.

THE MOUTH of the Susquehanna River is actually a brackish shallow tidal basin extending several miles upriver. Because of the tidal influence from Chesapeake Bay the water seldom freezes except under extreme cold conditions. When these conditions are prolonged, massive ice jams occur that can eventually freeze solid. This situation occurred during the winter of 1848-49, when PW&B had to let its passengers walk (or take wagons) across the ice or transport them by boat out into the Bay.

The most notable example occurred in the frigid winter of 1851-52 when the jam was so severe that water navigation was completely blocked. PW&B engineers took the ingenious – if dangerous – step of laying tracks on the ice and from 15 January to 24 February nearly 1400 cars carrying some 10,000 tons of freight, baggage and mail were moved across. The cars were released down the incline to the river and hauled by teams of horses to the opposite side where they were then pulled up the incline by a locomotive and cable arrangement depicted here. When it was deemed advisable to take up the track before the ice thawed, it was accomplished without a loss of a single rail or tie!

In January 1857 the river froze again but a channel was kept

R&LHS Bulletin /*Kalmbach Memorial Library*

open by repeated trips of the *Maryland*. However, one Saturday night the ice pack shifted and carried the steamer transporting a northbound passenger train 600 ft. downstream and then held it fast. This time a plank walkway was laid on the ice from Perryville and passengers and their baggage walked to shore. A 6-ft. wide walkway was then laid across the river, and passengers, baggage and mail transferred for four days until the ice thawed enough to release the steamer.

THESE MAKESHIFT, inconvenient and highly dangerous arrangements led to a growing public outcry for construction of a permanent bridge across the wide river. Extensive preliminary surveys were made in the summer and fall of 1853 and more detailed surveys were carried out in March and April 1854, resulting in three proposed alignments, generally following and approximately 1500-ft. above and below the ferry crossing. The upriver alignment was rejected because of the requirement for a longer bridge in deeper water. Bids were received for both of the other two routes and contracts signed on 31 May 1854. The "middle" route was finally selected on 12 August, with completion set for 1 January 1856.

It was an ambitious undertaking – because of serious questions on the ability of any bridge to withstand the treacherous ice jams and a shortage of funds following the Panic of 1857, construction was delayed until the summer of 1862. After careful planning it was decided to construct a single test pier in 42 ft. of water, the deepest ever attempted up to that time. The foundations were laid and work began on the pier itself on 15 November and was completed a month later, using "new engineering processes" to position it "with mathematical accuracy." The pier was then secured with rubble before the ice closed in for the winter, a lone sentinel to future progress.

R&LHS Bulletin /*Kalmbach Memorial Library*

After it held for three winters, the decision was made to build the remaining masonry piers. They were completed in 1866, utilizing stone from quarries opened in nearby Port Deposit. Work continued until the summer of that year when the wooden truss spans were nearly completed. Suddenly on 25 July Mother Nature wreaked havoc on the bridge when a violent tornado swooped down on the structure, destroying all but one of the spans. The mass of useless wreckage was cleared away, new trusses were erected and the bridge was *finally* completed in November. This placid view from the Havre de Grace side shows an early design for a fully covered wooden structure with a steamboat approaching the draw span.

THE FINAL DESIGN of the bridge, shown here during construction some time during 1866 – note the falsework under the spans – consisted of open, arch-reinforced wooden Howe trusses. The Perryville ferry slip is in the foreground.

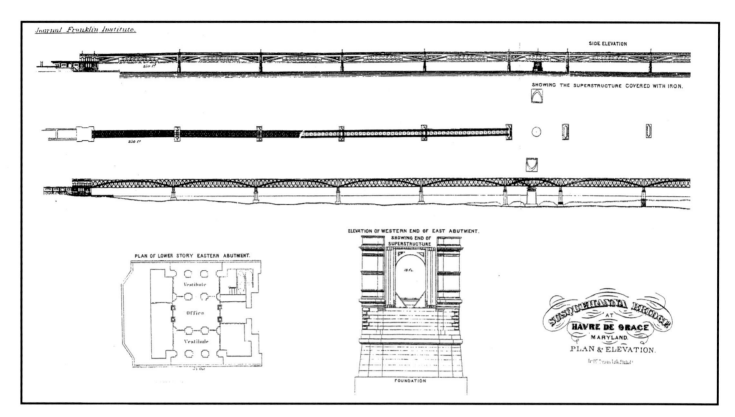

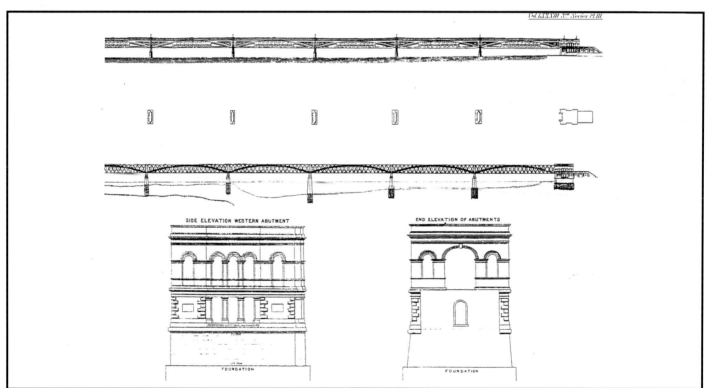

THE COMPLETED BRIDGE was opened for traffic on 26 November 1866, triumphantly giving the PW&B and the nation for the first time an all-rail route from Philadelphia to Baltimore – albeit a few years late. The $2,268,983 expenditure for the 3269-ft. structure was enormous – thanks to Mother Nature – reflecting the outlay for nearly two sets of wooden trusses. The single-track bridge consisted of 12 spans each 250 ft. in length, plus one 176-ft. draw span to accommodate river navigation. It was supported by 13 masonry piers and two massive and elaborate granite abutments housing offices at either end, plus two guard piers at the draw. The mean depth of water at the piers ranged from 10 to 45 ft.

Ted Xaras Collection

THIS VIEW shows the graceful bridge from the Havre de Grace end as it appeared in 1877. With the constant threat of bridge fires, the timbers were fireproofed with zinc chloride solution under pressure and the bottom chords were encased in 3/8"-in. thick plate iron (both for fireproofing and reinforcement) – al-

though we have found no evidence that the entire bridge was ever sheathed in iron as shown in the previous diagram. All together the massive structure took 500-1000 laborers five years to build and used 20 thousand cu. yds. of masonry, nearly 5 million feet of timber and 3 million lbs. of wrought and cast iron.

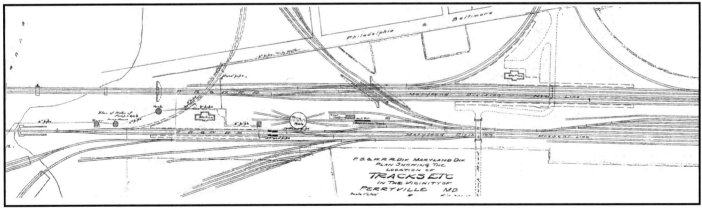

Hagley Museum & Librar

AS IMPRESSIVE as the wooden bridge was, it was rebuilt in place with an iron superstructure over the period 1873-79, with the draw span completed in March 1880. The cost was a little over $500 thousand – less than one-fourth the original expenditure (of course the ironwork only had to be done once). The iron bridge was in turn replaced with a double-track steel structure upstream of the original one in 1905-6, in conjunction with the multi-tracking and track elevation program on the division.

The complex track layout on the Perryville side is shown on this PB&W diagram dated 24 March 1906, before completion of the new bridge. At bottom is the original alignment, engine facilities, passenger station (inside the old wye to the C&PD Branch) and the marine terminal. V Cabin was located south of the station on the southbound side. Above that is the new elevated right of way with the new station and wye at right.

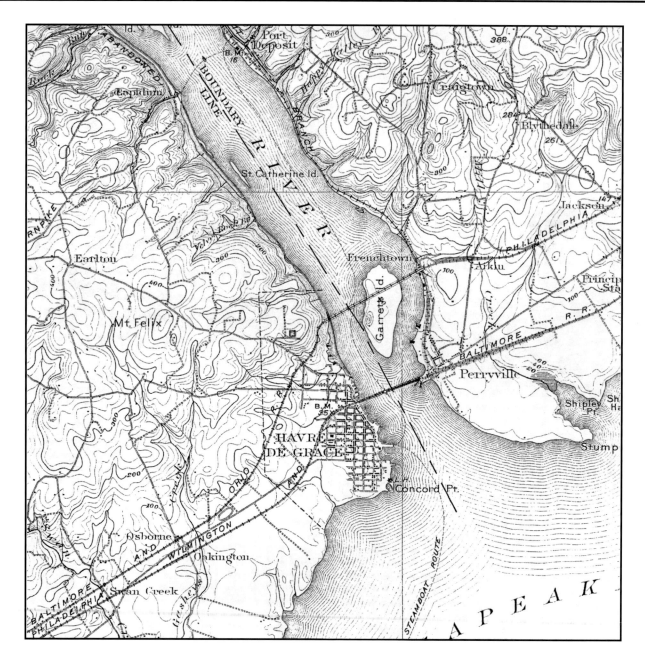

THE MOUTH of the Susquehanna River is shown in this 1900 USGS map, with the iron bridge still in place and the towns of Perryville, Havre de Grace and Port Deposit (upriver) – a dashed line denotes the old ferry route. But note that something else has intruded on the scene – the B&O Philadelphia line constructed in 1885. B&O boasted that its bridge location farther upriver offered better protection against scouring at the piers. Now let us follow the B&O line for an interesting story.

Note Garrett Island, Swan Creek to the west and Aikin to the right. Actually, the original name of the island was Palmers. Garrett's penchant for putting his name on everything like an Eastern potentate could not let that stand, so Garrett Island became. He also had a dream of creating a resort on the island, but fortunately that fantasy did not materialize.

The B&O bridge was single-track as built, but this was a minor impediment because there was very little traffic on the line. On 23 September 1908 an eastern span collapsed under a coal train (happily, without casualties) but this presented B&O with a *serious* impediment. Fortunately, PRR's new bridge was completed

as we shall see so PRR allowed B&O to use it.

A connection was built at Swan Creek, but trains had to back to reach PRR tracks. The other connection was at Aikin, reaching Perryville via C&PD tracks. Aikin is 50 feet higher than Perryville, so a short, savage grade had to be surmounted requiring helpers.

B&O's rebuilt bridge opened on 6 September 1910 and the Swan Creek connection removed. The Aikin-Perryville connection remains and was a factor in the abortive "Merger of Equals" between CSX and Conrail. discussed in *Triumph I*. Easing this grade was a major part of the proposed merger to allow Conrail traffic to reach Baltimore via the C&PD line.

For a banker, Garrett certainly did have a problem with arithmetic. His Philadelphia Division cost $17.8 million, and that princely sum did not include the Belt Line, or Howard Street Tunnel, in Baltimore nor other expenditures at the New York end.

This was more than PRR paid for PW&B, an amount Garrett would not pay eight years earlier. However, he did end up with a worthless island named for him.

HERE IS THE dramatic scene after the collapse. The bridge was being rebuilt in place because B&O had a rail and bridge loading problem on the Philadelphia Division. Obviously as to the latter, but just as important to the former. Why did PRR have so many Atlantic locomotives and B&O so few? Because PRR used heavier rail than B&O, so B&O was forced to stick with Ten Wheelers. The Garrett legacy.

F. A. Wrabel Collection

THE NEW PRR BRIDGE, a 4153-ft. long Howe deck truss structure consisting of 18 spans over the water (17 fixed plus one draw) and five stone arches, opened 29 May 1906. Its cost was $1.3 million – only slightly more than half that of the original wooden bridge 40 years before. This remarkable PRR photo shows the official inspection train crossing the bridge for the first time on that day – Office Car No. 2821 pulled by PB&W locomotive 5209. Unfortunately we can't make out who the officials are but Cassatt was President of PRR at the time and this bridge was of critical importance to his overall plan.

FORTY YEARS LATER a GG1-powered heavyweight train heads north across the impressive bridge in the early 1940s, not long after electrification. The draw span is visible beyond the train in this long view.

PRR engineer Forrwood "Fordy" Smith test-ran a light GG1 southbound to Perryville, reaching a peak of 165mph and regu- larly running at 125mph. Fordy related this story to Harry C. Eck at the B&O Museum, who in turn passed it on to us. Sadly, Fordy died on 13 November 2002 before we could interview him. Fordy also noted that the M1 was his favorite steam locomotive, praise shared by many PRR enginemen and historians.

WHEN the new steel bridge was com- pleted PRR converted the old one for highway and pedestrian use (replacing the draw span) in lieu of continuing to provide free transport service on sever- al trains across the river, as required in an odd provision in the original en- abling legislation. It was sold to a pri- vate company on 10 January 1910, which promptly imposed tolls, and then to the State of Maryland on 10 February 1923 – and subsequently de- molished with construction of a new highway bridge upstream. Both bridges are shown here in a 1913 post- card view looking southward.

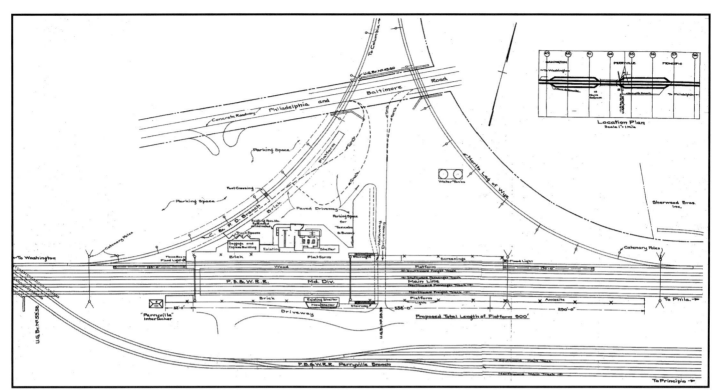

Hagley Museum & Library

BY 1942 the old wye had been removed and the residual line became the Perryville Branch, looping around to Perryville yards and then joining the C&PD Branch at Frenchtown (controlled by MINNICK Tower). This PRR diagram shows the proposed expansion of the passenger facilities to accommodate additional military personnel at the Bainbridge Naval Training Station located at Port Deposit, about 4-1/2 miles upriver on the C&PD Branch. This consisted of enlargement of the station, construction of a temporary baggage and express building, extension of the platforms and provision for busses. Note the location of the new PERRYVILLE Tower.

F. A. Wrabel Collection

BEFORE we continue farther south, we should take a closer look at Perryville (MP. 58.9), a town located on the north bank of the Susquehanna about a mile from where it empties into Chesapeake Bay. Originally a fishing community and also a shipping point for lumber and stone, its commerce increased with the coming of the PW&B and later the Columbia & Port Deposit RR extending up the river valley.

This PRR photo, also taken on 29 May 1906, shows the attractive new brick station constructed in 1901 replacing the earlier structure built in the 1870s. It is the only one we have come across that shows a passenger train at the C&PD platform, on the wye behind the building.

A NORTHBOUND passenger train roars by the station in 1932 before electrification was completed on the Division south of Wilmington. The station served not only the PRR mainline but also trains running on the Octoraro Branch to Octoraro Junction and continuing on the C&PD.

George F. Nixon/Maryland Rail Heritage Library

Fred W. Schneider, III

MOTIVE POWER of a much different sort – the early-morning Metroliner outruns the camera shutter as it hurtles past two girls watching it pass at Perryville station on 27 April 1969. Perryville had passenger service up to the last years of PRR when two southward locals, one southward mail and one northward local made station stops.

THIS VIEW shows us PERRYVILLE Tower and Amtrak Train 147, the Springfield (MA) to Washington *Bankers* as it speeds past the station, boarded up in November 1977. Actually the train is slowing from 80 to 60 mph before reaching the bridge. The tower was rebuilt in the 1940s.

William J. Coxey

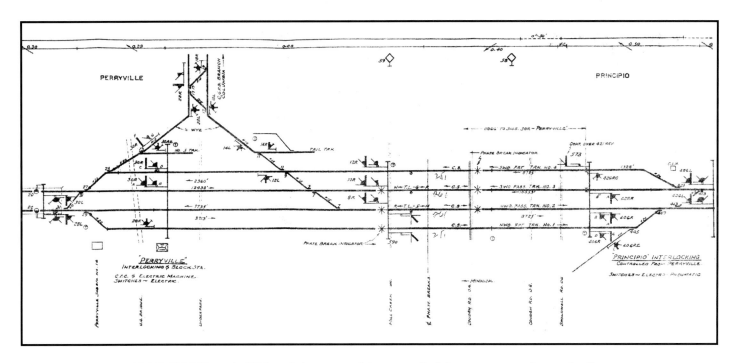

PERRYVILLE Tower's CTC and electric machine controlled the crossovers at the wye leading to the C&PD Branch plus the transition from two to four tracks at Principio interlocking and back again at the Susquehanna bridge. Note the phase break indicators in this March 1962 diagram.

William J. Coxey

AMTRAK Train 109, a four-car Metroliner set, quickly leaves Perryville and the tower behind it as it approaches the Susquehanna Bridge at 70 mph in November 1977. Note the traces of the PRR keystone logo on the front. Northward freights bound for the C&PD Branch used the crossover in the foreground to Track 3 and then switched to Track 4 and onto the wye. In the background is the switch leading to Track 1.

William J. Coxey

OUR PHOTOGRAPHER turns and catches the Metroliner as it heads out over the double-track bridge in November 1977. At this time the maximum speed for Metroliners south of Philadelphia was 100 mph while other passenger trains were limited to 80 mph. Now the *Acela Express* trains hit 125 mph in places and 90 mph across the bridge. Note the old bridge piers to the left, still enduring the river after well over 100 years.

George F. Nixon/Maryland Rail Heritage Library

IN AN EARLIER ERA a northbound steam-powered train crosses the bridge in 1932, which looks bare without the overhead catenary structure.

William J. Coxey

THIS VIEW gives us a better look at the drawbridge from the southward end as Amtrak Train 167, the New York Washington *Betsy Ross*, crosses the structure in November 1977. The old bridge piers are visible in the foreground plus the guard piers for the draw. Although the Susquehanna is navigable to Port Deposit, very few vessels are high enough to require a bridge opening, which has long required 24-hour advance notice.

BRIDGES GALORE – Underlining the value of this transportation corridor are the four current bridge across the Susquehanna from Perryville to Havre de Grace: Amtrak E60 956 hauls Amtrak Train 167 across the former PRR bridge, behind that is the replacement U. S. Route 40 highway bridge and then the black CSX (former B&O) structure – all deck truss bridges with central through spans for river clearance. Finally in the distance the I95 highway bridge is just visible.

William J. Coxey

HEAVY HAUL – Three GG1s in the stealth Conrail scheme power symbol freight B4 off the bridge into Havre de Grace in November 1977. The units are entering Track 4, which only extended 12 miles to the Bush River bridge where the line narrows again to two tracks. On the south side of the river freights were often routed via the two center tracks (Nos. 2 and 3), the reverse procedure from the north side.

William J. Coxey

125

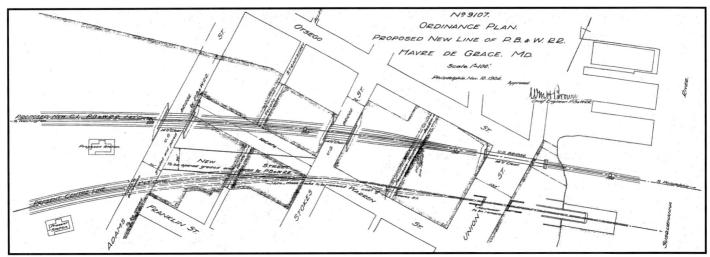

Hagley Museum & Library

THE NEW ALIGNMENT also produced changes at the south end of the bridge in Havre de Grace (MP. 60.1). The line was re-located on a raised fill with four undergrade crossings, three of which are shown here. The station was also relocated farther east, as indicated in this 1904 PB&W plan. The new passenger station was opened in 1906 and the old one was converted to a freight station two years later.

Overall the realignment for the new bridge and its approaches reduced maximum curvature from 2°5′ to 0°45′ and raised the elevation on the bridge from 31 ft. to 58.7 ft. above mean high water, drastically reducing the necessity for drawbridge operation.

William J. Coxey

AT HAVRE DE GRACE photographer Bill Coxey caught a Pepco unit train extra as it pauses with empty coal hoppers on Track 2, waiting for a northward passenger train to pass on Track 1 before proceeding across the bridge. At this time (November 1977) the station was unused – the last train, Washington to Philadelphia local No. 400, was discontinued in the mid-1960s.

Pepco (formerly Potomac Electric Power) has two generating plants on the former PRR Pope's Creek Branch (now CSX) – one is located at Chalk Point on the Patuxent River at the end of the Herbert Secondary and the other is on the Potomac River at Morgantown (near Pope's Creek). Several unit trains a day – now during the night – carry coal from western Pennsylvania (via Enola Yard and the C&PD line) in Pepco hoppers.

A SOUTHBOUND Conrail local headed by ex-PC, ex-PRR GP7 7102 crosses from Track 3 to Track 2 as it passes through Havre de Grace interlocking in May 1978. The freight is most likely MD119 that operated from Bay View Yard in Baltimore to Havre de Grace on a Monday-Wednesday-Friday basis and on the Pope's Creek Secondary south of Washington on Tuesday-Thursday-Saturday.

Note the interesting signal configuration – the lower signal heads provide the block condition for diverting routes, including crossovers. The least restrictive indication for the signals over Tracks 2 and 3 is Medium Clear (30 mph maximum). The right signal over Track 1 also has a similar lower head for the (relatively) high-speed Track 1-2 switch on the north side of the bridge – thus the yellow triangle to the left of the lower head – that indicates a least restrictive diverting route indication of Limited Clear (45 mph maximum). The metal boxes around the lower heads are sun shields for better visibility.

Tim Garner

A SOUTHBOUND Metroliner catches the sun as it passes under Maryland Route 7 south of Havre de Grace in November 1977. The classic Warren through truss bridge was later replaced and the tracks beneath it reduced to three.

Tim Garner

SPEEDWAY – A four-car Metroliner set takes advantage of the gently curving right of way north of Aberdeen as it as it speeds northward on 11 February 1977. The cars on the highway are about to witness a silver bullet.

Fred W. Schneider, III

MOVING SOUTHWARD, we come to Aberdeen (MP. 64.9), originally Hall's Cross Roads. The early PW&B passenger and freight stations at Aberdeen are depicted here ca. 1856. It was a small town surrounded by farms until the U. S. Army established the Aberdeen Proving Ground nearby on 20 October 1917, six months after the U. S. entered World War I, to provide a facility where the design and testing of ordnance equipment and ammunition could be done near the nation's industrial and shipping centers. However, it literally took an Act of Congress and two presidential proclamations to persuade the reluctant farmers to leave their rich agricultural lands, many of which had been in the same families for generations.

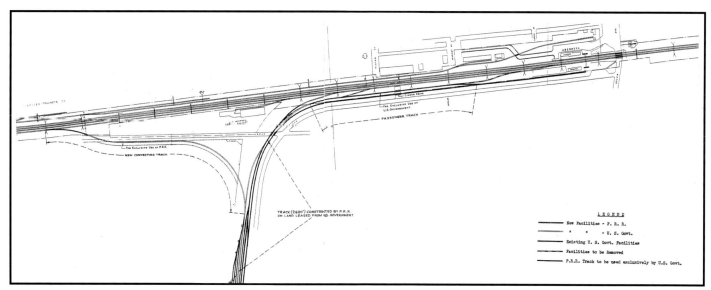

THE ARMY FACILITIES were enlarged in the 1930s and again during World War II. This 1944 PRR diagram shows the station area and additional sidings and trackage connecting the main with the Proving Ground. It was a major source of traffic and revenue for PRR, but the volume of wartime traffic was too much for PRR alone to handle, so B&O was granted access via a bridge over the PRR main and sidings within the government property. We used the artillery range at the proving ground for many years and an uncle was employed there. A father-in-law also worked there on the Manhattan Project. There are several splendid museums open to the public, although they may be closed in the present environment.

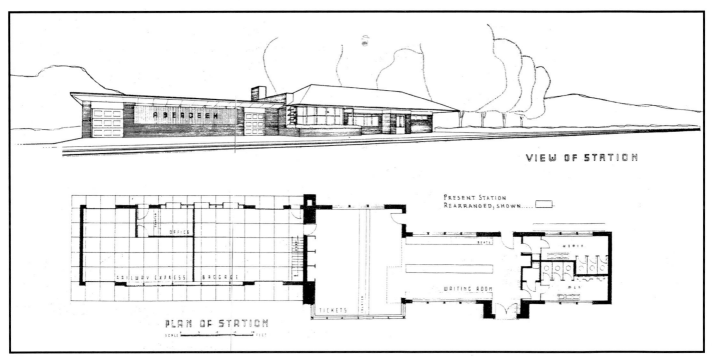

VIEW OF STATION

PRESENT STATION
REARRANGED, SHOWN......

PLAN OF STATION

THE STATION and northbound shelter were expanded as well to serve the large number of military personnel, utilizing the services of noted architect and industrial designer Raymond Loewy, who developed designs similar to these for a number of PRR stations. An underpass was built under the main for convenient troop access to the southbound station.

A SOUTHBOUND four-car Metroliner set hustles through Aberdeen station on 27 February 1978. Note the differences in pantograph design – the one on the 863 indicates a unit with GE equipment, the other is Westinghouse.

A PAIR of E44s hauls a southbound Penn Central freight as it approaches Bel Air crossing, just north of the Aberdeen station, on 8 February 1975. The PRR keystone on the lead unit is fading fast – but never to be forgotten.

Tim Garner

SOUTH of Aberdeen is the town of Perrymansville (MP 68.5), later shortened to Perryman. It was situated in an agricultural area noted for its heavy production of hay and grain. The early PW&B station is shown here.

PW&B 1856 Guide/Ted Xaras Collection

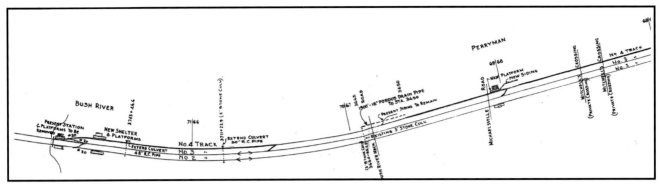

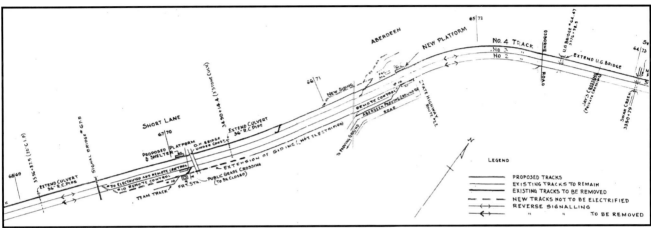

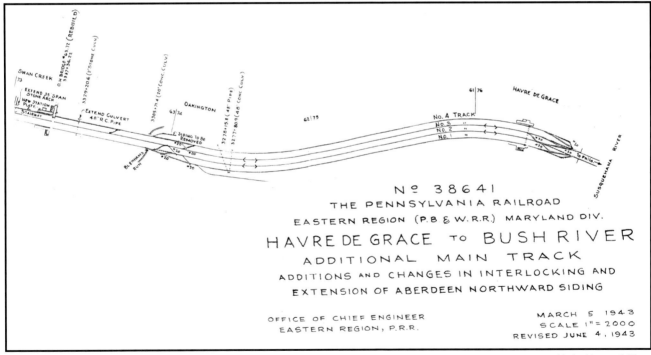

AS WE have noted, PRR experienced considerable delays because of heavy World War II traffic on double-track stretches south of Wilmington. Daily traffic between June 1941 and June 1943 surged from 129 to 199, a 54.2% increase. Because of a shortage of electric motive power, slower-moving steam locomotives were utilized for up to one-third of freight movements, further increasing the delays.

This diagram shows an additional project to lay an addi-tional section of third track between Oakington (south of Havre de Grace) and Bush River. The project included the construction, electrification and signaling of about 9 miles of additional main track, additional sidings and interlocking changes at Havre de Grace, Oakington and Bush River, along with modifications to stations at several intermediate points. The work was carried out during 1943-4 at a cost of $1.8 million.

SOUTH of Perryman is the Bush River which the railroad crossed on this 3,089-ft. long timber trestle. The Bush River, although nearly a mile wide, was really just an inlet from the Bay running inland only about 8 miles. This trestle was rebuilt in 1886 and in 1913 it was replaced with a 100-span, 2680-ft. double-track reinforced concrete structure.

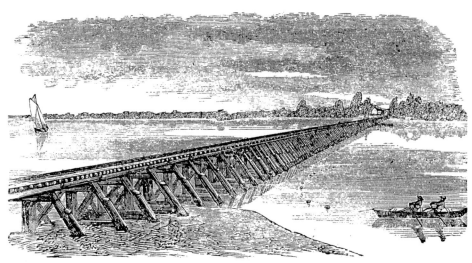

PW&B 1856 Guide/Ted Xaras Collection

Fred W. Schneider, III

FAMILY AFFAIR – All eyes are on the pair of Penn Central E33s as they power a southbound freight across the concrete bridge over the Bush River north of Edgewood on a warm August day in 1974. The mixed freight is headed for Potomac Yard.

EDGEWOOD (MP. 74.6) is located on the ridge that separates the Bush and Gunpowder Rivers. The early PW&B passenger station and dwelling was a two-story frame shelter, shown here.

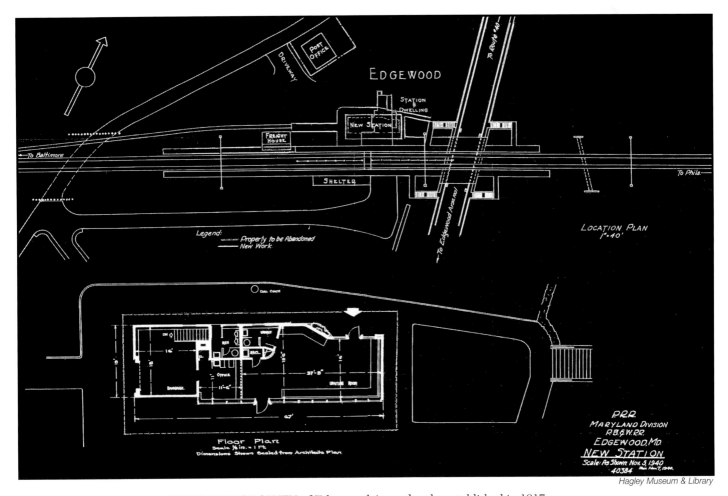

WITH THE GROWTH of Edgewood Arsenal – also established in 1917 as a chemical weapons research, development and testing facility – PRR replaced the old passenger and freight station with a combination station in 1940. It was another of designer Raymond Loewy's distinctive flat-roofed designs.

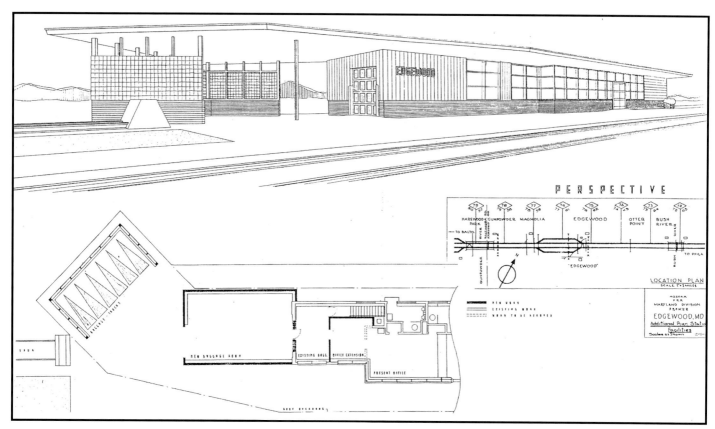

MILITARY TRAFFIC to Edgewood Arsenal continued to increase and 2-1/2 years later the station was enlarged by adding a 20 x 29-ft. baggage room and a 14 x 28-ft. shelter for baggage trucks – all in Loewy *moderne* style. The Arsenal became administratively part of Aberdeen Proving Grounds in 1971.

FLYING UNDER their fifth flag, Class E33 rectifiers 4603 and 4609 power a Conrail Potomac Yard-Enola freight on Amtrak rails approaching Gunpowder River Bridge north of Baltimore in June 1976. The 10 3300-hp. engines, originally numbered 4601-4610, were built by General Electric in 1956-7 to replace aging side-rod motors on the Virginian. A merger into the Norfolk & Western several years later made the electrification from the coal fields redundant and the almost-new electrics wound up on the New Haven roster as 301-10 in a bargain sale. Subsequent to the Penn Central merger, all through freight destined for New England was rerouted through Selkirk

Yard near Albany NY to avoid lighterage costs at New York Harbor (see *Triumph V*). The excess New Haven freight motors were then moved south to take the place of condemned GG1s. The ladies certainly got around.

Fred W. Schneider, III

BRICKS – Here we have another southbound freight, rolling past the Magnolia sign by a pair of Class E44 motors on 22 May 1976. These 4400-hp. units, an upgrade of the E33 design, were built by GE 1960-63. They utilized ignitron rectifier tubes, evaluated by PRR in the experimental electric units built by Baldwin 10 years before.

Tim Garner

NEARLY-NEW E60 963 leads a set of Amfleet equipment in the original color scheme near Magnolia, approaching the Gunpowder River. The date is November 1977.

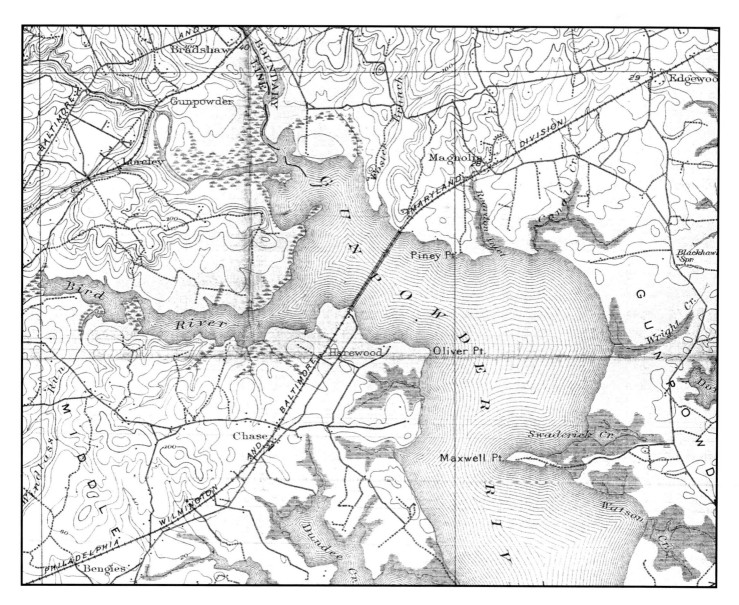

AS WE APPROACH the Baltimore area the main crosses the wide Gunpowder River, known for its numbers and variety of fish. Note the B&O is still with us at the upper left in this 1901 USGS map.

PW&B first crossed the wide river inlet on a 5238-ft. wooden pile trestle, shown here with a short draw span to allow the passage of small vessels. The trestle was rebuilt in 1886 and again in 1903.

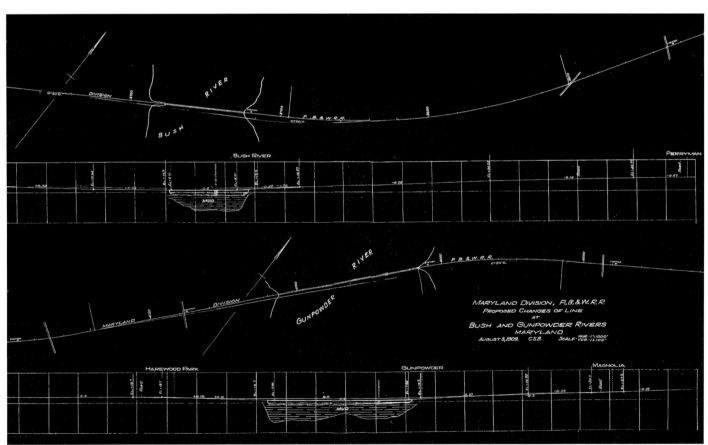

IN 1901 PB&W prepared this plan to realign the right of way and replace the old wooden bridges over the Bush and Gunpowder Rivers with new double-track reinforced concrete ones. It took three years and much deliberation over pier design and possible interference with fishing rights – including a review of the design by renowned consulting engineer Gustav Lindenthal (see *Triumph* V) – but the work was finally carried out in 1912-13 at a cost of $1.2 million. The Gunpowder bridge was a 188-span, 4853-ft. long structure plus a 30-ft. steel bascule draw.

John J. Bowman, Jr./Fred W. Schneider, III collection

A METROLINER SET crosses the concrete structure on 18 June 1976. The 60-plus years – and deferred maintenance – have taken their toll on the structure.

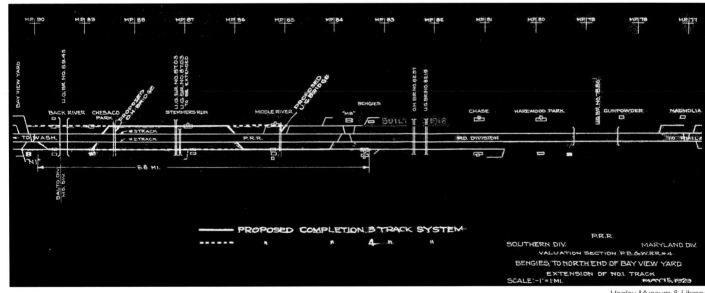

Hagley Museum & Library

COMPLETION of the four-track system from the Gunpowder Bridge to the north end of Bay View Yard in Baltimore was approved during USRA control (to facilitate World War I traffic) and a contract awarded on 28 June 1918. Work was suspended on 21 February 1919 after cessation of hostilities when it was only partially complete, and then carried out intermittently between December 1920 and November 1923, when it was again suspended.

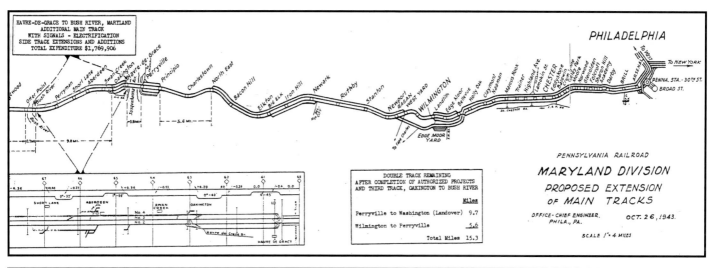

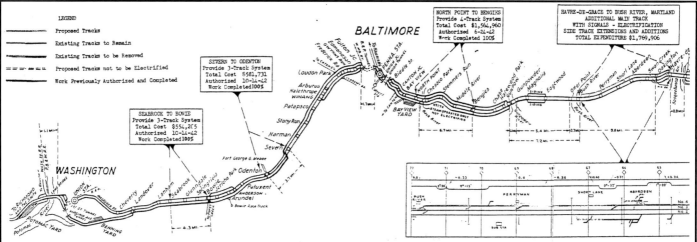

BY THE TIME the World War II traffic surge hit the railroad PRR had a four-track mainline between Philadelphia and Wilmington (RAGAN Tower). But between Wilmington and Baltimore there were only 20 miles of four tracks, 18 miles of three tracks and the remaining 28 miles were double-tracked. Between Baltimore and Landover, where the passenger and freight lines separated, there were 9 miles of four tracks, 14 miles of three tracks and 10 miles of double track.

PRR had to act – and quickly as passenger traffic in the first five months of 1942 had increased by a third over 1939 and freight traffic had nearly doubled. The most congested area was the 6.7-mile double-track section between Bengies and North Point, at the north end of Bay View Yard (see diagram), which had been left uncompleted after World War I traffic subsided. This double-track bottleneck seriously restricted the average traffic density of one train in each direction every 15 minutes – the result of increased all-rail Southern coal traffic to New York and New England, seasonal ore tonnage from the Great Lakes to Baltimore, heavy war materiel traffic in and out of the area as well as increased troop train movements and commuter trains for war plant workers. This $2.1 million project was completed in May of 1943, including electrification.

Two additional projects involved extension of the three-track system south of Baltimore between Severn and Odenton (3.7 miles, $1.1 million) and Bowie to Seabrook (4.3 miles, $1.3 million). Both of these were completed by October 1943. The fourth project shown on this diagram, expanding the three-track system

between Havre de Grace and Bush River, was discussed earlier. Completion of these projects left only 15.3 miles of double-track mainline between Wilmington and Landover.

North of Bay View Yard, note Chase and GUNPOW interlocking. On 4 January 1987 at about 1:30pm, three light B-36-7 units were proceeding north on No. 1 track with engineer Ricky Gates at the throttle. Spaced-out on drugs, Gates went through a restricting signal at the interlocking at such speed that all three units passed onto the northbound mainline and stopped. Northbound Train 94 *Colonial*, at a speed of about 90 mph, passed a clear distant signal only to have the home signal suddenly flash restricting in the engineer's face as Gates's units blocked the interlocking. *Colonial* could only slow a few miles-per-hour before the collision which resulted n 15 deaths and 176 injuries.

The toll would have been worse but for two factors. First, many passengers were returning from the New Year holiday and the conductor had closed the lead coach to provide for passengers who would board farther north. That car was demolished. Second, all cars were equipped with tight-lock couplers and the train did not part. Every car was jackknifed, but not one struck a catenary pole.

The bane of electrification is the poles. Solid steel anchored in concrete, when a car would strike one at speed the entire car would open up like a can opener, slaughtering everyone inside.

Gates was sentenced to five years in prison. We would have preferred the death penalty.

MIDDLE RIVER (MP. 84.8) was the site of the exclusive Maryland Yacht Club, an organization of "young men of Baltimore," which maintained a club, large farm and boat houses on the name-sake river. Many stations on the line provided living quarters for the agent and his family and this one shown in a 1927 view appeared to do so comfortably.

F. A. Wrabel

STEMMER'S RUN (MP. 86.4) was located in an area of sandy terrain, with some large farms nearby, but was also the site of deposits of a superior grade of iron ore, resulting in the establishment of early iron furnaces. The early PW&B station is depicted here.

PW&B 1856 Guide/Ted Xaras Collection

THE PW&B was well known for its fast passenger service between Philadelphia and Baltimore. Here high-stepping Class D14a 5023 upholds the tradition as it races southward north of Baltimore in the 1890s.

Ted Xaras Collection

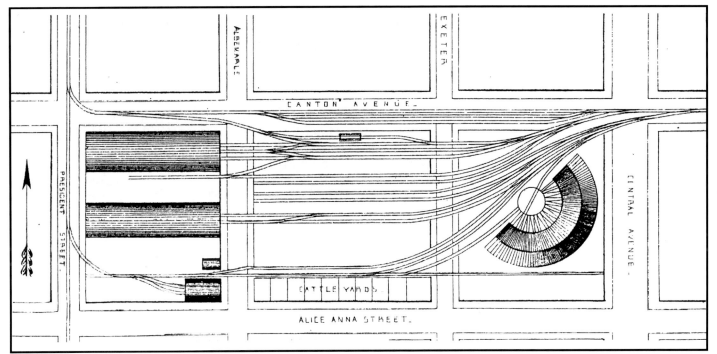

PW&B 1856 Guide/*Ted Xaras Collection*

WHEN the PW&B first arrived in Baltimore in the 1830s it initially rented space in the B&O's Pratt Street Station, which required moving cars via horse power (the slow-moving, four-legged variety). However, because of disagreements with its landlord and the inconvenience of street operations, it decided to build its own facility on President Street and Canton Avenue, which was opened on 18 February 1850. This allowed the use of locomotives all the way into the station. This diagram shows the terminal as it had developed by 1856, with passenger and freight stations, cattle pens and engine service facilities. Note that the tracks entering from the left connect with the B&O's Pratt Street line.

PRESIDENT STREET STATION was 66 ft. wide and 236 ft. long with a train shed "supported by iron pillars." It was set on fire in 1877 in conjunction with the strike and rioting in Pittsburgh, and militia once again fired on a mob in Baltimore (see Chapter 5). In 1883 the attractive "Railroad Roman" columned-front structure was converted to a freight shed – here labeled Shed A in a 1915 photo looking southeast at the intersection of President Street and Canton Avenue – and the new brick passenger station constructed farther to the east.

The head-house was partially restored and became the Baltimore Civil War Museum, opening in 1997 and winning a place on the National Register of Historic Places. There is a move afoot to recreate the building as a passenger station in a regional rail scheme, showing that fantasy dreams still abound in Baltimore.

THIS BUILDING later became Freight Shed B, shown here with horse-drawn wagons in a 1915 photo.

A THIRD freight warehouse was erected in 1899, a 66 X 480-ft. corrugated iron structure designated Shed C. The back of that building is at the left center in this westward view in 1915. The Union Box Company factory beyond advertises "Boxes of all kinds."

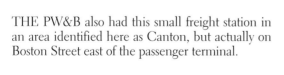

THE PW&B also had this small freight station in an area identified here as Canton, but actually on Boston Street east of the passenger terminal.

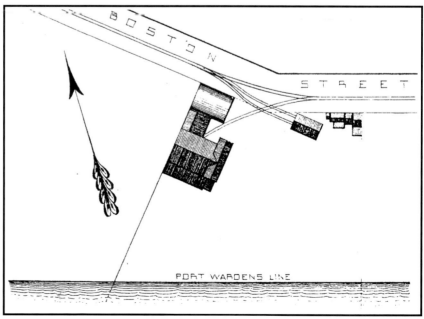

PW&B 1856 Guide/ Ted Xaras Collection

Chapter 3

Back Door Saga

The Octoraro and
West Chester Branches

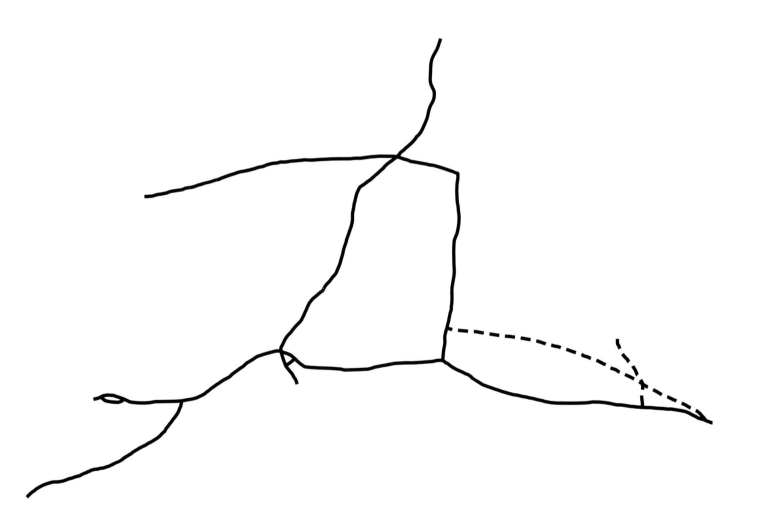

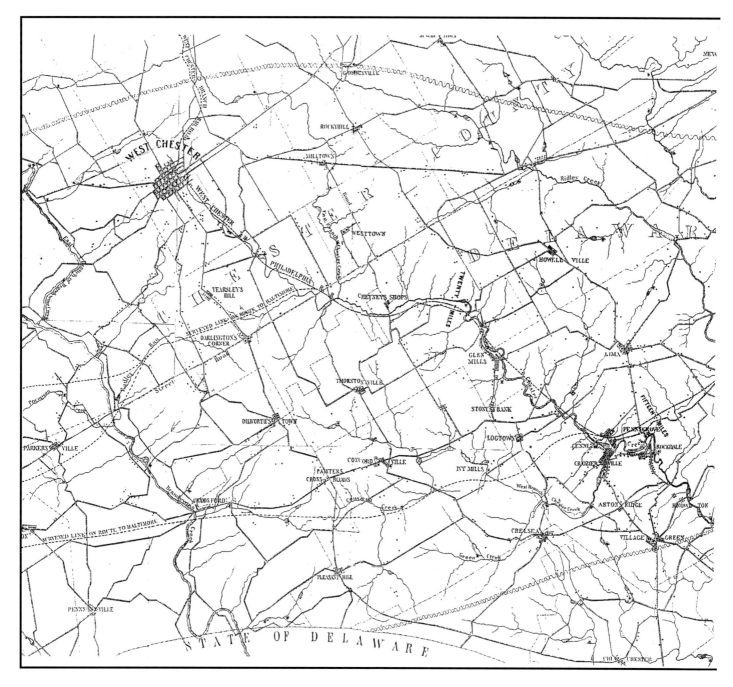

THIS HISTORIC MAP was issued by T. E. Sickels, the first Chief Engineer of the West Chester & Philadelphia, for that company's Third Annual Report in 1853. It shows the final "southern" route that followed the West Branch of Chester Creek, dipping to the south from the "direct route" proposed earlier by Edward Gay (see map page 150) and entered West Philadelphia parallel to the Delaware County Turnpike. The WC&P runs to its terminal at 31st and Chestnut, where a short dashed line (built in 1854-55) connects that road with the Philadelphia & Columbia (here labeled "Columbia Rail Road").

But note there is not yet a connection with the PW&B – this would come to fruition in the following decade with construction of the Junction RR. The PW&B is shown on its original alignment, prior to the Darby Improvement, and the West Chester RR (here labeled the "West Chester Branch Rail Road") extends north toward the P&C main at West Chester Intersection (later known as Malvern).

Interestingly, in addition to the WC&P the map shows three alternate routes proposed for the P&BC extending southward to Baltimore (dashed lines at left).

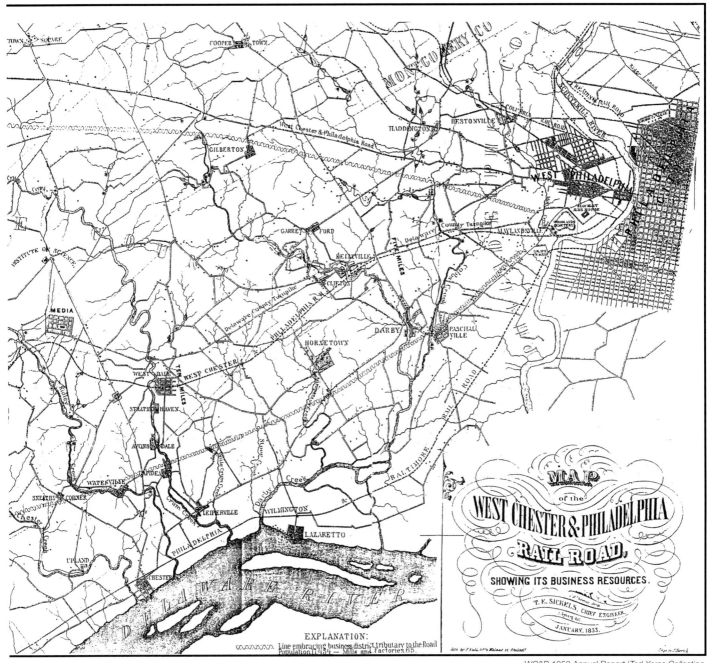

WC&P 1853 Annual Report/*Ted Xaras Collection*

Before we plunge into the conflicts and chaos inherent in the history of PRR and its predecessor lines in Baltimore, we need to examine a more peaceful – and lesser known, if not largely ignored – route planned to connect Philadelphia and Baltimore inland of the much better known PW&B main.

The first stirrings of a direct rail line between Philadelphia and Baltimore date to early 1831, when Samuel Dickey, the forward-looking president of the nascent Oxford RR, hired a young John Edgar Thomson to survey a line connecting the Philadelphia & Columbia RR (then still under construction) and Baltimore via Port Deposit. Thomson had started out as a rodman on the P&C and then gained additional experience as an engineer surveying portions of the Camden & Amboy in New Jersey, both under the guiding hand of Major John Wilson (see *Triumph II*).

Thomson's report of 30 May 1831 was extremely thorough and insightful, concluding that "the position of this rail way, situated as it is, between two of the largest commercial cities of the Union . . . gives it a character of national importance." He went further, predicting that "its completion will fully repay those whose enterprise may urge them to the undertaking, even were its cost ultimately to exceed the present estimate." Thomson's estimate was over $1 million but an insufficient number of investors felt the urge to support the project and it lay in the shadows of the lines closer to the coast that eventually became the PW&B.

But Dickey refused to give up and on 17 March 1853 he obtained a charter for the Philadelphia & Baltimore Central Railroad Company in Pennsylvania. A bit over a year later, on 20 June 1854, the Baltimore & Philadelphia Railroad Company was consolidated with it. The latter line had been authorized by the Maryland Legislature on 28 May 1852, granting $1.5 million to construct a road from Baltimore northward to connect with the Pennsylvania company, which in turn was given rights to construct a line from the Maryland border to intersect with the West Chester & Philadelphia RR "at or between" those two cities, "or to the city of Philadelphia." The proposed route generally followed Thomson's earlier proposal, although running somewhat farther to the west.

The area surrounding the planned route was largely farmland and it was hoped that the project would be supported by the local residents for transporting the fruits of their labors to market. That support was not forthcoming, however, and the projected line still did not offer much prospect to either Philadelphia or Baltimore investors compared to the increasingly heavily traveled PW&B route along the coast. That the road was able to raise funds at all was achieved only by offering substantial discounts on the sale of stocks, bonds and other notes. The route as laid out ran from Pennelton (later called Wawa) on the WC&P to Octoraro Junction on the Columbia & Port Deposit RR (see Chapter 4), where it terminated – the proposed extension to a connection with the Northern Central RR (see Chapter 5) and then to Baltimore was never built.

Construction began in 1855 and the road obtained authorization from both the Pennsylvania and Maryland Legislatures in the following year to allow issuance of bonds for an additional $1.5 million. In 1857 the company was authorized to change the routing to reduce sharp curves and steep grades, in addition to changing the northern terminus from Grub's Bridge on the WC&P to West Philadelphia, as long as the entrance to the City ran along the Philadelphia and Baltimore Turnpike.

The line was completed all the way to Oxford PA on 22 December 1860, but it requested an extension of time to finish the planned route because of difficult terrain and continued financing problems. A five-year extension was granted on 17 February 1863, along with authorization for an additional $350 thousand in preferred stock, allowing it to reach Rising Sun just across the Maryland border, on 19 March 1866. The road was finally completed to Octoraro Junction on the Susquehanna in December 1868, and revenue service to Port Deposit via the Columbia & Port Deposit RR (see Chapter 4) began on 12 April of the following year. During construction of the Maryland portion of the route a large vein of granite was discovered, and quarry operations began at the site.

To introduce an element of intrigue, in the summer of 1862 Samuel Felton, President of PW&B, secured control of most of the P&BC stocks and bonds after two years of effort. One faction of the original stockholders held out in the vain hope of keeping the line independent, but the financially troubled company was for intents and purposes bankrupt. Once this happened he "arranged" to have it connected to the PW&B, the first step in a fascinating drama, albeit on the sidelines.

Accordingly, on 13 January 1868 the P&BC leased the Chester Creek Railroad. This short (7 1/5-mile) road was chartered by the Pennsylvania Legislature on 16 April 1866 to run northwestward from Lamokin Street in Chester to Lenni in Delaware County, connecting with the WC&P. Strangely, this Act initially prohibited any connection with the Baltimore Central, but this was altered a year later, allowing an extension to the P&BC at Pennelton or any point between there and Lenni. Construction was completed in 1868, and the road began operations early the following year.

This line served as a short cut by-passing Philadelphia's increasingly congested freight yards, allowing traffic to move directly from the PW&B main to the P&BC. It also served a string of mills along Chester Creek, and in later years when these were converted from water power to coal-fired boilers coal became a major source of traffic for the short line.

The pioneering West Chester Railroad (not to be confused with the WC&P) is another piece of this back road puzzle. The relationship between this line and the WC&P – and ultimately PRR – is a fascinating story of convoluted maneuvering and conflict in its own right, rather more like a sideshow rather than a clash of titans but nevertheless part of the overall battle for power and supremacy between the giants.

The WCRR was chartered on 18 February 1831 to connect with the State-owned Philadelphia & Columbia (see *Triumph II*), allowing West Chester to have a much-needed line of commerce to Philadelphia. Major John Wilson, then Chief Engineer of the P&C, directed a preliminary survey of the route, which initially connected with that road at West Chester Intersection, now Malvern. The company organized shortly thereafter and Dr. William Darlington, a distinguished West Chester physician and member of the U. S. House of Representatives, was elected President and John P. Bailey was named as resident engineer. Bailey quickly (perhaps too quickly) laid out the route and construction began in June.

The road was formally opened on 13 September 1832, although the P&C itself was not opened until a month later. In the interim elated West Chester citizens were able to take excursions on horse-drawn trains to Intersection and back, but the line later ran regular service all the way to Belmont, opposite Philadelphia, where patrons descended into the Schuylkill Valley via the inclined plane and on into the City (see *Triumph II*). In 1845 the poorly constructed roadbed was rebuilt (but still using strap iron rail on wooden stringers) and the P&C provided steam motive power for WCRR trains, typically assigning older locomotives to the run.

The WCRR located a station in the West Chester House hotel on Broad Street in Philadelphia, reached via the City RR tracks on Market Street. About 1851 (after the P&C changed its approach into the City) the company moved to a new station on the south side of Market west of 18th Street (different from the WC&P facility at 18th and Market).

The road constructed a branch to the extensive limestone quarries in the Great Valley in 1834 and a short extension closer to the center of West Chester in 1836, but soon thereafter began to run into financial – and political – difficulties. It suffered from its chronically poor roadbed, continued operating delays on the P&C, exorbitant tolls on its shipments (and a generally poor relationship with the debt-ridden State road) and the usual financial constraints, resulting in a rail operation unsatisfactory to many influential West Chester business interests. Public agitation grew for an independent line directly into Philadelphia, bypassing the uncooperative State road altogether.

Thus the time was right for another rail line, and after public meetings advocating such an endeavor during the summer of 1847 the Pennsylvania Legislature chartered the West Chester & Philadelphia Railroad on 11 April 1848. An Acting Committee was formed, which secured the services of Edward F. Gay, a prominent Philadelphia engineer, to lay out the "best and most direct route between West Chester and the Permanent [Market Street] Bridge over the Schuylkill" into the City. This "direct route" was not accepted, however, in part because of its relatively steep grades and avoidance of settled areas.

The road was formally organized in 1850, with John S. Bowen elected its first President. T. E. Sickels was named Chief Engineer, who laid out the line to the south of Gay's proposed route (see maps) and let contracts for construction. Work began on 10 April 1852 about 6 miles east of West Chester. Construction was difficult because of the hilly terrain and winding stream valleys, which had to be crossed with high wooden trestles.

The road experienced difficulty in raising sufficient

funds over the next two years, leading to the resignation of Sickels on 30 May 1854. He was replaced by William H. Wilson, the son of Major John Wilson and later Chief Engineer of PRR. Wilson faced a major challenge – a few weeks after his appointment he was directed by the Board to suspend construction because of lack of funds, but with additional financing forthcoming, work was resumed on 1 August. By early September the five-span Crum Creek Bridge and other smaller bridges were finished and the road was officially opened between Philadelphia and Media on 19 October.

It would take another four years to complete the line to West Chester, and during that time the company was essentially in receivership, being operated by trustees appointed by the bondholders. This work was finally completed on 10 November 1858 and the entire road was opened for traffic the next day. Having fulfilled the task of completing the road, the trustees turned control back to the WC&P management – West Chester citizens *finally* had their own railroad that could compete with the WCRR.

Actually the "old railroad" had been steadily improving – again it upgraded its right of way, and in anticipation of completion of the WC&P it enlarged its West Chester depot and added a third daily train to Philadelphia, at least on a seasonal basis. In addition the State-owned P&C was taken over by John Edgar Thomson – now President of PRR – in 1857 (see *Triumph II*), and the previously lackluster WCRR suddenly became of interest to both PRR and the WC&P.

In the spring of 1858 the WCRR renegotiated more favorable terms with PRR for passage into Philadelphia. A year later the WC&P asked the WCRR (stay with us now) to enter into an agreement to set uniform freight rates – the WCRR, hoping to prevent a rate war with its rival, insisted on including passenger fares as well. The WC&P refused and relations broke off. Then on 1 April 1859 PRR reached agreement to take over operation of the WCRR for five years, and the line was operated as part of the PRR Philadelphia Division.

PRR made a number of improvements under the agreement, including new stations and some upgrading of the right of way. However, a few of the WCRR directors and several influential stockholders felt that PRR was letting their road wither on the vine, with intentions to purchase it for a bargain price when the

agreement expired, but in fact PRR refused an offer to purchase the line as too costly. Feelers were then quietly extended to the WC&P, and on 31 August that road purchased the entire capital stock of the WCRR at a premium $45 per share, right under PRR's corporate nose. PRR then "involuntarily" withdrew from WCRR operation at the expiration of the agreement on 1 April 1864, leaving the road as an operating subsidiary of the WC&P, which now held a monopoly on traffic to West Chester.

The WC&P rerouted through passenger service over its own line, leaving the track to Intersection for local trains or western connections on PRR. A connection between the two road's depots in West Chester was made – although use of the WCRR's facilities generally declined and the WCRR depot on Market Street in Philadelphia was sold, along with its West Chester enginehouse. This arrangement continued until 10 March 1873, when the WC&P entered into a formal 99-year lease of the WCRR, retroactive to 1 January.

However PRR had not lost interest in the WCRR – on the contrary. In December 1872 Thomson sent a letter to the WC&P indicating that he contemplated building a line from west of Frazer to West Chester, utilizing a portion of the WCRR route. The WC&P wasn't interested and instead tightened its grip on the WCRR under the long-term lease noted above.

But by the end of the decade the WC&P itself was in financial difficulty – isolated and having paid few dividends during its existence – so when PRR again made a move in its direction, the beleaguered directors reluctantly agreed. On 6 August 1879 they surrendered the lease of the WCRR, and stock control of the road was then taken over by PRR.

PRR immediately assumed active control of the WCRR, installing a new board, which duly named George Roberts (PRR First Vice President to Tom Scott – Thomson had died in 1874) as President. The planned extension to Frazer was built and the original route to Malvern abandoned. The right of way was upgraded and service to Philadelphia increased.

Now it was the WC&P's turn to wither – until a rapid-fire sequence of events took place that would permanently alter its future. On 1 August 1881, at the request of the stockholders of the P&BC, PW&B assumed operating control of that chronically financially troubled road, along with the WC&P. A month later the P&BC became the Central Division of the

PW&B, with headquarters at the WC&P's 31st and Chestnut Street terminal. On 31 October the WC&P was merged into the P&BC, which essentially ended the corporate existence of the former line.

As a result of this merger the mainline of the P&BC ran from West Philadelphia to Media and Wawa and continued on through rural southern Chester County to Octoraro Junction on the Susquehanna, and the line to West Chester became a branch – both routes to that town were again controlled by one company, only now it was PRR.

On 2 January 1882 the terminus for the Central Division passenger trains was shifted from 31st and Chestnut into PRR's new Broad Street Station. Trains operated via the Junction RR and through the 32nd Street Tunnel to a connection with PRR tracks into the new terminal (see *Triumph III*). The old station was remodeled and utilized for freight service (except for brief passenger use again when Broad Street Station was enlarged in 1893).

After the merger PW&B management carried out an intensive review of the branches. The former WC&P right of way was found to be in need of serious repair and improvements to bring it up to PRR standards. An extensive program was initiated, resulting in track improvements, new equipment and several new stations. The Media station was expanded to accommodate the offices of the Superintendent of the Division and opened for that purpose on 4 September 1882.

A program was begun to double track the line, beginning in 1882 from South Philadelphia to Angora (58th Street). Over the next several years double track (or long passing sidings) was laid, but the bridges remained a bottleneck. Finally with erection of new steel bridges over the major creeks by 1896 the entire line from Philadelphia to Elwyn was double-tracked.

There is one more small piece to this puzzle – on 30 June 1894 the P&BC took over operation of the 9.9-mile Philadelphia & Delaware County RR, extending from Fernwood to Newtown Square. This company had been chartered in 1872 as the Philadelphia & Chester County RR and had gone through successive reorganizations – and name changes – before being taken over and becoming part of the Central Division. This rural branch subsequently became the first in PRR territory to feel the impact of electric interurban encroachment on rail passenger operations (see photos), and in 1908 all passenger service was discontinued.

As noted previously, on 1 November 1902 the PW&B was merged with the B&P, forming the PB&W, which in turn took over operation of the P&BC. This arrangement lasted until 15 September 1916, when the P&BC was finally merged into the PB&W, and final consolidation into PRR took place on 1 January 1918.

As the years passed, traffic on the entire branch continued to decline with the growth of the automobile, trucks and busses. Freight traffic declined sharply after World War II and passenger service on the Octoraro Branch south of Wawa was discontinued in April 1948 – the line was finally abandoned in 1961. Several years earlier, on 28 June 1953, through service from Media to West Chester was ended and passengers had to change to a shuttle train to that destination. Through service returned for a time after the track was upgraded by SEPTA in 1983, but busses replaced all trains on that line south of Elwyn on 19 September 1986. The Newtown Square Branch, never a significant traffic route, was abandoned in 1963 from Grassland to its terminus, and the remainder in 1982.

In conclusion, it is useful to examine the similarities between PRR's actions here on the back road and the clear triumph achieved on the north-south main. Thomson's initial strategy in both cases was the same: secure a key line, even a short one (in this case the WCRR), upgrade it and by the power of PRR's vast economic resources force the competition (the WC&P) to eventually succumb.

The chronically weak Baltimore Central RR and its branches in and of itself was not a great prize – certainly not a triumph – but it did add what later became a valuable commuter operation on the northern end as the growing Delaware County towns became part of the expanding Philadelphia suburban complex, and on the southern end the agricultural area in Chester (Pennsylvania) and Cecil (Maryland) Counties, for a time shipping large amounts of produce to both Philadelphia and Baltimore markets.

Although we have not come across any evidence that either the B&O or the Reading ever made any moves to take over any of these lines (perhaps indicative of their low appeal), adding them did consolidate PW&B's – and later PRR's – hold on the entire complex of roads south of Philadelphia and kept the competition at bay in the overall clash of titans.

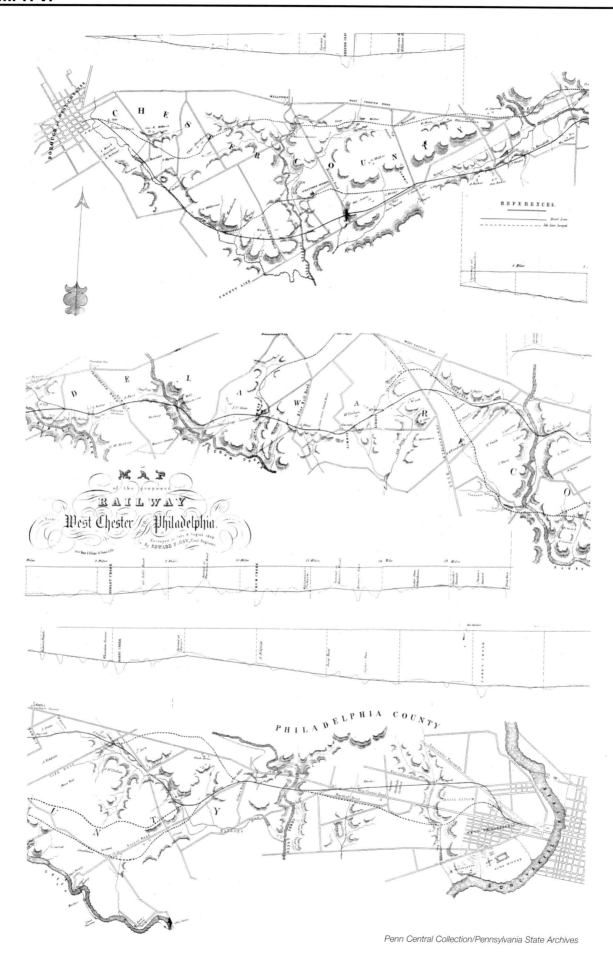

Penn Central Collection/Pennsylvania State Archives

(Caption for artwork on previous page)

SHORTLY AFTER the WC&P was chartered an Acting Committee hired civil engineer Edward H. Gay of Philadelphia to survey "the best and most direct route between West Chester and the Permanent [Market Street] Bridge over the Schuylkill." Mr. Gay followed his instructions closely, proposing a line in 1848 (solid line – the dashed lines are alternates considered) that cut across the undulating (to say the least) terrain of eastern Chester and northern Delaware Counties and five major streams to connect with the abandoned West Philadelphia RR right of way into West Philadelphia (the P&C would relocate to this latter approach to the City in 1850 – at the time of this map the WCRR trains ran over the original P&C alignment, using the Belmont Plane and crossing the Schuylkill farther upriver – see *Triumph II*).

In his 1848 report Mr. Gay strongly defended his proposed

route – particularly its grades (max. 0.95%) and cost (over $3/4 million, of which over $450,000 was for cuts, fills and bridges) – as essential to achieving a "direct route" into Philadelphia. It was not to be, however, and when the WC&P was formally organized two years later it selected T. E. Sickels as Chief Engineer, who laid out a line dipping farther to the south making use of the valley formed by the West Branch of Chester Creek (which it crossed several times as a result) for lower grades, running through more towns and approaching West Philadelphia from the southwest, along the Delaware County Turnpike. In so doing, it would thus provide convenient access to Philadelphia for the P&BC, the "Back Road" to Baltimore, as well as subsequently (in conjunction with the Junction RR) the PW&B to Broad Street Station. Note the Garret/Garrett names in the eastern part of the map. Since the B&O's Garrett did not appear on the scene until 1857, one notes this with wry amusement.

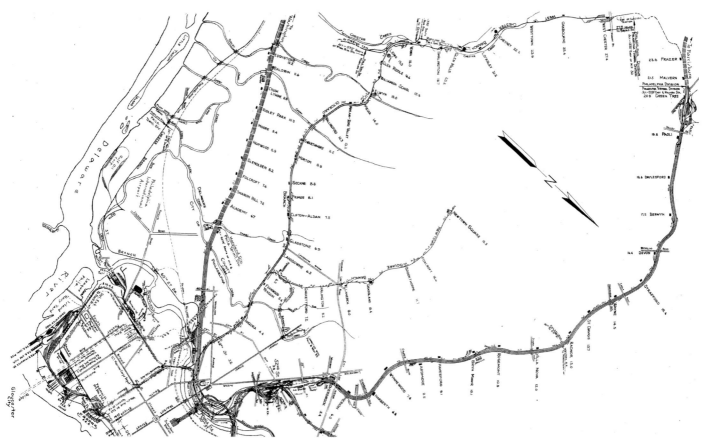

Andrew M. Wilson Collection

THIS PRR MAP from the mid-1950s clearly shows the relationship between those portions of the old Central Division that eventually became part of the Philadelphia Terminal Division – the Octoraro, Newtown Square and West Chester Branches, plus the tiny Cardington Branch and the north-south (former PW&B) and east-west (P&C) mainlines. The old PW&B alignment –

later the Reading Chester Branch – is shown as a light dashed line swinging toward the Delaware Riverfront, and the PRR 60th Street Branch extends south from Grays Ferry Yard and continues along the river as the Chester Branch. And, yes, the B&O main into Philadelphia is shown (partially) as a light double-dashed line where it crosses the yard south of Grays Ferry.

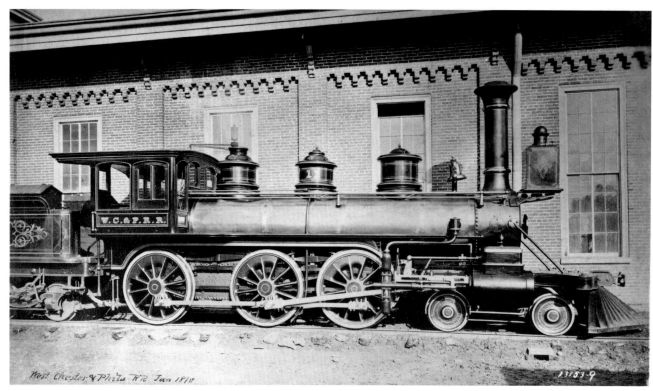

Ted Xaras Collection

THE WC&P located its Philadelphia terminal on several acres along the south side of Chestnut Street, between 31st and 32nd Streets. In 1854 it constructed an engine house, a 48-ft. cast iron turntable (replaced in 1867), a small passenger depot, freight house, car shop and milk shed. On 1 June 1867 a much larger (60 x 380 ft.) passenger depot was opened at the southeast corner of 31st and Chestnut, and expanded carshops were built, adjacent to the engine house and west of the depot. The passenger depot was rebuilt again in 1873-4 and a new engine house was constructed in 1887, replacing the original one. The WC&P also had a freight depot in the Bingham & Dock Commonwealth facility (see *Triumph III*) across the river at 18th & Market

Streets, reached by shared trackage over the P&C and the City-owned RR (and later PRR).

All of this changed when PRR opened its grand Broad Street Station in December 1881 and on 2 January of the following year WC&P trains began using the new terminal, along with the PW&B and P&BC. The passenger station at 31st and Chestnut was enlarged and converted for freight service, although it was used again briefly for passengers when Broad Street Station was expanded in 1893. In 1901 a new car shop was constructed in Media, and the old one demolished.

This superb photo shows the gold-striped WC&P ten-wheeler No. 11 gleaming in the sun alongside the car shop in 1870.

John J. Bowman, Jr./Fred W, Schneider, III Collection

IN THE 1880s and early 90s the Baltimore Central was double-tracked between Philadelphia and Media and new larger frame stations were built, usually on the inbound (toward Philadelphia) side with shelters serving the opposite direction. There were several early stations in the area west of 31st Street about which little is known but we do know that the station at 49th Street was opened in 1883 and enlarged in 1886. Here Train 726 (Media-Philadelphia) pauses at that location on 30 January 1960.

WC&P 1869 Guide Book/Ted Xaras Collection

ANGORA (MP. 4.4 – formerly Gray's Lane) was established in 1864 by the Callaghan Brothers as a mill town, with an extensive textile mill complex providing employment for the town's residents. A two-story brick station was built in 1867 to serve the inhabitants, at the time the first stop on the line. The brownstone mansion shown here in an 1869 rendering was built by the brothers for their mother.

In 1892 a new westbound shelter was built and the station grounds generally improved, along with several others on the line. However on 1 May 1905 loss of business to the streetcars on Baltimore Avenue forced the station's closing until 1911, when the freight station was remodeled for passenger use.

Ted Xaras Collection

IN A CLASSIC branchline scene, a southbound local freight makes its way past the shelter at Fernwood (MP. 5.4 – formerly Church Lane and later Fernwood-Yeadon) in 1949 and begins to turn westward onto the Newtown Square Branch. This location, the first stop in Delaware County, has had an interesting history. A stone station was opened on 4 May 1874, replacing an earlier frame structure which was moved to Abbotsford (53rd Street). New platforms were built in 1881-2 and in 1893 an addition was made to the freight house. In 1927 the stone passenger station was demolished to make room for the Chester Avenue bridge shown here.

Dave Cope/Ted Xaras Collection

IN ANOTHER delightful branchline scene, a local freight moves onto the Newtown Square Branch just west of the junction with the Octoraro (WC&P) Branch. The view looks eastward ca. 1940. The rural single-track line, initially chartered in 1872 as the Philadelphia & Delaware County RR, was taken over by PW&B in 1894 and made part of the Central Division. Its passenger service succumbed early to competition from the Philadelphia & West Chester Traction Company – it declined rapidly until being discontinued altogether in 1908, sadly never becoming part of Philadelphia's suburban rail network. Freight operations reached their peak after World War I when the area served by the branch underwent extensive industrial development, but the Depression and increasing inroads from trucking took their toll. Operations west of Grassland were abandoned in 1963 and the trackage and trestles removed in the late 60s and early 70s. Service on the remainder of the branch ended in 1981 and it was torn up in 1985.

THIS DRAWING from the *Philadelphia Times* of 18 July 1895 represents the "Battle of Llanerch Crossing," another interesting example of a crossing conflict (see the "Battle of the Frogs" in *Triumph V*) but this time with an interurban line. The rural setting was peaceful enough – the intersection of West Chester Pike and Lansdowne Avenue – but it was to witness a physical encounter and legal battles lasting for years.

The Philadelphia, Castle Rock and West Chester Railway Company was formed on 14 December to take over the old horsecar franchise of the Delaware County Passenger Railroad Company and build a trolley line along the turnpike from 63rd Street to Newtown Square and beyond. Short sections of track were laid at the Llanerch crossing in a deliberate attempt to block the Philadelphia & Delaware County RR

The Red Arrow Line/ Ted Xaras Collection

which was building a rail line to connect Newtown Square with the WC&P. This line would cross the turnpike and the trolley line at a sharp angle through a cut, making visibility at the intersection difficult.

When the P&DC crews reached the crossing in January 1894 they found the section of trolley line blocking their path. The trolley company, led by one John Shimer, had conveniently obtained a court injunction preventing the P&DC from removing their trackage and forcing the railroad to build a grade separation at the crossing. With the backing of PRR the P&DC went to court and got permission to rip up the offending trolley tracks – and the battle was on.

To complicate matters further, the City of Philadelphia and another trolley line, the Philadelphia & West Chester Traction Company, got into the act. The complex legal battle dragged on for years, but Shimer ultimately lost and PRR took over the P&DC, making it the Newtown Square Branch of the PW&B. Both the rail line and the P&WC trolley line were completed and the crossing remained – at grade – but despite their apparently peaceful coexistence, the trolley line clearly had an adverse impact on passenger service on the Newtown Square Branch, which was abandoned in 1908 because of meager traffic. The trolley line eventually became part of Philadelphia's famed Red Arrow Lines and subsequently was incorporated into SEPTA.

Ted Xaras Collection

ALL IS PEACEFUL at Llanerch crossing as a Newtown Square Branch local heads westward. The passenger station built in 1895 is at left in this ca. 1900 view looking east on West Chester Pike. At right are the P&WC trolley carbarns with the office building beyond.

Ted Xaras Collection

LOOKING WESTWARD 30 years later we see the passenger (MP. 9.0) and freight stations at right, with West Chester Pike and the trolley line at left. The passenger station was demolished a few years later.

EVOCATIVE of the rural nature of the single-track Newtown Square Branch in its early years we have diminutive Class F1 locomotive 182 steaming along with a lone combine in the 1890s somewhere west of Llanerch.

Ted Xaras Collection

RETURNING to the Octoraro Branch (WC&P) we come to Landsdowne (MP. 6.3 – originally Darby Road). The first frame passenger station was constructed in 1867-8, destroyed by fire in 1884 and rebuilt the following year. A passenger shelter was added in 1890. A brick passenger station designed by famed Philadelphia architect Frank Furness was built in 1901 and enlarged in 1905 – it is shown here after its restoration 90 years later. A new freighthouse was constructed in 1885, replacing one destroyed by fire the previous year, and this one was expanded in 1893 and again in 1905.

Ted Xaras Collection

THE WC&P had to span four major creek valleys along the route (Cobbs, Darby, Crum and Ridley) with seven smaller bridges over Chester Creek between Lenni and Westtown. All of these streams empty into the Delaware south of Philadelphia. The road constructed wooden truss structures initially, on high trestles where required. These bridges were rebuilt and strengthened several times over the years whenever necessary.

The original wooden truss constructed in 1852-4 over Darby Creek was replaced with a 274-ft. long, seven-span double-track steel and iron viaduct in 1892, which was further strengthened in 1900. Here H-class Consolidation 1377 leads a string of heavy-weight coaches across the bridge for a fan trip in March 1939.

COMMUTER RAIL SERVICE on the former PRR/Penn Central lines in the Philadelphia area is provided predominantly by the General Electric Silverliner IVs, new when this great shot was made on 17 July 1976. Here a trio of the cars approaches Clifton (MP. 7.5 – later Clifton-Aldan) while one of SEPTA's Red Arrow Division classic Brilliners glides below. The train passengers will get to Philadelphia long before the trolley riders complete their transfer to the Market-Frankford elevated at 69th Street Station.

L. R. Brittingham, Jr./ Ted Xaras Collection

CLIFTON served another textile mill town in the 19th Century as well as being the destination of President Tom Scott when visiting his county residence nearby. The two-story stone structure shown here was constructed in 1869 on the inbound side. In 1889 a frame freight station was built and the following year the outbound shelter was added – both are shown here on 17 February 1948. Note the end-door boxcar on the siding.

BY JULY 1979 only a few cars of the former PRR MP54 fleet of over 400 units remained in service, and they were limited to rush-hour service to Paoli and Media. Train No. 1749 (Philadelphia -Elwyn local) heads northward with 10 cars, most likely of the ca. 1950 modernized class MP54E6 units that had four traction motors per car (rather than two). Lead unit No. 448 features the then-new SEPTA graphics.

William J. Coxey

MORTON (MP. 9.9) was originally called Newton's, but was renamed in the 1860s in honor of the enterprising Judge Sketchley Morton, who had an elegant mansion nearby. The station was also used by President John Edgar Thomson who maintained a summer home in the area. A freight house was built in 1879 and a new passenger station was completed in February 1880 on a lot purchased from Thomson's estate. A frame shelter was added in 1892 and the station grounds landscaped. Here an eastbound SEPTA R-1 (Media-West Trenton) train pauses at the station in 1987.

Fred W. Schneider, III

A CLEAN MU CONSIST is nicely framed by a pair of signals as it heads southward under the wires between Morton and Swarthmore on 2 February 1957. Note the track signal connections.

John J. Bowman, Jr./Fred W. Schneider, III Collection

THIS GINGERBREAD-BEDECKED stone station was constructed in 1858 to serve the community then known as West Dale, named for the noted 18th Century painter Benjamin West. However, in the 1870s the community was renamed Swarthmore (MP. 11.2) after the college established nearby by the Hicksite branch of the Society of Friends (Quakers). In the background at left one can see Parrish Hall of the college under construction. When completed this magnificent edifice, which bore a striking resemblance to the Tuileries Palace (residence of the French Emperor), would dominate the campus.

The assembled multitude at the station (including those picking daisies) ca. 1867 is probably a reunion of the Friends' Social Lyceum that met several times on the new campus grounds.

Ted Xaras Collection

IN 1877 a new two-story brick passenger station was constructed, along with a frame freighthouse. In 1891 the freight station was replaced and the following year the entire station grounds were landscaped and improved. In 1906 the platforms and shelters were extended and a pedestrian subway was constructed to allow passengers to safely cross to the other side. The grade crossing in the foreground was replaced in 1930-1 by a highway underpass, necessitating new shelters and platforms on both sides of the track.

This 1928 view shows the station with a large, fashionably-dressed crowd assembled to celebrate electrification of the line, which was com-

Ted Xaras Collection

pleted all the way to West Chester on 2 December as part of the Philadelphia suburban program. This included the entire main trackage to West Chester, MU storage tracks at Media, Wawa and West Chester and sidings at Glen Riddle, Wawa, Glen Mills, Cheyney and Westtown.

THE CAMPUS of Swarthmore College is attractively landscaped and is the home of the Scott Arboretum and an extensive collection of trees, shrubs and unusual plants. Silverliner 255 making up Penn Central Train 731 passes the station on 9 August 1971 in an attractive setting reflecting that tradition. Between September 1982 and October 1983 this station was the terminus for commuter service when SEPTA rebuilt the Crum Creek bridge (about one-half mile south of the station) and generally upgraded the line all the way to West Chester.

Fred W. Schneider, III

WC&P 1869 Guide Book/Ted Xaras Collection

THE BRIDGE over Crum Creek, the longest on the branch, was completed by early September 1854, allowing the line to open between Philadelphia and Media later that Fall. That 90-ft. high structure is shown here in a dramatic 1869 rendering of the "lofty viaduct." It had been rebuilt in 1866 and further strengthened in 1873.

The following prose from the 1869 WC&P *Guide Book* is of interest: "In reference to the bridges which occur pretty frequently along this intricately-graded road, it is proper to say that these structures are, in point of fact, almost if not quite the safest places on the line. The trains are carried over them at a speed of not over four miles per hour, and it would be impossible for a train to be thrown off the track. The bridges have all been renewed recently, long before they had begun to show any signs of decay. A watchman is in attendance upon each, and makes a daily inspection of the bolts and fastenings, which cannot become insecure without the knowledge of the Company."

The old bridge was replaced in 1896-7 with a 17-span, double-tracked deck plate girder steel viaduct stretching 915 ft. across the valley.

Fred W. Schneider, III

MOYLAN-ROSE VALLEY (MP. 13.2) was originally known as Manchester until the late 1880s, when it became Moylan. The two-story brick station shown here was constructed in 1881 and featured a wooden platform with stairs that ran along the track side of the structure above the track-level platform. An inbound Penn Central Silverliner pauses at the station, still with its wooden platform, on 17 July 1976.

L. R. Brittingham, Jr./Ted Xaras Collection

IN EARLY 1855 the P&BC opened an attractive two-story brick passenger station at Media (MP. 14.0), the seat of justice in Delaware County and an important station on the line. In 1868 both the passenger station and the freight house (constructed in 1854) were expanded. The passenger station was enlarged again in 1881-2 to allow the Central Division Superintendent to relocate his offices from 31st and Chestnut Streets to Media, which opened on 4 September 1882. The double track was extended from Swarthmore to Media in 1887 and new platforms were built at the station. This view looks northward toward the Orange Street bridge on 1 March 1950, showing the impressive Victorian structure after its final expansion.

SADLY, in 1951 the structure was demolished and replaced by this utilitarian single-story brick station. WAWA interlocking was relocated to Media station and put into service on 28 June 1953 when the double-track line was cut back from Elwyn to just north of the Media station. WAWA Tower was closed on July 31, and the block stations at Glen Mills and Cheyney were closed in October. ELWYN and LENNI interlockings (controlled from WAWA) were eliminated, while WEST CHESTER block station lasted until September 1958.

In this project Track No. 1 was torn up and Track No. 2 south of the crossover became the single main track. The station trackage was rearranged to eliminate the old southward platform, the island platform shown here at left was built and the end of Track No. 2 became the stub-ended West Chester Shuttle Track. The end of old Track No. 1 became Yard Track No. 3, and two yard tracks were added (Nos. 4 and 5).

This view (from the rear of a Philadelphia-West Chester local) looks northward in June 1982, almost 100 years after the Central Division Superintendent relocated to Media. After the 1953 track reconfiguration the main track is the former southward main while the former northward main became the lead to the MU storage yard.

William J. Coxey

LOOKING SOUTHWARD on 7 March 1985 we have a look at Elwyn Local 9371 departing with former Reading Blueliner equipment while the West Chester shuttle waits on the stub track that once had been southward Track No. 2. One might think that the Reading cars would not have made an appearance on PRR rails until SEPTA began operations through the Center City Tunnel connecting the two lines in late 1984 (see *Triumph III*), but in reality they began operating in former PRR territory in the late 1970s when the MP54 fleet was rapidly shrinking.

THE FIRST RAILROAD BRIDGE over Ridley Creek was a single-track wooden trestle constructed by the WC&P between 1854 and 1858. The superstructure was replaced with a Howe deck truss structure on masonry piers that was described in 1869 as "long, high and perfectly substantial, its great length corre-spond[ing] to the extent of the charming valley it . . . spans." This photo shows a six-car train posing on the impressive structure in the 1870s. That "perfectly substantial" structure, however, had to be rebuilt in 1877 with iron trusses.

WC&P 1869 Guide Book/*Ted Xaras Collection*

THE VIEW FROM THE BRIDGE was described thusly: "To the left [headed southward] the hillsides, shaggy with woods, descend abruptly to the stream . . . . On the right [shown here] the opening is wider, and the eye commands a glorious prospect of rolling hills . . . fringed with glittering woods, bathed in sun and dew, and receding in height after height to a distance of several miles."

THE IRON BRIDGE was replaced with this double-tracked, 13-span steel deck plate girder structure in 1896-7. The 641-ft. long viaduct rises 103 ft. above the creek, the highest on the line. This was a major project involving new pier foundations, reworking the abutments and rebuilding the entire superstructure – the expenditures on this bridge and the one at Wallingford caused the P&BC to run a deficit of $69 thousand.

The northward track was removed in 1953 when the line was single-tracked south of a point just north of Media station. Here Saturday-only Philadelphia-Elwyn Local 1715 heads southward out of Media in November 1977.

William J. Coxey

William J. Coxey

ELWYN (MP. 15.0 – formerly Greenwood) was described in the WC&P 1869 *Guide Book* as an area of lovely landscape and picturesque woodlands. Little is known about the early passenger station other than it was a small, two-story house – a new freight house was constructed in 1896.

This 1977 photo shows Saturday-only West Chester to Philadelphia Local 0726 stopping at the new platform and shelters constructed by SEPTA. At this time the branch south of Media was operated in accord with manual block signal rules – trains required permission from the Media operator before running to West Chester.

THE STOP known as Williamson School (MP. 15.8 – originally Williamson) was established in 1890 to serve the nearby Williamson Free School of Mechanical Trades. At that time there was a small passenger shelter and frame freight house. On 1 December 1909 the attractive brick and frame structure shown here was opened opposite the freight house and also served as the local post office until 1953. The structure was also being used as a dwelling at the time of this photo in 1982.

William J. Coxey

THIS brick station was constructed in 1867 to serve Glen Riddle (originally Rockdale – MP. 16.6). A frame freight house was built east (north) of the station in 1890. This view looks southward ca. 1900. The passenger station was subsequently destroyed by fire.

Not far from the station was Glen Riddle Mills, originally established as a grist mill on Chester Creek in 1790. It was converted for spinning cotton yarn in 1822 and expanded several times over the years, the beginning of an extensive complex of textile mills on the creek.

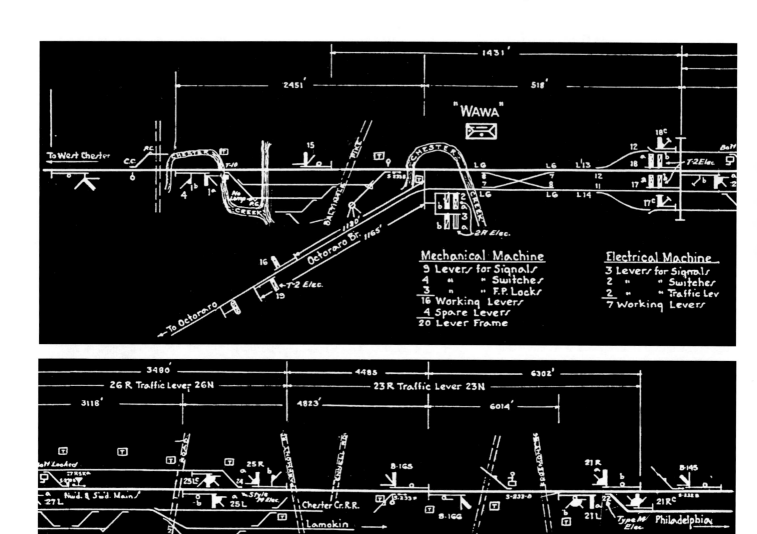

THIS INTERLOCKING DIAGRAM will serve to introduce the interesting area between Lenni and Wawa, including the junctions with the Chester Creek and Octoraro Branches. Prior to the 1952 "rationalization" the branch was single track south of Elwyn. A second track, 7/10 of a mile long and named the "Naught Track," ran from Lenni to Wawa. It connected at the north end to the Chester Creek Branch and at the south end to the Octoraro Branch (former Baltimore Central) at WAWA Tower. The former Chester Creek Branch right of way was paved over about 1990 to reach SEPTA's MU training center facility. At the time of this 1938 diagram (prior to its relocation to Media) WAWA contained a 20-lever mechanical machine and a seven-lever electrical unit.

LENNI (MP. 17.3) was the location of the junction with the Chester Creek Branch (RR) from Lamokin (Chester) on the PW&B main. The original ticket office was in a hotel and a freight house was constructed to the east (northward) in 1868. In 1880 a two-story brick station was constructed to serve both the WC&P and Chester Creek lines. In 1894 the hotel was converted to a freight station and the following year an enlarged coal wharf was constructed, also serving both branches. This undated postcard shows the two-story station.

WAWA was historically part of a tract of land granted by William Penn to the Pennell family, hence the original name of Pennelton. It was the junction with the P&BC and was referred to in the 19th Century as Baltimore Central Junction, West Chester Junction or simply Junction, depending on which railroad's point of view was taken.

This engraving shows us Baltimore Junction in 1869 looking northward from the station across Chester Creek. The train is located where the future yard will be laid out. The gauntlet track laid across the WC&P's single-track bridge connects the P&BC with the then-new Chester Creek RR at Lenni.

WC&P 1869 Guide Book/Ted Xaras Collection

THIS VIEW shows us the Junction over 75 years later on 24 March 1945. H9 3529 simmers quietly on the WC&P track – the Octoraro Branch curves to the right. Behind the locomotive is WAWA Tower, constructed ca. 1907 and used for many years as a training facility. Beyond is a frost-proof water tank, rebuilt in 1895. Alongside is a scissors crossover, later changed to a single.

J. R. Quinn/Ted Xaras Collection

H. L. Bongaardt

NEARLY 20 years have passed and the motive power for the local freights is now diesel, in this case Class BS10m 9434 built by nearby Baldwin shown here on 22 March 1963 as it shifts hoppers at Wawa.

WAWA STATION (MP. 18.0) and agent's quarters was constructed in 1867, replacing an earlier one from the 1850s. It soon became a busy junction – here passengers and their baggage transferred between the Baltimore Central and the West Chester lines. The 1876 edition of the WC&P *Guide Book* describes it thusly: "At this station, nineteen miles from Philadelphia, the road intersects with the Baltimore Central . . . . Passengers coming east [northward] on the West Chester road change cars here for Chester [via the Chester Creek RR] or for any place west [southward] on the Baltimore Central railroad. As many as three – and sometimes four – trains can be seen approaching this point at one time during the day, all coming together as regularly as clockwork, and intersecting so closely that passengers are immediately transferred from one train to the other, according to where they are bound."

The station was remodeled and enlarged in 1896, along with landscaping and paving to the appearance shown here in a ca. 1905 post card view. Other facilities at the junction included a coaling station, roundhouse and turntable, built 1885-6 for P&BC trains. The coal wharf was rebuilt and enlarged in 1895, the roundhouse was expanded in 1901 and a larger turntable was installed in 1904.

ON 26 JULY 1910 the old station was destroyed by fire and replaced the following year with this single-story brick structure, including a trapezoidal-shaped passenger shelter and a pedestrian tunnel serving both branches. In a classic 1947 view (20 years after the West Chester Branch was electrified) the morning commuter train from West Chester to Philadelphia stops to pick up passengers from the Oxford-Wawa "doodlebug" gas car. The baggage carts were often used to transfer mail and express between the two lines.

David H. Cope/Fred W. Schneider, III Collection

BY 1971 weeds were invading the platform as Penn Central Train 0744 (West Chester-Philadelphia) departs Wawa with a single Budd-built Silverliner. The track in the right foreground is the Octoraro Branch. In 1945 this branch began at ARSENAL Tower in West Philadelphia and extended all the way to the junction with the C&PD at Rock MD. The line from Wawa to West Chester was named the Wawa Branch. In 1949 the line from West Philadelphia to West Chester was renamed the West Chester Branch and became part of the Philadelphia Terminal Division. The portion south of Wawa became the Octoraro Branch, part of the Maryland Division.

Fred W. Schneider, III

AT THIS POINT we will continue to West Chester and then return to the Octoraro Branch. The station at Darlington (also known as Darling – MP. 18.7) was a non-descript structure built ca. 1881 and taken out of service in 1965. Here Train 0733 (Media-West Chester) heads west on 22 June 1957. At one time this was the heart of the butter district serving Philadelphia, and the name Darlington was "associated with all that is perfect and choice in the quality of the product."

John J. Bowman/Fred W. Schneider, III Collection

GLEN MILLS (MP. 20.2), location of more early textile mills, has another brick station designed by Frank Furness and built ca. 1881. It is considered by many to be the most attractive station on the West Chester Branch and has recently been restored, complete with PRR keystone station sign. The structure is shown here on 9 August 1971 with Penn Central Train 0739 (Media-West Chester) headed toward its destination.

Fred W. Schneider, III

Herbert H. Harwood, Jr.

HERE IS A FULL VIEW of this interesting station, date uncertain but probably in the same time-frame as the previous photo.

William J. Coxey

THE GLEN MILLS QUARRY, owned by General Crushed Stone since 1945, is still to this day supplying ballast for the Northeast Corridor main. In this June 1982 view looking northward the hoppers in the center are orange Amtrak work cars.

During PRR's last decade freight service on the West Chester Branch was provided by South Philadelphia-based Philadelphia Terminal Division local PT41/42, which turned here, along with a second train PT43/44. The Octoraro Branch was handled by Chester-based (Thurlow Yard) Maryland Division job MD47/48, while a Thorndale-based Philadelphia Division local served West Chester via the Frazer Branch (old WCRR).

Fred W. Schneider, III

A FLAG STOP was initiated at Locksley (MP. 21.5) as early as 1890, when a small passenger shelter was constructed, but it appears never to have had an agent. Penn Central Train 0723 (Philadelphia-West Chester) local heads southward past the shelter on 9 August 1971.

CHEYNEY (MP. 22.2) was named after an enterprising local merchant who built a frame passenger station here in 1867, along with a small freight house. In 1909 PRR purchased property from the Cheyney family for a replacement station, constructed the following year.

The passengers reading the notice posted at that structure in June 1982 are understandably concerned at the announcement that commuter rail service south of Elwyn will be discontinued effective July 1. Service was restored in October 1983 after the track had been rehabilitated. In 1986, to reduce an enormous $24.4 million deficit, SEPTA substituted bus connections for points south of Elwyn. The remains of the short (but electrified) siding are visible at left.

William J. Coxey

WESTTOWN (known as Street Road until 1884 – MP. 23.9) was the first stop on the Branch in Chester County. The first station was built in 1858 to serve the Westtown Boarding School, a facility established in 1799 by the Society of Friends. The two-story frame structure shown here in a 1971 view was constructed in 1881 and also served for many years as the local post office.

As Train 0745 (Media-West Chester) stopped on 9 August 1971 an attractive young woman stepped off and walked along the platform. Our enterprising photographer quickly descended to the parking lot to capture her smiling visage close up – until a car door opened and it immediately became apparent that her mother was picking her up. Nice try, Fred!

Fred W. Schneider, III

FORLORN PASSAGE – A pair of veteran MP54s comprising Train 0753 heads through the weeds towards West Chester on 9 August 1971. The location is south of Oakbourne (MP. 25.4, originally Hemphill, for most of its existence a flag stop). Hard to believe given the limited patronage, but train service would continue to West Chester for another 15 years.

Fred W. Schneider, III

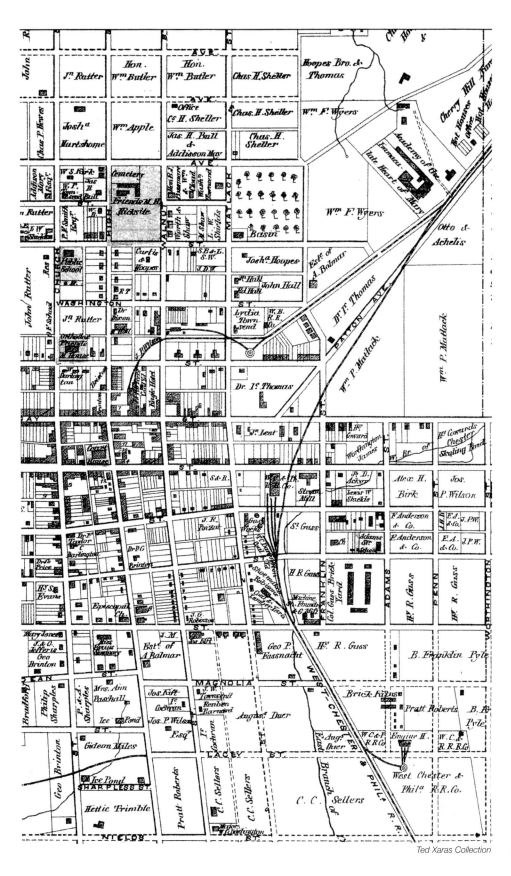

Ted Xaras Collection

AND NOW we reach historic West Chester, Chester County seat and "the gem of Eastern Pennsylvania." This 1873 map from Witmer's Atlas shows the two railroads serving the borough. The first, the pioneering West Chester RR, enters from the north to the depot and round-house at the corner of Chestnut and Matlack Streets. Sidings then ran several more blocks westward to serve a coal yard and other businesses.

The West Chester & Philadelphia entered from the southeast, utilizing the WCRR's depot for a time. In 1858 it constructed a three-stall engine house and turntable on Lacey Street and a freight station was built in 1867. The engine house was enlarged in 1903.

OPENING DAY of the line to West Chester (MP. 27.4) on 11 November 1858 brought everyone out to celebrate the long-delayed event, the men in their long coats and stovepipe hats and the women in their finery as well. The locomotive is believed to be the *Rockdale*, built by R. Norris & Son in 1854 and one of four engines (and six large passenger coaches like this one) owned by the road at this time.

Although the WC&P initially planned to build its own depot, the ever-present financial constraints and construction delays forced it to use the WCRR's facility on a joint basis for several years, which must have been a bit embarrassing for the backers who wanted a new and independent rail line to Philadelphia.

IN 1880 the WC&P finally had the resources to build its own station and imposing brick structure with a long shed terminating on Market Street. A frame freight station and larger roundhouse were constructed at this time as well. The passenger station was extensively damaged by fire in January 1885, but the repairs were completed by the end of the year. The freighthouse was enlarged in 1892.

THE STATION was gradually reduced bit by bit over the years. This view from the back on 22 June 1957 illustrates the facility with its train shed demolished and the boarding area reduced to two tracks and one platform shelter. It would be reduced still further to a small ticket office. What was left was razed in 1985 after being damaged by another fire, a year before the little-used train service was finally discontinued.

John J. Bowman, Jr./Fred W. Schneider, III Collection

MOVING down the Octoraro Branch, we have a typical rural scene on 27 March 1963 as another local freight rumbles across the road near Markham (MP. 3.3 from Wawa) behind Baldwin 5969. Note the classic cast iron oval crossing signs.

H. L. Bongaardt

Dave Cope/Ted Xaras Collection

HEADED NORTH we find a northbound mixed consist led by G5 5725 making a statement of its own as it moves out of Chadd's Ford Junction (MP. 8.9) and across the plate girder Brandywine Creek viaduct in 1940. At the junction the line crossed the Reading's Wilmington & Northern Branch running down the Brandywine to Wilmington.

IN A DRAMATIC PHOTO, Train 4605 (Sunday only Wawa-Perryville) pauses at the water tower north of Kennett Square on 10 March 1940. The classy G5s – the 5716 this time – gets some lubrication and TLC from the crew. These engines, never built in large numbers, were relegated to branchline service by the E and H classes for mainline passenger and freight duty, respec-tively, but performed these duties well. Note the R50b express reefers in the consist, in this and the previous photo. Express traf-fic on the branch consisted primarily of mushrooms (Kennett Square is often described as the mushroom capital of the world) as well as flowers and milk from several creameries.

THIS 1984 VIEW shows the former PRR freighthouse in Kennett Square (MP. 15.4) being used for equipment storage for the short line Octoraro Railway. The brick passenger station was demolished in 1949.

William J. Coxey

ELKVIEW VIADUCT was erected in 1898, replacing a wooden trestle over Big Elk Creek. The steel plate girder bridge extended 853 ft. across the valley and rose 62 ft. above the creek. A short local freight, with the cabin car sandwiched in the middle, pauses on the long bridge on 27 March 1963.

H. L. Bongaardt

ALTHOUGH passenger service was discontinued on the Octoraro Branch on 30 April 1948, the gas car emerging from the fog (here running as a West Jersey Chapter NRHS special on 10 October 1984) was typical of those assigned to the line after the West Chester Branch was electrified in 1928. The PRR Class OEG350 was originally built by Pullman in 1929 with a pair of Winton gasoline engines, which were replaced with two Cummins diesels in 1942. The restored car was placed in service on the Wilmington & Western tourist line in the spring of 1980, after 13 years and 11,000 hours of dedicated labor.

William J. Coxey

OXFORD (MP. 31.0) was at one time the primary passenger and freight center of the Octoraro Branch, where a three-stall engine house and turntable were constructed in 1893. Here our local freight reaches the brick station, built in 1903. At right in this 1963 photo is the Oxford Grain Company elevator.

H. L. Bongaardt

THIS 1984 view of the station looks southward, with the rail fans enjoying lunch on the platform. By this time it was being used by the borough for municipal services including the police department. The siding in the foreground once served the grain facility.

William J. Coxey

THE FREIGHTHOUSE just to the south of the passenger station was built in 1905, replacing an earlier one constructed in 1891. The large building at the left was once the Oxford Furniture Company, last used by a feed distributor. It is little wonder that the Octoraro Railway shut down – there was very little rail business left on the branch.

William J. Coxey

FINAL DESTINATION – Train 4605 – minus the three R50bs – reaches Perryville after its trip down the branch on 10 March 1940, concluding our journey down the line as well. Note the entrance to the pedestrian tunnel leading to the passenger shelter on the northward side.

Chapter 4

Up The Valley

The Columbia & Port Deposit RR

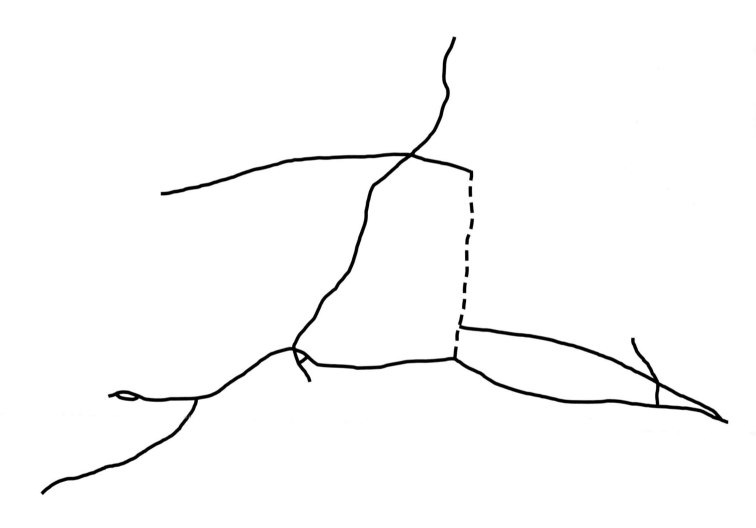

(Caption for artwork on next page)

THIS MAP of the southern end of the Columbia & Port Deposit Branch gives us an opportunity to see its relationship to other lines near the mouth of the Susquehanna River. As we have seen previously, it connects with the PW&B (PRR) main at Perryville (prior to the 1905-6 realignment). At Octoraro Junction it con-nects with the P&BC Branch of the PW&B, which used the C&PD to complete service to Perryville and points southward. This 1900 USGS map predates the Conowingo dam on the lower Susquehanna, but still shows the abandoned Susquehanna & Tidewater Canal on the west bank of the river.

We also need to examine two lines running from the Baltimore area up the Susquehanna Valley, connecting with the Low-Grade east-west passenger main to Harrisburg and westward.

The first of these is the Columbia & Port Deposit Railroad, which was originally formed as the Washington & Maryland Line RR, incorporated in Pennsylvania on 30 April 1857 by local investors in Columbia to run down the Susquehanna Valley. Its purpose was to connect the terminus of the Pennsylvania Canal and the Philadelphia & Columbia RR at Columbia with the canal and shipping operations at Port Deposit and continue on to Baltimore and (via the C&D Canal) to Philadelphia. In 1860 the name was changed to the Columbia & Maryland Line RR and four years later to the Columbia & Port Deposit RR (a second company, also known as the C&PD RR, had been formed in Maryland in 1858 and on 27 September 1864 the two were merged).

After nearly 10 years of legal maneuvering, name-changing and fundraising, construction of the road finally began in September 1866 – it was completed between Perryville and Octoraro Junction in 1868. During its construction PRR management perceived that the line formed a potentially useful alternate route from Baltimore up the Susquehanna Valley, with lower grades than the Northern Central (see Chapter 5). Thus when operations did not generate enough revenue to pay the interest on two bond issues (1868 and 1875), the property in Pennsylvania was sold to the highest bidder – PRR. On 13 June 1877 PRR agreed to operate the entire line on completion of construction in July of that year, and in 1890 it purchased the Maryland portion as well, operating both as part of the Philadelphia Division.

On 1 May 1882 the short Port Deposit Branch of the PW&B, running between Perryville and Port Deposit, was transferred by lease to the C&PD, and on 12 May 1893 the entire C&PD line was assigned to the PW&B, becoming part of the Maryland Division. On 15 September 1916 it was incorporated into the PB&W.

As built the 43.5-mile line followed an easy grade on a light right of way, hugging the north bank of the Susquehanna River and extending from Perryville to Columbia where it connected with the Columbia Branch of PRR.

There were little or no improvements to the line until 1905, when dramatic events happened at both ends. In that year, during the heavy construction of the Low-Grade Line (Atglen & Susquehanna Branch – see *Triumph II*) that ran parallel to and on the bluffs above the C&PD from Shenks Ferry to Creswell, such difficulty was encountered in operating the branch because of constant rockslides that all operations were suspended between Benton and Washington Boro. The tracks on the C&PD were removed and the right of way turned over to the contractor until the blasting, excavation and grading on the Low-Grade Line was completed. During that time material from side-hill blasting operations on the A&S was shot down and allowed to fill up the old roadbed of the C&PD – thousands of tons of rock and gravel were blown clear into the river.

When the A&S was finally completed it was decided to raise the grade of a portion of the C&PD to elevate it above the frequent ravages of high water and ice (the Safe Harbor bridge over Conestoga Creek was destroyed in March 1905 because of ice jams and the resultant flooding). Thus an entirely new roadbed was constructed from Creswell to Shenks Ferry. In addition an undergrade connection was built at Creswell to avoid crossing the A&S Branch at grade.

In 1906 the right of way from Shenks Ferry to Benton was elevated, moved back from the river and widened in conjunction with the construction of the 60-ft. high McCall's Ferry Dam at Holtwood, about 19 miles south of Columbia (see maps) – the first of three major hydroelectric projects on the lower Susquehanna that would gradually result in the transformation of the line from a winding branch carrying light traffic to a heavily-trafficked freight line. During this construction it was again necessary to suspend operations over a portion of the line.

At this time the southern end of the road was also altered in conjunction with the reconstruction of the Susquehanna River Bridge at Perryville and the new alignment from Principio to Oakington. When the grade of the PB&W main was elevated the C&PD had to be raised to meet it. The old right of way was converted to a freight yard and was then operated as the Perryville Branch of the C&PD. A new connection was built and named the Perryville Branch of the PB&W (got that?).

The C&PD is usually thought of as a freight line running from Enola Yard (constructed as part of the

Low-Grade Line project) to the Baltimore area and points south, but in 1916 there were two daily passenger trains each way between Perryville and Conowingo and four each way between Perryville and Octoraro (continuing onto the Octoraro Branch, as shown in the previous chapter). At one time PRR even considered transferring through passenger service between Baltimore and Harrisburg from the Northern Central and onto the Port Road (see Chapter 5).

There are few bridges on the C&PD and there are no large ones except the 295-ft. deck plate girder structure constructed over Conestoga Creek at Safe Harbor in 1906, replacing the previous bridge destroyed by ice jams. There are a number of short girder spans bridging the numerous small streams that cross the right of way, along with a considerable number of culverts. Most of these from Benton to Columbia were built (or rebuilt) between 1905 and 1908 during the rebuilding and elevation of the line. For months after the new line was put into service considerable difficulty was encountered from frequent washouts, and numerous additional pipes and culverts had to be installed. PRR was eternally busy keeping up with the forces of Mother Nature, especially in the Susquehanna Valley!

The right of way was initially ballasted with local stone (mostly mica schist), which was found to be unsatisfactory. When the road was rebuilt, large quantities of cinders (from the engine terminals at Harrisburg and Columbia) and granulated slag (from the steel mills at Marietta on the Columbia Branch – see *Triumph II*) were hauled in and used for both fill and ballast.

Although another power dam on the river was proposed as early as 1906, it was not until 1923 that planning work began for the second major upheaval that would result in the final transformation of the C&PD to a heavy freight line. The McCall's Ferry Power Company had originally planned to construct this one 15 miles south of the first – it was to be 4630 ft. long and 90 ft. high, with a roadway on top. Slack water would extend nearly to the tail race of the earlier dam, again requiring elevation of the trackage through the area. With through freight traffic between Baltimore and Harrisburg increasingly shifted from the Northern Central Branch (see Chapter 5) PRR decided not only to carry out the required elevation of the right of way and realignment of the connection with the Octoraro Branch, but also to grade the excavation for double track. The initial estimate for this project, extending approximately 16 miles from Rock Run to Fishing Creek, was about $4.5 million – a figure that ultimately proved too low.

The undertaking was delayed for a time while the original power company went into bankruptcy and the Philadelphia Electric Company took over the project. Actual construction on the Conowingo Dam began in March 1926. It was another massive undertaking, involving a continuous succession of cuts and fills, three tunnels and three new multiple-span concrete arch bridges. Approximately 1.5 million cu. yds. of earth and rock (about two-thirds through solid granite) had to be blasted and excavated. To avoid rock cuts 130-145 ft. deep, three tunnels totaling 875 ft. in length were driven through solid rock. No lining was necessary! Reinforced concrete arch bridges were constructed over streams at Octoraro and Conowingo MD and Peach Bottom PA along with nine smaller arch bridges and numerous pipe culverts.

Considerable difficulty was experienced in this project. The bluffs were so steep at many points that the new line was almost directly above the old one. This required extreme precautions during both blasting and filling operations to keep the line open and to protect the heavy traffic moving on it.

But if the physical obstacles of Mother Nature to the heavy construction as the work progressed were not enough, the vagaries of human nature entered the picture at the southern end. The plan called for a 0.35% compensated westbound grade from east of Port Deposit to the maximum height of 70 ft. above the new dam. This necessitated elevation of the tracks through a portion of the town – the new right of way at Port Deposit station would be 6-1/2 ft. above the old line and 15 ft. above it at Rock Run (see maps).

When the town officials of Port Deposit were approached in early 1927 for their approval of the project, they instead called "a mass meeting of the citizens at which it was unanimously decided to oppose the elevation . . . . not one resident of Port Deposit is in favor of the change in grade."

PRR (PB&W) took the thorny issue to the Public Service Commission, which ruled on 12 August that the railroad did not have the right to "destroy" the town. Typical of government bodies it rendered a compromise, setting the grade at 0.38% (instead of the 0.4% demanded by the town), thus reducing the elevation to 2 ft. at the station. However, PB&W promptly appealed the ruling to the Maryland Court of Appeals, which rejected the PSC's position and directed them to allow the railroad to proceed with the 0.35% grade as proposed. It was a small PRR triumph, but a triumph nonetheless.

In March 1936 Mother Nature struck the line again. Unprecedented floods and associated ice jams occurred in many of the major rivers in the eastern U.S., and the Susquehanna was no exception. Severe and prolonged cold during the winter produced heavy snow accumulations and thick ice cover on the river and the streams feeding it. A sudden thaw melted much of the snow cover, saturating the ground and filling the streams. The flooding passed down the river, with relatively minor damage along the way. But then heavy rains caused the already overburdened streams, and the river, to rise again to levels much higher than originally predicted.

The resulting surge produced record water levels and flow rates. For comparison, the great Johnstown Flood of 2 June 1889 (see *Triumph I*) caused the Susquehanna River to rise to a record 26.8 ft. at Harrisburg with a peak water flow of 700,000 cu. ft. per *second*, considered by many to be the worst flood level the river would ever reach. However on 19 March those numbers would reach 30.33 ft. and 875,000 cu. ft. per second.

The massive surge of water and ice wreaked havoc on PRR lines, especially the trackage in Columbia and just to the west (see *Triumph II*), and caused considerable damage at the Holtwood power dam and washouts along the Port Road. Heavy pack ice jammed against the ice sheet on the river was blamed as the primary cause of this damage, but the dams actually served to break up the ice, reducing damage downriver.

The damage repaired, catenary was installed on the C&PD in 1937-8 in conjunction with electrification of the east-west freight lines in the Philadelphia Division (see *Triumph II*), the Low-Grade Line and Trenton Cutoff, and the P5a became the primary power beginning on 15 April 1938. Several track relocations were also carried out at this time, especially through and just south of Columbia. Centralized traffic control was installed in 1940.

Traffic on the Port Road peaked during the World War II years, with an average of 47 freight trains daily on the line. The line continued through Penn Central and on into Conrail, its role largely unchanged. Although Conrail abandoned electric power in 1981 because of high fees imposed by Amtrak (the third power dam constructed at Safe Harbor provides power to the east-west main), the Port Road remains a viable route, especially for coal traffic, although overall traffic diminished with the elimination of classification at Enola Yard in 1993. With the renewal of this function under Norfolk Southern aegis, however, the future of the C&PD as of this writing seems considerably brighter. Most of the trains operate at night, to avoid interference with heavy daytime passenger traffic on the Corridor.

(Caption for artwork on next page)

THE ENTIRE C&PD Branch from PERRYVILLE to COLUMBIA (later COLA) is depicted in this 1941 track diagram. The branch is predominantly single track with passing sidings in several locations – notably the long section from Midway to McCalls, which is reverse signaled. Other features include the Perryville Branch, the junction with the Octoraro Branch (to Philadelphia), the undergrade connection with the A&S Branch (Low-Grade Line) at Creswell and the junction with the Columbia Branch (to Lancaster and Marietta) at Columbia. Built as a light-duty line to tap the Baltimore traffic in the Susquehanna Valley, it was upgraded several times and soon outshone the rival Northern Central route because of its lower grades.

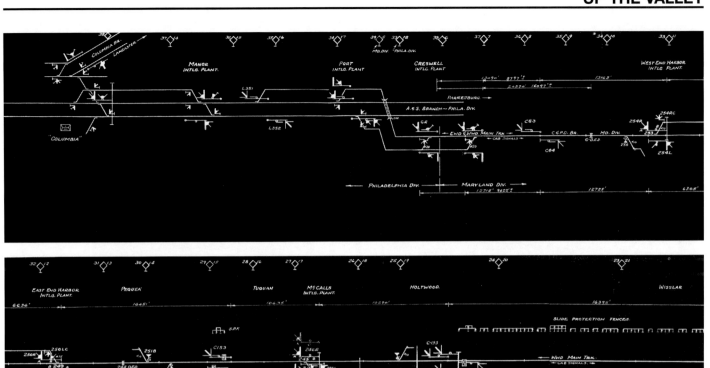

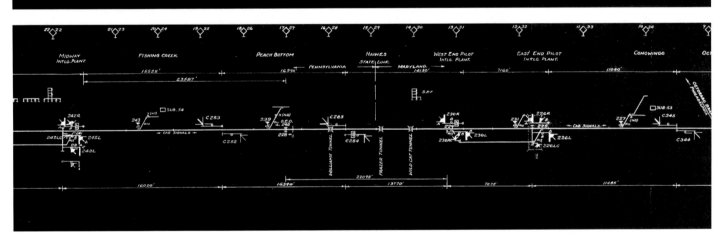

REVERSE SIGNALING ~ MIDWAY TO McCALLS.

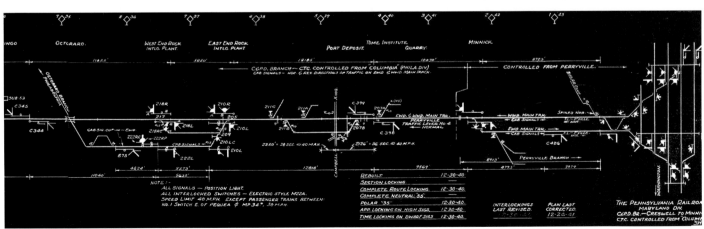

William J. Coxey

WE BEGIN our journey on the C&PD Branch on the main at Perryville as northbound Conrail freight WAENA (EC5), with an early morning departure from Potomac Yard, edges onto branch trackage in November 1977. At this time Conrail operated two daily Potomac Yard-Enola freights in each direction on the Port Road.

William J. Coxey

HERE the train squeals around the sharp curve on the south leg of the wye where the maximum speed was 15 mph. The maximum speed on the branch was then 40 mph, although there were speed restrictions to 30 mph at several curves along the river.

ALTHOUGH the C&PD is normally considered a freight line, through passenger service (if it could be called that) once operated on the branch along with the trains turning onto the P&BC at Octoraro Junction. Here Class D16b 3317 leads a short consist in a photo from the early years of the 20th Century.

W. M. Moedinger, Jr./Fred W. Schneider, III Collection

Fred W. Schneider, III

WITH ELECTRIFICATION of the line in 1938 the P5a became the predominant power. Here a pair of the veteran motors leads a coal train southward in an undated photo.

Tome Station, P.R.R., Port Deposit, Md.

James Cassatt, Jr. Collection

THIS TRIM STATION, shown here in an undated postcard view, was built at Tome (MP. 3.8) in 1916 to serve the nearby Tome Institute, a private boys' school established by Jacob Tome. The school property was later taken over by the U. S. Navy ca. 1940 for construction of the Bainbridge Naval Training Station.

Jacob Tome was an interesting individual. As a wealthy Port Deposit banker he was for a time considered the foremost financier between Philadelphia and Baltimore. In addition, he served as a Director on the PW&B for 30 years as well as the C&PD and the Baltimore Central, which gave him considerable leverage on these lines. He utilized this influence to secure completion of the C&PD from Perryville to the connection with the P&BC when that latter road was in one of its early financial crises.

AS WE HAVE NOTED EARLIER, the Susquehanna River is notorious for massive ice jams (also see *Triumph II*), and the low-lying C&PD is particularly vulnerable to Mother Nature's wrath. This photo dated 3 January 1910 shows a contorted Port Deposit station (MP. 4.2) caught in the grip of a hellish mix of ice, rock and gravel. The humans with their puny shovels seem no match to the formidable task of digging out the line.

F. A Wrabel

P. R. R Station, Port Deposit, Md.

WHAT WAS LEFT of the badly damaged structure was torn down and replaced with an attractive stone and frame combination station the following year, shown here in a postcard view mailed 2 July 1938. We wonder if they made use of the abundant supply of stones already delivered to the site.

James Cassatt, Jr. Collection

Fred W. Schneider, III

A SOUTHBOUND FREIGHT passes through Port Deposit in decidedly warmer temperatures in the spring of 1969. GG1 4876 and sister are in charge on the elevated right of way through town. All was not always so peaceful here, however. Local citizens vehemently protested the elevation of the tracks necessitated by construction of the Conowingo Dam upriver.

A WARY OPERATOR poses for the camera at ROCK block station at the junction with the Octoraro Branch in 1940. Note the common tools of the trade and the strategically placed horseshoe.

F. A Wrabel

THE OCTORARO BRANCH was long gone when this photo was taken at the junction, now known as WEST ROCK, on 5 May 1978. The view looks southward.

Tim Garner

A CONRAIL FREIGHT heads northward between Octoraro and Conowingo on 5 May 1978. Conrail discontinued use of the overhead because of high fees charged by Amtrak, owner of the power supply to this and the Low-Grade Line. The Penn Central logos on the Geeps were quickly painted over after the takeover.

Tim Garner

ALL IS QUIET at Conowingo (MP. 9.6) on this day in 1928, although earth was being blasted not too far away.

F. A Wrabel

THE SUSQUEHANNA RIVER drops 227 feet in its 43-mile journey between Columbia and tidewater, making it potentially useful for hydroelectric power development. In 1906 the McCall's Ferry Power Company began construction of the first of three hydroelectric power dams that would be built across the lower Susquehanna to harness the power of the restless river. The strategic location chosen was at Minqua (later known as Holtwood) near McCall's Ferry. The surrounding hills provided a natural enclosure for a reservoir. Work was begun in January 1906 but because of the high costs of the project, increased by a dam break in September 1907, the original company went into receivership and the project was taken over by the newly-formed Pennsylvania Water & Power Company (later Pennsylvania Power

& Light). Final closure of the dam took place in August 1910 and power from the first generating unit began on 23 October.

The dam is 55 ft. high and nearly 2400 ft. long (excluding the powerhouse), the largest in the nation at the time. The lake created by the dam covers 3.75 sq. miles and extends 8 miles upriver, impounding 6.3 billion gallons of water. The dam is shown here under construction in a postcard view with temporary tracks laid to haul concrete.

By the way, a pact between Maryland and Pennsylvania allowed the latter all electricity rights and the former water rights. A water tunnel from the river to the Baltimore water system was built and used during droughts, most recently in 2002-3.

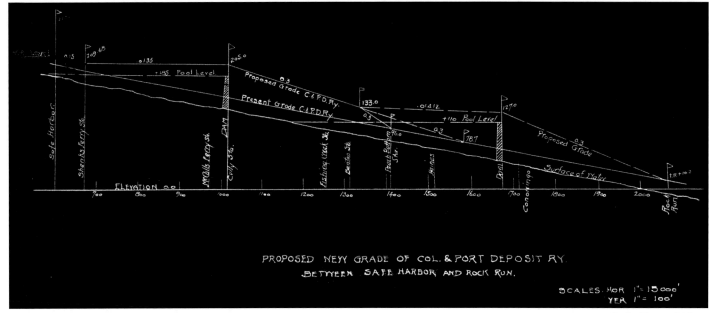

PROPOSED NEW GRADE OF COL. & PORT DEPOSIT RY.
BETWEEN SAFE HARBOR AND ROCK RUN.

SCALES. HOR 1" = 15 000'
VER 1" = 100'

BECAUSE the dam (the left one on this 1926 diagram) would raise the level of water at McCall's Ferry 60 ft., with slack water extending up to Safe Harbor, it was necessary to rebuild the C&PD for 13 miles between Benton and Safe Harbor to elevate it above possible flood levels behind the dam. The maximum grade on the new line was planned to be 0.3 %, with a run-down grade of 0.5% at Benton. At the dam site itself the new tracks were to be 25 ft. above the old right of way.

The $1.25 million contract to rebuild the line was let by the power company to H. S. Kerbaugh of Philadelphia (contractors for Enola Yard and much of the Low-Grade Line – see *Triumph II*). Work began on 1 August 1906 and remarkably finished on 12 September 1907. Operations on the line were suspended be-

tween Benton and Safe Harbor to facilitate the work of blasting side-hill cuts in the steep rock bluffs above the river.

In doing the engineering design work for this large project it seems that someone forgot to include the costs to fill in the gap (far left in the diagram) between Shenks Ferry and the new grade to Safe Harbor. Since the power company refused to pay for any trackwork north of Shenks Ferry it took an "I beg leave to hand you herewith" letter on 26 April 1906 from typically reticent Second Vice President Charles Pugh to anything but reticent A. J. Cassatt asking for an additional $100,000 to cover the oversight. We would like to have been a proverbial fly on the wall in Cassatt's imperial office in Broad Street Station during that discussion!

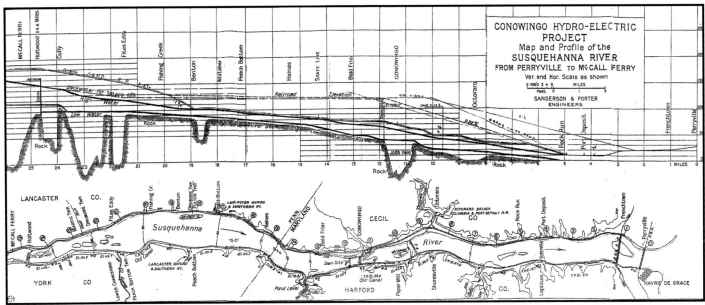

SOME 20 YEARS LATER the Philadelphia Electric Company (which had taken over the second planned hydroelectric project from the defunct McCall's Ferry Company) began work on a 4630-ft. long, 90-ft. high concrete dam south of Conowingo. This again necessitated elevation of the C&PD, this time for 16 miles between Port Deposit and Fishing Creek. It was a massive undertaking involving excavation of 1.5 million cu. yds. of earth and rock (largely solid granite) in side-hill cuts on the steep slopes above the river. To avoid further cuts up to 145 ft. deep, tunnels were blasted through solid rock in three locations.

The elevated line ascended a 0.35% compensated grade through Port Deposit, the subject of intense legal challenges as noted, to a point 70 ft. above the old right of way at the dam, and then continued for 10 miles on a nearly level grade 12 ft. above the full reservoir water level. The right of way was graded for double track, although it was laid with single track with three 100-car sidings. Maximum curvature through the rugged terrain was held to 6° and that only at a few locations.

Note the "Old Canal" notation on the diagram, a remnant of the S&T complex. Interestingly, PRR considered developing a rail line on the west bank of the river along the canal towpath between Havre de Grace and Wrightsville and possibly to a connection with the Low-Grade Line. The issue first arose in 1906 as a possibly cheaper solution than elevating the C&PD and then again in 1929 to serve potential industrial development associated with the Conowingo Dam. Philadelphia Electric built a single-track access line from Havre de Grace to the foot of the dam along a portion of this route, but the cost (estimated at over $5 million in 1929) precluded PRR taking over this line and extending it farther northward.

THIS VIEW dated 27 February 1927 shows the Conowingo Dam in the background at left, with excavation progressing for the new right of way at the far right – at least this section near the outlet of Conowingo Creek was mostly dirt!

Hagley Museum & Library

IN SOME AREAS it was necessary to construct dykes to protect the right of way and towns along it, such as the one at Cromley's Mountain Station shown here in an interesting photo taken on 24 May 1928. There appears to be a tracklaying operation going on here, with the ties and rails neatly stacked at left. Note the cattle pen just east of the station.

Hagley Museum & Library

THE C&PD is not generally noted for its bridges, but as part of the Conowingo Dam project three heavy reinforced concrete structures were constructed where the new line crossed major streams – Octoraro MD (six arches), Conowingo (five arches) and Peach Bottom PA (three arches).

The one at Octoraro Creek is shown here in October 1927. All of them were double-track, solid-barrel, rock-filled structures with 70-ft. arches. Nine similar but smaller bridges were built in addition to the three major ones.

IN ADDITION to the bridges relocation of the line necessitated drilling
three tunnels in locations where blasting deep cuts of 130-145 ft. would have
been needed through the rock outcrop-
pings. These were located north of the
dam at Wild Cat Point, Frazers Point
and Williams Point. The one at Wild
Cat Point was located on a tangent, but
the other two had 6° curves. All of them
were unlined and 30-ft. wide and 24-ft.
high, large enough for double track.
This October 1927 view of the west end
of the Williams tunnel looking downstream shows the difference in elevation
between the old and new right of ways.
Note the westbound passenger train on
the old line.

Hagley Museum & Library

GONE FISHIN' – For a time the
Washington DC-Harrisburg section of
the *Broadway Limited* ran via the Port
Road (and the Columbia Branch) to its
mainline connection. Here the train
runs on weed-infested trackage at the
southern end of Pilot Interlocking just
north of Conowingo in August 1974.
The dam is just visible in the distance.

Fred W. Schneider, III

A NORTHBOUND Penn Central freight winds its way along the curving banks of the Susquehanna south of Peach Bottom on a sunny 5 September 1970. The two freight motors are Class E33 – former Virginian locomotives purchased by the New Haven RR and then inherited by Penn Central in the 1968 merger. They were one of the few bright spots in that ill-fated venture.

Fred W. Schneider, III

NOT ALL THE ACTION on the C&PD was through traffic. Here a local freight led by veteran Baldwin diesel switcher 7940 ambles along the line in a peaceful setting south of Peach Bottom on 1 September 1970. The access road looks well used.

Fred W. Schneider, III

A PAIR OF E44s, still in PRR lettering, stirs things up as they power a southbound freight through rugged Wildcat Tunnel in June 1969. Note the slide protection fences, necessary to shield the right of way at the foot of the sheer rock face which seems poised to engulf even these powerful beasts at any moment.

AND NOT ALL E44 RUNS were followed by long strings of freight cars. Here we have a pair leading a northbound "cabin extra" near Peach Bottom on a sunny September day in 1970. The real cabin at the left overlooks the outlet of Peter's Creek into the river.

Fred W. Schneider, III

AS USUAL everyone, including an apparently unhappy beagle, posed to have their picture taken in front of the classic frame depot at Peach Bottom in a ca. 1910 postcard view.

James Cassatt, Jr. Collection

OOPS – Looking like something more akin to a beached whale than a superb and versatile locomotive, hapless GG1 4829 rests precariously on the banks of the Susquehanna north of Peach Bottom on 3 June 1946. The crew of L1 597 and the rest of the workers seem perplexed at what to do next.

The GG1 ran into a rockslide and tipped over. Wreck trains were dispatched from Wilmington and Enola to fish her out, but to make matters worse the train from Enola ran into a slide as well and the crane rolled over. Talk about a bad day!

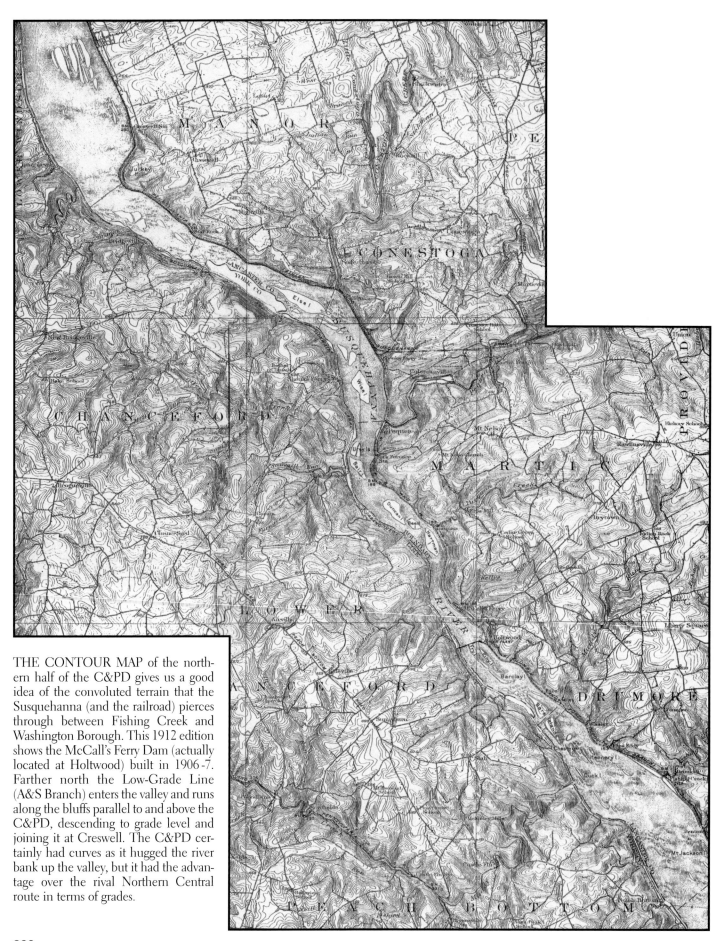

THE CONTOUR MAP of the northern half of the C&PD gives us a good idea of the convoluted terrain that the Susquehanna (and the railroad) pierces through between Fishing Creek and Washington Borough. This 1912 edition shows the McCall's Ferry Dam (actually located at Holtwood) built in 1906-7. Farther north the Low-Grade Line (A&S Branch) enters the valley and runs along the bluffs parallel to and above the C&PD, descending to grade level and joining it at Creswell. The C&PD certainly had curves as it hugged the river bank up the valley, but it had the advantage over the rival Northern Central route in terms of grades.

IN A LATTER-DAY REINCAR-NATION of a favorite William Rau tableau, a pair of Penn Central E33s moves a northbound freight across the solid stone arch bridge at the outlet of Fishing Creek on 5 September 1970. The boaters and the locomotive fireman exchange traditional waves.

Fred W. Schneider, III

ROCKS – With the line occupying a narrow ledge along the river bank, rocks were everywhere on the C&PD. In what could be a model railroad scene GG1 4869, recently repainted in Penn Central black, joins a colleague still in the PRR wide-stripe scheme in moving Train B4 south of Drumore. The date is 30 May 1969, one year into the ill-fated merger.

Fred W. Schneider, III

FRAMED – Fred Schneider turned and caught the cabin car still bringing up the rear of the train, nicely framed by the trees and set against the rugged rock face.

Fred W. Schneider, III

F. A. Wrabel

McCALL'S BLOCK STATION looked like this in a view up the peaceful Susquehanna in the summer of 1922. The interlocking was located at the west end of a long passing siding, but it appears that the operator didn't have a good view of approaching eastward trains. Note the tiny necessary facility.

As for the interesting semaphore, the 1924 Maryland Division employees' timetable offers the following: "A yellow semaphore arm with a black circle on the face of the arm in a diagonal position is equivalent to block is not clear, proceed with caution; name, permissive signal." The arm in the stop position covers a yellow light that results in two horizontal yellow lights at night when the permissive signal is shown – hence PRR obtained a second indication that in automatic block territory indicated "prepare to stop at next signal; name, approach." According to this timetable these signals (home and distant) were in use at this time on the C&PD as well as the Octoraro Branch, the Newark & Delaware City and the Chester Creek RR.

THE BOYS in the motorboat seem oblivious to the pair of E44s rumbling southward across the concrete arch bridge at the outlet of Pequea Creek on 16 July 1964. The bridge railing provides a convenient (?) place to tie up a boat. The Low-Grade Line also crossed this creek on a high bridge farther upstream (see *Triumph II*).

Fred W. Schneider, III

Fred W. Schneider, III

AS WE MOVE up the valley, we reach the point where the east-west Low-Grade Line approaches the C&PD. In this high-level eastward view at Safe Harbor the catenary poles of that line are just visible on the bluffs at upper left as a westbound Conrail freight passes below on 24 June 1978.

LOOKING WESTWARD in the wintertime, we have an interesting low-level view of the dual bridges over the outlet of Conestoga Creek at Safe Harbor – and more ice jams on the river. This ca. 1910 postcard view, taken only a few years after the entire area was completely rebuilt (see *Triumph II* for dramatic construction photos), shows a freight headed eastward on the newly-completed Low-Grade Line.

James Cassatt, Jr. Collection

203

Fred W. Schneider, III

IN OUR VIEW the most spectacular location on the C&PD, the dual bridges at Safe Harbor provide a look at heavy railroad infrastructure at its best, combined with that of the hydroelectric plant. In a superb photo taken in 1962 an eastbound freight led by two P5a motors heads down the Port Road. The 295-ft. deck plate girder bridge carrying the C&PD over the creek was constructed in 1906 on a new elevated right of way to replace the previous structure destroyed by an ice jam. Note the ice – just a thin layer this time – on the river. Towering above it all is the long viaduct of the Low-Grade Line as it descends westward towards the river and just behind the bridge is a large electric substation.

At the left is the Safe Harbor dam, the third on the lower Susquehanna. This was another undertaking by the Pennsylvania Water & Power Company, successor to the short-lived McCall's Ferry Power Company. Work on this project began on 1 April 1930 and final closure of the dam was made on 19 September 1931. Power was first delivered on 7 December of that year. It required rebuilding of 9.5 miles of the C&PD.

The dam is 62 ft. high and nearly 4900 ft. long, including the powerhouse. The lake covers 11.5 sq. miles and extends 10 miles upriver. The storage volume is 22.5 billion gallons.

THE MASSIVE INFRASTRUCTURE of the Safe Harbor Dam towers above the human visitors. This May 1962 view looks back at the rock cliffs. At their base the C&PD line is about on a level with the top of the dam and the Low-Grade line is just visible half-way up.

AN EASTBOUND FREIGHT awaits clearance to enter the CTC-controlled C&PD at Creswell interlocking where the Port Road and the Low-Grade actually join. Note the locomotive – not a GG1, but a modified P5a. The date is a gloomy day after Christmas 1956 and the swollen, ice-laden Susquehanna again threatens.

SPEAKING of the river threatening, these two photos portray the ice jam and flooding that occurred at Creswell in January 1957 when the water covered the tracks to a depth of 4 ft. (the electric switch motor, controlled from Columbia [COLA] Tower, was safely removed to higher ground before the flood).

This photo shows the home signal that governs the entrance to the Port Road. Chet Fuhrman, who took the photos, was stationed at Creswell to hold the signal shown until a train was almost upon it, at which time he phoned COLA and had it set to Clear. This gave trains approaching both Approach and Stop aspects, causing them to run slowly enough so as not to damage the traction motors.

Chester D. Fuhrman

WADING through the icy waters – does a GG1 really wade anywhere? Anyway, this photo shows a train approaching the signal in the flood, ready to continue its journey southward. It's a fine example of dedication under adverse conditions, Chet, but did the train really proceed through 4 ft. of water? Water and electricity do not mix.

Thus we end our story of the C&PD as it began, with ice everywhere.

But what of the river itself? What is its history and why the name? Well, it seems that back in deep Indian history there was a tribe called the Algonquins that lived in a valley *long gone*. Their chief was Chippewa who, with wife Shawnee, gave birth to a daughter named Susquehanna, or Hannah for short. She developed into a lovely woman who spurned all advances from eager braves to the extent that her parents feared her lot would be spinsterhood.

Then one day a brave from a distant tribe named Octorora arrived with a message for Chippewa. Hannah and Octorora met, sparks flew, a wedding followed and Little Octorora soon arrived.

Father and Son were on a hunting trip when a violent storm swept through the valley and Father was struck dead by lightning.

A search party found the Father's body with Son in a depressed state that, sadly, never healed.

Then a vicious drought struck the valley. The tribe was starving. Hannah, still troubled by grief and a depressed Son, announced that the Great Spirit had been offended and offered herself and Son as a sacrifice, plunging from a rock into the dry valley.

Within days a vast wall of water inundated the valley, forming a whole new wide river. The tribe named the river Susquehanna in her memory.

This delightful story, clearly labeled as fiction, was written by Leonore Taylor, daughter of B&O Aikin Towerman W.L. Taylor, and appeared in B&O Magazine issue of January 1923.

Fiction? Of course. Yet geologists have determined that, during the Pleistocene Ice Age, the river drained central New York State but the tributaries were blocked by morainal deposits and the water level shrank. A submarine channel has been found extending eastward from the mouth of the present river across the Continental Shelf, the remnant of a former valley.

All this could just be coincidence. Yet all pre-recorded history is oral, passed down by word of mouth through countless generations.

Fiction? We hope not.

Chapter 5

Route of Invasion

The Northern Central Railway

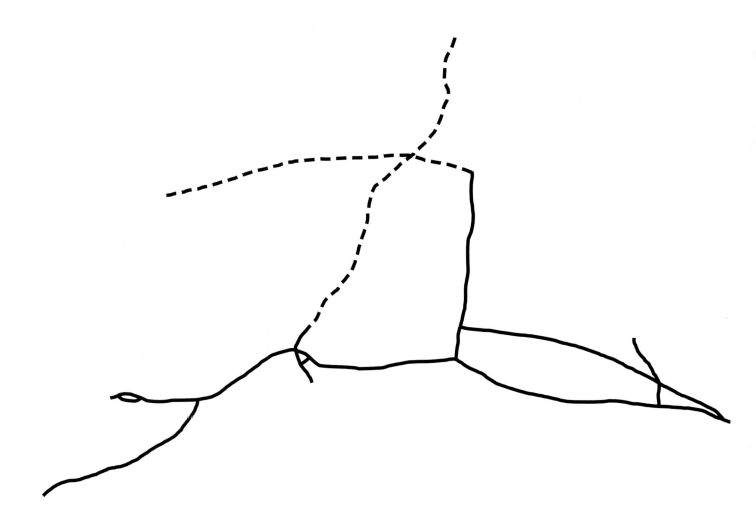

(Caption for artwork on next page)

THE ENTIRE Northern Central Railway is depicted in this map dated February 1913, the last year of its independent existence. The Baltimore Division (shaded line) is covered in this chapter – the remaining divisions (and other PRR lines in north-central Pennsylvania and New York) will be discussed in a subsequent *Triumph* volume. The Northern Central emerged in 1854 as a consolidation of the Baltimore & Susquehanna and three other lines resulting from Baltimore's determined effort to build a rail line up the Susquehanna Valley. It funneled heavy freight traffic down the valley – primarily anthracite, grain and lumber – from numerous branches, from diverse online industries and from the West via its PRR connections. In its heyday it also had a significant passenger business, everything from through travelers to tourists to commuters.

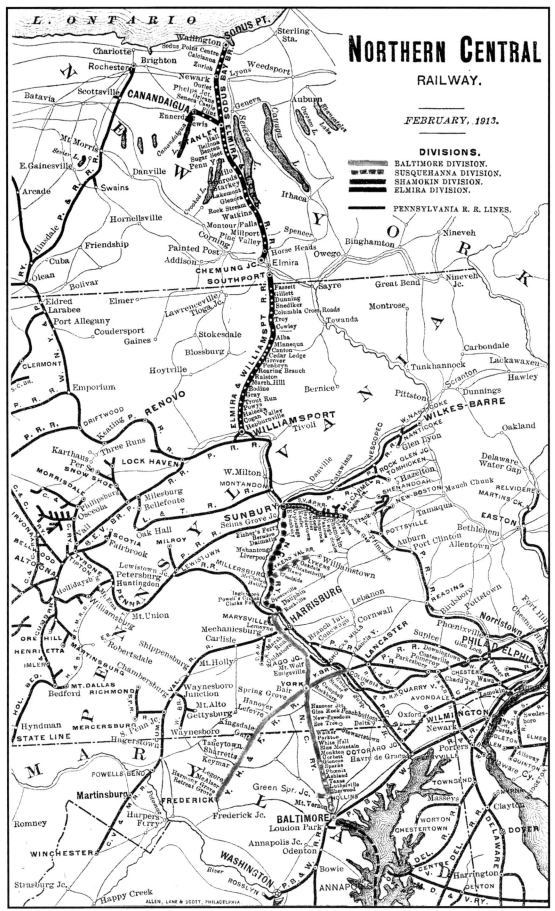

Gunnarsson Collection / Railroad Museum of Pennsylvania (PHMC)

The second line running from Baltimore up the Susquehanna Valley was the Northern Central Railway, a name that evokes a rich panoply of historical events, railroad and otherwise. It arose out of a complex corporate reorganization process. To recite the facts – it was formed on 4 December 1854 under the provisions of an Act of the Maryland Legislature dated 10 March of that year (concurrent with one in Pennsylvania dated 3 May) authorizing the consolidation of the York & Maryland Line RR, the York & Cumberland RR and the uncompleted Susquehanna RR (all incorporated in Pennsylvania) with each other and with the Baltimore & Susquehanna RR (incorporated in Maryland).

These railroads encompassed the main line between Baltimore and Bridgeport (across the river from Harrisburg) along with the extension northward into the coal regions. Curiously not included in the consolidation was the Wrightsville, York & Gettysburg which the Northern Central continued to operate as a separate entity until 1870. The new company officially took over the property and the debts of the old companies on 1 January 1855.

But looking beyond the cold facts, the new company also took on all of the simmering political sensitivities inherent in the longstanding Philadelphia-Baltimore rivalry. The Maryland Legislature, with at least one eye on the road's potentially lucrative coal traffic, included a provision that authorized financing to allow the Northern Central to complete the line northward to Sunbury, gateway to the anthracite region. Their Pennsylvania counterparts, as always looking out for Philadelphia interests, inserted wording that would have in effect turned over the line from Harrisburg to Sunbury to the Philadelphia-backed Sunbury & Erie RR if the parties could not agree on a new charter.

The Northern Central proceeded to float a $2.5 million bond issue with two objectives in mind – completing the road to Sunbury and extending at the southern end to the Baltimore port area at Canton. Only the most critical expenditures were made at this time along the remaining portions of the line.

The section between Dauphin and Millersburg (see map) was completed by 1857 and the Northern Central built an interchange with the Lykens Valley RR, allowing it to initiate the crucial anthracite shipments to Baltimore using PRR's Rockville Bridge temporarily to cross the Susquehanna until its own bridge could be constructed. That structure, known as

the Dauphin Bridge, was opened for freight service in March 1858 and four months later the line was completed and through service to Sunbury on its own trackage began.

Completing the extension to Sunbury was probably the Northern Central's most important accomplishment up to that point – the only portion of the line built new by that company, the other extensions were by acquisition. But it too was caught up in the seemingly never-ending Philadelphia-Baltimore conflict. City fathers in Sunbury were opposed to traffic being routed south to Baltimore by an "encroaching enemy" instead of eastward to Philadelphia. Consequently they initially refused to let the Northern Central enter the city itself and thus passengers had to board horse-drawn coaches to the S&E station. Freight had to be transferred to heavy wagons. Eventually the Northern Central took over operations of the S&E line to Williamsport and Lock Haven, but that is a story for another *Triumph* volume.

The other extension mandated by the State of Maryland under the Act establishing the Northern Central was a line to the Baltimore inner harbor area, known as the "Basin." As soon as the line was complete to Sunbury the surge in coal and lumber traffic quickly began to overwhelm the already congested old City Dock area. Consequently, in 1858 the Northern Central attempted to construct a line to the undeveloped area on the east side of the harbor known as Canton. Like earlier attempts, however, this one came to a halt because of legal action and problems in obtaining property rights.

Thus the railroad turned to a badly needed upgrading of its right of way, installing new iron rails (on the main at least), replacing bridges, building new stations and engine service facilities and expanding the still valuable canal junction operations. Large numbers of new locomotives and cars were purchased, although the burgeoning anthracite traffic found the road chronically short of cars to haul what had rapidly become a major business – black diamonds.

In addition to anthracite, iron ore was an early source of traffic – and revenue – for the line. In 1854 iron ore was discovered in several locations along the recently completed Hanover Branch RR and for the next three decades thousands of tons of ore were hauled in both directions to smelters via the Northern Central. Two mile-long sidings were laid at Hanover Junction to make up long trains of ore cars. Interestingly, many of the cars were owned by local gentry and rented to the Northern Central on a ton-mile basis. These enterprising individuals reaped a substantial reward from their role as forwarding agents.

Although traffic was steadily increasing, all of the heavy expenditures put the Northern Central back into a precarious financial state. This situation would be remedied by two dramatic events looming on the horizon – the rapidly gathering storm clouds of the Civil War and the entry of PRR.

PRR's entry into the Northern Central realm is a tale of political intrigue and corporate machinations that included a cast of characters that we have met before in the *Triumph* series, with one notable newcomer – Simon Cameron. Simon Cameron, a nationally prominent member of the fledgling Republican Party, was one of the most influential, colorful, and corrupt public figures of his day. His construction firms had been involved in building the extensions of the B&S, and he became president of the Harrisburg, Portsmouth, Mountjoy & Lancaster RR (later a part of the east-west PRR main. But by far his most enduring characteristic was an uncanny ability to derive personal profit from a wide range of public endeavors.

In late 1860 the State of Maryland instituted a foreclosure suit against the Northern Central, pushing the chronically ailing road to the edge of financial disaster and striking fear into hearts and minds of the ever-hopeful stockholders. The road's desperate situation was poignantly characterized by then President John S. Gittings: "To meet our engagements with the State of Maryland, pay the interest on our bonded debt, meet the floating debt, pay for the material, rolling stock and cars absolutely required is *impossible*." The financial crisis was temporarily alleviated by a personal loan from Gittings, but a more permanent solution was clearly needed.

Enter PRR.

John Edgar Thomson had been eyeing the Northern Central for some time as an outlet for Western traffic seeking the Baltimore market, and Cameron had urged Thomson and Vice President Tom Scott in mid-1860 to join forces to take control of the line (Scott and Cameron had become political bedfellows in the tonnage tax debate – see *Triumph II*). But PRR was prevented from acting by the control exerted by the road's major stockholders and PRR corporate antagonists, our old friends the B&O and the Reading.

Cameron already owned a sizable block of North-ern Central stock and Thomson quietly began purchasing shares himself. Early in 1861 both Garrett and the Reading unloaded their holdings. Thomson personally purchased nearly 13,000 shares (over 28% of the total), which were held in a broker's account and subsequently transferred to PRR by special Act of the Pennsylvania Legislature in April allowing any railroad chartered in the Commonwealth to hold stocks in other lines. The two blocks together represented nearly 50% of the total outstanding shares. Two years later PRR purchased another 2500 shares, making it the largest single stockholder and enabling it to secure working control of the road.

And herein lies a mystery. Garrett and his wife owned a substantial number of NC shares. Why did he sell such potentially valuable stock?

In what appears to be an early example of insider knowledge, it is easy to assume that Garrett knew well in advance from his pals in Annapolis that foreclosure had been decided, perhaps as part of a well-worn scheme to drive down the share price only to buy it back later at a lower price and, in the process, pickup additional shares and get a lock on this property so vital to the future of B&O, Baltimore and Maryland. With his banker mentality and conviction that he was in fact a "Boy Wonder" in all matters railroad-related as he was touted when he took over the presidency of B&O in 1858 after the Panic of 1857, such a scenario is quite plausible.

Even today, a century and a half later, we cringe at the thought of Garrett thinking he could outwit the PRR team. His only hope was that they would die laughing before administering the final blow.

Though it was like taking candy from a baby, through this bold – and triumphant – stroke Thomson had gained direct access to Baltimore, greatly enhancing PRR's competitive position vs. Garrett's B&O. From 1861 onward the Northern Central board was controlled by PRR officers, Cameron family members and others friendly to Pennsylvania – rather than Maryland – interests thus thrusting a sword deep into B&O's heretofore sacrosanct arena. This move unleashed a chain of events that subsequently enabled PRR to seize control of the main north-south route and gain an entry to the South from which it could undertake its own campaign to build a southern domain.

But all that lay in the more distant future – the immediate future was increasingly, and ominously, stormy.

The storm, or more accurately, whirlwind was the Civil War.

We have thoroughly related this story in our book *East End* (1992, 2003), particularly in Chapter 10 "The Uncivil Civil War", in all its gore and fury. The student of this subject would do well to study this chapter.

Pertinent to this book, however, we will just extract some facts.

1. The reign of Simon Cameron and Thomas A. Scott, Secretary of War and Assistant Secretary respectively, is one of the ugliest episodes in the nation's history. They gave avarice and corruption a bad name.

2. This duo closed down vital B&O, rigged all rates skyhigh, stiffed PB&W by diverting traffic to PRR and NC lines and lined their pockets with loot. Real patriots.

3. When the stench reached Lincoln's nostrils in early 1862, he banished Cameron to Russia while stating, in his apt prose, that he "was so corrupt that he would steal everything in sight except for a red-hot stove."

4. Cameron later left his mark on history by defining an Honest Politician as one who "once bought, stays bought."

5. Scott, being congratulated by Joseph R. Potts on his appointment as Assistant Secretary of War, stated "Yes, this place is worth $100,000 a year to me." Lincoln sent him back to PRR.

6. Thomson, as usual, let his minions do the dirty work.

Our readers know that we do not think highly of Garrett, but even we can sympathize with him facing the depredations of this cabal. He may not have been very bright, but he was an honest servant of the Republic.

The surge in traffic generated a bonanza of revenues, enabling the Northern Central for the first time in its life to attain stable finances, and to rebuild and even expand the line.

The Northern Central's first role in the looming conflict actually began well before active hostilities erupted. The original B&S, developed by interests based in Maryland – lest we forget a slaveholding state – was a preferred route for a different kind of railroad, the clandestine network known as the Underground Railroad to transport fugitive slaves across the Mason-Dixon line.

After the passage of the Fugitive Slave Act in 1850 the Northern Central's official policy was to provide the means to capture and return runaway slaves to their owners. The road even established holding pens and maintained strings of boxcars for the purpose at the town of Freeland – an odd choice given their function, although it was the first stop south of the Pennsylvania border. However, unofficially many individuals along the route – and perhaps even station agents at locations such as Cockeysville, White Hall and Parkton – aided the slaves in their perilous journey to freedom.

The role of the railroads in the impending conflict was further underlined by abolitionist leader John Brown's bizarre attack on a B&O train as it arrived at Harpers Ferry shortly before dawn on 17 October 1859. A company of Federal troops (interestingly led by then Colonel Robert E. Lee) boarded a train in Washington and moved on the B&O (via Relay) to the site of the attack and quickly rounded up Brown's small band of troublemakers. The B&O resumed operations the next day, but its Civil War travails had just begun.

The hostility erupted into open conflict when Confederate artillery bombarded Fort Sumter on 12 April 1861 and the Northern Central was quickly drawn into the battle. As a result of the attack on a Federal fort, Lincoln immediately called up 75,000 volunteer troops and forces from the North were quickly dispatched to Washington to provide protection for the capital.

These troops had to pass southward over either of the two rail routes into Baltimore from the north – the PW&B main from Philadelphia and the Northern Central from Harrisburg – and their cars hauled (city ordinance insisted on animal power for this arduous task) through the congested city streets to the B&O, which at that time controlled the only rail link to the nation's capital over its 40-mile long Washington Branch. Thus trains from the PW&B had to be broken up and the cars hauled from its President Street terminal (see maps) along Pratt Street trackage to the B&O's Camden Station. Likewise, cars from the Northern Central were transferred from the Bolton Depot southward on Howard Street to the Pratt Street line. Large horse stables were built at the Bolton Yards to accomplish this task.

This unwieldy situation, known as the "Baltimore Bottleneck," was clearly a weak link in the Union's vaunted rail system (Philadelphia was another, as we have noted, but Baltimore was closer to the thick of the action), and Confederate sympathizers wasted no time in making their sentiments known to the Union troops moving slowly through the city streets. The troops passed through the mile-long hostile gauntlet on the first day, 18 April, without serious difficulty but when the news of a Confederate attack on Harpers Ferry reached Baltimore, things became much worse.

The "Baltimore Riot," also known as the "Pratt Street Riot," not only produced the war's first casualties, it would have far-reaching consequences for the PW&B, and more profoundly, the Northern Central. As troops of the Sixth Massachusetts Volunteer Regiment began the slow journey along Pratt Street the next morning, the crowd grew in both size and hostility, stoning the last car when it suffered brake problems during its slow move west toward Camden Station.

The troops retreated to President Street Station, causing the crowd to think they were returning to Philadelphia. But instead they reorganized and began a fast march across town. Suddenly blocked in this move, the soldiers in desperation fired on the angry crowd, which fell back, allowing them to finally reach their 13-car waiting train that eventually moved on to Washington. When it was all over eight rioters, three soldiers and one onlooker had been killed, and three dozen from both sides were wounded – the first casualties of the long and bloody conflict to come.

As the day progressed rumors spread through the city that Union forces would retaliate as a result of this "heinous" incident. Officials hastily convened a meeting that evening to plan the city's defense, and when they heard that additional Federal troops were being sent from Harrisburg over the Northern Central, the decision was quickly taken to cut all the rail lines from the North into the city.

Early on the morning of the 20th two groups of militia were sent out to "break the bridges" of both the PW&B and the Northern Central. One group commandeered a PW&B train and set afire the long wooden trestles across the Gunpowder and Bush Rivers (as noted in Chapter 2). The second group, with orders to burn all of the bridges on the Northern Central to the Pennsylvania border, succeeded in destroying trestles at several locations.

The bridge burning, along with destruction of the telegraph lines along the way, largely came to an end on the 24th – although vandalism continued for some time – but the rumors of a Federal invasion persisted, with troops "prepared to shoot their way through

Baltimore." These rampant rumors, as it turned out, were the primary result of orders to do just that from none other than Simon Cameron, in his new role as Lincoln's Secretary of War. Furious at the irresponsible behavior of his Cabinet appointee, Lincoln directed General-in-Chief Winfield Scott to quickly revoke the order and by arrangement with Felton, send the troops instead by ship down the Chesapeake Bay to Annapolis. This allowed matters to cool down and prompted the Maryland Legislature to vote against secession.

Lincoln was under heavy political pressure to replace Cameron and Scott, which he did in January 1862. Edwin M. Stanton was appointed and proved to be a more effective cabinet officer. Cameron was subsequently relieved of his duties and exiled to become Minister to Russia.

In an effort to calm the tense situation Lincoln summoned Maryland Governor Thomas Hicks and fiery Baltimore Mayor George Brown (both of whom had authorized the raids on the railroad bridges) to Washington and agreed to send no additional troops through the city. Although a proclamation to this effect had the desired calming influence, Lincoln subsequently ordered the city occupied and the rail lines secured by Federal troops anyway.

In retrospect, the precipitous actions by Baltimore city officials had further inflamed an already tense and dangerous situation. They had not only clearly underestimated Lincoln's unyielding determination to preserve the Union – and to keep Maryland within that fold after Virginia's secession – but they had also been responsible for destruction of the strategically valuable rail lines at a particularly critical time.

The bridges were promptly rebuilt and the lines repaired. Revenue service on the Northern Central was restored on 13 May, some say because of Cameron's enduring influence. Both the PW&B and the Northern Central charged the city for the damages, not only for replacement of the bridges (nearly $118 thousand on the latter) but also for the loss of business.

After Federal troops occupied Baltimore in May of 1861 and stationed themselves along the line, the Northern Central entered a brief period of relative peace and prosperity. Although the war continued in earnest, the major battles were to the south and west and the line benefited heavily from the burgeoning traffic. When Confederate troops effectively shut down Mississippi River commerce, agricultural products from the Midwest moved eastward primarily by rail – bumper grain harvests in the Midwest coupled with European crop failures and frequent closings of the B&O lines further boosted east-west traffic on PRR and the other two eastern trunk lines. Aided by military contracts (initially dispensed by Cameron) – and the wartime inflation – the Northern Central's revenues nearly tripled during the war years.

The millstone of huge debts a thing of the past, the revenues were put to work rebuilding the right of way to handle both coal and military traffic. Double-tracking was begun in 1861 and expanding the line directly into the anthracite fields in 1863. Except for a few minor raids at both ends of the line it was largely a period of calm – for the Northern Central at least.

But the calm would be shattered by the clash of 150,000 men from the two major armies, both inexorably moving toward their rendezvous with destiny at the tiny town of Gettysburg. General Robert E. Lee's Army of Northern Virginia and the long-suffering Army of the Potomac, headed by the newly-named General George Gordon Meade. Lee had reorganized his forces and feeling that time was running out for the Confederacy, decided to make a strategic thrust into the heart of the Union – into the Susquehanna Valley. Early on the morning of 3 June, Lee divided his forces and began his move northward in parallel groups on either side of the South Mountain – the first time that a major Confederate force had invaded the North.

News that Confederate troops were marching northward set off near panic in the border states, and on 27 June when initial units of Lee's forces descended on York, nervous citizens of Baltimore erected barriers in the streets. York itself was spared the torch, thanks to a controversial deal with General Jubal Early that allowed his forces to occupy the town unopposed. As the armies moved closer to his state, Pennsylvania Governor Andrew Curtin issued a proclamation asking the citizens of the Commonwealth to protect and defend "their own homes, firesides and property."

As we have discussed in previous *Triumph* volumes, PRR personnel assisted the Union Army staff in providing extremely valuable scouting of Lee's movements. In response to the imminent threat PRR set up a comprehensive defensive plan for the road, moving large numbers of locomotives and cars on both sides of the river to the safety of more northern and eastern areas, as well as packing up much of the valuable shop equipment at Altoona. Northern Central officials sus-

pended most operations south of Harrisburg on the 15th and by the 25th traffic on the threatened line was halted altogether.

Moving ahead of the main body in their usual role as the eyes and ears of the army, General J.E.B. Stuart's cavalry and other units under General Jubal Early began their deadly work of cutting the rail lines that they knew were crucial to the Union's supply network – the Northern Central main plus the line to Hanover and Gettysburg. The specific targets were the Northern Central Hanover Branch between Hanover and Hanover Junction, bridges north and south of York and the line to Wrightsville.

The fast-moving Confederate forces wreaked havoc against the road, defended by relatively small Union forces stretched thinly along the line from the Pennsylvania border to Harrisburg. They burned bridges, tore up rail, cut telegraph communication lines and destroyed equipment and other facilities. As the enemy troops neared Wrightsville, the fearful residents of Columbia across the river, aided by the 10th Pennsylvania Militia, set the Columbia-Wrightsville bridge afire on 30 June to prevent Lee's main forces from crossing the river (see *Triumph II*).

Portions of Lee's army moved to Bridgeport with the apparent intent to capture Harrisburg, but he instead wandered into a meeting engagement with Meade's army and pulled them away from the river, leaving PRR itself unscathed. It was to be the farthest northern advance of Confederate forces, but the cavalry had done their job well on the Northern Central: over 30 bridges and trestles were destroyed, large sections of rail were removed and twisted into grotesque shapes and long stretches of telegraph wires were cut into unusable pieces. And of course there was the Columbia-Wrightsville bridge to be rebuilt.

Although the Union Army's greatest challenge was stopping Lee's invasion of the North, the critical importance of the Northern Central to the overall war effort was clearly recognized. Repair of the line was given the highest priority in Washington. The formidable task was assigned to General Herman Haupt, Chief of Construction of the U. S. Military Rail Roads, established in February 1862 by newly-appointed Secretary of War Edwin Stanton. Haupt was an outstanding civil engineer who had done early survey work west of Harrisburg and was later Thomson's trusted assistant in PRR's formative years. In addition he was familiar with the Northern Central, having laid out the bridges on the Wrightsville line.

As head of the U.S.M.RR, Haupt assembled a group of skilled craftsmen, rugged frontier woodsmen and even freed slaves to fashion a railroad construction force that went on to produce spectacular railroad engineering accomplishments. He soon developed innovative techniques of using prefabricated components that allowed quick replacement of destroyed bridges, along with field methods to rapidly repair damage trackage.

He demonstrated a penchant for new techniques to fit particular situations. To support the Union attack on Lee's troops approaching Fredericksburg in late 1862, Haupt's forces constructed transfer bridges and developed a new float bridge design to move loaded freight cars down the Potomac from Alexandria to a nearby landing site. He even recommended to General Burnside that Union forces move quickly before Confederate troops became entrenched on the heights above the city. The attack failed, in part because Burnside waited too long and was not very bright but it was one of the earliest attempts, "to transport cars by water with their cargoes unbroken."

Haupt also demonstrated a genius for organizational skills. Upon taking over a rail line he quickly reorganized it, instilling timetable or train order discipline to efficiently operate it under often difficult conditions.

Responding to the invasion of Pennsylvania, he wasted no time, traveling via the PW&B main to Philadelphia and then westward on PRR, arriving in Harrisburg late in the evening on 30 June as acrid smoke from the smoldering bridge still hung in the air in the valley. After conferring with Scott and Curtin, the indomitable Haupt returned to Baltimore the next day and immediately set in motion an emergency program to restore the devastated line.

Haupt selected Westminster MD as the supply depot for Meade's army – it could be reached via the undamaged lower portion of the Northern Central, over the Green Spring Valley Branch and onto the Western Maryland, which was only partially completed. Haupt summoned Adna Anderson and 400 construction workers under the U.S.M.R.R. These forces labored around the clock to simultaneously repair the damaged sections of the Northern Central and upgrade the Western Maryland to handle the traffic volume needed.

As the two armies maneuvered into position and then clashed at Gettysburg, Haupt and Anderson had somehow managed to route 15 convoys (groups of five or six trains running together with armed guards on board for protection) into Westminster by 2 July with critical supplies for Meade's forces. When the fierce three-day battle that in many ways decided the nation's future finally ended, Haupt's rail operations had carried 1500 tons of materiel *daily* to supply the troops in the battle zone – and then returned with 2000-4000 wounded. Haupt's use of armed convoys and the prompt unloading and return of empty cars was crucial to the success of this undertaking.

The Herculean task of rebuilding the devastated rail lines was completed and all routes were returned to service on 15 July. Although most of the repair work was actually carried out after the cataclysmic battle was over – and consequently had little impact on the outcome – it did expedite the grisly task of evacuating the wounded to hospitals in Hanover, York and Baltimore. Haupt directed that the empty supply trains carry the wounded, some 11,000 of them "regardless of uniform," a decision that won him accolades from both sides after the war was finally over.

In a little over two weeks the military construction crews performed a near miracle. They repaired or rebuilt 33 bridges and laid several miles of new track and telegraph lines, all at no cost to the Northern Central. However the railroad still had the task of clearing away the huge piles of debris from the burned bridges, buildings and cars as well as additional repairs to the right of way. To make matters worse, as the work was nearing completion Mother Nature brought her own destruction to bear, unleashing heavy thunderstorms on 13-14 July, destroying several bridges that had just been rebuilt and causing the beleaguered line to shut down again for five days while this work was carried out. The cost of the cleanup work, plus lost business while the line was out of service, amounted to over $350 thousand.

The work completed, the Northern Central and the Hanover Branch had one more task to carry out associated with the Battle of Gettysburg. Lincoln traveled up the line on 18 November to make a few remarks at the dedication of a national cemetery on the site of the bloody battle. The two hours of stemwinding oration from Edward Everett were soon forgotten by the crowd of 15,000 present, but the less than 300 words that Lincoln spoke have resounded down through history.

There would be one more raid on the Northern Central, often referred to as the "Johnson and Gilmor Raid" after the officers leading it. This was another swift cavalry strike, part of a larger operation undertaken in July 1864 by General Early directed against Washington and to rescue Confederate prisoners being held near Point Lookout MD. The cavalry operation headed by General Bradley Johnson and Major Harry Gilmor was designed to cut rail lines and telegraph communications into the nation's capital, rescue the prisoners and destroy the Ashland Iron Works that supplied the Union Army. These forces arrived in Cockeysville on 9 July and set about their now familiar task.

They succeeded in destroying four large trestles and six smaller bridges south of Cockeysville as well as tearing up rail and cutting telegraph wires (including chopping down the poles). Although the raid disrupted rail transportation (including the Western Maryland) into Baltimore and Washington from the north and west for five days, the Union forces did prevent the prisoner release.

As an interesting sidelight, John Merryman, a Confederate sympathizer at whose estate, "Hayfields," Johnson and Gilmor set up headquarters during their brief stay in Cockeysville, convinced Johnson to spare the Ashland Iron Works and the nearby station, possibly in return for intelligence information.

The U.S.M.R.R. construction crews were engaged elsewhere at the time so the Northern Central quickly repaired the damage itself, at a cost of nearly $35 thousand. It was the last raid on the line and in fact the last Confederate incursion of any significance into Northern territory.

At this point we should reflect briefly on the role of railroads in the Civil War in general. The vaunted network of rail lines in the North certainly gave the Union Army a tremendous advantage in terms of moving both troops and materiel to the battle areas, but in the combat areas themselves the rail lines were at times both a blessing and a curse. If the forward rail lines were destroyed by enemy forces the armies dependent on rail transportation had to wait, sometimes for agonizing weeks, before moving into battle. None other than General William Tecumseh Sherman growled that, "Railroads are the weakest things in war . . . a single man with a match can destroy and cut off communications," and in his devastating march through the South he chose to have his armies live off the land rather than wait for supplies to be shipped over vulnerable extended rail lines.

Nevertheless, in January 1862 the war Congress authorized Lincoln to take over any railroad, "when in his judgment the public safety may require it." This authority was seldom used in the North, except to force the rail lines to keep rates down and give precedence to military traffic. As we have noted, following recommendations from then Assistant Secretary Scott in February, Stanton formally established the U.S.M.R.R. to operate the lines and rebuild them whenever, and wherever, necessary. Stanton appointed Daniel McCallum, a highly-effective former Erie RR executive, as superintendent on 11 February 1862, and at its peak the Military Railroads operated and maintained over 2100 miles of right of way, mostly in the South.

In the spring the U.S.M.R.R. would have one final operation to carry out before being disbanded. The long war was finally over, and the task was in many ways as much a part of rebuilding the nation as its construction operations had been. The somber assignment was to convey the assassinated President's body back home to its final resting place in Illinois but by a circuitous route to allow the maximum number of grieving citizens to view the casket. The route bore a striking resemblance to the President-elect's triumphant journey to Washington in 1861. Leaving the nation's capital on 21 April 1865 after the body had lain in state in the Capitol rotunda, the train proceeded via the B&O to Baltimore, where thousands of mourners paid their last respects to the slain President in the Exchange Building– a vastly different response than four years before.

From Baltimore the train followed a roundabout route, moving over the Northern Central to Harrisburg (see *Triumph II*), over PRR rails to Philadelphia, to New York City, north to Albany and then headed west toward Chicago. The entire operation was handled with the utmost dignity and precision. Everywhere its progress was marked by bells tolling and crepe hanging over doorways and the outpouring of a shocked citizenry mourning and paying its final tribute to their lost leader with a profusion of flags and flowers.

Starting even before the Civil War disruptions the Northern Central had embarked on a much-needed program to rebuild the line, and the wartime traffic bonanza provided the funds to do the job. Double-tracking the entire main between Baltimore and Harrisburg began in 1861 and continued with only brief interruptions during the raids. The work was completed as far as Relay House in 1862, Cockeysville in 1863 and reached York by the end of 1865.

The trackwork actually moved forward reasonably

well, but rebuilding the many bridges slowed progress. Double-tracking north of York as far as Sunbury was not completed until the early 1870s. The road also undertook to upgrade some of the coal-hauling branches, which were in generally poor condition.

The Northern Central again attempted to construct the Canton extension. Additional property was acquired and some work was actually carried out, but once again the project collapsed because of continuing legal problems and persistent uneasiness over the war.

However, the Northern Central's Baltimore terminal facilities were greatly improved during this period. On 1 April 1865, just as the war was finally winding down, the road opened a large new brick freight depot on Centre Street, just north of Calvert Station, which then was used for passenger service only. New stations were also constructed at Cockeysville and York, and the road purchased new locomotives and large numbers of freight cars, especially for hauling coal.

In 1863 President Anthony Warford (who was Simon Cameron's brother-in-law) resigned because of ill health and Cameron's son, J. Donald, assumed the office. The younger Cameron served for 11 years, guiding it through the war years and its postwar rebuilding and expansion. He also succeeded his father in the U. S. Senate and inherited his father's political power, albeit with considerably less controversy. His years marked the end of a turbulent era – after he resigned in 1874 the Cameron family's influence on the road would come to an end, and the position of president would henceforth be filled by a PRR executive.

After the war the Northern Central consolidated its control over several rail feeder lines for the transport of anthracite – as well as entering, along with PRR and the Reading, into the highly competitive field of coal production itself. We will explore these lines in some detail in a later volume in the *Triumph* series, but suffice it to say that by the early 1880s the Northern Central routed considerable tonnages of black diamonds to tidewater at both Philadelphia and Baltimore (and in 1884 northward to a terminal at Sodus Point, New York, on Lake Ontario).

In the process the Northern Central itself increasingly became a strategic partner in PRR's emerging role as one of the three or four eastern trunk lines. But PRR had a problem – actually several problems – all demanding solutions that quickly assumed the form of strategic objectives. The first was to somehow gain direct access to Baltimore's port facilities, bypassing the bottleneck through the nightmare of the congested streets. The second was to outmaneuver B&O and establish its own New York-Philadelphia-Baltimore-Washington route.

The New York-Philadelphia segment is discussed in *Triumph III* and *V* and the Philadelphia-Baltimore link in Chapter 2 of this volume, but we need to examine in detail how the crucial last portion between Baltimore and Washington was accomplished.

Like all of Thomson's efforts it involved obtaining control of a short but critical local line and then brandishing the sword to vanquish the enemy – in this case the B&O – in its own sacrosanct territory.

Well aware of both B&O's strong power base in Maryland – it had secured a state-authorized monopoly on the line to Washington – as well as being viewed as a foreign road in the state, Thomson shrewdly utilized three railroads appropriately chartered in Maryland to not only solve PRR's problems but also launch a very real invasion. In so doing he would pull off a spectacular corporate triumph virtually without equal.

The three companies were first and foremost the Northern Central, already poised to further invade B&O's hallowed ground, and two local independent roads, the Baltimore & Potomac RR and the Union RR. The B&P would provide PRR with its own legally sanctioned – albeit somewhat devious – route to the nation's capital, and the short Union RR would at long last enable it to not only access Baltimore's port area but also establish a key connection with the PW&B main to Philadelphia.

The decision to take over the B&P grew out of Garrett's hostile refusal to accept through service between Harrisburg and Washington. Cars were no longer transferred and baggage couldn't be checked through to the final destination – passengers had to use cabs to connect between the two lines (the Northern Central refunded the cost). It was Garrett's petulant and shortsighted unwillingness to cooperate on this endeavor – and on traffic rates in general – that set the wheels quietly but inexorably in motion.

To understand the background of this fascinating scenario, we first need to go back to 1833. In that year the State of Maryland had agreed to provide substantial financial support for the construction of the B&O's Washington Branch, in return receiving a percentage of the passenger revenues on the line. To protect the investment of both parties the agreement prohibited any new lines from being constructed between the two cities, thus giving the B&O a seemingly ironclad monopoly on the route.

But Thomson, this time with the willing assistance of Northern Central President Donald Cameron, found a way to break it. The key was a little-known line chartered in Maryland on 6 May 1853. This road's initial purpose was to build a line from Baltimore southward to the tobacco producing area in southern Maryland, but nothing was done for several years. Finally in December 1858 the company was formally organized and a decision taken for a route extending to a terminal on the Potomac River at Pope's Creek. From here the road envisioned a car ferry to Aquia Creek, Virginia, and then via the Richmond, Fredericksburg & Potomac RR to Richmond.

Surveys of the planned route were carried out in the following year, but lack of sufficient funds delayed the start of construction. And then on 12 July 1860, Oden Bowie, leader of a prominent tobacco-growing family in the region, was elected President of the struggling company. Bowie immediately went to Garrett for capital to build the line. Seeing no value in the enterprise, Garrett unwittingly turned him down. Bowie, who was also an astute politician well aware of PRR's desire to reach Baltimore's port facilities as well as gain access to Southern markets, then turned to Thomson and Cameron for support. Enough was forthcoming to allow some preliminary construction work to take place, but the outbreak of hostilities further delayed substantial progress.

In 1866, after the war had ended, a mysterious figure entered the arena. George W. Cass, a former PRR director and President of the Pittsburgh, Ft. Wayne & Chicago (one of PRR's prime western connections), and a group of investors associated with Lines West stepped forward and purchased the B&P outright. The reason for such a move became apparent the following year, bringing us to 1867. Suddenly Thomson and Cameron each came forward and invested $400 thousand in the nascent line, giving it the capital – for the first time in its existence – to undertake serious construction.

Thomson's real intent here was not to build an agricultural line to southern Maryland, but to take advantage of a provision in the original B&P charter allowing "lateral" branches "not to exceed 20 miles in length." Thomson and Cameron shrewdly envisioned that a line routed through Bowie MD would allow a "branch" to be built to the nation's capital and Baltimore fully within the terms of the charter. Bowie himself, now governor of Maryland as well as still President of the B&P, duly cooperated by pushing a bill through the Legislature enabling construction.

Triumph.

The line had been drawn in the sand of the arena, and Thomson and Cameron had boldly crossed it. Garrett, and for that matter, the State of Maryland, had been outwitted. We are forced to add that if this was a clash of titans, there was a gladiator missing from the arena or at least asleep on his sword while the others adroitly maneuvered around him. Again.

Construction work on the Pope's Creek line began in 1868 and was nearly half completed by the end of the year. The Washington "branch," however, ran into political difficulties – the line had readily obtained approval from District of Columbia officials, but the U. S. Congress was another matter. Thomson marshaled a formidable lobbying team led by heavyweights Tom Scott and Donald Cameron, working with now-Senator Simon Cameron. The stakes were enormous, but in the end they delivered – in spades – securing congressional approval for not only a route carrying the line across the center of the Mall to an impressive terminal at 6th and B Streets, but also providing direct access to the railroads entering the city from the South.

This was accomplished by means of the "Long Bridge" across the Potomac, constructed by the U.S.M.R.R. during the war to provide secure military access to Virginia. Operation of this key bridge was assigned to the Alexandria & Washington RR, which connected with the B&O, and Garrett entertained his own ideas about using it to extend his line southward after the war. But PRR again emerged with a spectacular triumph, winning congressional legislation in June 1870 that not only gave it access but amazingly, *exclusive* use of the bridge – once again thwarting Garrett's ambitions.

The outcome was a spectacular testament to PRR's influence – and an unabashed display of its rapidly growing political clout. The titans had clashed, and the PRR team had emerged with a glorious victory. To make it even sweeter, this time the arena was the hallowed – albeit occasionally raucous – halls of the U.S. Congress.

The "branch" to Washington was opened on 2 July 1872, but the difficult entrance into Baltimore was progressing slowly, and the B&P had to use a temporary station at Lafayette Street in West Baltimore.

Thomson's strategic plan was gradually coming together, but the final critical links between the Northern Central, the B&P and the PW&B would take a while longer. We sometimes wonder if Garrett knew what was really happening to his railroad, and if he did, whether he comprehended that he didn't stand any real chance of doing anything about it. But that didn't stop him from trying, at every available opportunity.

Within the city of Baltimore, Thomson and Cameron had three primary challenges remaining: 1) to connect the B&P to the Northern Central to allow through service to Washington, 2) to join the B&P with the PW&B – providing the vital link in routing through traffic between New York, Philadelphia and Washington – and 3) to finally extend the Northern Central to the Canton waterfront.

The solution to all of these challenges was to build two tunnels across the north side of the city. The first, actually three tunnels end-to-end, would allow the B&P to enter the city and connect with the Northern Central. The second tunnel extended the line eastward to connect with the PW&B, allowing a branch to the Canton dock area. Between them a new "union" station was constructed at Charles Street to serve the B&P, the Northern Central, the PW&B and also the Western Maryland (the latter line used Northern Central and B&P trackage from Fulton Junction, just west of the B&P tunnels).

The first set of three tunnels, together known as the "B&P Tunnel," was the longer and – because of the terrain and location under a growing residential area – the most difficult to construct. Most of its 7500-ft. total length was built using the cut-and-cover method – the remaining 1000 ft. used the costly "drift" method to minimize disruption of existing streets and buildings. This involved digging small holes from the top, inverting "crown bars" and then excavating the tunnel downward, installing the lining as it progressed.

As part of this project the Northern Central main into the city was relocated, providing better gradients. It originally entered the city through the Jones Falls Valley, left the valley to reach Bolton Depot, and then reentered it again at Chase Street to access Calvert Station and the old branches to the waterfront. The new right of way continued down the valley to a point just east of the tunnel, where it connected with the B&P line. This connection alongside Jones Falls became forever known as "B&P Junction." The line then continued southeastward through the new Union Station to rejoin the old line near Chase Street.

The B&P tunnel project was completed and opened for traffic on 29 June 1873. The entire $3 million cost was underwritten equally by PRR and the Northern Central. Once the tunnels were opened both the Northern Central and PRR through trains began operating on the route to Washington, stopping at Union Station (also known as Potomac Station because of its connections) and then continued on to Calvert Station, convenient to the downtown area.

The old line was then abandoned and torn up, although the northern portion remained as a short freight spur into Bolton Depot. Extensive new car and locomotive shops were constructed at Mt. Vernon Yard on the original main just north of North Street. The old shops were torn down and Bolton Yard was converted to a coaling facility.

When the "Union Tunnel" was completed a month later the link to the PW&B was made, and through New York-Washington PW&B trains could then travel on this route, avoiding the incessant conflicts with the B&O over rates. Thomson's vision for a PRR-controlled East Coast line was moving closer to fulfillment.

The second tunnel project also allowed the Northern Central to build its long-delayed extension to the Canton dock area. These two objectives were accomplished by means of the second independent line, known as the Union Railroad, whose background is a fascinating one as well.

As discussed earlier the City of Baltimore had agreed to provide financial support for the Northern Central when it was chartered in 1854, provided that extensions were built on the northern end to Sunbury and on the southern end to the Canton dock area, thus facilitating anthracite (and flour and grain) traffic into the city. However the Canton extension became bogged down in seemingly endless litigation and then was further delayed by the war. As a result the city finally sold its holdings in the Northern Central back to the road (at a loss) in 1865.

The prolonged legal challenges against the B&S and later the Northern Central for access to the Canton area, as it turns out, were largely the result of behind the scenes political and legal maneuvering by the B&O, which feared the loss of traffic on its Pratt Street line and because of its investment in the Locust Point terminal which it opened in 1849 on the south side of the harbor.

To access the harbor in its early years the B&S had initially built a line in 1839 jointly with the B&O from

Bolton along Howard Street to the B&O's Pratt Street line. The B&S then used this trackage to access the piers (using animal power) along Pratt Street and the City Dock area on the east side of the harbor. Because of continuing friction with the B&O under this arrangement, the B&S built its own line to the City Docks in 1840. It was still agonizingly slow, involving animal power plodding through increasingly congested city streets, but at least it had its own trackage.

The Canton Company had been chartered in 1828 to develop the large waterfront area known by that name on the southeast side of the harbor. This large undeveloped area offered excellent potential for deep-water piers, but it had no rail access even though the PW&B main ran through its northern edge. Efforts by the B&S and then the Northern Central to reach the area had come to no avail, thanks to the B&O machinations, and development of the property languished for several years. The partially completed trackage built by the B&S was torn up and the right of way eventually sold.

Because of the years of conflict and inaction, after the war the idea was advanced by forward-thinking Baltimore merchants, city officials and others to construct a union line to the Canton waterfront open to all railroads willing to provide financial support. The impetus for action was the prolonged delays caused by the now notorious Baltimore bottleneck, particularly during the war, which clearly demonstrated the need for improved rail access.

In 1866 the Canton Company itself obtained a charter for the Union Railroad, authorizing it to connect with the Northern Central at Guilford Avenue and the PW&B just north of Canton and extend to the waterfront. The B&O was invited to join in this open "federation of railroads,' but Garrett adamantly – and once again shortsightedly – refused to participate because it already had its own extensive marine facility at Locust Point and at the time he had no plans to expand the road's operations north of Baltimore.

Construction work began in 1867 but was interrupted several times over the next several years. Finally on 2 May 1870 the Canton Company took over the line, investing heavily in the struggling road. With added financial aid from PRR and the Northern Central, construction resumed in the spring of 1871.

Completed on 24 July 1873 at a cost of $3 million, the double-track line ran from Union Junction, just east of Union Station, through a 3410-ft. tunnel and then southeastward to Bay View where it connected with the PW&B main. A branch then ran from a point just west of Bay View to the Canton waterfront.

Opening service to the Canton area had a salutary effect almost immediately. Foremost among the industries, not surprisingly, was flour – the Canton Company constructed a 100,000 bu. elevator known as "Gardner's Union Elevator," and in 1876 the Northern Central built a large 300,000 bu. structure (Elevator No. 1), followed by a still larger one (No. 3) three years later. Other industries moved in, including iron works and ore and coal piers. As a result Northern Central anthracite traffic increased 500 per cent the first year. Over the next few years a whole range of commerce developed, including distilleries (well, there was bountiful grain to be had), produce and petroleum terminals and even textiles.

Although awash in hyperbole, Baltimore could now boast of having the "finest port on the Atlantic," and PRR could take satisfaction in the published article that concluded that "the stranglehold that the B&O held on the port was destroyed."

It was all too true.

In 1880 the Northern Central purchased property for construction of a large rail yard to serve the rapidly growing terminal. When this facility was completed six years later it would have a capacity of over 2000 cars, testament to the volume of traffic on the line and the potential value of the Canton terminal. During this period the Northern Central entered into negotiations for the purchase of the Union RR, which was completed in the spring of 1882.

With the Baltimore connections in place Thomson had achieved his goal of a PRR-controlled line from Harrisburg to Washington, and more importantly, put in place the strategic links to anchor a critical East Coast north-south route from New York City to the nation's capital and the South. By the time the Baltimore terminal connections were completed he had secured his own line from Philadelphia to the New Jersey waterfront, opposite New York (see *Triumph II, III* and *V*). Although the remaining middle link from Philadelphia to Baltimore was still in the hands of the independently-owned PW&B – which continued to handle both PRR and B&O traffic – at least the PRR-controlled lines through Baltimore bypassed the bottleneck street operations that the B&O still had to endure.

However the cost of the southern terminal improvements and the necessary rebuilding of the northern branches as well as upgrading of the mainline to handle the steadily increasing traffic took its toll on Northern Central revenues. As a result pressures from stockholders who had holdings in both roads had surfaced during the war to lease the road to PRR, and the issue arose again in 1873, when an independent-minded stockholders' committee voted to make an offer to its financial benefactor.

Things came to a head on 8 December 1874 when Cameron and the entire Northern Central Board, apparently tired of the whole issue, suddenly resigned *en masse*. A stockholder delegation made its proposal to Scott (who had replaced Thomson after his death in June), but the combination of the Panic of 1873 and an investigation of PRR's finances by its own rebellious stockholder committee (see *Triumph II*) prevented him from accepting any further expansion opportunities at that time. After protracted negotiations it was finally agreed that the Northern Central would continue with its own operating management, but under the direction of the PRR executive as its president.

It was the end of the Cameron family era just as the road was entering its "glory years." Revenues grew dramatically during the 1880s, rising from $5 million to $13.5 million in 1913, the road's last full year of independent operation. This was largely because of a corresponding growth in anthracite traffic, but grain and lumber were major contributors as well. During this period several other roads, including of course PRR but also the Erie and the Philadelphia & Erie, operated trains over the Northern Central under trackage rights agreements.

Under new President George Roberts (Scott resigned on 1 June 1880 because of ill health) the Northern Central – and indirectly PRR – extended its control at both ends of the line. After PRR completed its takeover of the PW&B in 1881 (see Chapter 2) the Northern Central purchased all of the outstanding shares of the Union RR in the following year, giving it direct ownership of the Canton road. That same year, at Roberts' direction, a new line was laid along the Susquehanna west of Harrisburg, connecting the Northern Central to PRR's recently-rebuilt double-track Rockville Bridge and the Northern Central's wooden Dauphin Bridge was abandoned.

In 1884 the Northern Central fulfilled a long-sought dream of its original Baltimore investors by taking over the Sodus Bay & Southern, giving it a Great Lakes terminus at Sodus Point – although by this time it was a part of PRR's overall strategy to ex-

pand its coal operations rather than a Baltimore-based endeavor.

Finally in 1889 the Northern Central built a short spur from the Canton yard to connect with the Baltimore & Sparrows Point RR, constructed and owned by the Maryland Steel Company (a subsidiary of the Pennsylvania Steel Company), to serve that company's large new steel mill. This essentially completed the Northern Central's expansion, although several feeder lines were built in the last decades of the 19th Century.

During the 1890s the Northern Central – at the direction of PRR – embarked on its last complete upgrading as an independent line. Steel rail was laid, old iron and wooden bridges were replaced with new steel or stone ones (some quite impressive) and several stations were rebuilt, notably the ones at York and in Baltimore itself where a substantial new brick and stone Union Station, with a large iron train shed, was opened on 1 April 1886 in place of the original frame structure. In January 1893 the Northern Central completed the elevation of the Union RR right of way within the city limits to avoid the congestion at grade crossings and two additional tracks were opened in November of that year on the elevated line between Canton Junction and Biddle Street.

This program of rebuilding and consolidation was followed by an even stronger one after George Roberts died in early 1897 (followed by the brief interim presidency of Frank Thomson) and the reigns of power were assumed by A. J. Cassatt. Cassatt's grand vision for PRR was to substantially improve the railroad's physical plant, constructing new bridges and yards – and even entire lines where necessary – to allow it to efficiently handle large increases in freight traffic with minimal interference with fast passenger operations (see the preceding, and subsequent, *Triumph* volumes for various aspects of his wide-ranging 1902 Improvements program).

For the Northern Central, Cassatt's plans significantly improved its connections and facilities, but at the same time set in motion a diminishing role for the line in the overall scheme of things, largely because of its grades. First was a simplification of freights operations in the York area and in Baltimore. Operation of the York & Wrightsville (originally part of the B&S main) and the York, Hanover & Frederick Branches, both previously operated by PRR, was transferred to the Northern Central on 1 June 1902, giving it control of both lines from York.

In Baltimore, the Northern Central on 1 November 1904 assumed operation of local freight operations on the southern end of the old PW&B main (which had become the PB&W President Street Branch) between Bay View Yard and President Street Station, into the inner harbor. Passenger trains continued to operate over this route, from Bay Junction (Orangeville) to the station. In 1913 the Northern Central took over the Baltimore & Sparrows Point RR, giving it a direct route to that growing plant.

But the greatest improvement on the Northern Central after the turn of the century came in the Harrisburg area. The capital of Pennsylvania had become the center where PRR's Susquehanna and Cumberland Valley operations and the east-west passenger and freight mainlines came together, creating another major traffic bottleneck. Cassatt's bold solution was to construct a vast new yard along the banks of the river at Enola, on the opposite side of the river from the city. This yard was intended to replace the Northern Central's yard at Marysville, which was hemmed in from further expansion by the surrounding mountain ridges. It would serve the Northern Central, C&PD, Philadelphia & Erie, the CV – and the Atglen & Susquehanna, a new low-grade freight line running parallel to the east-west main (see *Triumph II* for construction photos of Enola and the Low-Grade line). After completion of Enola in 1905-6 freight traffic would increasingly be routed over other, lower-grade lines, e.g. the A&S and the C&PD, and diverted off the Northern Central.

Cassatt planned improvements north of Harrisburg as well. The Northern Central Connecting Railway, a 32-mile cutoff between Selinsgrove Junction, south of Sunbury, and Aqueduct Station, west of Duncannon, would have provided a bypass of the Harrisburg area for bituminous coal traffic to northeastern destinations vs. Sunbury. This project never came to fruition, however, and like a number of Cassatt's plans, expired with his death in 1906. However a new yard at Northumberland, just north of Sunbury, was completed and put into operation on 6 August 1911, greatly improving the classification of coal trains headed both north to Sodus Point and south to Baltimore.

A massive new Union Station was opened in Baltimore in 1911 (see Chapter 6), replacing the previous structure less than 20 years old. Although this station was built primarily for New York-Washington traffic, Northern Central trains continued to use it. Many local trains still terminated at Calvert Station, closer to downtown.

The Northern Central during its glory years became a valuable connecting rail line to the West. Reflecting its status, it constructed many new stations, some following a standardized frame design, but several were unique, architecturally distinctive structures designed by commercial architects including noted Philadelphia architect Frank Furness. These new stations were built to accommodate a growing tourist clientele, attracted to the line's beautiful scenery and resort destinations, including the Susquehanna Valley, the Finger Lakes Region in New York State and even Niagara Falls (the latter via a New York Central connection).

Just as the coal and resort traffic was reaching its peak several events occurred that would cause the Northern Central to begin a long decline. Particularly damaging to the road, with its heavy dependence on coal traffic, was the federal Hepburn Act, passed in 1906 as part of Theodore Roosevelt's wide-ranging reform efforts. The "commodities clause" of this legislation, enforced by Federal legal actions to follow, prohibited the nation's railroads from owning the sources of the freight commodities they carried, particularly mining companies. Thus the Northern Central – and ultimately PRR itself – were forced to divest themselves of their coal mining holdings, reducing revenues from these operations.

The impact of the Hepburn Act was further exacerbated by the general – and rapid – decline in the use of coal, particularly anthracite on which the Northern Central was heavily dependent. Although bituminous coal was still in heavy demand, increasingly petroleum products were being used by industry, in home heating and of course in transportation.

A lesser factor was the equally rapid decline of the canal system on which the Northern Central was also dependent for traffic at transfer sites. The S&T Canal between Wrightsville and Havre de Grace was abandoned in 1894, and the notorious 1889 flood (see *Triumph I* and *IV*) destroyed large portions of Pennsylvania's Susquehanna Canal, with the last operating section between Columbia and Northumberland abandoned in 1901. On top of these elements, the depression of the 1890s and the mergers of the 1896-1902 period combined with the short-lived but serious Panic of 1907 resulted in the closing of a large number of mills and factories along the line, further reducing traffic and revenues.

The declining financial outlook resulted in the

resurfacing of the idea of leasing the Northern Central to PRR in 1910. In 1911, after lengthy discussions and analysis of the road's options, a special stockholder's committee recommended leasing the entire railroad, effective 1 January of that year. The proposal was overwhelmingly approved by the stockholders (other than PRR), but lawsuits filed in both Maryland and Pennsylvania opposing the lease caused PRR management to defer implementation.

In 1912 a dramatic downturn in coal traffic put the line in further peril, causing the opponents of the lease to withdraw their objections. This led to Samuel Rea, now joint President of PRR and the Northern Central, to openly support the lease. Thus on 29 July 1914 the Northern Central officially ceased life as an independent railroad, ending 60 years of sometimes turbulent, sometimes glorious existence and making it a full member of the growing PRR family. The name was rather quickly removed from timetables, locomotives and cars, but in the hearts of the local patrons it was still the Northern Central, and PRR remained the outsider.

Under the 999-year lease all Northern Central lines came under the control of PRR operating divisions. On 1 January 1918 PRR leased the PB&W – which by that time included the B&P – and on 1 April of that year it also leased the Union RR, thus giving it direct control of all of its diverse operations in the Baltimore area. A massive modernization program was initiated for the Northern Central, gradually bringing most of the line up to PRR standards.

Although some local passenger runs were discontinued, in the pre-World War I years an impressive array of trains still operated on Northern Central trackage. Some 35 trains departed Calvert Station daily for Harrisburg and/or intermediate points, nine trains operated between Harrisburg and Sunbury and nine trains each way plied various portions of the Columbia-Frederick Branch via Wrightsville and York. Through trains on the main offered parlor, sleeper and dining car service – through sleepers were operated between Washington and such distant points as Rochester, Buffalo, Pittsburgh, Cleveland, Cincinnati, Detroit, Chicago and St. Louis. Even under PRR aegis the Northern Central still retained elements of its glory years.

Consideration was given to reduce grades and curvature on the line during the early years of World War I and again in 1929 as an alternative to shifting the passenger trains to the C&PD, but neither plan was carried out.

World War I brought heavy traffic to the line – which took its toll on both equipment and the right of way – but increasing integration with overall PRR freight operations began to have their impact as well. From the 1920s onward through freight traffic in the Susquehanna Valley was gradually routed over the C&PD (see Chapter 4) because of its significantly lower grades, and by 1930 the Northern Central was utilized primarily for passenger service, local freights and traffic specifically to York. As overall freight volume on the Northern Central declined, so did the economies of the local communities it served and ultimately the entire line suffered.

PRR electrified the heavily-traveled New York-Washington main beginning in 1928 (see Chapter 2) and the Low-Grade and Port Road freight lines 10 years later, but traffic density on the Northern Central didn't warrant the investment and it remained under steam power (wires were strung on the multiple-track section between Wago Junction and Enola along the A&S Branch). As part of the north-south mainline electrification program PRR announced plans to enlarge both the B&P and Union Tunnels in Baltimore (see Chapter 6). A second Union Tunnel, parallel to the original bore, was completed and opened on 12 November 1934, but the B&P Tunnel had to settle for only a partial renovation. The B&P project was to include a new station and wye connection with the Northern Central, eliminating the need for Harrisburg trains to run backward between Washington and Baltimore, but these plans never came to fruition.

With increasing use of motor vehicles – and in some areas interurban trolley lines – by the late 1920s PRR began to decrease its local passenger service everywhere and because of its primarily rural nature the Northern Central was particularly vulnerable. Through trains generally continued, although shorter in length, but local service on the main and on several branches was cut in half. Where it remained, economical Brill gas-electric cars took over the duties on several lines from locomotive-hauled trains. These were affectionately referred to as "doodlebugs" elsewhere, but on the Parkton locals they were derisively dubbed, "Ruxton Rockets."

The Depression took a further toll on the road, and by 1939 local service all but disappeared, except the five remaining Parkton trains. Surprisingly, although it too was reduced, through train service continued to operate. One could still ride a sleeper from Washington to Midwestern points, and in 1938 PRR even re-equipped the *Liberty Limited*, its flagship Washington-Chicago train (intended to compete with the B&O's prestigious *Capitol Limited*), with streamlined cars.

World War II brought a temporary reprieve from the decline, but severely strained the line's capability in the process. During the war years passenger traffic quadrupled and freight tonnage more than doubled on the line. Trains hauling coal, steel products and other wartime materiel to Canton, Sparrows Point shipyards and East Coast military supply depots were given priority, followed by troop trains to the various bases.

Once the war was over the decline resumed, slowly at first but then it accelerated to the point that by the late 1970s the Northern Central and many of the towns it served were ghosts of their former selves. They were victims of all the sinister forces affecting PRR and most other eastern railroads – the dramatic growth of government-subsidized highway and air travel, high labor costs – and for the Northern Central in particular the virtually complete loss of anthracite traffic. The process was painful but inexorable. Each reduction in service in turn adversely affected the remaining business.

Through passenger service was drastically cut back in the late 1950s and on 27 June 1959 the near-legendary Parkton local was discontinued, thus ending the remaining suburban operation. The Green Spring Branch, which saw very heavy military traffic during the war, was partially abandoned in 1959 and torn up the following year. Reflecting this decline, the second main track was removed beginning in 1954 and by the end of the decade the Northern Central was essentially a single-track line between Baltimore and York.

Surprisingly, through passenger service lingered into the 1960s – in reality mostly mail traffic and thus patronage was light – and by the time of Amtrak's takeover of all intercity passenger operations in 1971 there was only one lonely train remaining on the line between Baltimore and Harrisburg, and even lonelier alternate-day service north of there to Buffalo. Amtrak refused to take over either run, and thus on 1 May 1971 the last ghostly remnant of the once-proud Northern Central passenger service came to an end.

As for freight operations, PRR optimistically inaugurated through TrucTrain piggyback service between Baltimore and Midwestern terminals in the mid-1960s. This train ran on the Northern Central for

a time until tunnel clearances on the Port Road could be enlarged, and then was rerouted. Local service, however, continued to be cut back. The bridge across the Susquehanna to Columbia was demolished in 1964, and the York-Wrightsville Branch itself was abandoned in 1969. As anthracite traffic dried up, the branches north of Harrisburg were gradually abandoned, and other traffic was shifted to former New York Central lines after the Penn-Central merger. With the 1976 Conrail takeover of the branch to Shamokin, that traffic was rerouted to former Reading trackage – this line was later sold to a private operator (we will deal with these northern lines in a later *Triumph* volume). After the collapse of Penn Central many of the remaining branches simply withered on what was left of the vine.

The ultimate killer of the Northern Central (and many other mid-Atlantic rail lines), however, was Mother Nature, in the form of Hurricane Agnes – officially downgraded to a tropical storm but still capable of dumping torrential rains on the area. The resultant flooding in late June 1972 ravaged the entire line, particularly the section between Cockeysville and York where numerous bridges and sections of track were washed out. Penn Central refused to restore anything but the Baltimore-Cockeysville segment, despite an order from the Maryland Public Service Commission.

A long, complex process ensued, involving endless ICC hearings, fervent boosterism by local businesses and of course intense political maneuvering. Reminiscent of earlier rivalries, sections of the line became political footballs between Maryland and Pennsylvania – on 27 June 1973 the Pennsylvania Department of Transportation acted independently purchasing the line from New Freedom to York to provide a connection for the Stewartstown RR, which was largely untouched by the storm. All the efforts to retain the line between Cockeysville and the Pennsylvania line proved futile, however, and the ICC approved the abandonment in 1975. The track was completely torn up by early 1976.

On April 1 of that year Conrail took over operation of the line between Baltimore and Cockeysville, from York northward to Williamsport and between Elmira and Sodus Point in New York State. The resurgent Ma & Pa (with little of its own trackage left) obtained the lines within York and from York to Frederick although sections of this branch were later abandoned. One success story was the New Freedom-York segment, which was restored with Pennsylvania state funds and the Stewartstown RR as designated operator. The rehabilitated line was reopened on 14 January 1985, although traffic remained light.

After seemingly endless studies and numerous proposals over several years, the State of Maryland in 1990 purchased the Conrail branch from Baltimore to Cockeysville for new light-rail commuter service, with Conrail retaining freight trackage rights, primarily to the large quarry at Texas MD. Service began two years later to suburbs that had first developed along the Northern Central in its glory years.

The Frederick Branch

The Frederick Branch, one of the feeder lines into the Northern Central, actually developed independently from the main and then moved through a rather convoluted corporate history for such a short segment. This branch resulted from a consolidation of three short, end-to-end lines that in turn connected with the Y&WRR, the original B&S line to Wrightsville. The first segment was the tiny (7-mile) Littlestown RR, built between Hanover and Littlestown and completed in 1858. This railroad soon came under control of the Western Maryland through the connecting Hanover Junction & Gettysburg. The second section of this branch was the Frederick & Pennsylvania RR, built from Frederick MD to a connection with the Littlestown RR and opened on 8 October 1872.

These lines provided the small town of Hanover with two rail connections – both to Baltimore – via the WM directly and to the B&O at Frederick. With all their earlier enmity directed at Philadelphia, the citizens of York County nevertheless looked toward an additional rail outlet north to Harrisburg and eastward to the Quaker City. With this objective in mind, the Hanover & York RR was chartered on 21 April 1873 and the line between these two towns was completed in 1875.

And then an interesting development changed the entire orientation of this small complex of lines. Although PRR had turned down a lease of the Northern Central the previous year, it did obtain control by lease of the H&Y on 5 July 1875 and took over operation of that road, thus thwarting both the B&O and WM from securing these links.

Things remained largely unchanged on the rural lines for nearly 20 years until the H&Y RR took over the Littlestown RR in 1892, after the WM completed its line to Hagerstown and decided to construct its own branch to York. In 1896 PRR purchased the moribund F&P at foreclosure, reorganizing it as the Frederick & Northern RR, and on 1 January 1897 it consolidated the F&N with the H&Y, forming the York, Hanover & Frederick RR.

The first President of the YH&F was none other than Samuel Rea, who just happened to be a PRR Vice President (see *Triumph V* for more on Rea's successful career with the parent road). PRR took over operation of the combined York & Wrightsville and YH&F on 1 March. As previously noted control of these lines was transferred to the Northern Central in 1902 and then included in the PRR lease of that road in 1914.

Operations on the Frederick Branch were generally similar to the Northern Central except without the through traffic and on a smaller scale. Passenger service initially ran round trips between Frederick and Columbia (actually Lancaster, where they connected with east-west mainline trains), plus intermediate runs – Columbia to York, Columbia to Littlestown and Bruceville (later Keymar) to Frederick. Service was cut in the pre-World War I years because of competition from the York Railways interurban line and gradually reduced further during the Depression years until it was finally discontinued altogether after World War II on 14 August 1948.

Local freights primarily served the industrial centers of York (where it was based) and to a lesser extent Wrightsville, Spring Grove and Hanover. PRR and WM had joint trackage rights along their parallel right of way through the West York industrial district, and interchange occurred at Lincoln Yard. Traffic declined steadily because of truck competition, and in 1958 the connection with the Low-Grade Line at Columbia was severed and five years later the line was abandoned to Hellam, west of Wrightsville, and the historic Columbia-Wrightsville bridge torn down.

Traffic continued to decline until the line was divided up among several small operators – the Ma & Pa, the Maryland Midland and the Walkersville Southern – thus the former PRR branch came full circle to being run by several independent lines, with a mainline connection at York to a large system.

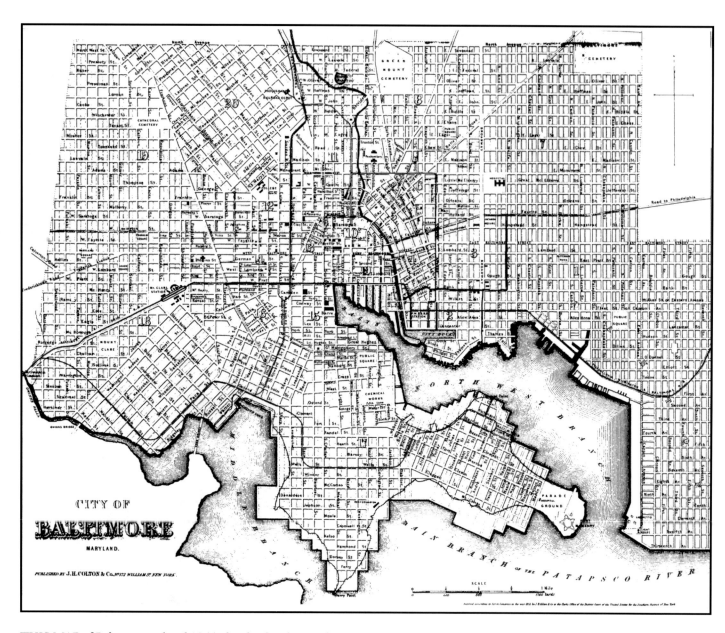

THIS MAP of Baltimore is dated 1855, shortly after the Northern Central was formed. The original B&S mainline enters the city through the Jones Falls Valley (top center), climbs out of it and runs along Cathedral Street to Bolton Station. From there it swings eastward and follows Jones Falls again to its main terminus at Calvert Station, opened in 1850. A freight branch runs east from the main on Monument Street and then turns south on Central Avenue to the City Dock area. Another freight branch runs south from Bolton Depot on Howard Street to the B&O's Pratt Street line.

Also shown are the B&O main to Mt. Clare Station at left, the freight branch following the waterfront to the terminal at Locust Point and the line connecting them to Camden Station.

CHARTERED one year after the pioneering B&O, the B&S was the result of an earnest desire on the part of Baltimore merchants and investors to build a railroad up the Susquehanna Valley to tap the riches of central Pennsylvania as well as transshipment of Baltimore-bound river traffic. Frustrated by the less than stellar results from earlier efforts with turnpikes and canals – and Pennsylvania's repeated thwarting of these nevertheless valiant attempts – Baltimore turned to railroads as their salvation, first the B&O to the West in 1827 and then in the following year the B&S.

Launched in 1829 with the appropriate celebrations, festive parade and the requisite oratory, the line suffered repeated fits and starts caused by financial, political and natural obstacles, but it finally reached York (via the York & Maryland Line RR) in 1838. Obviously wanting to convey the message that the trains were finally *running*, the line published this broadside on 1 June 1840 when the line was opened to its terminal on the Susquehanna at Wrightsville. At this time it offered one passenger train in each direction daily between Baltimore and Wrightsville, plus one additional local between York and Wrightsville, with connections to the Philadelphia & Columbia and the Pennsylvania State Canals at Columbia.

J. W. Wolf/F. A. Wrabel Collection

HORSEPOWER – The date of this photo is 1917, but things looked very much the same in the 1850s, when Baltimore's early railroads – B&O and B&S alike – were forced to use animal power to haul freight along the street trackage in the downtown area. This "string team" was paused from its labors on the City Block Route.

HORSEPOWER of a different sort. Baltimore's famous (they were also used in Jersey City), if ungainly, electric tractors were built by Altoona in 1916-17 to replace the string teams. The battery-powered units were housed and recharged in "the stable" (as opposed to garage or enginehouse) located east of the Calvert Station yards, property later sold for expansion of the jail. Amazingly, they remained in service at least until 1955. Here we see unit 5 assigned to the New Street area posed with its train crew ca. 1917.

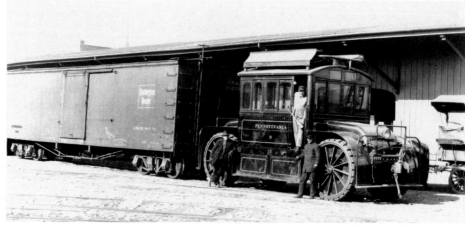

Gunnarsson Collection/Railroad Museum of Pennsylvania (PHMC)

ALTHOUGH the infamous 1861 Baltimore Riot involved Union troops attempting to travel through the streets from the PW&B to reach threatened Washington DC via the B&O, it was the Northern Central that suffered by far the most severe and extensive damage at the hand of inflamed Baltimore citizens attempting to cut off further Northern troop movement through their city. The ensuing clash, an ominous portent of things to come that resulted in the Civil War's first casualties and railroad damage, was the direct consequence of hauling rail cars by animal power through Baltimore's congested city streets – and which ultimately led to vastly improved rail connections in the city after the bloody conflict was finally over.

IT'S DIFFICULT to know how to best characterize Simon Cameron: banker, business entrepreneur, railroad officer, scoundrel, astute and powerful politician – and a charismatic public servant with an extraordinary talent for using public offices for personal gain. Yet he was a critical player in Thomson's grand strategy to gain control of the Northern Central for its thrust into Baltimore that vanquished the B&O's monopoly control and ultimately led to PRR's triumphant takeover of the critical New York-Washington corridor.

As Lincoln's controversial first Secretary of War and a director of the Northern Central, he used his positions and pervasive influence to dispense war contracts to the line that substantially increased traffic and revenues. After the April 1861 Baltimore riots he ordered Northern troops to fight their way through the rebellious city, but Lincoln countermanded the order in an effort to restore calm. The embarrassed president finally appointed Cameron as ambassador to Russia in 1862 to get rid of him.

However the irrepressible Cameron resigned the post in the following year and was re-elected to the Senate in 1867 and in that role again assisted PRR in securing exclusive control of the Potomac River bridge into Washington. An early supporter of Lincoln and the fledgling Republican Party (which landed him the Cabinet position in the first place), he built a powerful state machine in Pennsylvania that controlled the state government in the 1860s and 1870s. He resigned from the U. S. Senate in 1877 over President Rutherford B. Hayes' refusal to extend the appointment of Cameron's son as Secretary of War, and eight days later the compliant Pennsylvania Legislature named his son to succeed him in the Senate. The elder Cameron retired to his 120-acre estate, Donegal, in Lancaster County, where he died on 26 June 1889 at the age of 91.

Gunnarsson Collection/Railroad Museum of Pennsylvania (PHMC)

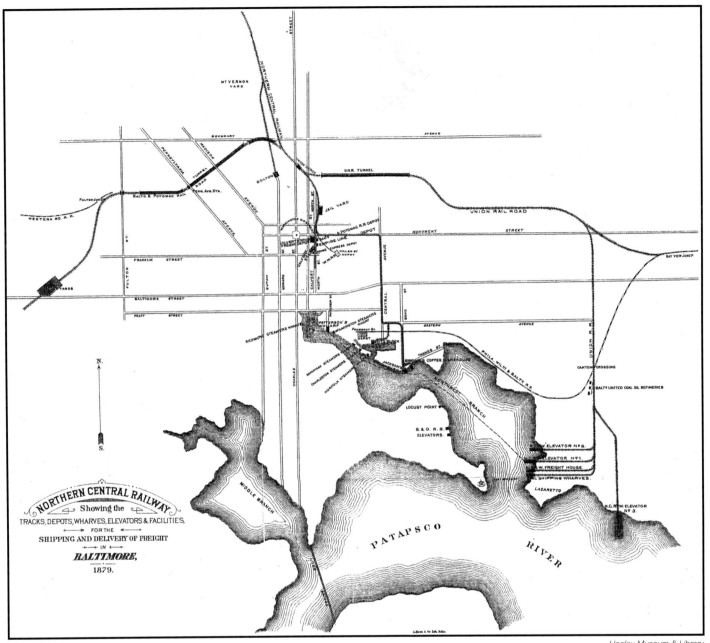

Hagley Museum & Library

BETTER THAN ANY OTHER that we have found, this superb Baltimore map clearly shows the Northern Central, Baltimore & Potomac and Union Railroads as well as the Western Maryland in 1879, after completion of the PRR-sponsored reworking of the connections through the city to eliminate the street bottleneck – the B&P and Union Tunnels, the strategic PW&B connection and the long-delayed Canton extension (B&O trackage is conspicuously missing, perhaps representing a tactical withdrawal as a result of the PRR-engineered invasion of its home arena).

The map is worthy of close study to identify the already numerous "depots, wharves, elevators & facilities for the shipping and delivery of freight." At the top center are the Mt. Vernon Yard and Shops, at the junction of the spur (the remnant of the old B&S right of way) connecting the main to the Bolton Depot, at this time used as a local passenger station and freight transfer facility. Following the relocated mainline we come to the first Union Depot and then continue south to the Calvert Street passenger and freight depots. The B&P line enters through the three tunnels from the west (railroad southward), connecting with the Northern Central at B&P Junction (the WM also used this revised routing, continuing on to its Hillen Street depot).

The Union RR runs east from Union Junction to the strategic connection with the PW&B at Bay View, with the PW&B continuing on to its President Street terminal and the Canton line running south to the elevators and wharves on the east side of the harbor. The old freight line also runs from Calvert Station east and then south to the old City Dock area, with additional wharves and warehouses lining the waterfront on either side.

IT TOOK two tunnels and several new connecting lines – constructed at a cost of over $6 million – to overcome the bottleneck. This view shows the southern end of the Union Tunnel ca. 1910 – at right is the original location of CS Tower.

F. A. Wrabel Collection

THIS FAMOUS DRAWING shows B&P Junction at Jones Falls near the east portal of the B&P Tunnel as it appeared in 1889. The Northern Central main extends westward from left to right, joining the B&P trackage which then runs southward to Washington through the tunnel. The tracks at left continue to northward to Union Station.

Gunnarsson Collection/Railroad Museum of Pennsylvania (PHMC)

COMPLETION of the Union RR finally allowed the Northern Central to reach the Canton waterfront directly. This wonderful 1874 broadside provides multiple views of "Gardner's Union Rail-Road Depot" and the 100,000-bu. grain elevator. This historic structure was destroyed by fire on 11 April 1883 and never rebuilt, being supplanted by other much larger structures.

Hagley Museum & Library

Maryland Rail Heritage Library

THE DIRECTORS of the B&S were determined to erect a terminal in their home city that would impress the investors, shippers and traveling passengers alike. Work began on the terminal in 1848 and the imposing station was opened early in 1850, consolidating all of its offices for both passenger and freight service and operations under one roof. Known as the Calvert Street Station, the two-story head house fronted diagonally at the intersection of Calvert (left) and Franklin Streets, with the Adams Express building shown at right in this mid-1890s photo. The noted Baltimore architectural firm of Niernsee & Neilson created an impressive two-story Italian Renaissance structure, further enhanced by a pair of three-story towers at each corner. The expansive waiting room was heated by huge fireplaces topped by large black marble mantels. The upper floor of the elegant structure, also heated by the fireplaces, housed the offices of the railroad and a boardroom. When originally built this building handled both passenger and freight traffic. The "Blue Line" cable streetcar passengers are enjoying the open car on a pleasant day over a century ago.

THE TRAIN SHED, or Car House as it was initially designated, shown here ca. 1915, measured 112 ft. wide and 315 ft. long. Its massive "Triumphal Arch" styling and rock-solid construction (literally – the pillars were cut granite) reflected the Italianate influence of the main building in front of it. The sheet-iron roof was supported by iron trusses spanning 100 ft. Inside were two passenger tracks and platforms and three "tonnage tracks," with broad covered receiving and distribution platforms along the sides.

Later PRR engine crews on trains entering the station reportedly blasted columns of cinders at the electric trolleys overhead when passing under the elevated structure – and promptly received clouds of sand in response. More later.

231

WITH ITS BUSINESS GROWING the Northern Central constructed a separate general office building at the corner of Calvert and Centre Streets. Completed and occupied on 1 March 1876, the four-story, 50 X 80-ft. brick structure complemented the style of the passenger station, shown in the background of this late 1890s photo. The office space in the passenger station was then used exclusively by the President, Board and executive officers of the company.

AS FREIGHT TRAFFIC GREW, the original station was overwhelmed and in 1865 a large new freight depot was constructed along Guilford Avenue just north of the passenger terminal, facing Centre Street. This ca. 1915 photo shows the freight office and behind it what later became known as Freight Shed A.

In the background is a structure that appears in the next several photos. It was an early elevated street car line, known in Baltimore as the trestle, viaduct or "vidock" in Baltimorese. It ran above Guilford Avenue for nine blocks (about three-quarters of a mile) to clear the PRR trackage and yards. The first electrified elevated line in the U.S., it was double tracked (widely-separated), rose on solid masonry inclines at both ends and was supported by steel girders, with a truss over some areas. The first trip on the line was on 3 May 1893, the last run was on 1 January 1950 and it was torn down in May 1951. On 10 May 1948 a PRR gondola derailed and rammed a supporting column, putting the line out of service for about a month.

IT WAS INDEED an impressive structure – at the time it was labeled by the *Baltimore American* as "the largest and probably best railway depot building in the United States." This 1915 view emphasizes the length of the 150 X 383-ft. building, which contained two tracks inside.

With its traffic declining in the 1920s, Calvert Station became embroiled in a prolonged dispute between PRR and the city. An ordinance passed on 27 June 1929 directed the railroad to remove the existing station and build a new one. Years of protracted negotiations ensued. Finally in 1943 the masonry train shed was demolished and five years later the venerable Calvert Station itself fell victim to the wrecker's ball as well to make way for a new printing plant for the Baltimore *Sun*. With a modernized façade Shed A then became the "new" Calvert Station, also serving as the Railway Express Terminal.

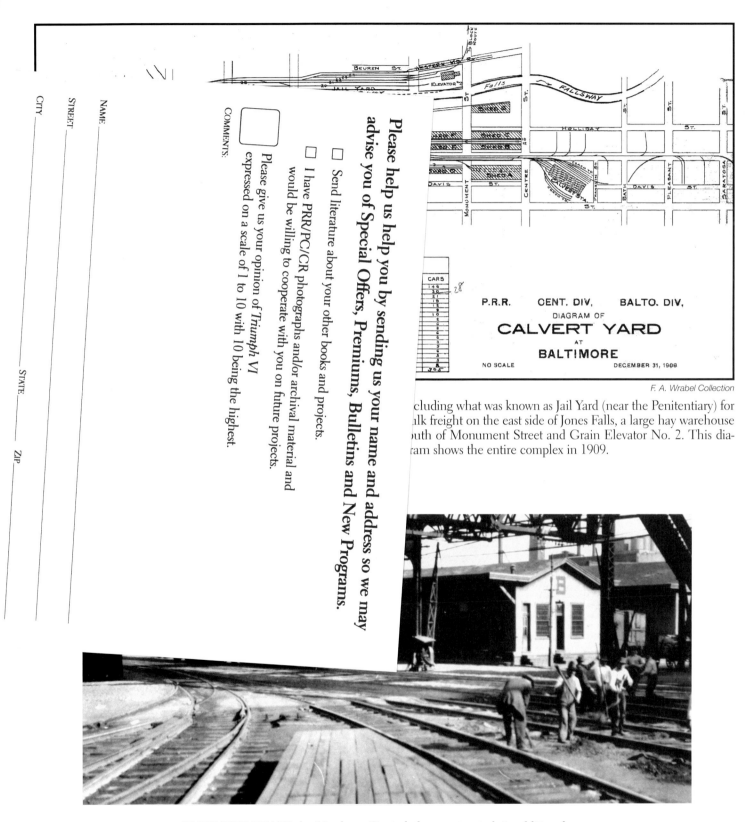

P.R.R.   CENT. DIV,   BALTO. DIV,

DIAGRAM OF

CALVERT YARD

AT

BALTIMORE

NO SCALE   DECEMBER 31, 1909

F. A. Wrabel Collection

...cluding what was known as Jail Yard (near the Penitentiary) for ...lk freight on the east side of Jones Falls, a large hay warehouse ...uth of Monument Street and Grain Elevator No. 2. This dia-...ram shows the entire complex in 1909.

OVER THE YEARS the Northern Central also constructed six additional corrugated iron freight sheds, designated B-F. Shed B, shown here in a ca. 1915 view in the shadow of the viaduct, is typical of the group. The track supervisor, in business suit, gets right in there with the work gang for some needed repairs.

GRAIN ELEVATOR No. 2, located at the northwest corner of Monument and Beuren Streets, was completed and put into operation on 20 August 1891. With a capacity of 300,000 bu., it was used for handling and storage of oats, corn and other grain for city delivery. It is shown here in a 1915 view.

Prior to construction of this facility the delivery of grain at Calvert Street Station was made directly from boxcars, using the "weigh bag" system, which was time-consuming, costly and the cause of much consternation by customers.

This ca. 1915 view shows the diagonal main tracks at left and the crowded team track area, with a fascinating collection of period freight cars. The viaduct runs northward at the left and the Jones Fallsway rises northward at right.

THIS VIEW looks at the Jail Yard team tracks ca. 1915, with what appears to be a hay unloading operation visible to the left of the two shanties. The viaduct is in the background.

Tom Hollyman - Penn Central Railroad Collection/Pennsylvania State Archives

BY 1953 when this fascinating aerial photo of the lower Jones Falls valley was made, several changes had taken place in downtown Baltimore. To help orient the reader we are looking south toward the Inner Harbor – prior to its development as a tourist attraction. In the center of the photo Elevator No. 2 stands vigil. To the immediate right of it is the Jones Falls "Fallsway" snaking down to the waterfront. Farther to the right are the six remaining PRR freight sheds including the large Shed A, converted to the "new" Calvert Station after the original one farther south was demolished to make room for the Baltimore *Sun* printing plant. The elevated viaduct over Guilford Avenue has also been demolished.

In the foreground to the right of the Fallsway are Madison Yard and the remains of Eagle Yard. To the left of the Fallsway is Jail Yard and the old Penitentiary is to the left of that. Beyond the elevator to the left is the Western Maryland Hillen terminal.

F. A. Wrabel Collection

WE NOW MOVE farther north up the Jones Falls valley to the site of Baltimore's Union Station. In 1873, as part of the what we could call the initial Baltimore Improvements program, the first Union Station was constructed east of B&P Junction jointly by PRR, the B&P and the Northern Central for use by these roads and through service with the PW&B (and initially by the Western Maryland until it built its own terminal near Calvert Street Station three years later). It was a modest frame structure with a wooden train shed, built in an area still notably rural in character at the edge of the business district. This rare photo shows the facility shortly after opening

ADDITIONS were made to the frame structure in 1882, but it still fell short of the growing traffic needs on the four roads. Thus in 1885 work was begun on a new Union Station, which opened on 1 April 1886. Similar in layout to its predecessor, this rather impressive Mansard-roofed brick structure consisted of a three-story office building, two-story waiting room and baggage area, and behind it a large open train shed. In the foreground are a horse-drawn streetcar and an assortment of wagons and carriages on Charles Street.

Maryland Rail Heritage Library

A SOMEWHAT LATER VIEW ca. 1900 gives a better view of the large train shed. This facility must have been a fascinating place to watch passenger train operations in the Golden Age, handling as it did a wide array of through trains on the PB&W/B&P (New York/Philadelphia -Washington), Northern Central/B&P (Washington/Baltimore-Harrisburg and diverse northern and western points) as well as Northern Central locals running to and from Calvert Street Station.

HERE'S JUST ONE EXAMPLE – B&P 4-4-0 318 catches the early morning sun as it waits at the Union Station train shed with three stately wooden cars before moving southward in this classic 1880s view. Note the high arched windows on the elegant parlor-observation.

AFTER COMPLETION of the second Union Station the Northern Central established the Guilford Avenue Engine Terminal at Union Junction to serve the growing traffic. This 12-stall enginehouse, which replaced an old two-stall one located near Calvert Station, became the primary service facility for locomotives assigned to both Calvert and Union Stations. In this 1891 view a Northern Central locomotive heads toward Calvert Station, while a PW&B train heads into Union Station. The array of locomotives represents various D-classes that are lettered for PRR, Northern Central, B&P or P&BC – PRR D3 937 at the far right held the distinction of being designated the "President's Engine."

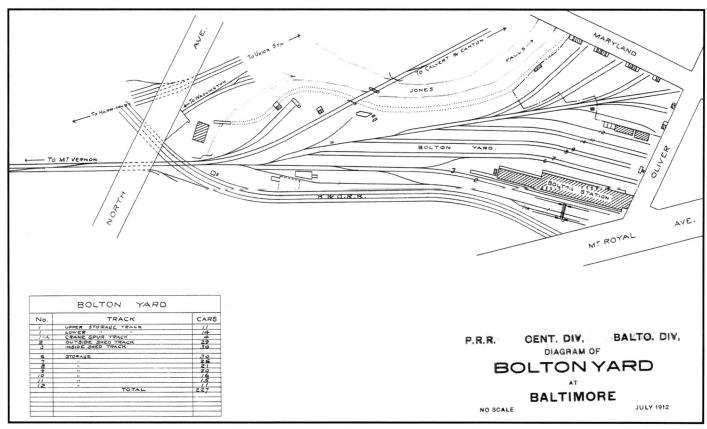

IN 1832 the B&S began construction of its first major terminal facility in an area known as Bolton, named after the estate of George Winchester, first President of the road. This complex eventually included Bolton Station, a passenger depot serving the "uptown" section of the city, along with offices, freight sheds, machine shop, engine house and yards. This diagram shows the layout of the complex in 1912 – note the proximity of the B&O line to Philadelphia.

F. A. Wrabel Collection

THE GRADE from Calvert Station to Bolton was so great that all passenger trains required assistance from a pusher to make the climb. After the difficult right of way into the city was relocated in 1871 as part of the Union RR improvements project, the old line south of the station was abandoned, but trains still used the remaining spur as a northward connection to the Northern Central main. This ca. 1915 photo shows the station at the intersection of Oliver Street and Mt. Royal Avenue – note the gantry crane at left.

F. A. Wrabel Collection

WITH THE OPENING of Union Station farther south in 1873, Bolton gradually diminished in importance as a passenger terminal. However its coal facility, team tracks and produce yard remained in operation for a number of years. The entrance to the freight station, including the coal trestle, produce yard and team tracks are shown here as they appeared ca. 1915. Horse-drawn wagons are still in abundance.

Note the sign promoting Bismarck Beer, testimony to the large German population in Baltimore and Maryland. Things German were quite popular in the United States from the mid-19th Century until 1917. High Society's debutante cotilion was called the "German," at least in Baltimore, and Maryland's laws had to be printed in German as well as English. By 1914 trade with the "Central Powers" exceeded that with Great Britain, particularly out of Baltimore, and the British blockade of Germany caused much friction with the United States. It remains our historic view that we were suckered into World War I by British portrayal of the Kaiser as a Hitler when in fact he was not, but Franco/British conduct at the end of the war virtually guaranteed that a Hitler would arise, with unspeakable consequences. By 1917, trade with the Allies was booming and war was declared followed by one of the most outrageous programs ever promoted by a national administration. To fan war fever, a deliberate campaign of anti-German propaganda was initiated by the Woodrow Wilson administration *against our own citizens* that resulted in horrific acts of violence in Baltimore and elsewhere that cowed a significant portion of our population. Citizens attacked on the streets, businesses burned, property destroyed, laws and street names changed . . . altogether a disgusting performance. We assume that Bismarck Beer did not survive the unpleasantness. Since German and Beer are the stuff of legend, along with truth this was still another casualty of war.

MOVING up the Jones Falls Valley we find a local freight working hard as it charges westward past KN block station in January 1930. The Mt. Vernon shelter shed can be seen at the lower right, and above that the Mt. Vernon Mills, a loyal Northern Central/PRR shipper.

F. A. Wrabel Collection

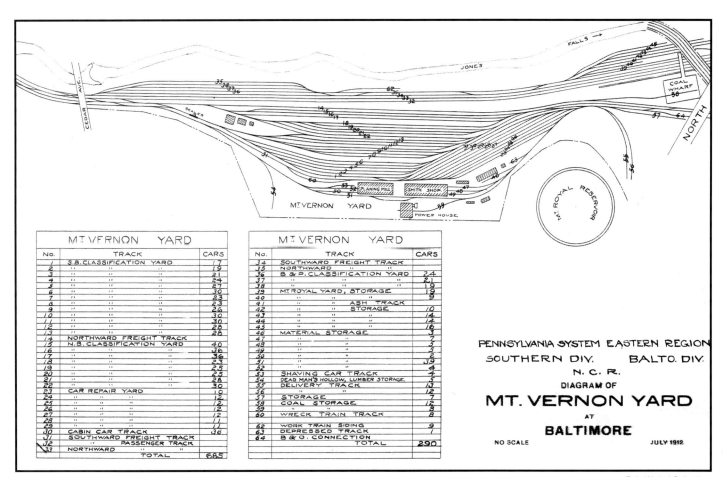

No.	MT. VERNON YARD — TRACK	CARS
1	S.B. CLASSIFICATION YARD	17
2	" " "	19
3	" " "	21
4	" " "	24
5	" " "	27
6	" " "	30
7	" " "	23
8	" " "	23
9	" " "	26
10	" " "	30
11	" " "	30
12	" " "	28
13	" " "	28
14	NORTHWARD FREIGHT TRACK	
15	N.B. CLASSIFICATION YARD	40
16	" " "	36
17	" " "	36
18	" " "	23
19	" " "	25
20	" " "	25
21	" " "	28
22	" " "	30
23	CAR REPAIR YARD	10
24	" " "	12
25	" " "	12
26	" " "	12
27	" " "	12
28	" " "	11
29	" " "	11
30	CABIN CAR TRACK	36
31	SOUTHWARD FREIGHT TRACK	
32	" PASSENGER TRACK	
33	NORTHWARD "	
	TOTAL	685

No.	MT. VERNON YARD — TRACK	CARS
34	SOUTHWARD FREIGHT TRACK	
35	NORTHWARD " "	
36	B & P. CLASSIFICATION YARD	24
37	" " "	21
38	" " "	19
39	MT. ROYAL YARD, STORAGE	9
40	" " "	
41	" " ASH TRACK	
42	" " STORAGE	10
43	" " "	14
44	" " "	14
45	" " "	16
46	MATERIAL STORAGE	3
47	" "	7
48	" "	5
49	" "	5
50	" "	2
51	" "	39
52	" "	4
53	SHAVING CAR TRACK	4
54	DEAD MAN'S HOLLOW, LUMBER STORAGE	5
55	DELIVERY TRACK	13
56	" "	12
57	STORAGE	7
58	COAL STORAGE	12
59	"	8
60	WRECK TRAIN TRACK	8
62	WORK TRAIN SIDING	9
63	DEPRESSED TRACK	1
64	B & O. CONNECTION	
	TOTAL	290

PENNSYLVANIA SYSTEM EASTERN REGION
SOUTHERN DIV.   BALTO. DIV.
N. C. R.
DIAGRAM OF
MT. VERNON YARD
AT
BALTIMORE
NO SCALE   JULY 1912

F. A. Wrabel Collection

AS PART OF the relocation of the right of way the Northern Central shops were moved to a new facility north of North Avenue on property once part of the Bond estate. Extended several times over the years, the Mt. Vernon complex provided the Northern Central with a large new classification yard, engine terminal, turntable and repair shops. This diagram shows the complex still near its full configuration in 1912.

THIS ca. 1915 view looks northward up the Jones Falls Valley along the crowded yard tracks, with the main at the extreme right.

CLEAR THE WAY – In 1911 the enginehouse was destroyed by fire, and subsequently the old car shops were removed and new engine facilities constructed at Orangeville (see Chapter 6), jointly owned by the Northern Central and the PB&W. The remaining shops at Mt. Vernon are pictured here in 1930 on the eve of their demolition to make way for a new Produce Terminal. Several buildings and yard tracks have already been removed.

F. A. Wrabel Collection

J. W. Wolf/F. A. Wrabel Collection

POMP AND CIRCUMSTANCES – On 21 July 1931 the new Produce Terminal was completed and opened in grand fashion, perhaps to offer hope to a Depression-ravaged economy. Built at a cost of $750 thousand, the brick and reinforced concrete structure was 82 ft. wide and 660 ft. long, providing the city with a large and modern outlet for fresh produce. This photo shows the new complex, with a presumably uncomfortable marching band and color guard sweltering in the summer under their World War I-style metal helmets, heavy uniform and boots – but nevertheless arrayed in precise formation to dedicate the facility. A host of railroad and public officials attended the event, including the Mayor of Baltimore and the Governor of Maryland.

Tom Hollyman - Penn Central Railroad Collection/Pennsylvania State Archives

HERE'S an aerial view of the Produce Terminal in 1953, looking northward up the valley. The delivery yard included 10 tracks in pairs, separated by 60-ft. wide concrete aprons providing easy access to every car for unloading. There was an elevated platform between each pair of tracks for the convenience of inspectors. The tracks were 2300 ft. long with a total yard capacity of 325 cars.

In addition to the reefers in the Produce Terminal, note the strings of hoppers and gons alongside the main. At the right is the Ma & Pa yard, engine terminal and roundhouse.

FOREIGN VISITOR – The Rexall Train is shown here on display in the Produce Terminal yard on 1 September 1936. New York Central Class L-2c Mohawk 2873 was leased from PRR's arch-rival, fitted with oil burners and given a streamlined shroud almost identical to that applied to its more famous cousin, Class J-1e Hudson 5344 used to head that road's *Commodore Vanderbilt*. This locomotive, smartly decorated in Rexall blue and white, led a matching 12-car train on a 29,000-mile tour across the U. S. and Canada, acting as a stirring traveling exhibit and meeting headquarters for some 10,000 druggists and 20,000 sales representatives. Note the vintage autos and the classic Mack tank truck refueling the locomotive.

F. A. Wrabel Collection

LOCOMOTIVES had to work hard to move freight tonnage up the valley as dramatically demonstrated by this double-header charging up the grade just north of Mt. Vernon Yards in 1901. The Meadow Mill is at left and behind it is the Clipper Mill.

Gunnarsson Collection/Railroad Museum of Pennsylvania (PHMC)

WE NOW BEGIN a tour of the Northern Central line, a railroad that for most of its years took considerable interest in the communities it served. Those communities ranged from residential suburbs to large manufacturing centers, from resorts to mill towns – and in most of them the station was the center of commerce and even social activity. Those in the Baltimore suburban area, like this frame structure at Melvale (MP. 2.4 from Calvert Station) built in 1888, had two stories to accommodate living quarters for the agent.

National Archives

POOLE & HUNT foundry and machine works, located in Woodberry (now Baltimore City – MP. 3.3) was typical of the diverse industries – both large and small – that developed along the Northern Central. Established in 1853, this facility developed into a large producer of castings and industrial machinery. Among other products the firm produced the components for the magnificent cast iron colonnade supporting the grand dome of the U. S. Capitol. This drawing depicts the complex – belching smokestacks signifying a thriving industry – as it appeared in the 1880s, with a northbound Northern Central passenger train passing by.

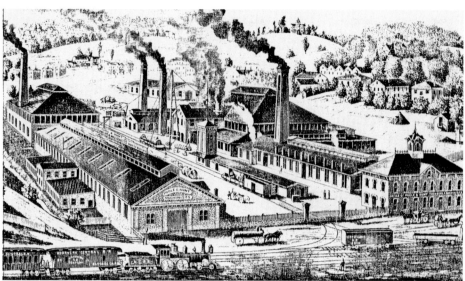

Gunnarsson Collection/Railroad Museum of Pennsylvania (PHMC)

MT. WASHINGTON station (MP. 6.0) was a board and batten design with Gothic touches typical of late 19th Century construction with ample room for the agent's quarters. It is shown here in 1916.

National Archives

THIS VIEW shows the freight station at Mt. Washington in 1957 just before demolition for a new warehouse for the National Biscuit Company. This stop was once a major destination for many of PRR's famous horse express cars during the racing season at nearby Pimlico Racetrack.

F. A. Wrabel Collection

THE B&S track reached what is now the Lake Roland area in early 1831. As with most lines of this early period it was laid with strap iron rails on wooden stringers secured to wood ties. A small station was built there the following year, known as Relay because it was the point where horses tired from the long climb out of the city were changed for fresh ones (because of confusion with B&O's Relay Station, used for the same purpose, the name was changed to Hollins in 1874). The replacement structure shown here was built in 1876 and depicted as it appeared ca. 1880. The mainline is at the right. The tracks curving to the left are the Green Spring Branch, which is a convenient segue to a fascinating story.

THE GREEN SPRING BRANCH was for a time the projected mainline of the B&S in its effort to reach the Susquehanna. Because of the protracted battle to secure a charter from the hostile Pennsylvania Legislature, the B&S in 1831 decided to turn westward from Relay through the Green Spring Valley toward Westminster and beyond. Although the company continued some work on the original planned route toward York, it was necessary for the road to reach the businesses in Owings Mills in order to survive. On 14 June 1832 the line was opened as far as the Green Spring Hotel which also served as the station. The hotel is shown here as it appeared ca. 1857 with large additions to the left of the original building. The frame structure was destroyed in a spectacular fire in 1860.

The line was opened the two additional miles to Owings Mills on 14 August 1832, and between the flour mills there and mines and other mills (flour, textiles and powder) in the lower Jones Falls Valley, the road slowly began to build traffic. It did well enough to purchase its first steam locomotive, the *Herald* (originally an 0-4-0, but rebuilt as a 4-2-0 to negotiate the sharp curves). The Green Spring line itself, however, was never profitable, and as soon as the charter battle was resolved later that year the plans to extend the line to Westminster were abandoned and construction resumed north of Relay.

Although operation ceased by 1845 the story of this short branch doesn't end there. On 1 October 1857 the Northern Central sold it to the Western Maryland which gained entrance to

Baltimore via trackage rights from Relay southward. Then in 1873 the WM constructed its own right of way into the city, using the B&P to reach the depot as part of the PRR-sponsored relocation project and the Green Spring line again became a rural branch, living out its life in obscurity until finally being torn up in 1960.

THE STATION at Hollins (MP. 7.1) – somewhat modified – was still standing when this Valuation photo was taken in 1916. It too was destroyed by fire, this time shortly after the photo was taken.

National Archives

245

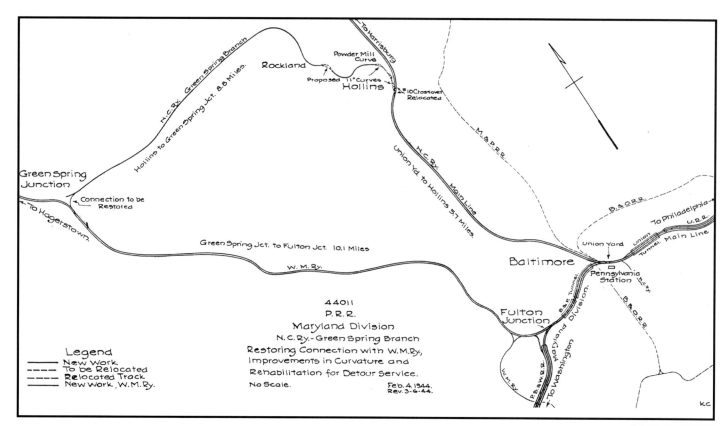

F. A. Wrabel Collection

THIS 1944 map gives us an opportunity for a quick look at the rural Green Spring Branch, whose location enabled it to serve as a bypass into the city when the Northern Central or B&P main was tied up. It was briefly equipped with passing sidings and block signals to serve in that capacity for both PRR and WM trains while the B&P tunnel was being improved just prior to World War I (see Chapter 6). The line was again pressed into service as a detour during World War II improvements, as indicated here.

HERE WE SEE a gutsy Class H8 Consolidation pulling a local freight westbound around the 11° "Powder Mill" curve in March 1916, showing one of the passing sidings.

F. A. Wrabel Collection

IMPROVEMENTS OR NO, derailments still occurred. This 1916 view captures one at PC Block station. A perplexed (disgruntled, furious – take your pick) track supervisor appears to be trying to figure out how to clean up the mess. Note the wheels buried in the cinders.

THE HOOK has now arrived and things seem to be making progress. Note the "NCR" markings under the standard PRR lettering on the crane. Track workers or foremen, hats again prevail. The operator and block station survived, not always the case in such incidents.

SIGNAL MAINTAINERS at PC, probably recorded during the derailment described above. Note the artifacts of the day – the keystone over the door, and the new switch light and dry cell batteries to the right of the switch lamp. The keystone was cast into this concrete structure and was painted the same color red as the road's station signs. The road's initials never appeared on this application. No further identification was needed!

F. A. Wrabel Collection

END OF THE LINE – PRR at least. Here we see GJ block station and Kirk station on the Western Maryland in a quiet March 1916 view. Lower-quadrant semaphores still prevail.

F. A. Wrabel Collection

E. G. Hooper/Herbert H. Harwood, Jr. Collection

THE NEXT TWO STATIONS on the main exemplify more so-phisticated designs befitting their suburban location and status. Ruxton (MP. 8.4), built in 1892 to replace a small frame build-ing, is shown here in a 1904 photo as a southbound Northern Central train speeds past, led by a trim D16. There's nary a weed in sight nor a blade of grass uncut. The center (third) track, which ran to the next stop at Riderwood, facilitated locomotive runaround, returning locals and as an express track in the com-muter district. It was torn up in the late 1920s with declining traf-fic and improved signaling.

The attractive stone and frame structure, part of the upgrading program implemented by George Roberts, was built to serve a planned suburban development begun in 1887. It served as a community center for decades until finally, and sadly, being de-molished in 1963.

National Archives

RIDERWOOD (MP. 9.2 – formerly Sherwood) station was designed by noted Philadelphia architect Frank Furness in 1903. This facility, which also included a post office, is shown here in a 1916 view. It eventually be-came a private home.

LUTHERVILLE (MP. 10.5), developed in 1852 by two Lutheran clergymen, Drs. Benjamin Kurtz and John Morris, was one of the first planned suburban communities in the U.S. located outside a major city and joined to it by a rail link. Similar to several of Baltimore's early suburbs, as well as later communities on Philadelphia's Main Line, Lutherville became both a summer resort for affluent professionals from the city and home to many year-round residents.

The B&S built its first station in 1853, a frame structure that was replaced in 1876 by this substantial stone building. The station is depicted here as it appeared in 1978.

F. A. Wrabel

A STATION of more modest proportions, but neat and trim nevertheless, served the patrons at Timonium (MP. 11.7) – shown here as it appeared in 1916 not long after it was built. The main passed close to the grandstand of the well-known Timonium Fairgrounds.

National Archives

Milton A. Davis

A LEGEND IN ITS TIME – Similar to the role served by Paoli for Philadelphia commuters on the PRR Main Line, the Northern Central established Parkton, Maryland as the limit of its Baltimore north suburban commuter district. Service began on 23 November 1861 and over the years was gradually expanded to carry hundreds of thousands of Baltimore commuters safely to and from Calvert station. Like its northern counterpart, the service became a part of local folklore. Here we see Train 441, the evening local, at Timonium in the spring of 1941.

By the way, E5s 6528 (Juniata, 1913) carried a bit of notoriety of her own. She was the last of the E5 Atlantics. Altoona started building E6s's the following year. The last of the litter.

Milton A. Davis

COCK OF THE WALK – Most PRR power was big-boilered but few gave such an impression of size as did the two K5s engines. Here is Baldwin's 5699 (5698 was built by Altoona) in July of 1941 at Timonium with a Baltimore-Harrisburg train. Note the graphited boiler front emphasizing her chestiness, the bell under the headlight, the slatted pilot, the ubiquitous P70 coaches, the position light signal, the train control box. The scene shouts pure PRR. Built as potential successors to the K4 engines, they were initially assigned between Philadelphia and Pittsburgh but then bounced to the Northern Central's curves and choppy grades to put their power to good use.

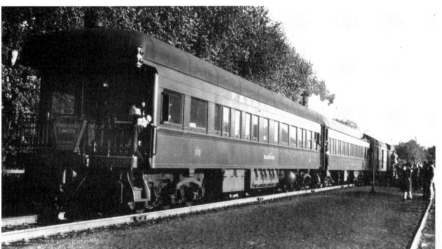

Milton A. Davis/F. A. Wrabel Collection

ROYAL VISIT – Aside from crowds attending the annual Maryland State Fair, Timonium was a peaceful stop. This October 1941 view reminds us, however, that royalty could embrace even relatively remote locations in an era when railroads still dominated passenger transport. The Duke and Duchess of Windsor elected to detrain at Timonium rather than continue on to Penn Station in Baltimore. The heavyweight observation *Baltimore* is taking time off from its regular duties on the *Pennsylvania Limited*.

THE STATION SIGN says Texas – Maryland, that is (MP. 13.5). Originally constructed by the B&S, the stone station was 90 years old when this photo was taken in 1916. In the mid-1880s the facility was kept busy with business from early lime kilns and marble quarries nearby. The stone and lime traffic continued to grow through the years and in fact the much enlarged stone quarries at Texas became the single largest customer in the declining years over 100 years later. The historic structure was gutted by fire in the late 1950s.

National Archives

National Archives

COCKEYSVILLE (MP. 14.9) was just a small town located on the Baltimore-York turnpike, but it grew quickly with the coming of rail service. The gingerbread-bedecked two-story station shown here in a 1916 photo was constructed in 1866 and by the mid-1880s it became the center of Northern Central Baltimore suburban passenger operations as well as serving as crew change headquarters, communications center and town post office. It was also a center of freight operations with a large yard and sidings to various local industries including lumber mills and furniture manufacturing.

J. W. Wolf/F. A. Wrabel Collection

ALTHOUGH the station hadn't changed much in the intervening period, we couldn't resist this photo both for its depiction of classic V Cabin and the delightful overall crossing scene, complete with vintage autos ca. 1926.

ALTHOUGH Parkton was the limit of Baltimore commuter service, Cockeysville was the terminal for most of the trains. The 1904 timetable shows an impressive 18 weekday locals making the daily roundtrip with seven additional trains continuing on to Parkton. Several through trains also stopped at Cockeysville, like this southbound headed by K4s 3361 in October 1921.

George F. Nixon/Maryland Rail Heritage Library Collection

HERE WE HAVE the Cockeysville freight station as it appeared in 1971, shortly after renovation by Penn Central (did someone forget to paint two of the roof brackets?). The local freight agent at the time, Edward F. McGarity, made a valiant effort to work closely with shippers from the nearby Greater Baltimore Industrial Park. By 1973 Penn Central could no longer justify the expense and the office was closed and later leased as warehouse space to a succession of private individuals.

F. A. Wrabel

COMPARED TO Cockeysville, the small station built in the mid-19th Century at Ashland (MP. 15.8) looks like a dollhouse. Ashland was a true company town, established in 1844 around the local iron works. From primitive beginnings the Ashland Iron Works grew steadily through the ensuing years, absorbing the Oregon furnace in 1852 and barely escaping destruction by Confederate raiders in 1864. The Works provided substantial tonnage for the Northern Central which hauled the key raw materials – iron ore, lime and anthracite – from primarily on-line sources to the furnace. It then shipped high-quality pig iron to Baltimore, York and other locations. Several sidings were laid into the facility in the early years of the Civil War, and a coal trestle was constructed there in 1875.

National Archives

Despite the improvements, however, the Ashland Works succumbed to new technology in the 1870s and early 80s as the more efficient Bessemer process spelled the end of small furnaces. Henceforth iron and steel production would be concentrated in large centers like Pittsburgh. The Works declined rapidly. It was closed in 1884 and sold the following year. It was briefly reactivated in 1887 by the Pennsylvania Steel Company but two years later that firm opened a larger and more efficient plant at Sparrows Point MD and in 1892 the old furnace was dismantled. In an ironic twist the scrap was shipped to the new facility.

THE residence-like station at Phoenix (MP. 17.8) was constructed in the mid 1870s. A homey picket fence connects it with the nearby freight shed.

National Archives

SPARKS (MP. 19.6) was still a thriving "tank town" when this photo of the attractive passenger station built in the early 1880s was taken in 1915. The freight house is in the background.

National Archives

GLENCOE (MP. 20.5) was typical of the small resort communities that were located in the hills surrounding the Gunpowder Falls valley. The early station, shown here in an 1880s engraving, later became a private home. Note the interesting Bollman through truss across the Falls at right.

AND HERE IT IS – now a private residence and still standing in 1984.

F. A. Wrabel

THAT STRUCTURE was replaced with this frame combination station in the late 1880s, utilizing one of the Northern Central's standard designs. It is shown here in 1916.

National Archives

AN ALMOST IDENTICAL structure was built about the same time in Corbett (MP. 22.3) and is shown here as it appeared in 1916. The town, which grew up to serve a steam sawmill established in 1885, was named for Isaac Corbitt (*sic*) who donated the land for the depot. Several sidings were constructed in the late 1880s for the mill and associated lumberyard.

National Archives

255

MONKTON (MP. 23.0) was typical of the stations built in 1897 during the late Roberts era of facilities upgrading and is shown here in 1916. The station is extant and used as a bike path facility.

THE HAZARDS of heavy traffic on the twisting and hilly Northern Central are recorded in this 18 August 1913 view after Extra 5062 derailed east of the Blue Mount (MP. 25.0) station. In that era derailments on the line were so common that PRR main-tained wrecking crews at Baltimore, Parkton and York just to serve the Northern Central. On a more positive note Blue Mount also featured a large stone quarry that supplied a major portion of the rock ballast for the Maryland Division.

VETERAN photographer Frank Wrabel snapped this shot of a renumbered Penn Central Alco RS-11 (PRR Class AS18m) rolling freight B-95 down the valley near Blue Mount in December 1971. It captures the scenic beauty of the line, even in its declining years.

F. A. Wrabel

(*below*) AND NOW we arrive at Parkton (MP. 28.8), final destination of the commuter locals. Parkton was just another small town on the old York Turnpike that was literally transformed when the Northern Central selected it as the northern terminus for Baltimore suburban commuter service as early as 1861. The town grew rapidly as a result and by the turn of the century new facilities were needed. A new station was built and the yards and engine service facilities were expanded to support additional trains. The station itself was another creative design by Frank Furness that also contained agent's quarters and telegraph office. Note the signal tower in this 1916 view.

National Archives

DECLINE – The Parkton station is shown as it appeared in 1957 just prior to the removal of the block station in conjunction with removal of the second mainline track southward to Glencoe. Parkton local service was discontinued two years later on 27 June 1959, the end of an era. Note the work cars in the distance.

F. A. Wrabel Collection

NEW FREEDOM Pennsylvania (MP. 37.1) could be considered perhaps the epitome of what Northern Central towns were all about – both a manufacturing community and a primary railroad center. Located just north of the Mason-Dixon line, it was situated on the ridge separating the Gunpowder Falls valley from the Codorus Creek watershed. Trains had to climb the steep ruling grades in both directions and thus the town became the center of helper operations. A small yard was built here in 1881 and four years later this station was constructed, following a standardized design.

In that same year the yard was enlarged to serve the Stewartstown RR, an agricultural short line opened to its namesake town. The road operated both passenger and freight service for a time, connecting with Northern Central trains. Amazingly the tiny road not only survived the decline and fall of the Northern Central itself, it inherited the section of the main from New Freedom to York.

THE STATION at Shrewsbury (MP. 38.6) was located in this building that looked more like an old hotel or tavern than a railroad structure. The year is 1916.

DEFINITELY NONSTANDARD – The combination station at Seitzland (MP. 39.1) offered the bare minimum of facilities to the small community. The interesting structure is shown here in 1916.

GLEN ROCK (MP. 41.8) was originally named Heathcote Station after the owner of a water-powered sawmill on the Codorus Creek. The name was changed to Glen Rock in 1843 with the arrival of the B&S – at the recommendation of William Heathcote himself – after the prominent rock outcropping near the right of way. In 1852 the sawmill was converted to a flour mill, and several other industries were established over the next decade. In 1918 the flour mill began production of delightfully-named "June Bug Poultry and Livestock Feed," well known in the surrounding area.

The station, which is shown here in the mid-1950s, was located in a nondescript former commercial building. Look at the weeds. It is good that Thomson did not live to see it.

York County Heritage Trust, PA

Gunnarsson Collection/Railroad Museum of Pennsylvania (PHMC)

MYSTERY PHOTO – This famous image taken at Hanover Junction purportedly shows President Abraham Lincoln's train returning to Washington after he delivered the Gettysburg Address on 18 November 1863. According to this scenario, Pinkerton security men are stationed atop the cars and the 16th President is the tall figure with the stovepipe hat on the station platform. Although this description has been questioned, we can affirm that the track curving to the right is the Northern Central main northward, the track that the locomotive is standing on is the Hanover Junction RR (later the Western Maryland branch to Hanover) and that the brick building at left is the Junction Hotel, later a private residence.

THIS PHOTO shows the bridge just north of the Hanover Junction station that was destroyed by Confederate General Jubal Early's cavalry onslaught into Pennsylvania just prior to the pivotal Battle of Gettysburg. Taken from a train on the Hanover Junction RR, it shows the bridge after it was quickly rebuilt by Herman Haupt's hardworking USMRR crews, here sitting on the structure.

Gunnarsson Collection/Railroad Museum of Pennsylvania (PHMC)

HERE WE HAVE a view of Howard Tunnel, considered by some to be the first railroad tunnel in continuous use in the U. S., if not the world, located 7 miles south of York. It was named after Revolutionary war hero Colonel John Eager Howard, landowner, civil engineer and one of the original advocates and investors in the B&S. Following his suggestion it was cut through a 90-ft. high ridge of solid rock for 300 ft. using sledge hammers, hand drills, blasting powder and pickaxes wielded by the Irish immigrant laborers. Progressing at a rate of 4 ft. per day, it took two years (1836-8) to complete a rough single-track bore, which was finally finished in 1840. This photo was taken shortly after the tunnel was widened for double track and brick-lined in 1868-70. A picnic ground was laid out nearby in 1872 which became a favorite destination for Sunday School and factory worker excursions from York.

Gunnarsson Collection/Railroad Museum of Pennsylvania (PHMC)

YORK (MP. 57.2), the county seat and situated at an important turnpike crossing, was a hotbed of early citizen activity favoring a rail line up the Susquehanna Valley. It became the original terminus of the York & Maryland Line RR, the road borne of the compromise worked out in the Pennsylvania Legislature finally allowing the B&S to obtain a charter in that state. It was the first railroad into the town and freed merchants and area farmers from their former dependence on canals and toll roads. As with other communities along the line with the coming of the railroad York expanded rapidly. Flour mills, iron furnaces and numerous manufacturing plants all became dependent on the successor Northern Central for their raw materials – grain, iron ore and an-

thracite – as well as shipping their finished products.

This 1927 USGS map shows the main (still labeled Northern Central) approaching the town from the southwest, traversing the easier terrain north of Codorus Creek and then following it more closely to the north of the town center. The Western Maryland York Branch enters from the west, and the Ma & Pa and the Northern Central line to Wrightsville enter from the east at right. Note the York Electric and other interurban lines radiating from the town at this time which hastened the demise of local passenger service before disappearing themselves, both ultimate victims of the automobile's onslaught.

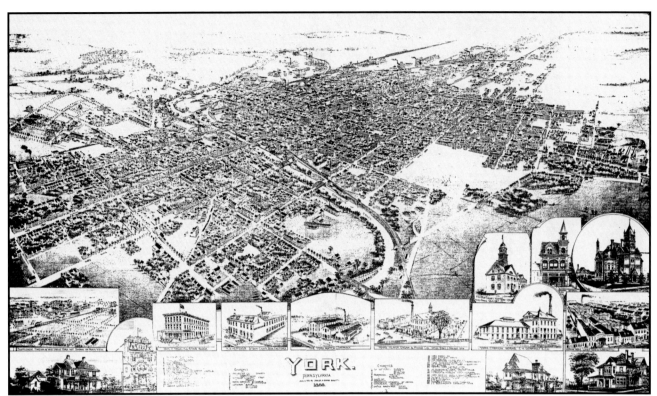

YORK WAS ALREADY a thriving industrial center in 1888 when this fascinating lithograph of York was made. It depicts a train on the Northern Central main as it approaches the center of town along Codorus Creek and then continues northward at top center. Another train on the Hanover & York enters from the left and a third on the York & Wrightsville runs eastward at the top right – the Ma & Pa enters at the upper right. The Western Maryland branch was not yet built and the West York industrial district was under development.

THE B&S constructed its first station in York in the 1840s, shown here on 3 June 1857 surrounded by a crowd upon the arrival of James Buchanan. We're not sure of the occasion for the tumultuous reception but the fifteenth President had served his native Pennsylvania as a state legislator as well as U. S. representative and Senator prior to being elected President in 1856. He maintained his estate, Wheatland, in nearby Lancaster during his term as Secretary of State during the Polk administration and presumably used the B&S and successor Northern Central to travel to and from Washington.

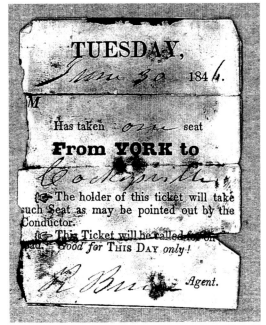

THE FIRST TICKET issued by PRR for inauguration of passenger service from York to Baltimore on the B&S is dated 30 June 1846, not long after the parent road was chartered. It granted the holder passage from York to Cockeysville and exhorted that "the holder may take such seat as may be pointed out by the Conductor."

York County Heritage Trust, PA

THE SECOND STATION constructed to serve York is shown in a rare photo ca. 1873. Note the ghost image in the center.

York County Heritage Trust, PA

ALL IS QUIET at the passenger station in a 1916 view. The impressive brick structure was built in 1889-90, the third serving the growing manufacturing community.

National Archives

THE TRACK SIDE of the structure is shown here on a gloomy 22 November 1963, a somber day known for an event unrelated to the railroad or the weather. After taking this photo veteran photographer Ed Weber turned on his car radio only to hear the shocking news that President Kennedy had been assassinated in Dallas. This view shows the long platform shelter still remaining on the northbound side. The southbound shelter has been considerably shortened. The freight office was located in the three-story building across the street at right.

Edward H. Weber

John J. Bowman, Jr. /Fred W. Schneider, III Collection

TRAIN 549 (Baltimore-Harrisburg) pauses at York on 15 August 1964. It was one of three remaining through trains on the line that endured into the 1960s. However, in 1968 the *Northern Express/Southern Express*, an overnight train running between Washington and Buffalo, was discontinued. By 1971 there was just one meager train left, which Amtrak refused to continue, thus ending over 130 years of through passenger service on the line on 1 May of that year.

BY THE turn of the century the Northern Central had developed three rail yards and numerous freight warehouses and loading facilities in York. The Duke Street Team Tracks and Freight House Tracks along with a network of industrial sidings provided a substantial complex serving local customers.

This map of York shows the yard facilities, the Baltimore-Harrisburg main (lower left to upper right, forming an S-curve through the city), the branches to Wrightsville/Columbia (lower right) and Frederick (upper left) and the junction with the fabled Ma & Pa (lower center). The passenger station is at center left, and east of there is the YORK Tower (center).

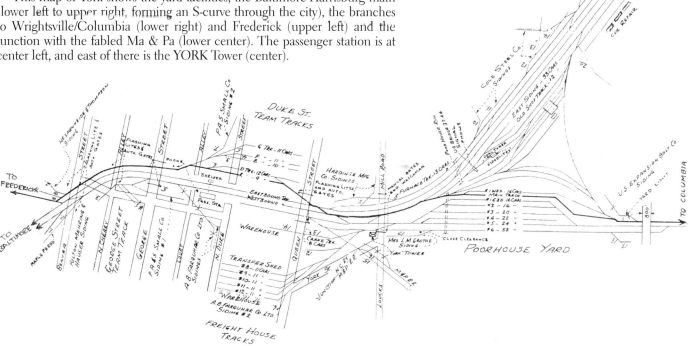

THIS 1916 photo shows the front of the freight station, a substantial 61 X 534-ft. structure.

THE FREIGHT FACILITIES in York also offered this 50-ton P&H gantry crane, with a 27-ft. span. The date is 1916.

THE OCCASION for this assemblage of workers and officials was a special double-headed train of 3000-ton (!) vaults destined for Japan from the York Safe & Lock Company. The photo of the somber-faced group was taken alongside the plant in 1930.

YORK SWITCHING – This insurance photo provides a brakeman's-eye view of typical York switching operation in 1938. The cars at left are on Siding No. 1 alongside the original plant of the P.A. & S. Small Company, with George Street crossing behind the locomotive and the tracks to Baltimore curving to the left in the background. Note the immaculately maintained brick and gravel areas between the tracks.

F. A. Wrabel Collection

ANOTHER YARD was located farther north along the main that served the car shops that at one time turned out both freight cars and elegant passenger equipment, and Poorhouse Yard, named after a nearby almshouse, which was the main classification yard located east of YORK Tower. This structure built in 1891 served as the Carpenter Shop. Modelers – take note of the profusion of clutter, even in 1916!

National Archives

THE SUPERVISOR'S OFFICE responsible for managing the facilities in York was located in this attractive Italianate building built in 1856 and shown here as it appeared in 1916.

National Archives

HERE WE HAVE an overall view of the York engine terminal area ca. 1951 showing the concrete coaling tower, steam crane and hoppers of company coal for the tower. The L1-Class locomotive in front of the enginehouse in the background was used on the "Beany," the once-daily freight operated between Lancaster and York in the 1950s. Because of the sharp curve on the west end of the bridge at Columbia, the locomotive had to be literally walked around it by the train crew.

John Bucher/David S. Bucher Collection

F. A. Wrabel Collection

AFTER REACHING York in 1838 the B&S made the decision to build a line east toward the Susquehanna River at Wrightsville rather than continue northward to York Haven, its original objective. After overcoming both financial and bridge engineering problems (the latter with the brilliant assistance of the then 23-year old civil engineer Herman Haupt), the Wrightsville, York & Gettysburg RR reached its river terminus in 1840, paralleling a portion of the Lancaster Turnpike down a gentle stream valley.

This view from YORK Tower on a cold day in 1932 shows the historic junction. The track that extends to the right, between the signals, marks the original alignment of the B&S (Y&W) line to Wrightsville. The multiple-track line that curves to the left past the shops was the later Northern Central extension to York Haven, Harrisburg and Sunbury. The engine terminal, shops and coaling trestle supported the Northern Central and the Frederick and York Branch locals. The tracks at the right foreground extend to Poorhouse Yard.

HELLAM (MP. 6.1 from Columbia) is located about half-way between York and Wrightsville. The delightful photo presented here captures a long-ago scene at the station team track ca. 1910 with a wagon being used to unload a boxcar while a young boy wearing a straw hat keeps Dobbin steady.

York County Heritage Trust, PA

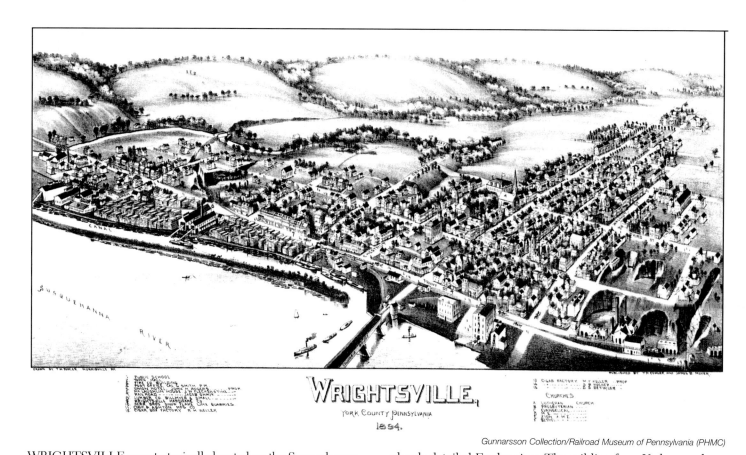

Gunnarsson Collection/Railroad Museum of Pennsylvania (PHMC)

WRIGHTSVILLE was strategically located on the Susquehanna at the head of operations on the S&T Canal and directly opposite Columbia, the western terminus of the Philadelphia & Columbia RR and the eastern end of the Pennsylvania Canal. These connections enabled Wrightsville to become an important canal junction town and it remained as the main northern terminal for the B&S for the next decade.

The thriving town is depicted here in 1894 in another meticulously-detailed Fowler view. The rail line from York runs along the base of the ridge in the background and curves into town at the left center, running along Front Street to the station, located at the wooden bridge crossing the river to Columbia. The entrance to the S&T Canal is just to the left of the bridge. The Billmyer & Small lumber mill dominates the waterfront along the canal, and the Kerr Bros. "Snow Flake Lime Quarries" are at the far right.

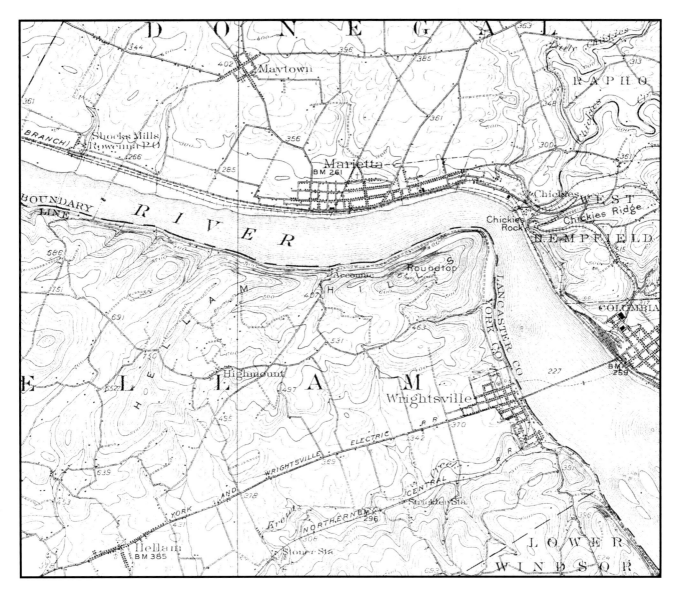

BY 1908, when this USGS map was published, both Columbia and Wrightsville had diminished in importance in terms of both water and rail commerce although the rail yard and engine service facilities still operated in Columbia (see *Triumph II*). The parallel York & Wrightsville interurban line offers competition to the Northern Central and the Low-Grade Line runs along the north bank of the Susquehanna, adjacent to the Columbia Branch and the now-abandoned Pennsylvania Canal bed (dashed line).

THIS VIEW of the brick replacement station at Wrightsville (MP. 69.1) looks west from the western end of the Columbia-Wrightsville bridge on 6 May 1956. At the left is the Lincoln Highway (U.S. Route 30) bridge. The speed limit on the tight curve onto the bridge was 4 mph at this time!

Edward H. Weber

269

Gunnarsson Collection/Railroad Museum of Pennsylvania (PHMC)

PANIC – This drawing depicts the chaotic scene at Columbia on 28 June 1863 during the evacuation of Wrightsville in the face of invading Confederate forces that "burned every one" of the railroad bridges between there and York. On 30 June the panic-stricken – but apparently resourceful – citizens of Columbia, assisted by the 20th Pennsylvania Militia that had retreated from Hanover Junction, set fire to the bridge to prevent the Southern troops from crossing and gaining access to the iron furnaces and other critical industries (see *Triumph II* for views of the replacement bridges at this crossing).

The 5620-ft. long wooden bridge existing at the time of the Civil War was erected in 1834 to replace an earlier one built in 1814 that had fallen victim to an ice jam. It was a versatile structure with provision for wagons and foot traffic as well as a double-deck towing path to haul canal boats back and forth across the river. The B&S laid two tracks on the bridge to allow a rail connection with the P&C at Columbia. No steam locomotives were allowed on the bridge – cars were towed across by mule teams. However, with the imminent threat of invasion by Southern troops, the locomotives – with their high stacks removed – were hauled across the bridge by mule power.

F. A. Wrabel Collection

THE FOURTH AND LAST Columbia-Wrightsville Bridge is shown as it appeared in 1930 shortly after the new Route 30 highway bridge allowed separation of road and rail traffic across the river. It was constructed in 1896-7 as a replacement for the previous one destroyed in a hurricane and was dismantled in 1963.

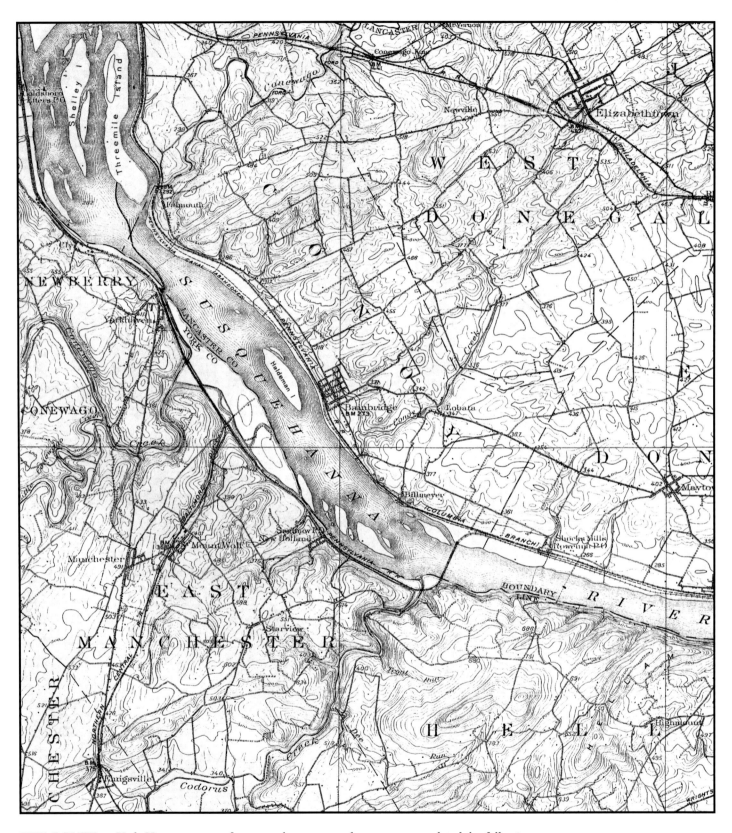

THE ROUTE to York Haven was not forgotten, however, and with the landmark chartering of the Pennsylvania RR in April 1846 to build west from Harrisburg, the state capital became the new focus of the B&S. In the same historic month the York & Cumberland RR was chartered to construct a rail line from York northward through the Codorus Creek valley and then across the low hills toward York Haven. Construction began in 1850 and was completed the following year.

This 1908 USGS map shows the junction of the Northern Central with the A&S Branch of the Low-Grade Line, which crosses the river on a high stone arch bridge at Shocks Mills (see *Triumph II*). The Columbia Branch continues westward on the north bank of the river and the east-west PRR mainline to Harrisburg cuts across at the top, descending to join it.

AS IT LEFT the Codorus Creek valley the line passed through Emigsville (MP. 61.6), where this standard design combination station was built in 1886.

National Archives

THE LINE continued on through Mt. Wolf, location of another standard combination station constructed in 1884 and shown as it appeared in 1916 with the station agent and others posing for a Valuation photo.

National Archives

THIS tiny shelter served the small community of Wago. Just beyond this point, at Wago Junction (MP. 66.7), the Northern Central met the Atglen & Susquehanna Branch, part of the Low-Grade freight line that was constructed alongside the original right of way to Enola Yard.

National Archives

YORK HAVEN (MP. 68.5), located on the Susquehanna some 14 miles from Harrisburg, was an ideal location for transshipment of river traffic to a projected rail line down the valley. Thus when the B&S reached the town in 1851 it quickly became an important canal junction, and it grew rapidly. Numerous grist mills began shipping flour to Baltimore and several iron furnaces also used the line. From the 1850s to the 1870s the town prospered and grew, but its role as a river terminal gradually shifted to points farther north and by 1880 the area had deteriorated noticeably. However there was still enough traffic on the Northern Central to warrant construction of this combination station in 1884, shown here in 1916. By then this portion of the line (alongside the Low-Grade Line) was part of the Philadelphia Division.

National Archives

ANOTHER standard design, the station at Cly (MP. 69.9) sits very close to the multiple-track right of way in a 1916 photo.

National Archives

GOLDSBORO (MP. 72.5) was another standard combination station, built in 1891 and shown here in a 1916 photo. Note the iron fence to protect passengers on the Northern Central from the heavy freights on the Low-Grade Line.

National Archives

THE SHELTER at Marsh Run (MP. 75.4) was only slightly larger than the one at Wago. It was also constructed in 1891 and shown here looking northward along the dual-service right of way in 1916.

National Archives

THE STATION at New Cumberland (MP. 80.4) was originally a board-and-batten structure built in 1886 to the standard design for both freight and passenger service but had new sheathing applied and was freight only when this photo was taken on 14 June 1964. Note the superb rail and roadbed condition at this late date.

Edward H. Weber

(caption for artwork on next page)

FROM YORK HAVEN the two lines followed the west bank of the Susquehanna to a junction with the Cumberland Valley RR at Bridgeport (later Lemoyne), opposite Harrisburg. This USGS map shows Harrisburg as the center of several rail lines, making it the hub of rail traffic in central Pennsylvania. The PRR main and Columbia Branch approach along the north bank of the river, and the Northern Central and Low-Grade Line run along the south bank. The PRR Cumberland Valley Branch and the Reading's Philadelphia, Harrisburg & Pittsburgh Branch (which although ambitiously named did give the Reading its long-sought freight connection to the Western Maryland) enter from the west. The Northern Central Marysville line and the PRR main then

continue westward, with the mainline crossing the river on Rockville Bridge (the location of the demolished Northern Central Dauphin Bridge is indicated by a light dashed line). The Reading's Lebanon Valley Branch completes the array.

Sharp-eyed historians may discover that the lower portion of this map (dated 1906) shows the multiple-track right of way reflecting the recently-built Low-Grade Line, while the upper portion (dated 1899) shows the track along the river prior to construction of Enola Yard – and why the Marysville area between the mountain ranges where the Northern Central had their yard was too confining for Cassatt's bold vision of PRR's growing freight traffic needs.

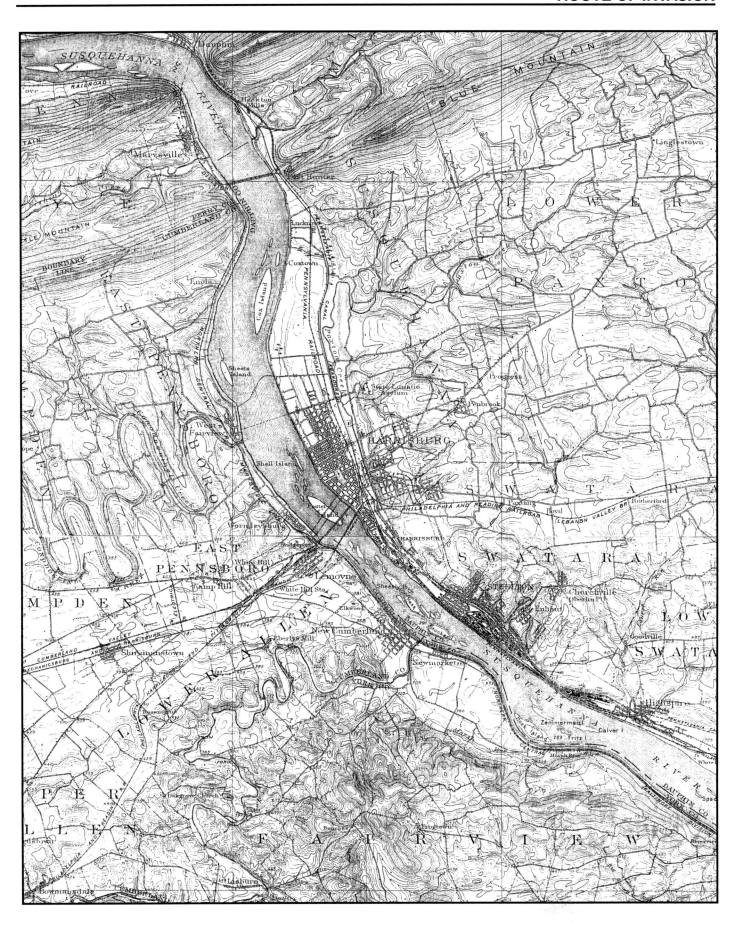

THE YORK & CUMBERLAND RR ran along the west bank of the Susquehanna to Bridgeport (later Lemoyne), where it connected with the Cumberland Valley RR (later a PRR branch) and used that line's wooden bridge across the Susquehanna into the state capital. The first bridge was completed in 1839 and burned in 1844. It was rebuilt in 1844-6 and replaced with an iron structure in 1887. That one lasted until 1915, when it was finally rebuilt as a stone arch bridge. This 1874 engraving looking across the river toward Harrisburg shows a southbound train on the second bridge.

Gunnarsson Collection/Railroad Museum of Pennsylvania (PHMC)

LEMO (Lemoyne) Tower is shown here on 14 June 1964. The view looks northward on the electrified Northern Central/Low-Grade Line at the junction with the Cumberland Valley Branch (the connecting track is in the background). LEMO (originally J) faced the branch when it was built in 1855 but was later turned to face the Northern Central and Low-Grade tracks as shown here (see *Triumph II* for an interlocking diagram of this interesting junction). It was carefully dismantled and reassembled at the Strasburg RR in 1984 after the junction was abandoned.

Edward H. Weber

COMPLETION of the landmark Rockville Bridge across the Susquehanna by PRR in 1849 finally allowed that road to utilize its trackage westward from Harrisburg. This view of the original wooden deck truss bridge from the Harrisburg side also shows the experimental through-arch truss across the Pennsylvania Canal designed by Herman Haupt. After this bridge was rebuilt as a double-track iron structure in 1877 (see *Triumph II*) a connecting line was laid along the river, allowing Northern Central trains to use it, and the wooden Dauphin Bridge was abandoned.

Gunnarsson Collection/Railroad Museum of Pennsylvania (PHMC)

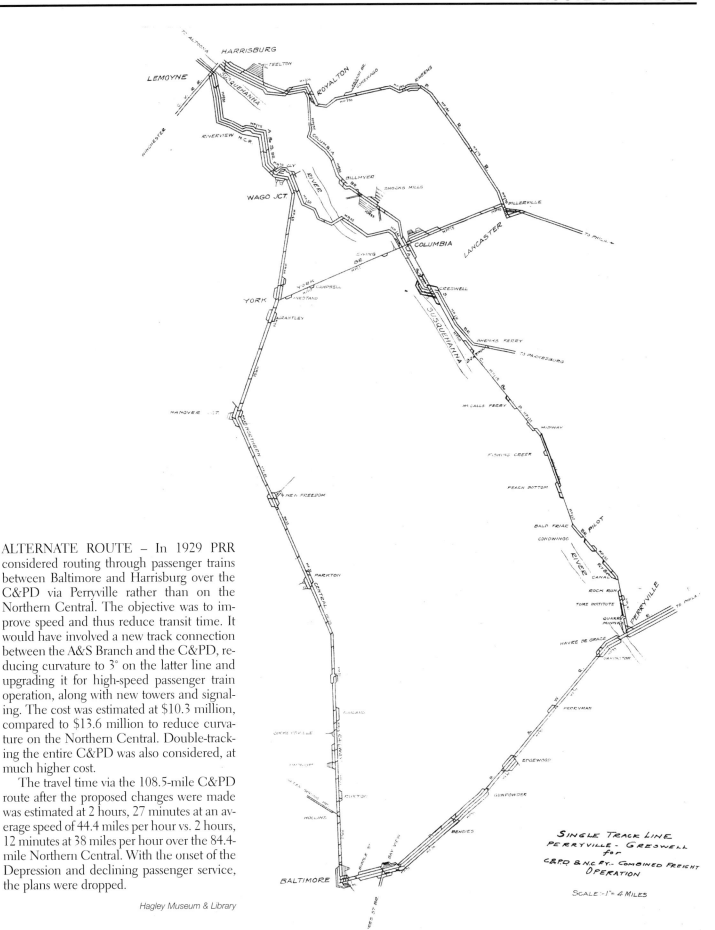

SINGLE TRACK LINE
PERRYVILLE - CRESWELL
for
C&PD & N.C. RY.- COMBINED FREIGHT
OPERATION

SCALE: 1" = 4 MILES

ALTERNATE ROUTE – In 1929 PRR considered routing through passenger trains between Baltimore and Harrisburg over the C&PD via Perryville rather than on the Northern Central. The objective was to improve speed and thus reduce transit time. It would have involved a new track connection between the A&S Branch and the C&PD, reducing curvature to 3° on the latter line and upgrading it for high-speed passenger train operation, along with new towers and signaling. The cost was estimated at $10.3 million, compared to $13.6 million to reduce curvature on the Northern Central. Double-tracking the entire C&PD was also considered, at much higher cost.

The travel time via the 108.5-mile C&PD route after the proposed changes were made was estimated at 2 hours, 27 minutes at an average speed of 44.4 miles per hour vs. 2 hours, 12 minutes at 38 miles per hour over the 84.4-mile Northern Central. With the onset of the Depression and declining passenger service, the plans were dropped.

Hagley Museum & Library

AND NOW we turn to the Frederick Branch. The Hanover & York RR was chartered on 21 April 1873 in response to the needs of the growing businesses located in Hanover and Spring Grove to reach York with its valuable rail connections to Harrisburg and Philadelphia. In 1897 PRR consolidated the H&Y and two other lines extending to Frederick MD to form the York, Hanover & Frederick RR. This line was in turn combined with the original York & Wrightsville to form the Frederick Branch, a line extending from Columbia through the industrial complex of York to Frederick.

This 1885 stock certificate was never issued.

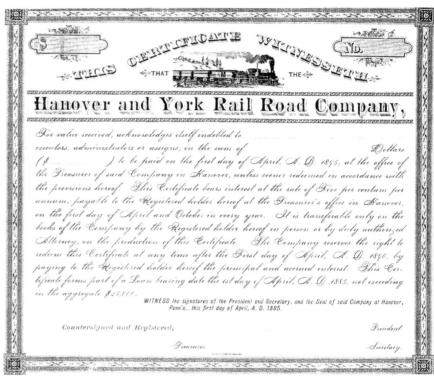

Railroad Museum of Pennsylvania (PHMC)

THE BRANCH crossed Codorus Creek on this 224-ft. long, two-span through plate girder bridge. The photo looks eastward into York in 1915.

National Archives

SPRING GROVE (MP. 23.2 from Columbia) was one of the industrial centers that generated traffic on the Frederick Branch. This view looks northward from the combination station on 22 November 1963.

Edward H. Weber

THE P.H. Gladfelter Paper Company in Spring Grove was one of the largest customers on the Frederick Branch extending westward from York. This 1881 engraving shows the mill on the then Hanover & York RR after it was leased to PRR. Begun in 1864 by P. H. himself, the longtime family-run business had already assumed a substantial output by this time.

A MODERN-DAY VIEW of the P. H. Gladfelter plant is shown here. It provided PRR with substantial carloadings on the Frederick Branch. Many years ago we purchased a lot of paper from this splendid firm which is still quite active.

ATTRACTIVE insulated water tanks were located on the line at Spring Grove, Keymar and at Frederick. This shows the one built in 1898 at Spring Grove in 1915.

Gunnarsson Collection/Railroad Museum of Pennsylvania (PHMC)

THE Union Passenger Railway Depot (as it was known) at Hanover (MP. 31.7) is just visible above locomotive 993 at right. A PRR local pauses ca. 1885 at the depot which served both PRR and the Western Maryland.

F. A. Wrabel Collection

THE YARD at Littlestown (MP. 38.8) is shown here in a westward view ca. 1915. The structures behind the water tank are, l. to r., the freight station annex, the original freight station, and across the tracks to the right, the passenger station. Note the two gentlemen (one smiling, one scowling at having their picture taken) next to the standpipe drain.

THE STATION at Taneytown (MP. 46.5) offers an interesting variation on the combination station design with its integral high-level platform. This view looks eastward on 22 November 1963.

Edward H. Weber

MOVING farther west we get a look at the Taneytown yard as it appeared in 1920. The station is in the background at the right opposite a feed mill.

J. W. Wolf/F. A. Wrabel Collection

THERE ARE several girder bridges on the Frederick Branch and the viaduct spanning Rock Creek at Keymar is an interesting example of railroad bridge architecture. The 720-ft. long structure was made up of 15 steel deck plate girder spans, replaced at various times from 1885-1903, and of varying lengths – five 30-ft., one 40-ft., one 45-ft., two 47-ft., five 62-ft., and one 79-ft. The bovine residents seem unimpressed.

National Archives

END OF THE LINE – This view shows the freight station in Frederick in June 1928 with a local extra (flying white flags) in the street beyond, sent from York to investigate a grade crossing accident. The PRR facilities here for both freight and passengers were meager to say the least, and two proposals were made to improve them – the most elaborate was developed in 1914 and called for a new freight station. The second plan drafted in the early 1920s featured a modest combination station to be built on the site of the freight shed shown here. In the end, nothing was done and the branch began its gradual decline. After all, this was a B&O town.

J. W. Wolf/F. A. Wrabel Collection

THIS VIEW shows the passenger station with the extra at left. Wooden passenger equipment would be gone by the end of 1928 as PRR proudly announced the "passing of the wooden passenger car from our railroad" in October of that year. The station originally featured a large platform that surrounded the building, but this was removed because of deterioration and to reduce maintenance expenditures.

J. W. Wolf/F. A. Wrabel Collection

BASKET CASE – Extra 5026 stops as officials inspect the outcome of a grade crossing accident at the Jacobs Mills station stop. The old D16sb locomotive was originally built for the PW&B and was serving out its last days on the branch. The twisted remains of the vehicle appear destined for the scrap heap. Then, now and forever – it does not pay to tangle with a locomotive.

J. W. Wolf/F. A. Wrabel Collection

F. A. Wrabel Collection

HERE'S A CLOSEUP look at a PRR Class D16sb – the 1223 (Altoona 1905). Polished up for the occasion, she was displayed at Taneytown in connection with that town's bicentennial celebration held on 27-31 July 1954. When it was built it was the last word in fast passenger power – it and other engines of the day did much to further PRR's reputation as the Standard Railroad of the World. She was the last of her breed, happily preserved today in the Railroad Museum of Pennsylvania.

Chapter 6

Arena of Conflict

The Port of Baltimore

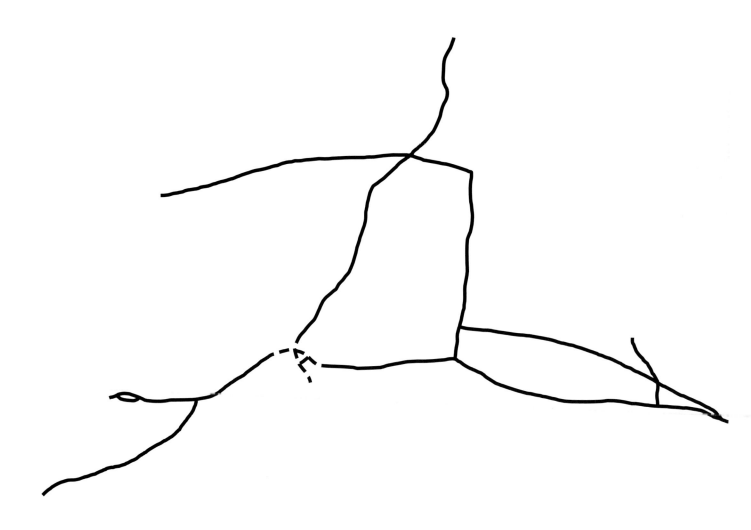

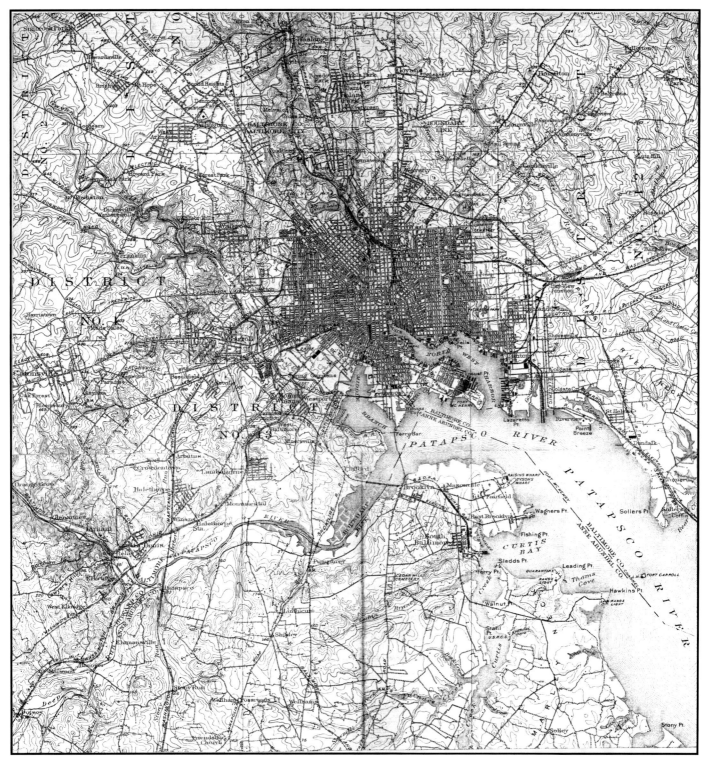

THE COMPLEX ARRAY of rail lines radiating out from Baltimore is depicted in this 1904 USGS map. The inlets at the mouth of the Patapsco River formed a natural harbor around which the city consolidated with its neighboring port areas to become a premier East Coast port.

Starting at the lower right and moving counterclockwise we have the Northern Central Sparrows Point Branch, the PB&W and then the B&O mains to Philadelphia. The PB&W main continues through the Union Tunnel to Union Station while the original line runs to President Street Station, with the Union RR line to the Canton marine terminal complex. The B&O

main runs all the way around the Belt Line to Camden Station.

Continuing counterclockwise, we have the colorful but lowly Ma & Pa RR, the Northern Central main from Calvert Station to Harrisburg, the WM main and Tidewater extension, the PB&W (B&P) main to Washington and finally the B&O main to Washington and the line to its Locust Point marine terminal.

In this chapter we will explore the development of PRR facilities in Baltimore after 1900 – the stations, towers and yards, port areas, the contentious Baltimore Improvements – and of course the constant conflicts with the B&O in its home arena that continued well into the 20th Century.

Arena of Conflict, or perhaps it should be Tunnels and Turmoil, take your pick. Whatever the terminology, arguably no other PRR division witnessed the conflicts – railroad or otherwise – than the Maryland Division, with Baltimore as its focus.

The conflict began early, as we have noted in Chapter 1, over the earnest desire of both Baltimore and Philadelphia to tap the riches of central Pennsylvania and the overland traffic slowly moving eastward through it from the West. Discouraged but unbroken by constant battles with Pennsylvania over attempts to build a canal up the Susquehanna River, it was with determination and a resounding spirit of optimism that Baltimore merchants and investors turned to railroads to gain an advantage over Philadelphia – first the pioneering B&O in 1827 and a year later the B&S up the Susquehanna Valley – only to meet a new set of obstacles from their hostile neighbor to the north.

While these two roads fought the endless dual battles of politics and Mother Nature, a third railroad venture – this time to Philadelphia – entered the scene. The Baltimore & Port Deposit RR, which had begun a rail line northward out of the city in 1832, merged with two other connecting lines in 1836 to form the PW&B.

Out of necessity these three lines built primitive interchange tracks through the increasingly congested city streets of Baltimore. The B&S and B&O established a connection along Howard Street, and the B&S built a line eastward along Monument Street and then southward on Central Avenue to interchange with the PW&B. The B&O and PW&B utilized trackage along Pratt Street, which subsequently became the major rail route connecting New York City and Philadelphia with the nation's capital.

As traffic on these cumbersome street interchanges – all of which by city ordinance involved animal power to haul the cars – continued to increase, all of the lines realized the limitations of their makeshift terminals. The first road to complete a new facility was the PW&B, which opened President Street station on 19 February 1850. Steam locomotives could then haul trains over its own trackage directly into the station, although interchange with the B&O to Washington still required animal power.

The B&S was not far behind – it opened Calvert Station closer to the downtown area on 3 June, also using its own right of way. Notably, it was the largest railroad station constructed to date. This facility was an immediate success, resulting in construction of a separate freight station in 1865.

The success of these two terminals was not lost on the B&O, which was still struggling to complete its line westward. To make matters worse, B&S successor Northern Central had made connections with PRR near Harrisburg to establish its own route for Midwestern traffic, which was handled by several enterprising Main Line freight forwarders. Finally in 1852 the B&O completed its long-delayed line to Wheeling VA (until 1863) and turned to improvement of its own Baltimore facilities.

It contracted with Niernsee & Neilson, the same firm responsible for Calvert Station, to design a new station – deliberately larger and grander than the two others. Camden Station, located to the west of President Street, was partially opened in 1857 but the B&O's precarious finances and the turmoil associated with the ominous national conflict swirling around the city delayed its completion until 1865.

Having effectively assured operating control of the Northern Central in 1864, PRR immediately began to upgrade the line, including improvement of its Howard Street interchange for though service between Harrisburg and Washington. But the B&O's prickly John Garrett refused to cooperate on this endeavor – or much of anything else involving PRR – and declined to sell through tickets, run trains or even forward baggage through the city.

It was against this background of blatant and short-sighted hostility that Thomson carried out one of the most ingenious and strategically brilliant moves ever devised in the history of rail transportation – Garrett's subsequent clumsy attempts to gain control of the PW&B notwithstanding – that would forever vanquish the B&O to third place in its own arena and elsewhere. Taking over the charters of the little-known B&P and Union railroads allowed construction of the "branch" to Washington and the critical connection to the PW&B line to Philadelphia. Having secured the line from Philadelphia to New York at the northern end in 1871 and now anchoring the vital connection for PRR to Washington at the southern, Thomson set the stage for PRR to gain control of the PW&B 10 years later – a move that would have disastrous financial consequences for the B&O which felt forced to build its own line to Philadelphia in 1886.

To establish a center of control for its new lines through Baltimore, PRR located a new "Union" station between the B&P Tunnel leading southward across the western portion of the city and the Union Tunnel to the east and north. Its primary function was for through trains between New York and Washington, although Northern Central trains from Calvert Station as well as local service also used the facility. Because of the alignment of the B&P-Northern Central connection, however, trains between Washington and Harrisburg had to operate "backwards" between Washington and Baltimore.

The original Union Station opened in 1873 was less than optimum. Surprisingly, given the eloquence of the other stations in the city, it was a relatively crude frame affair. It was enlarged in 1882 but was still inadequate to serve the growing needs of the PW&B, Northern Central, B&P and the WM. A new and "commodious" Union Station was built on the same site and opened on 1 April 1886. The new station was ideally situated to serve the growing residential area of the city, while Calvert Station continued to handle traffic in and out of the business district.

Passenger traffic throughout the 1880s and 90s continued to grow, severely taxing the capacity of Union Station and the tracks serving it. Little was done, however, and PRR came under increasing criticism – the beginning of much more to come – to improve its passenger facilities.

In the meantime the B&O established its "Royal Blue Line" service to Philadelphia and New York City in 1895 (via the Reading and Central RR of New Jersey on the northern end) and a newly-electrified Howard Street Tunnel (ironically utilizing the engineering talents of later PRR President Samuel Rea). In addition, it opened its attractive Mount Royal Station the following year, three blocks from Union Station. Still PRR did nothing, focusing its attention on construction of an electrified line into New York City under the enduring vision of Alexander Cassatt and the experience of Rea.

As traffic and congestion continued to increase, however, PRR was strongly pressured to join with the B&O in a true union station, but Cassatt took his time. Suddenly in 1901 a dramatic development occurred. Increasingly concerned that several weaker eastern rail lines (i.e., B&O, Chesapeake & Ohio, Norfolk & Western and the Reading) would engage in ruinous rate wars, Cassatt and William H. Newman of rival New York Central went along with the urgings of imperious financier J. P. Morgan to establish "communities of interest" and stabilize the ailing roads by acquiring a controlling interest in them.

Under the plan PRR did just that with the B&O in 1901. The next step in the grand plan was consolidation of the PW&B and the B&P into the PB&W. With both the B&O and the PB&W under his control, Cassatt then developed a plan for new union stations

in both Baltimore and Washington, which would support the increased traffic between New York and the nation's capital that he envisioned would result from the bold new terminal project planned for Manhattan.

The plan called for an elevated line along the old Pratt Street route across downtown Baltimore, with a true union station to serve the PRR-affiliated lines, the B&O and the WM. But while the controversial project was still under discussion, PRR, fearing anti-trust action by an aroused federal government, suddenly divested its holdings in the B&O. The result was a dramatic reduction in Cassatt's willingness to construct a new union station with the B&O. After lengthy scrutiny the plan was dealt a fatal blow by the ever-hostile Maryland Legislature, which refused to grant the right of way through the city.

Faced with criticism of his proposals from both the city and the Legislature, Cassatt now favored building the new station on the existing site – without the B&O – but Baltimore would have to wait a while longer. Cassatt died at the end of 1906, but successor James McCrea moved forward to complete his program – opening a new Union station in Washington in 1907 (see Chapter 7) and New York City in 1910 (see *Triumph* V). These grand new terminals at either end of the line had the desired impact on PRR passenger traffic between them, but Baltimore took on the burden of a decidedly undesirable name – *bottleneck*. This referred to the tunnels, the yards and the station itself.

Finally PRR in 1908 decided to proceed with construction of a new station on the existing site. A competition was held and the winner was Kenneth W. Murchison (previously with the prestigious firm of McKim, Mead & White that designed Penn Station in Manhattan) who submitted a design similar to his DL&W station in Scranton PA. Both stations incorporated the innovative Bush trainshed (developed by Lincoln Bush, Chief Engineer of the DL&W), featuring platform shelters with arched roofs slotted over the tracks to allow smoke to escape. The Baltimore station was the first use of this feature below grade level.

Construction of the new station began in 1910 and was officially opened to an admiring public on 14 September 1911. What Baltimore citizens were presented with was an imposing structure executed in classical style in gleaming Mitford pink granite. The main building was 60 ft. deep and 275 ft. long, looking large from the front but narrow from the side. It contained a street-level main waiting room 65 ft. deep and 95 ft. long, featuring massive Doric columns and walls of Pandellic marble with skylights inlaid with round stained glass panels. Ticket offices, rest rooms and dining facilities were located around the waiting room.

The concourse was made up of a covered lobby 28 ft. wide and 330 ft. long extending along the track side of the building plus a 50-ft. wide extension across the seven passenger tracks. Eight stairways descended to the train platforms, which were 20 ft. wide and ranged in length from 600 to 1000 ft. Baggage and express rooms and train service facilities were also located at track level.

Even though the station was surrounded by rail yards and bypass tracks, as well as the open channel for Jones Falls, the city made the best of it, laying out an attractive landscaped plaza known as St. Paul Gardens on the south side of the curved waterway. Although Baltimore citizens were visibly impressed at the official opening – as was the local media, which was uncharacteristically outspoken in its praise – experience showed that the waiting room was really too small, especially during peak holiday travel periods, and that the benches blocked access to the ticket windows.

As traffic congestion increased, Baltimore officials again became dissatisfied with their railroad stations and proposals for a new union station resurfaced. The most significant was one developed during USRA control that once again proposed a joint PRR-B&O freight bypass of the city and a new multi-level station facing Mt. Royal Avenue, between St. Paul Street and Maryland Avenue, and spanning Charles Street. This proposal envisioned abandoning both the B&O's Mt. Royal station and the WM's Hillen Station, plus construction of expanded local freight facilities in the Calvert-Hillen station area along with additional tunnels and new track connections that would facilitate traffic flow through the city.

Another USRA proposal called for building a new station at Edmondson Avenue in West Baltimore to serve Northern Central trains that would utilize a new wye connection to B&P Tunnel, thus bypassing Union Station completely. The Edmondson Avenue station was actually built (but not the wye connection), but U. S. railroads were returned to private management on 1 September 1920 and old rivalries resumed with a vengeance, thus dooming further implementation of the USRA plans.

William Wallace Atterbury assumed the presidency of PRR in 1925 after returning from Europe, bringing his expertise to bear that would result in a more efficient organizational structure, better coordinated transportation operations – and most critically for Baltimore, electrification.

Operations of PB&W, the Northern Central and the Union RR were further consolidated, PRR adopted the more realistic title of Pennsylvania Station for its main depot and efforts were made to close Calvert Station because of declining commuter traffic on the Northern Central. Strong opposition from wealthy residents of the northern suburbs prevented implementation of the latter plan, but gas-electric motor cars and even buses were introduced on several local routes instead of locomotive-hauled trains.

In 1928 Baltimore mayor William F. Broening made one last attempt to resurrect the idea of a union station by either expanding or rebuilding Pennsylvania Station for this purpose – this time it was B&O President Daniel Willard, at the time investing heavily in its rival "Royal Blue" service between Washington and New York City who adamantly refused to participate with arch-enemy PRR in such a venture.

In that same year Atterbury made the dramatic announcement of the first phase of a bold new program that would electrify the PRR main from New York to Wilmington, later to be extended to Baltimore and Washington. What this would ultimately mean for Baltimore was not only the eventual elimination of steam trains through the smoke-filled tunnels, but also a comprehensive program for the city that came to be known as the Baltimore Improvements.

Underscoring its importance, the following entry appeared in the 1929 Annual Report:

> "Agreement was reached during the year with the City of Baltimore, Md., relative to proposed improvement and expansion of the lines and facilities in and near that City. The agreement, *which has been under negotiation for several years* [italics added], covers extensive station, platform and track improvements in and through that City, including the construction of two double-track tunnels and the electrification of lines. The completion of these new tunnels will enable your railroad to operate a four track main line through Baltimore from the eastern to the southwestern City limits, a distance of six miles. It also provides for the rebuilding of Calvert Station, construction of warehouses adjacent to that station and the elimination of grade crossings. These improvements will greatly benefit the City of Baltimore and will enable the New York-Wilmington electrification to be extended to Washington DC giving your System a total of 799 miles of line and 2,759 miles of track electrically operated upon completion of the electrification program outlined in the 1928 Annual Report."

PRR then went on to paper over the years of rancor and rejected proposals with the following olive branch:

"The active co-operation and constructive attitude of the City authorities in reaching conclusions which permitted the inauguration of this important improvement program are cordially acknowledged."

Diplomatic statements from PRR notwithstanding, the city was evidently still skeptical, forming a municipal railroad commission and passing several restrictive ordinances holding PRR's nose to the grindstone. Nevertheless the agreement was reached and implementation of the program begun: The yards at Pennsylvania Station were modified in 1929-30 to accommodate a new Post Office building, built on the site of the old coach yard east of St. Paul Street. Work began in 1931 on elimination of grade crossings – elevation of the tracks in some areas and lowering it in others.

By 1933, however, the Depression hit hard and traffic and revenues plunged. Funds for electrification south of Wilmington and completion of the Baltimore Improvements – despite a $27.5 million loan from the Reconstruction Finance Corporation – were depleted and the work was suspended. In August of that year PRR officials began urgent discussions with representatives from the newly-formed federal Public Works Administration (PWA), which hoped that additional funding would not only allow resumption of the project and put thousands of laid-off workers back to work but also have a wide-ranging effect on the severely-depressed economy.

On December 29 PRR reached agreement with the PWA providing a $77 million loan to complete the project. These funds allowed completion of the new Union Tunnel, grade crossing elimination, station and right of way improvements and of course the all-important electrification. However the proposed additional B&P Tunnel proved too costly (upwards of $8 million, depending on the exact configuration), and it was never carried out – nor was a new Calvert Station.

Thus it came to pass that a special train left Washington Union Station on a frigid 28 January 1935. On its way to Philadelphia it stopped at Pennsylvania Station for Baltimore officials to board – among them ironically Daniel Willard, who must have felt strange at the sight of PRR's awesome new physical plant that would further reduce B&O's competitive presence, its continued public relations campaigns notwithstanding. Regular electrified passenger service began on 10 February.

With the completion of the electrification program PRR changed the focus of operations through Baltimore from east-west (Washington-Harrisburg and westward) to north-south (Washington-Philadelphia-

New York). The decision was made not to electrify the Northern Central, and instead freight traffic was increasingly routed on the C&PD line, which did receive the overhead wires, connecting with the Low-Grade Line into Enola, also electrified. It was the beginning of a slow death for the scenic line. In July 1938 the old Baltimore Division was combined with the Maryland Division, further reducing the status of the Northern Central.

World War II brought a surge of traffic though Baltimore – both passengers and freight. In response to the delays Bay View Yard was greatly enlarged in 1943, becoming the central PRR classification yard for the city, and yards in the Camden area were expanded as well. A new freight station was opened to the west of Bay View in 1945.

Pennsylvania Station, besieged with upwards of 400,000 passengers (on Christmas weekend in 1944), endured the war with the indignity of its stained glass and Bush trainshed covered over with solid roofing. A successful but modernistic USO lounge, designed by Lester Tichy of Raymond Loewy Associates, was added on the east end of the station.

As the war drew to a close, PRR again submitted plans for station improvements to the city, but these were sharply criticized as inadequate – the city insisting on adherence to the ordinances passed two decades before for electrification of the line to Calvert Station and construction of a new terminal on that location. Faced with the escalating costs of maintaining the old structure for the few remaining trains on the old Northern Central line, PRR demolished the original terminal in 1949 and remodeled a portion of the 1865 Freight Shed and dubbed it Calvert Station. With traffic declining, PRR managed to escape the requirement for electrification of the line.

On 27 June 1959 the legendary Parkton local was discontinued, and the commuter platforms on the south side of the station, constructed in 1934 as part of the Baltimore Improvements, were removed.

With reduced maintenance and declining through passenger service in the late 1950s – PRR in general but especially on the Washington-Chicago route, B&O on its Baltimore-New York "Royal Blue Line" service and the WM passenger operations out of the city altogether – Pennsylvania Station became a dingy and forlorn presence, commercial vendors and a cheap game room notwithstanding. But its historic liabilities – inadequate size and distance from the business district – actually contributed to its survival through the Penn Central debacle and into the formation of

Amtrak in 1971. Several proposals emerged for modernization of the station, the most ambitious involving using it as the focus of a new transportation center.

But the preservationists wanted the station restored to emphasize its original character – in 1975 it was listed on the National Register of Historic Places and with the takeover of the Northeast Corridor by Amtrak in 1976, the victory had been won. Some $6.7 million of the $2.2 billion for the Northeast Corridor Improvement Project was allocated to the station for both exterior and interior architectural restoration.

Interior work began first, with removal of the roof covering the skylights, restoration of the stained glass domes over the waiting room and the unique Rookwood tiles in the Concourse, and cleaning and repointing the marble walls and mosaic tile floors. This phase was completed in 1982 and a dedication ceremony held on 16 May 1983.

The second phase involved construction of a large landscaped plaza in front of the station, providing improved traffic flow and much needed additional parking space, as well as renovation of the upper floors for commercial tenants.

The trackage through Pennsylvania Station was rebuilt to improve train movements in conjunction with the implementation of Amtrak's CETC, controlled electronically – and ironically – from Philadelphia. Tracks A and B (in front of the station) as well as main Tracks 1 and 5 were removed and Track 2 was realigned to provide improved clearances for intermodal freight traffic. UNION JUNCTION Tower was closed on 17 March 1987 and B&P JUNCTION was likewise shut down on 27 October. Many of the former PRR and B&O commuter operations were taken over by MARC rail and MTA light rail lines.

Thus relative harmony and peace has come to Baltimore, a city that has probably seen more than its share of turmoil and conflict.

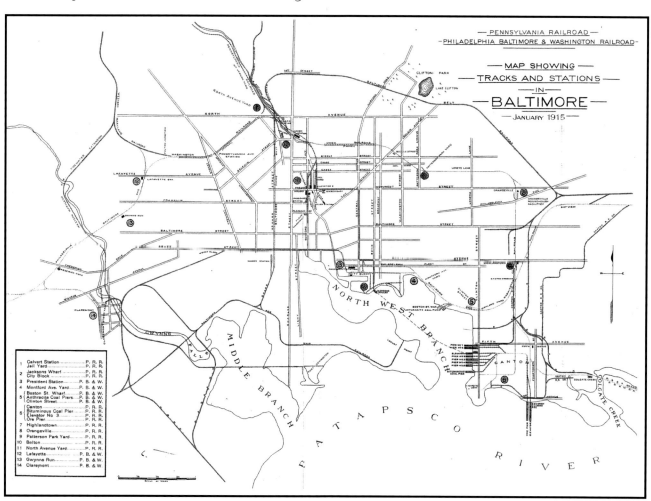

Hagley Museum & Library

WE HAVE SOMEONE in the PB&W to thank for another superb map of Baltimore – this time thoughtfully with only the major streets showing – that allows a clear depiction of the major rail lines through the city as of 1915, after the PRR takeover of the PB&W. Compare this one to the earlier 1879 map. The B&O and Canton RR trackage has at least been included for reference. The map key locates the major PRR stations and yard facilities.

F. A. Wrabel

WE WILL BEGIN our exploration of the development of PRR facilities in Baltimore at North Point Block Station, shown here with a solemn-faced track gang and a group of more jovial supervisors on 9 February 1928. Although in many ways North Point was the gateway to Baltimore – it was the location of the division post between the old Baltimore and Maryland Divisions for a number of years – it looks here more like an outpost at the North Pole rather than an entry to a major city on the East Coast.

BECAUSE OF restricted yard space within the city limits and rapidly-growing interchange traffic with the B&P and Union RRs, PW&B in 1880 purchased extensive property for a new yard in the Bay View area, near the junction with these lines. This new facility allowed makeup of trains outside of the city limits for the first time. Continued traffic growth forced expansion of the yard in 1889-90.

This view looking southward shows the crowded yards in 1915, with a variety of cars and loads – close inspection of the photo reveals what looks like a gun barrel mounted on a flat car.

WITH CONSTRUCTION of B&O's Baltimore Belt Line in 1890-96, Bay View also became an interchange point with that road. This photo was taken 16 April 1926 looking northward at the original BAY VIEW block station. The B&O interchange track, yards and main are visible behind the tower.

F. A. Wrabel

ELECTRIFICATION and reworking of the trackwork required rebuilding of BAY VIEW interlocking and tower, shown here in a 1934 view. Steam power still operates under the newly-installed overhead, which was not yet fully operational at this time. The B&O connecting track is now in front of the tower – a B&O tower is just visible at the left of the photo.

F. A. Wrabel

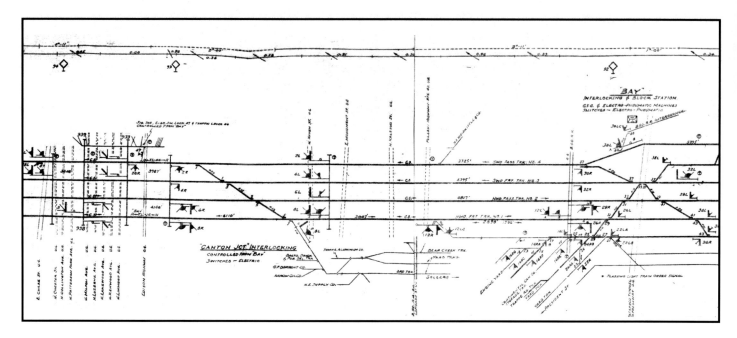

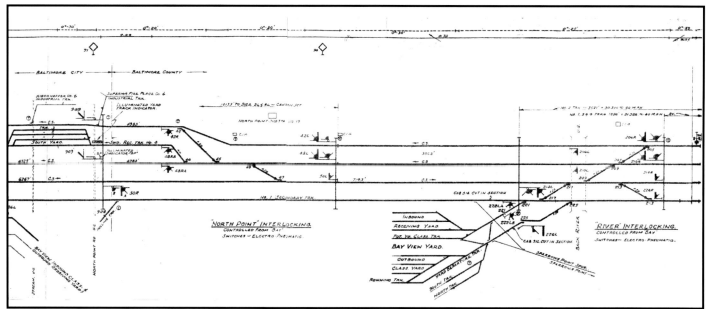

THIS DIAGRAM dated 15 April 1946 shows the series of interlockings, RIVER, NORTH POINT and CANTON JUNCTION, all by this time controlled from BAY Tower, which was equipped with CTC and electro-pneumatic machines. These installations protected both ends of Bay View Yard and interchange with the B&O as well as smaller yard tracks, sidings and the line to Canton Yard and President Street Station.

REVENGE – Perhaps expressing frustration and feelings of helplessness because of declining numbers caused by electrification, L1s 3280 appears to have tried to bring down the overhead in a 1941 wreck scene. It didn't succeed, but it certainly caused the wreck crews plenty of headaches. This view looking northward at Bay View shows two cranes – the one at right still lettered Northern Central – trying to untangle the mess while a host of onlookers watches the proceedings. Note the short-lived Futura lettering on the tender.

J. W. Wolf/F. A. Wrabel Collection

WITH OR WITHOUT WRECKS, the catenary requires constant maintenance to insure smooth and trouble-free operation. Here we have a steam-powered wire train and crew at work at CANTON JUNCTION in 1935. A cigar-chomping foreman oversees the operation.

F. A. Wrabel

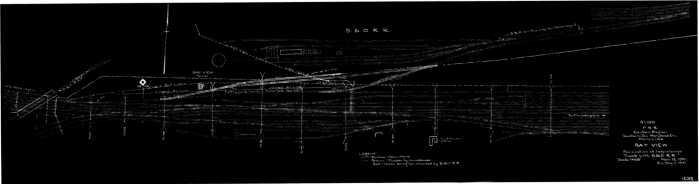

Hagley Museum & Library

WORLD WAR II brought massive traffic surges to Bay View and the yard was greatly enlarged in 1942-3. One of the first tasks was to increase the capacity of the B&O interchange, which had seen a 55% increase from 1939 to 1941. It was originally a single track holding 52 cars connecting with the No. 4 (southbound) passenger track through a hand-thrown switch. This necessitated light engine movements several times daily. The connection was moved farther south and double-tracked, as shown here in a 1941 diagram. And yes, B&O did cooperate on this one, reworking their tracks accordingly.

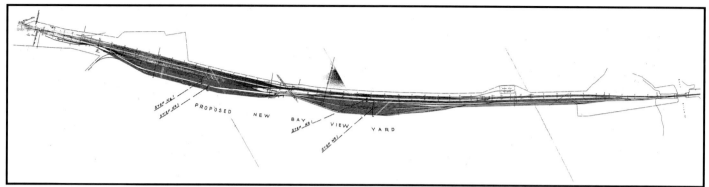

LACK OF adequate centralized yard facilities in Baltimore had long been a source of delay in both road and yard operations in the multiplicity of existing yards, leading to high operating costs, tying up motive power and sub-standard service to shippers. The situation was aggravated during the years leading up to World War II by the increasing traffic flow in and out of the city itself and through the port areas. With increasing train length, the fact that none of the existing yards could handle a train greater than 85 cars without blocking other yard or main tracks became a serious problem, requiring an excessive number of inter-terminal movements and resulting in intolerable delays.

Bay View was chosen as the logical location for such a central yard, consolidating classification operations divided between the existing Bay View, Highland (just to the south on the President Street Branch) and Canton Yards. The complete yard layout shown here provided sufficient capacity for classification of inbound trains for all Baltimore destinations except Canton (ex-panded yards were constructed at Canton at the same time) and assembly of all outbound loads and empties.

The project involved excavating and grading 375,000 cu. ft. of soil, laying nearly 150,000 lineal feet of track (of which 100,000 ft. was electrified), construction of a new bridge over North Point Road and the installation of a new signal system at BAY VIEW Tower. As completed in 1943 the yard included the following: Inbound Receiving – three tracks, capacity 289 cars … Inbound Classification – 16 tracks, capacity 812 cars … Outbound Receiving – six tracks, capacity 358 cars … Outbound Classification – 21 tracks, capacity 1064 cars, plus a cabin car track 400 ft. long, two car repair tracks and three running tracks for a total of 52 tracks with a capacity of 2649 cars. The initial cost estimate approved on 14 January 1942 was for approximately $2 million, but increasing costs after the U. S. entry into the war pushed the total to over $3 million. PRR at last had a real classification yard in Baltimore and it was ideally sited for interchange with B&O.

THIS AERIAL VIEW of Bay View Yard looks at the southern half of the facility in 1953 – the Inbound Classification Yard is at the left center stretching along the main, with the Outbound Receiving Yard to the left of that. A pair of Baldwin switchers works the hump near the hump tower and yard office in the foreground. To the right of center is the new plant of the Kieckhefer Container Company. In the background at the right are the B&O yards and to the left of center are BAY VIEW Tower and the B&O branch to Canton crossing over the PRR main.

That B&O yard brings back memories. During World War II Father was pulled from his office and assigned to this yard as a clerk to help with the congestion. He took us along on several occasions as an unpaid assistant to help with the war effort. The B&O high-speed main ran through the middle of the yard which, as one can see, was on a curve – surely the most hazardous arrangement possible.

We recall walking down a string of cars checking car numbers (with great caution) when we reached the end of the string. One is never quite sure where one is in this situation, *(continued on next page)*

(continued from previous page)

so we peeked around the end of the car only to discover that we had found the mainline. Just then an eastbound passenger train flashed by at about 70 mph just two feet in front of us. Frozen in our memory is the sight of the engineer, an old man by our reference, leaning back in his seat with his feet up and in total, casual control of this roaring behemoth. Awesome. One could see why a young man would rather be an engineer than President.

The yardmaster was, if memory serves, a gentleman named Hartung. We remember when a brakeman came off a road engine and complained to Mr. Hartung that there was grass growing around a switchstand to the east. Mr. Hartung snarled as follows: "This war is going to be over one of these days and you'll be back eating with the birds."

The yardmaster shack (and it was just that) was next to the receiving track. Please understand that in railroading, as with the infantry, one must bellow to be heard over ambient sound. When a train arrived, the yardmaster would shout out and signal the track to which the train was assigned – done with alacrity to keep the train moving. Thus the window to the shack was always open.

We owe a relative this story. After the war a trainee was assigned to this post, but the yardmaster was too busy to have time for him. This young man, eager to make himself useful, noticed that his window was filthy so he cleaned *and closed* it. As a train arrived, the yardmaster lunged through the window to shout up orders. The window shattered along with the yardmaster's temper. We don't know the fate of the trainee.

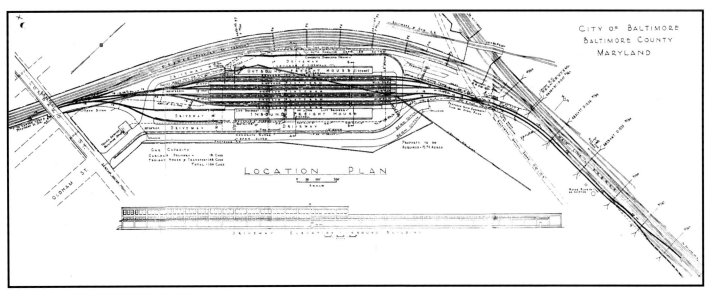

Hagley Museum & Library

THE FINAL STEP in the expansion of the Bay View area was construction of a new freight station. Although both Calvert Street and President Street freight stations and yards had been expanded several times, both were inadequate for the volume of wartime traffic – and difficult to access. In 1945 PRR opened this large new LCL facility, located on Lombard Street near the south end of Bay View Yard and the junction of the President Street Branch and the main (still labeled PB&W on this diagram). It consisted of an inbound and outbound freighthouse and three covered platforms serving eight tracks holding a total of 164 cars. Note the B&O crossing.

ON 12 JUNE 1911 the Northern Central opened an enginehouse, shops and small yard at Orangeville just west of Bay View Yard. This became the central PRR service and repair facility for all through passenger and freight locomotives as well as switchers used at Bay View, Calvert Street, Canton, Gwynns Run, Mt. Vernon and Sparrows Point. This southward view shows the Orangeville Shops and engine terminal ca. 1915, with the mainline swinging to the right and the Continental Can plant at the left.

National Archives

HERE'S a close-up view of the massive 1060-ton coal wharf, looking from the opposite direction in 1915. This would make a challenging modeling project.

THIS TINY SHELTER, shown in a 1915 photo, served as the station at Orangeville, primarily for the convenience of railroad shop personnel. Note the pole-mounted lanterns.

HERE'S THE LAYOUT of the Orangeville engine terminal in a 1949 diagram, with the steam locomotive facilities still largely intact.

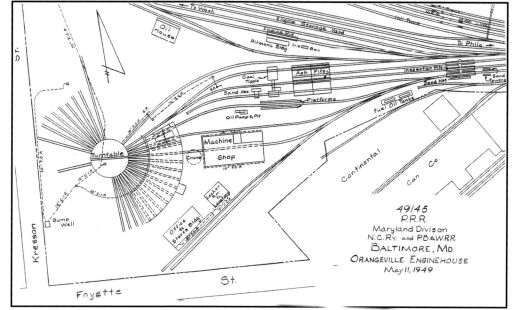

F. A. Wrabel Collection

WITH ELECTRIFICATION of the main, Orangeville was also assigned the task of servicing the P5a and GG1 fleet. It was expanded during World War II and handled over 100 locomotives per *day*. Here we see GG1 4861 and colleagues under the glow of floodlights during the early 1970s.

Maryland Rail Heritage Library

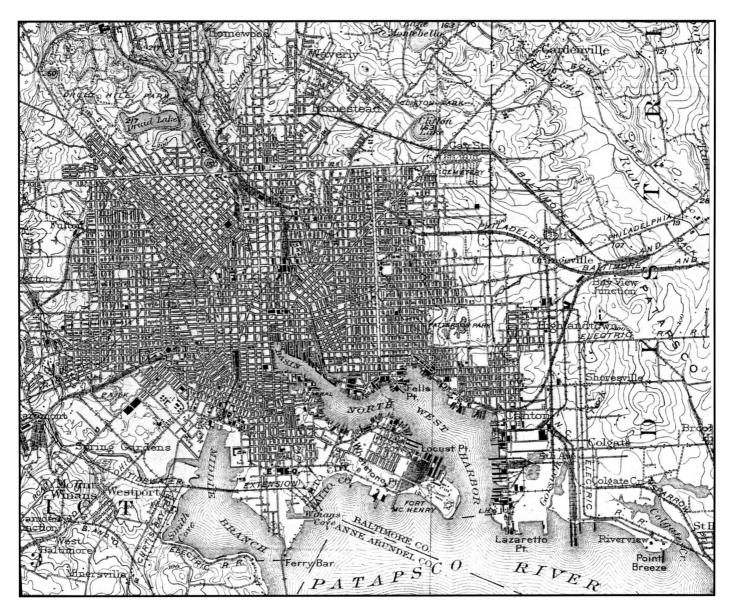

WE NOW MOVE to the Canton pier area, site of PRR's bold thrust into B&O's harbor trade. To help us understand the complexities of Baltimore Harbor in general and the Canton area in particular, we present a closer look at the facilities from the USGS map shortly after the turn of the century – 1904 was the year that fire destroyed a large portion of the Pratt Street waterfront area. It was soon rebuilt and had minimal impact on the Canton waterfront which lines the western edge of the Northwest

Harbor area, directly opposite historic Fort McHenry and B&O's main terminal area at Locust Point.

Both B&O and PRR suffered extensive fire damage to their respective grain elevators and other pier facilities from the 1890s to the early 1930s, when reinforced concrete structures replaced wooden ones (please refer to the superbly detailed map on the rear endpaper to see the growth of the entire Canton area – both the piers themselves and the extensive rail yards serving them).

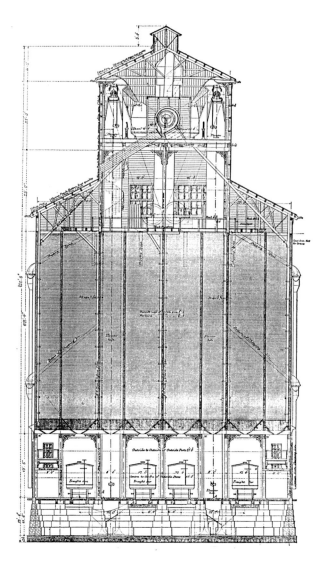

TO SUPPORT the burgeoning grain and flour trade and foment its invasion of B&O's arena, the Northern Central and subsequently PRR constructed a series of elevators in Canton and nearby areas. Elevator No. 1, with a storage capacity of 500,000 bu., was built by the Northern Central and put in service in 1876. It is shown here in a meticulously-detailed engraving in Dredge's laudatory treatise on PRR technology.

F. A. Wrabel

FIRES and even explosions in grain elevators are a constant danger because of the highly combustible nature of the dust given off during handling plus the threat of lightning strikes, but Elevator No. 3 had a particularly tortured history. It was built by the Northern Central in 1879 with a storage capacity of 600,000 bu. This elevator was completely destroyed by a spectacular fire on the night of 13 January 1890. It was rebuilt and enlarged on the original site at the foot of 14th Street with a capacity of 1,000,000 bu. and put in operation on 10 August 1891. The elevator suffered extensive fire damage on 1 January 1903 and was rebuilt with 32, 25-ft. diameter concrete storage bins added in 1906-7. The ill-fated elevator once again succumbed to fire in 1916 and was replaced by this massive fireproof reinforced concrete and steel structure in 1920. The old wooden Elevator No. 1 was demolished at this time.

This superb view of the elevator shows stored ships from the PRR-owned Baltimore, Chesapeake & Atlantic and Maryland, Delaware & Virginia steamship lines.

WITH the new elevator PRR could boast a fireproof storage capacity of 4.25 million bu. By means of four mechanical car unloaders (located at the center of the photo above the bow of the right-hand ship) the facility could unload 40 box cars (about 80,000 bu.) per hour. There was space for three ships to berth at the pier at the same time. In this 1953 view the 32 smaller, partially enclosed silos that face the water were part of the old Elevator No. 3 built in 1906-7.

The Ore Pier is at left – this wooden pier, 64-ft. wide and 1200-ft. long, was originally constructed in 1887 and re-built in 1939. It was served by the yard extending northward behind it and four surface tracks extending the full length of the pier. It was the site of intense activity during World War II when domestic ore was shipped here by rail, loaded into barges and then moved to the Bethlehem Steel facility at Sparrows Point. Activity had diminished considerably by the time of this photo.

Also visible in this view are the rebuilt Yard No. 3 behind the grain elevator, the dust-enshrouded National Gypsum plant (right), Crown Cork & Seal (right background) and the Standard Oil tank farms (background).

Tom Hollyman – Penn Central Railroad Collection/Pennsylvania State Archives.

B&O RESPONDED by building its own new fireproof concrete grain elevator for export service, shown under construction in early 1924. Located at Locust Point across from Canton, it replaced two smaller elevators destroyed by fire on 2 July 1922 (this time by lightning – although PRR had made a titanic thrust into the area, to our knowledge it did not have control over lightning strikes). To quote the B&O Engineering Department report dated 24 May 1926, "The new facilities, which have just been placed in service, provide the Port of Baltimore and the patrons of the Baltimore & Ohio with a grain terminal equal to the best."

Well, not quite. Not only was its storage capacity (3.7 million bu.) and car unloading rate (32 cars – about 60,000 bu. per hour) less than that of the PRR elevator, but also both PRR (and later Western Maryland) whittled away at B&O's near-monopoly on grain exports

from Baltimore during the period 1897-1924, and in several of those years both roads equaled or even surpassed B&O's tonnage.

As an aside, in studying this photo we are struck by what it must have been like for the residents of the rowhouses at the left to look out their back window and see the mass of 112-ft. high towers and the 206-ft. high elevator blocking out the sky.

AT THE SAME TIME that PRR constructed the greatly expanded general classification yard at Bay View, it also expanded the yards in the Canton district. The new yard at Holabird Avenue, just east of Clinton Street, was enlarged so that all the switching and classification work needed for the various Canton piers previously performed at several widely-separated points could be consolidated in one area. The new yard had 30 tracks, with a capacity of 600 cars, primarily serving Piers 1 and 11.

This 1953 view looks south over the new yard in the foreground toward the Grain Elevator and Ore Pier. In the background at the far right is Pier No. 11, then leased by PRR from the Canton Company, and to the right of it Pier No. 10. At left are Yard No. 3 and the smaller 5th Avenue Yard, serving the grain elevator and ore pier.

Tom Hollyman - Penn Central Railroad Collection/Pennsylvania State Archives

J. W. Wolf/F. A. Wrabel Collection

SPEAKING OF Pier No. 11, here's the front view of the facility ca. 1940, with shiny vintage automobiles and a classic Schwinn bicycle gracing the scene. The pier measured 200-ft. wide by 1623-ft. long and provided berthing space for three ships. The two-story shed itself was 91 X 921 ft. and contained 324,600 sq. ft. The pier had a single-track apron alongside the shed.

The other half of the pier, designated No. 10 and belonging to the Canton Company, was 197-ft. wide and 1483-ft. long. It contained a one-story shed measuring 100 X 501 ft., with a double-track apron alongside. In addition there were several tracks between the sheds with a total capacity of nearly 140 cars.

AND HERE'S the working end of Pier No. 11, with crated International trucks being loaded – seemingly rather casually – on board ship from gondolas (modelers take note). It was originally constructed primarily to serve the Baltimore Mail Line passenger service prior to World War II, but by the time of this photo was used only for freight. It was equipped with freight elevators and chutes and protected by firewalls and a sprinkler system.

J. W. Wolf/ F. A. Wrabel Collection

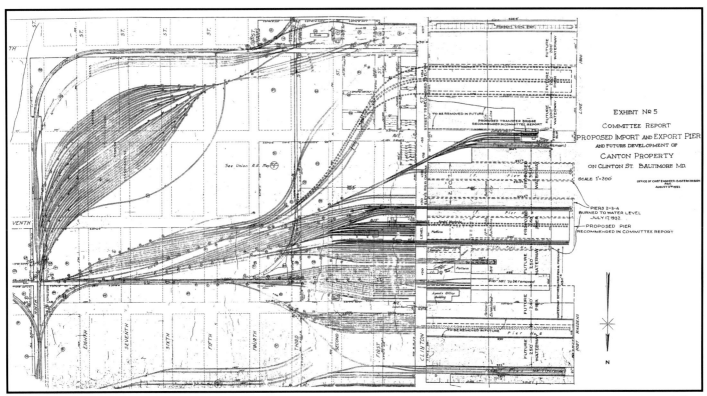

Hagley Museum & Library

ON 17 JULY 1932 Piers 2, 3 and 4, located north of the Coal Pier, burned to the ground (okay, water level). In typical PRR fashion a committee was quickly formed to examine the issue and in a report dated 5 August it duly recommended construction of a large new Pier No. 1 to replace the three destroyed piers, along with old Piers 1 and 6 (right center of this diagram). Note also the location of the Coal Pier (top right) and coal storage yards (top left).

WHAT RESULTED was a modern, two-story fireproof pier of steel and concrete, 223 ft. wide by 930 ft. long. At the time promoted by PRR as one of the most modern facilities of its kind in the world, it was designed for export and import of a wide variety of nonperishable goods. It provided wharf space for four oceangoing ships at once and was served by a sprawling yard and 4400 ft. of trackage extending inside the shed and on the side aprons (as built the structure had a heavy-duty forced ventilation system to remove smoke). The pier included a three-story office building at the bulkhead end, shown here ca. 1940 with Clinton Street in the foreground, with a two-story freight shed beyond covering an area measuring 173 X 895 ft. Costing $2 million, it was supported on 4501 reinforced concrete piles, a new technology for piers at the time.

F. A. Wrabel Collection

THIS 1953 VIEW shows Pier No. 1 after lengthening to 1100 ft, including a one-story addition to the shed and adding a second 15-ton gantry crane on the double-tracked south apron. At right is the Rukert warehouse on Pier No. 5, and in the background are the American Mining & Smelting Works (upper left) and the yards (upper right) serving the Coal Pier.

Tom Hollyman - Penn Central Railroad Collection/Pennsylvania State Archives

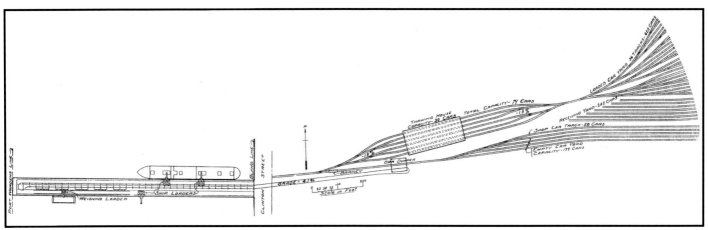

COAL was a major source of revenue for the Northern Central from its early years, especially after the northern extension and branches into the anthracite fields were built. After anthracite traffic diminished, bituminous coal shipped from its PRR connections remained an important revenue source both for use within the Baltimore area and for export.

After taking over the Northern Central, PRR in 1916-7 constructed a new reinforced concrete and steel Coal Pier, replacing an older wooden structure farther to the north constructed in 1881 and expanded in 1888. The new structure was located on Clinton Street at the foot of Keith Avenue.

IN OPERATION strings of loaded hopper cars were pushed by locomotives from the 1000-car storage yard up an incline to a kickback where they rolled one-by-one back to a barney that in turn pushed them onto a car dumper. There they were picked up and turned over, emptying the coal into a 100-ton receiving hopper. Small 4-ton cars, shown here in a 1917 photo, were then loaded from the receiving hopper (stay with us now) and pulled by a continuous cable system out onto the trestle along the center of the pier and dumped into four traveling unloaders with a capacity of 1000 tons per hour at any location desired. From these unloaders the coal was conveyed by telescoping chutes into the holds of waiting ships.

STORAGE BINS, which are shown in this 1917 photo of the nearly completed facility, were also constructed at the foot of the pier for different grades of coal for local harbor use. Boats for this trade were loaded via a small traveling unloader. In order that the work of unloading hoppers could continue in cold weather, a steam-heated thawing house with a capacity of 30 cars was located at the yard throat. This entire coaling facility, which cost $225,000, was constructed for PRR by the Arthur McMullen Co. of New York, according to designs made by the Cleveland Dock Engineering Co.

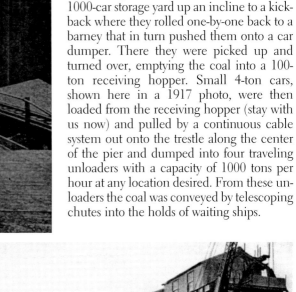

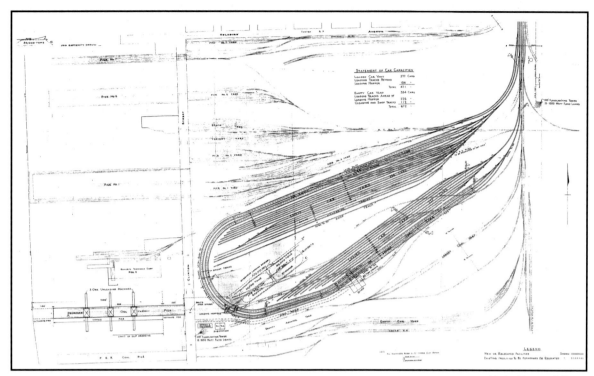

AFTER World War II PRR seriously considered construction of a new ore pier in the Baltimore harbor area. It examined sites as diverse as Soller's Point, Todd Point, Bay Shore Park and Black Marsh before proposing in 1950 a $10 million facility to be located right in Canton, between the Coal Pier and Pier No. 5. It would have involved new yards north of the coal yard and because of limited space, making use of a complex conveyor system from the pier to four loop tracks to permit continuous unloading.

The project ran into a convoluted political situation involving the City of Baltimore, U. S. Steel (which wanted to build its own facility) and the Canton Company, which carried out a $1.5 million upgrade of its own pier west of PRR's old one, effectively causing a frustrated PRR management to, "find itself jockeyed completely out of position for the ore traffic in the Baltimore harbor." Even PRR couldn't win them all, although it did construct a new ore pier in 1952-4 at Greenwich Point in Philadelphia (see *Triumph III*) where the political climate was decidedly friendlier.

PRR also maintained marine facilities northwest of Canton, at the old Boston Street wharf area along the President Street Branch – the original PW&B line into Baltimore. At the time of this 1953 photo the float bridge was being used to unload car floats containing reefers of bananas. The National Brewing Company brewery (lest we forget, another grain product!) is at the upper right. Maryland's unofficial title "Land of Pleasant Living" was created for "National Bo."

THE Mountford Avenue Yard was located just northwest of the Boston Street facility, serving the piers at Jackson's Wharf and City Block. Here hoppers and strings of vintage boxcars occupy the yard in a ca. 1915 view.

BEFORE LEAVING the immediate Baltimore harbor area, we need to examine the giant steel complex at Sparrows Point, southeast of Canton. This area was originally accessed by the Northern Central Sparrows Point Branch, built to serve the steel mill originally constructed by the Pennsylvania Steel Company, partially owned by PRR. This branch connected with the original Union RR line east of Canton and extended to Colgate Creek where it continued the remaining 4 miles to the plant as the Sparrows Point RR, built and owned by the Maryland Steel Company.

Highlandtown station was located just north of the junction of the PB&W President Street Branch and the Union RR at Eastern Avenue – a Canton RR spur extended northward from Fifth Avenue to this point. This 1915 view shows the small passenger station with the team track and freight shed beyond.

THE TINY Fifth Avenue station was located on the Sparrows Point Branch at, not surprisingly, Fifth Avenue. This ca. 1915 photo looks northward – the buildings at the right are on Fourteenth Street (leading southward to the Grain Elevator and Ore Pier), and beyond them lie tracks of the Canton RR and the later B&O branch to Sparrows Point.

SUTTON was a station stop on the Branch used mostly by blue collar workers who kept the plants running on the southeast side of town. A lone pooch (left of the tracks) warily eyes the photographer ca. 1915.

ANOTHER shelter was located at Colgate Creek shown here in a ca. 1915 view looking south. The PRR branch actually ended here at this time – just beyond the station a string of hoppers rests on a spur of the Sparrows Point RR which continued on to the mill complex

THIS PHOTO at Colgate Creek taken on 14 November 1918 shows a PRR local crossing the wide creek on the trestle at left. In the center are the heavy Baltimore Gas & Electric pipelines and electrical service to the mill and at right is the Baltimore Transit line.

Maryland Rail Heritage Library

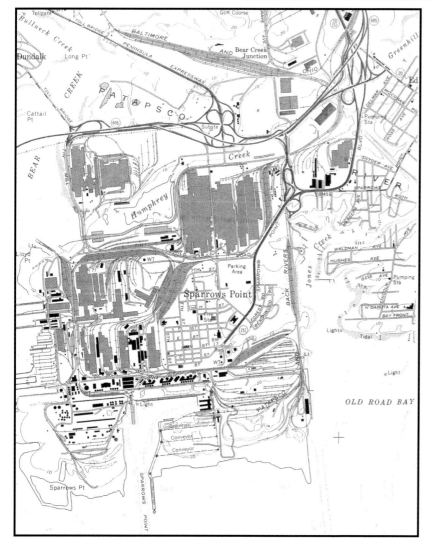

THE SPARROWS POINT mill, later taken over by Bethlehem Steel and greatly enlarged, was designed to receive most of its iron ore from South American and European sources, but during World War II the ore was shipped by rail from Great Lake ports because of the threat of Nazi U-boat attack. The ore was transferred from hoppers at the PRR ore pier into barges, which were then towed to Sparrows Point to be unloaded at the ore docks there. At its peak operation over 2 million tons of ore were delivered to the site by PRR in this manner.

The sprawling facility – and the rail yards serving it – is depicted here in a USGS map revised to 1974. Both Penn Central and B&O lines enter from the north – the raw material yards are at center and lower right, with the blast furnaces at lower left, the open hearth furnaces above that and the rolling mills at the upper right. The famed shipyards are at the left.

One of Father's closest friends, Vic Ryan, was a master for the Calmar Lines, Bethlehem's shipping subsidiary. When in port he would visit with Father and other pals in friendly poker and crap games. Naturally we witnessed the events from the top of the steps and used knowledge gained in our own crap games.

Captain Ryan hauled ore from South America to Sparrows Point. In early 1942 he was in port and we heard him, quite shaken, talk of his latest northbound trip. In *one day* a total of five ships were torpedoed on his route. Those were grim days indeed.

Tom Hollyman - Penn Central Railroad Collection/Pennsylvania State Archives

IN this 1953 aerial view the lime and scrap yards are in the foreground and the scrap sorting area is at right center, with the blast furnaces (center) and open hearth furnaces (right) in the background.

Tom Hollyman - Penn Central Railroad Collection/Pennsylvania State Archives

MOVING IN CLOSER we see another scrap yard (the facility was served by both PRR and B&O), with the long open hearth furnace structures behind. The shipyard is just visible in the background.

AND on the output side, here's a look at the hot strip mill. The broad Patapsco River is in the background. As is evident from these photos, the domestic steel industry in its heyday was a major source of traffic for U.S. railroads, particularly PRR.

IN A STIRRING EXAMPLE of raw materials being converted to finished product at one location, here we have the famed Bethlehem Steel shipyards as they appeared in 1953 with at least four ships under construction. This facility was responsible for turning out an enormous number of ships during World War II. Bear Creek is visible in the background.

AS WE LEAVE the harbor area, we come to Biddle Street station which was located on the elevated PB&W main just east of the Union Tunnel. This ca. 1915 view of the station – used for local trains – was taken after heavy rains soaked the area and turned the street into a muddy mire.

F. A. Wrabel Collection

WE NOW RETURN to the Union Station area, focus of a prolonged conflict between PRR, B&O and the City of Baltimore. During the late 1880s and through the 1890s PRR greatly expanded its passenger operations, including through sleeping and parlor car service through Baltimore and completely overwhelming the capacity of the 1886 facility. Not only was the station itself inadequate to handle the traffic, passengers were required to cross the station tracks in the trainshed, creating a serious safety hazard. At least three plans were developed to enlarge the station, including this one in 1898, which would have provided additional office space and dining facilities, but done nothing to improve the safety of the trainshed. None of these plans were implemented, perhaps because of the conservatism that plagued the road during the latter years of the administration of George Roberts.

HARD TO PLEASE

CALVERT STATION.

LORD BALTIMORE: "Please, sir, won't you build me a new station?"

MR. CASSATT: "Do you want the earth? Don't you see that I am busy giving Calvert Station a nice, new coat of paint?"

Baltimore News/Hagley Museum & Library

THIS delightful editorial cartoon from the 5 December 1906 Baltimore *News* ridicules Alexander Cassatt for his perceived foot-dragging on a new Union Station for the city. Cassatt, not usually known for foot-dragging on much of anything, was seriously ill by this time and saving his remaining strength to concentrate on completing the tunnels into New York City. In addition PRR was strongly opposed to a union station with the B&O and was also awaiting the outcome of the proposal for a possible joint PRR-B&O freight bypass of the city before committing to any new station project.

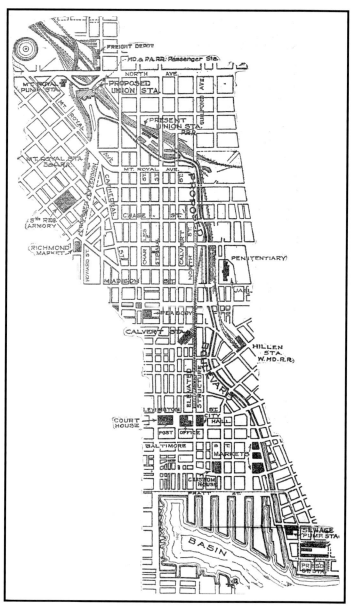

THIS PROPOSAL for a new Union Station at North Avenue and Jones Falls was made by Calvin W. Hendrick, chief engineer of the Baltimore Sewerage Commission (no comment) and summarily rejected by Cassatt as being too close to the B&P Tunnel and not allowing convenient interchange with Northern Central trains. The plan envisioned the new station as part of a proposed urban redevelopment program that situated it at the northern terminus of a proposed boulevard over the Falls that would extend southward to Baltimore Street. It also proposed that the B&O's Camden Station be used for freight only and the Mt. Royal Station be converted to a school or central marketplace. Fat chance. The latter, by the way, did end as an art school.

F. A. Wrabel Collection

AFTER Cassatt's untimely death new President James McCrea frostily opposed the Union Station proposal – for essentially the same reasons as his predecessor – and the project was shelved for a time. It was revised and resurrected in 1908 by the Baltimore Commission for the Improvement of Railway Terminal Facilities. What emerged was this "splendid" design that faced south toward an extension of Howard Street for street car and carriage traffic, which would pass under the tower to the dual waiting rooms at street level and then connect with North Avenue over short bridges.

Passengers would descend one flight of stairs to the B&O tracks (left) or down an additional flight to the PRR platforms (right). Under the PRR tracks were concrete tunnels through which Jones Falls would flow – hence the interest by the Sewerage Commission. Although favored by B&O and the city, it continued to be opposed by PRR – and thankfully never saw the light of day.

FRUSTRATED by continuing attempts by the city to force it into a union station with the B&O, PRR elected to build a new Union Station of its own at the same location (although Western Maryland trains continued to stop, it was later renamed Pennsylvania Station). The old station was demolished in March 1910 and a new one quickly began to arise in its place. This photo taken from St. Paul Street later that year shows the new station under construction and the access ramp to the temporary passenger facilities at the right.

The stunning new structure, of classical genre, was designed by New York City architect Kenneth M. Murchison, who had previously worked for the famed architectural firm of McKim, Mead & White and who was also responsible for the DL&W stations in Hoboken NJ and Scranton PA (which it resembles). Murchison's design was selected from eight competing plans by a committee of PRR officials. Interestingly, because a request by McKim, Mead &

White (which had been awarded the New York City Penn Station contract by Cassatt) to have a representative on the committee, the firm abruptly withdrew from the competition.

PENNSYLVANIA STATION was opened for public inspection – before it was fully completed – on 15 September 1911, when several thousand curious Baltimore citizens enjoyed a warm reception. The fourth largest on the PRR system at the time, the new station was 60 ft. wide and 275 ft. long. It was constructed of gleaming Mitford pink granite with trim of terra cotta, brick and ornamental metalwork. The main floor at street level (one floor above the tracks) contained the main waiting room surrounded by ticket offices, news stand, men's and women's "retiring rooms," lunch and dining rooms and baggage and parcel rooms. A 50-ft. wide lobby extended across the Bush train shed (the first of its type in a depressed location covering seven tracks and four platforms.

The lower level contained the baggage rooms and Station Master's office. The Northern Central RR offices were moved to the upper two floors. This photo shows the south side of the station shortly after opening.

Ted Xaras Collection

FLAGS FLYING, a busy Pennsylvania Station rises above the smoke and steam in this classic 1920s scene looking southward at the track side of the building. Note the concourse extending over the Bush trainshed, visible through the heavy trusswork of the St. Paul Street bridge. Steel passenger cars are making inroads for mainline service, but several wooden cars still occupy the coach yard at left.

MOVING just a bit farther west (railroad north) we see the Guilford Avenue engine terminal – also known as the Falls engine terminal – as it appeared ca. 1915 shortly after the Northern Central roundhouse had been demolished. The brick tower in the center controlled the movements in and out of Calvert Station from 1903 until 1911, when CS Tower opened.

At the left is the Northern Central line from Calvert Street, which joins the PB&W main (right) from Philadelphia in front of CS Tower, just visible in the background between the old brick tower and the middle pier of the ornate iron Guilford Avenue bridge. The freight line to Mt. Vernon Yard curves sharply to the left and continues along Jones Falls in front of the station. A passenger locomotive enters the turntable at center left, which remained in service until the mid-1950s.

F. A. Wrabel Collection

ALTHOUGH PRR had expended some $1 million on the new station and embellished the main waiting room with a stained glass ceiling, Doric columns and finished it in stunning Pentellic marble – used in the Parthenon in Athens – city officials and local citizens alike were disappointed in not having a true union station. They were both nevertheless glad to have the new facility with its airy Bush train shed – at least compared to the old one. This view of the impressive columned front façade shows the taxi loading ramp running between St. Paul and Charles Street, in the foreground. The date is 2 August 1923 – the flags are now at half-mast and the canopy is draped in black in memory of President Warren Harding, who died earlier in the day.

THIS AFTERNOON PHOTO shows the front façade of Pennsylvania Station during the mid-1940s, the tracks now electrified but with the grime of accumulated steam locomotive smoke evident. At this time the stained glass ceiling was blackened to reduce city lights that might aid enemy submarines and remained so until rehabilitation of the station in the mid-1990s. Note the south side platform for Northern Central trains running to and from Calvert Station.

J. W. Wolf/F. A. Wrabel Collection

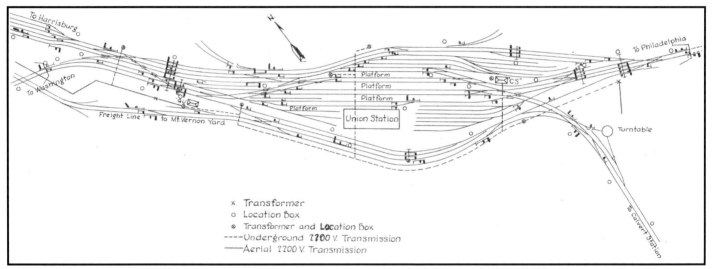

Signal Engineer/Kalmbach Memorial Library

THIS 1913 DIAGRAM shows the track configuration and the two electro-pneumatic interlocking plants as originally installed at Union Station. It would be changed several times over the years. The two towers, "new" CS at the north end and GU at the south end, initially handled approximately 300 passenger train movements on the PW&B, Northern Central, Western Maryland and Baltimore & Sparrows Point RRs every 24 hours. In addition

an estimated 350 freight train movements, including through and local trains plus shifting for train makeup, were handled daily on the PB&W and the Northern Central.

During construction of the station 13 track rearrangements were made between 12 December 1910 and 22 June 1912. When completed on that date, CS Tower contained a 107-lever machine and GU controlled a 95-lever installation.

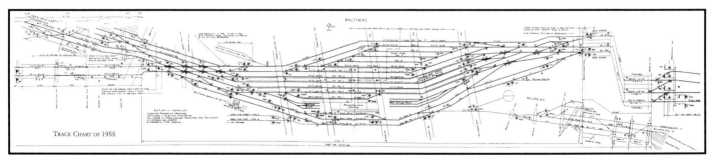

F. A. Wrabel Collection

AFTER the Baltimore Improvements and subsequent changes the track configuration looked like this in 1955. CS and GU

Towers have been rebuilt and renamed UNION JUNCTION and B&P JUNCTION, respectively.

BECAUSE of complaints about overcrowding in the Waiting Room, plans to expand the facility began shortly after opening. This early (1915) proposal featured an expanded concourse over the main tracks, extending to a new three-story annex on St. Paul Street. It was never constructed.

AS AUTOMOBILE TRAFFIC to and from the station grew, the lack of convenient parking became apparent. Consideration was given over the years to locations on the north side along Lanvale Street between Charles and St. Paul Streets and on the south side including the area over Jones Falls. One proposal in 1941 envisioned a bridge connecting a lot on the north side to the south side loading ramp – this was rejected because of the cost, over $1 million.

A more modest proposal, costing about $300 thousand, is shown here involving covering the tracks on the south sides and extending over Jones Falls, which is closer to what was finally built.

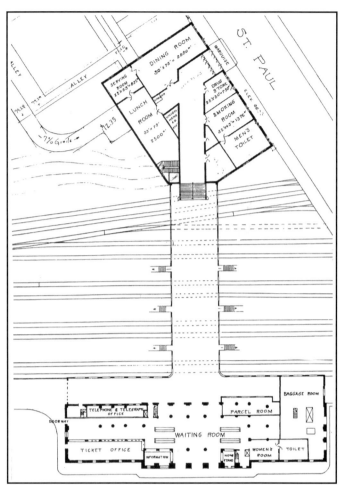

F. A. Wrabel Collection

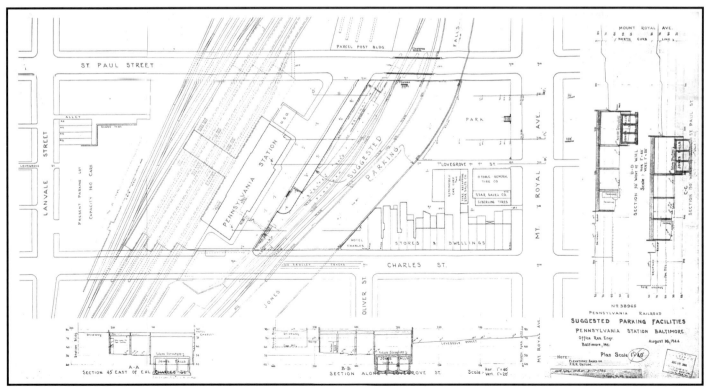

Hagley Museum & Library

HERE WE HAVE a grand aerial panorama of the area around Pennsylvania Station in 1953. This view looks northwestward up the Jones Falls valley from Guilford Avenue (lower right) to the Produce Terminal along the Northern Central (upper left). The north-south streets, from r. to l., are Guilford Avenue, Calvert Street, St. Paul Street, Charles Street, Maryland Avenue and Howard Street, with North Avenue crossing below the Produce terminal.

The north-south (ex-PB&W) main runs past the station, the 1930 Post Office building and the remains of Bolton Yard (left)

and then swings to the left into the B&P Tunnel just in front of the North Avenue bridge under the smokestack while the Northern Central trackage continues up the valley with the Ma and Pa tracks to the right leading to their tiny "Station" at North Avenue. The B&O main to Philadelphia snakes under North Avenue and over the PRR tracks (Mt. Royal Station is just out of the picture at center left, at the bend in its namesake avenue). Note no parking area has yet been constructed on the south side, although there is a lot cleared on Lanvale Street.

THIS VIEW looks southeastward down the valley, with the harbor in the distance. In the foreground the B&O main to Philadelphia curves past Bolton Yard in the center of the photo. Mt. Royal Station is at upper right. The entrance to the B&P Tunnel is marked by the smokestack in the center of the photo at the point where the B&O tracks pass under North Avenue.

This view clearly illustrates why the B&S utilized the Jones Falls valley to climb northward out of the city, why Bolton Ter-minal was located where it was and why it was later necessary for the B&P and Union RRs to tunnel out of it to make connections to Washington and the PW&B line to Philadelphia. In a later era the Jones Falls Expressway (I 83) would sweep up the valley as well.

In the 1950s we commuted in and out of both Penn and Mt. Royal Stations through these tunnels. We also lunched (brown bag) in the park on Mt. Royal Avenue overlooking Penn Station, watching trains. There were a lot of them.

WE NOW drop down to ground level in the station area and catch a Class E3sd locomotive striking a classic pose as it makes its presence known passing UNION JUNCTION Tower enroute from Falls Engine Terminal to Pennsylvania Station in 1930. The Guilford Avenue bridge is in the background. This tower, by the way, was removed and reassembled in Sykesville MD by railfans near B&O's Old Main Line and "Baldwin" Station in that town. Irony.

F. A. Wrabel Collection

THIS VIEW taken ca. 1915 shows the station looking west from the Guilford Avenue bridge, with the Calvert Street bridge (and behind it St. Paul Street) crossing the valley before electrification was installed. Behind the Calvert Street bridge is the old coach yard where the Post

Office building was later constructed. In the foreground is Jones Falls walled in concrete and at left is the edge of the landscaped St. Paul Gardens. This view clearly illustrates how the narrow station was surrounded by trackage.

JUMBLE – Here we have the aftermath of the wreck involving MD12 and Extra 4728 on 22 July 1946. A crew of sidewalk supervisors lines the Calvert Street bridge as two steam cranes try to sort out the mess under the wires – at least seven freight cars remain. One small consolation is that they didn't have to worry about the high-voltage wires, safely buried through the area at the insistence of the city. E5s 1750 is in wreck train service at right, near the Post Office building.

J. W. Wolf/F. A. Wrabel Collection

RARE BIRD – PRR 5267, a Class B6sb 0-6-0, simmers under the wires on a rainy 25 April 1937 as passengers board the coaches. This locomotive was one of the few oil burners owned by the road.

RECENTLY SHOPPED K4s 3856 – anything but a rare bird – paused under the St. Paul Street bridge on New Year's Day 1940. It has just brought Train No. 542 down the Northern Central line from Harrisburg.

AND OF COURSE there were the stalwart GG1s – here engine 4840 brings Train No. 126 *The President* under the Howard Street bridge – and the marvelous maze of overhead – into the station area. The date is 7 April 1940 and the train will continue on to Penn Station, New York City, where it will arrive shortly after noon.

THIRTY-SEVEN YEARS have passed, and the GG1s are still performing yeoman service, in this case handling Train No. 89, the New York-Savannah *Palmetto* departing on Station Track 7 in March 1977. The two-year old E60s were still having teething problems, and it was not uncommon at this time to see trains pulled by a GG1 with an E60 following to provide HEP power for the Amfleet cars. The head end of the train is passing under the Maryland Avenue bridge, and the old Ma & Pa interchange track is visible to the left of the GG1.

AND YES, there were MUs in Baltimore. At this time Penn Central MP54s were assigned to the two remaining Monday-Friday Baltimore-Washington commuter locals – the photo was taken on a Saturday in March 1977 so they are stored in Baltimore over the weekend. The three-track coach yard appears to be unused. Not visible in this picture to the right are Station Track B (once used by the famed Parkton locals) and northward freight Track A.

We rode these MUs to Halethorpe in the 1950s. On B&O, Budd RDCs were used. There was no comparison.

We also used the New York sleeper which was positioned on one of these sidings. You boarded about 10 pm and awoke at Penn Station in New York about 8 am. B&O had a similar service.

William J. Coxey

George F. Nixon/Maryland Rail Heritage Library Collection

VISITOR – As we move west (railroad south) of the station area we encounter a PRR train on the B&O line. This was most definitely *not* what John Garrett had in mind when B&O was forced to construct its own line to Philadelphia after being vanquished by PRR. No matter, some degree of cooperation between the two roads was involved to allow a southbound PRR train to detour over the line ca. 1949. The photo was taken looking northward from the North Avenue bridge.

AND NOW we turn to the saga – and it is a saga, still ongoing in the Amtrak/CSX era – of PRR's tunnels in Baltimore. The story is a long and complex one, fraught with conflict, formidable engineering challenges and equally complex political machinations involving the city, the B&O (who had its own Howard Street bore) and of course PRR. Interestingly, although the Union Tunnel eventually received most of the attention and expenditure for improvements, it is the B&P Tunnel that remains, to this day, the most hated and difficult bottleneck through the city.

As the size of locomotives and the frequency of trains increased accumulation of smoke and hot gases became a major problem, both for visibility and health of the crews and passengers. In 1892 a ven-

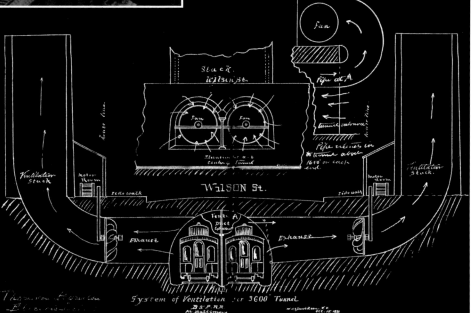

Hagley Museum and Library

tilation system consisting of large fans was installed in the Wilson Street section of the B&P Tunnel, leading to a 160-ft. high brick stack to remove the fumes. This system remained in operation until electrification, and then dieselization, rendered it unnecessary. It was abandoned and the tower finally demolished in 1966.

AT PENNSYLVANIA AVENUE, PRR constructed this Italianate station at an open cut with stairways descending from the waiting room at street level down to the platforms. Shown here in a ca. 1915 view, it was utilized by both PRR and WM trains.

THE REAR of this station was actually a tunnel portal, shown here in an 1887 drawing. PRR later modified the upper part of the structure to include a large fan to further improve ventilation as engines increased in size.

F. A. Wrabel Collection

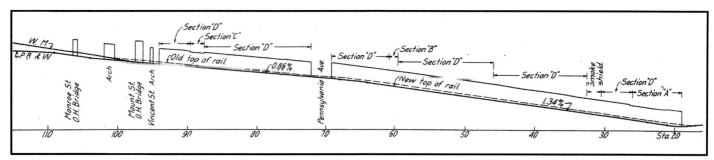

Railway Maintenance Engineer/Kalmbach Memorial Library

BY THE LATE 1800s, traffic through the Baltimore tunnels had become so heavy that PRR considered several possible ways to reduce the congestion. In 1907 a proposal was put forth for a freight bypass – either alone or jointly with the B&O – to route freight traffic around the northeastern quadrant of the city. This controversial project was soundly defeated in the Maryland Legislature. Several years later PRR proposed a radical solution – construction of a new line through Canton and then tunneling under the harbor. This project was likewise met with strong opposition and was subsequently dropped. It was in 1915 that PRR first proposed new tunnels parallel to the existing Union and B&P Tunnels, but this also met with a mixed reception.

In 1917, faced with constant rejection of its major proposals, PRR embarked on a more modest project to improve clearances in the B&P Tunnel, the worst bottleneck. This work, done under heavy traffic and on one track at a time, consisted of lowering the track grade about 2 ft, 6 in., installing a new concrete lining and enlarging the rock side walls to a minimum of 27 ft. in width. These changes allowed continued double-track operation with larger equipment coming into use.

To facilitate this work a detour was constructed by extending the Green Spring Branch to a connection with the WM tracks plus building a wye connecting between the PB&W and the WM south of the south portal at Fulton Junction. In addition, a smoke shield was constructed down the middle of the tunnel to protect the workers during construction. Even so, we can't imagine being inside the tunnel when a train blasted through!

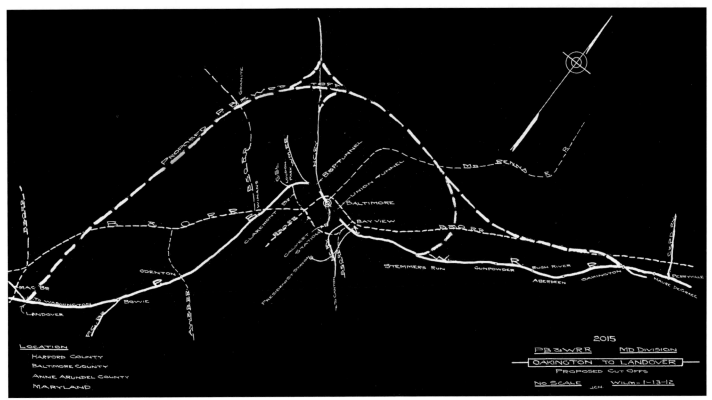

THE DIFFICULT GEOGRAPHY of Baltimore is such that once PRR and the B&O located their main passenger stations where they did, it was out of necessity that they resorted to tunnels and tortuous curves to run trains between Washington and New York City. B&O was the first to use electrification to solve the onerous problem of smoke and dangerous gasses in their Howard Street Tunnel but it still proved to be a traffic bottleneck.

The idea of an alternate, possibly joint, line through Baltimore was the subject of intense, and ultimately futile, interaction at the highest levels of both PRR and the B&O involving a profusion of plans, letters, memos and meetings over several years.

Cassatt and Lenore F. Loree (PRR's puppet B&O president during PRR control) supported by their respective chief engineers began discussions with each other in the early 1900s. The initial proposal that emerged was for a *six-track* elevated line (to be known as the Baltimore Terminal RR) running from east of Bay View Yard, dropping down and running parallel to Pratt Street and then connecting with the B&O at Carroll Junction and continuing on to Halethorpe Station. Connections would be made with PB&W and the B&O at the northern end, with the Northern Central in the city and with the B&P and B&O lines at the southern end. The line as initially proposed would have had a maximum grade of 0.8% in either direction (vs. 1.14% northbound and 1.21% southbound on the Union/B&P route), and there would be no tunnels.

The focus of this elevated line was to establish a "general terminal" either between Pratt and Lombard Streets or between Camden, Sharp and Howard Streets near Camden Station. The total cost of this "extravagant" proposal (there were later, less ambitious ones), including roadway construction, terminal and property acquisition, was a staggering $14.5 million.

However, after PRR relinquished control of the B&O – and Cassatt's interest in a union station waned – emphasis shifted to consideration of a freight-only line, either by a cutoff bypassing the city to the north or utilizing a less elaborate version of the Pratt Street elevated concept. Many route proposals were ad-

vanced, with various connecting points at either end.

In an impassioned letter to Edwin Warfield, then governor of Maryland on 6 April 1906, Cassatt voiced his strong opposition to pending legislation that would have restricted the construction of new railroad lines within the city limits. He indicated that construction of either a bridge or tunnel across the harbor would be impractical and cost prohibitive, and therefore a line north of the city (but not too far north) was the only feasible solution. However, the most desirable route would still pass within the restricted area.

As he had done in New York City, Cassatt offered carrots – reduced congestion within the residential areas of the city by rerouting freight traffic on the bypass and construction of a new grain elevator at Canton – but concluded with a stick: "If, therefore, the Bill now before you becomes a law, the Philadelphia, Baltimore & Washington R.R. Co. and the Northern Central Ry. Co. cannot construct any line connecting their lines to the North and South of the City of Baltimore to relieve the now existing condition in the tunnels and in the valley between them in the City of Baltimore."

Cassatt's appeal was to no avail. The Act was passed and signed by the governor and PRR subsequently proceeded to rebuild its own new station. Cassatt died, but the idea of a freight bypass refused to die, at least not right away. Discussions between the new administrations and proposals by both roads continued for several more years. This 1912 PRR plan for a line from Oakington to Landover is representative. But the impasse ultimately resulted in PRR proposing the Baltimore Improvements, which provided electrification to solve the smoke problem, a second Union Tunnel and improved right of way and resultant traffic flow through the city, but left the B&P bottleneck largely untouched and the B&O with nothing to show for its efforts but stacks of plans.

One of the more sensible World War I proposals was to put all passenger trains on PRR and all freights on B&O, exactly the way it evolved a half-century later.

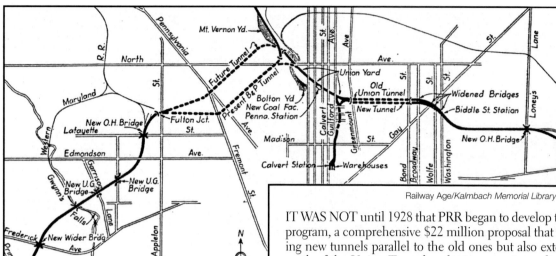

IT WAS NOT until 1928 that PRR began to develop the Baltimore Improvements program, a comprehensive $22 million proposal that included not only constructing new tunnels parallel to the old ones but also extending the four-track system south of the Union Tunnel, reducing curvature, eliminating several grade crossings and electrifying the entire main through the city. This time the road made a valiant effort to work closely with city officials through the tortuous approval process, smoothing – at least partially – the way toward success.

Prior to beginning the Improvements program the four-track main from the north extended only as far as the Biddle Street station, about 1-1/3 miles east of Pennsylvania Station. Beyond that point it continued as a double-track line through the city to the west end of the B&P Tunnel, where it expanded to six tracks for 1-1/2 miles to the Gwynns Falls bridge, where it became double-track again to Loudon Park.

Under the new arrangement the four-track system was extended from Biddle Street to the Union Tunnel by adding a track on either side of the existing right of way. The southbound tracks then came together into one track, which passed through the old tunnel, changed to single track downgrade. The two northbound tracks passed through the new tunnel, allowing for separate passenger and freight movements in this direction.

THIS VIEW looks northward from the east end of Union Tunnel in 1931, during the four-tracking phase of the Baltimore Improvements. A Washington-bound train hauled by a Class K4s overtakes a light Class B6sb engine movement – most likely running from Orangeville engine-house to Union Station. A standard PRR watch box and tool house frame the mainline, and the American Brewery – a Baltimore landmark - towers over the scene at the extreme left.

THE NEW TUNNEL was constructed in three sections – a cut-and-cover portion 295 ft. long at the east (northward) end, with a concrete arch – a shield-driven tunnel 2085 ft. long, lined with cast iron – and a 946 ft. long cut-and-cover section at the west end, also with a concrete arch. All three portions had the same cross section, 33 ft. wide at the base of the arch and 22 ft., 3 in. high above the top of the rail. The grade inside the tunnel was 1.2% northbound.

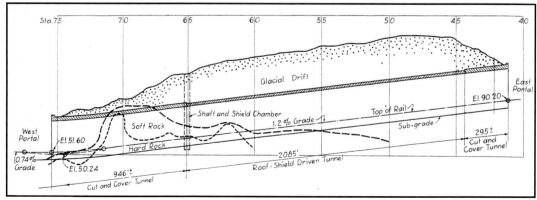

J. W. Wolf/F. A. Wrabel Collection

THE CUT-AND-COVER METHOD was used at the ends of the tunnel because of the relatively shallow thickness of the earth above the opening. This view looking west in 1933 shows the cut-and-cover portion of the new tunnel under construction. Improvements or no, the local residents must have been less than thrilled to see this giant trench slice through their neighborhood!

F. A. Wrabel

THE SHIELD METHOD was utilized for the main tunnel because of the thick overburden and a glacial drift formation overlying layers of hard and decomposed gneiss alternating with a mix of sand, gravel, clay and mud. After an 18-month delay because of the Depression, work began in earnest on 17 July 1933 from the western end of Valley Street and proceeded upgrade, using a main shield 36 ft. in diameter – the largest used in the U. S. at the time.

After driving side wall drifts, using small shields 11 ft. in diameter, concrete side walls 5 ft. 10 in. high were poured on either side. The main shield was then erected and traveled along the top of the side walls – it was moved forward by twenty 200-ton hydraulic jacks pushing against the cast iron lining erected behind it.

The lining was made up of 30 in. wide segments with 14 in. wide flanges, bolded together with 1-3/4 in. bolts and caulked with lead.

Excavated material was removed by means of a mucking machine that loaded 2 cu. yd. dump boxes that were picked up by a gantry crane and set on narrow gauge flat cars and then moved to electric elevators in the access shaft. After the west end cut and cover section was completed, the dump boxes were unloaded into standard gauge air dump cars and hauled to the west portal by an electric locomotive.

This view shows the workers posed in the tunnel interior under construction in 1933.

THE new Union Tunnel was holed through on 7 Sept 1934, marked the next day by a brief ceremony. The Baltimore *News* of that date characterized the event as "one of no little moment to Baltimore," marking "the completion of one stage of the electrification project of the Pennsylvania RR in this city."

On 27 September, after the linings and track were completed, PRR officials got their first look at the new tunnel by means of an inspection train shown here emerging from the tunnel as it moved to Pennsylvania Station. Typically all of them were somber faced, and of course all wore hats.

Hagley Museum & Library

F. A. Wrabel

AFTER the new tunnel was completed the old tunnel was stabilized and then waterproofed for electric operation by means of a gunite lining applied over the old five-ring brick arch, which had been worn considerably by years of stack-blast action, particularly over the southbound (upgrade) track.

Because roof clearances in the old tunnel were too low to accommodate catenary wires for two tracks, one track was removed and the remaining one aligned to the center. Through Pennsylvania Station the tracks and platforms were lowered by 18

in. to make room for the overhead, the platforms were lengthened and the track arrangement was modified to improve traffic flow. Because city fathers refused to allow PRR to run the 132,000-volt transmission line towers over the tunnels, the lines were installed inside 7-in. diameter steel conduits along the tunnel walls, with oil circulated under pressure for both insulation and cooling. The conduits are just visible on the portal at left.

This view shows the east portals of the completed tunnels in 1935 – the new tunnel at the left, the old one at the right.

AS FOR the B&P Tunnel, PRR originally planned to run a new double-track bore roughly parallel to the old tunnel but at some distance to the north. The plans called for the new tunnel to leave the main just south of Mt. Vernon Yard, curve (4.2°) to the southwest and run parallel to the old bore, through a gentle (2°) curve under Pennsylvania Avenue and then rejoin the main at Fulton Junction. In addition a short single-track tunnel was planned to run from the entrance to the old tunnel and curve around to join the Northern Central northward, forming a wye that would have allowed a direct route for trains between Washington and Harrisburg (construction of this connector was actually begun when the original tunnel was built in the 1870s but then abandoned).

Herbert H. Harwood, Jr.

The overall plan was to utilize the old Union Tunnel and the new B&P bore exclusively for passenger trains and run freights through the new Union Tunnel and the old B&P bore. This route was laid out and the plans carefully presented to the city fathers – in fact much of the property had been secured. But as the Depression deepened and PRR's finances became depleted (even with substantial loans from the PWA and the RFC) the expenditure of an additional $5 million for construction of the new B&P tunnel and the North Avenue wye was postponed again and again, and finally abandoned altogether.

Thus the worst bottleneck on the New York-Washington line remained – the result of a combination of tight clearances, a nasty 1.34% southbound grade and harsh curves. In 1959 PRR implemented a partial solution involving chipping away areas of the walls and ceiling and installing a gauntlet track through the Pennsylvania Avenue curve to improve clearances for piggyback traffic. The tunnel has seen its share of disasters which have maintained the dubious distinction of being Baltimore's worst bottleneck.

The north portal of the hated tunnel is portrayed here in May of 1967 as triple-headed GG1s lead a southbound freight into the bore.

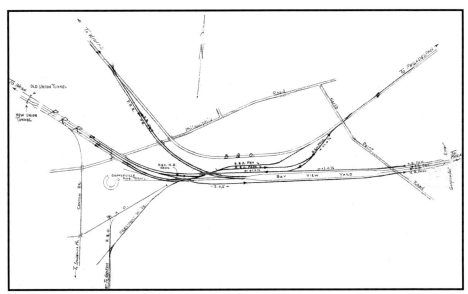

Hagley Museum & Library

DURING the Baltimore Improvements PRR considered the possibility of combining operations with the B&O through the city. After extensive analysis it was concluded that PRR trackage could satisfactorily be used for passenger operations by both companies, while the B&O line was not considered satisfactory for PRR trains. It was further concluded that "The B&O line would of necessity have to be used as the freight line for both companies, but for the P.R.R. freight movement it would not be as satisfactory as the present P.R.R. line."

Several alternate plans were put forward, with the total costs ranging from about $3 million to nearly $8 million, including electrification of the B&O trackage to Washington and increasing clearances in the B&O Howard Street Tunnel. This diagram shows one proposal for the northern connections at Bay View.

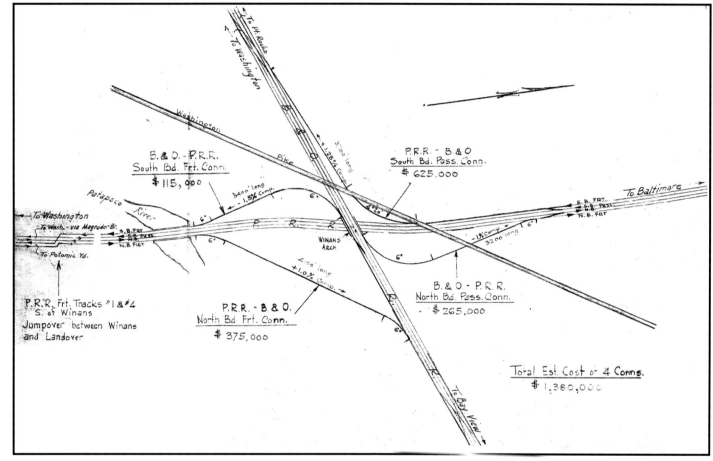

THE CORRESPONDING proposed southern connections at Winans are shown here. PRR was un-enthusiastic at best on this whole scheme, as it was judged (correctly, as it turned out) that the B&O would only be willing to pay for the passenger connections at Bay View and Winans.

Now follow the Washington Pike over B&O and PRR tracks, locate the northbound connection and the legend "1% comp 3200' long." Grandfather Stewart's house was in this "V" and would have been removed. It went anyway. In 1937 the State replaced the bridge over PRR tracks and took the property.

Chapter 7

Southern Invasion

Baltimore to Washington

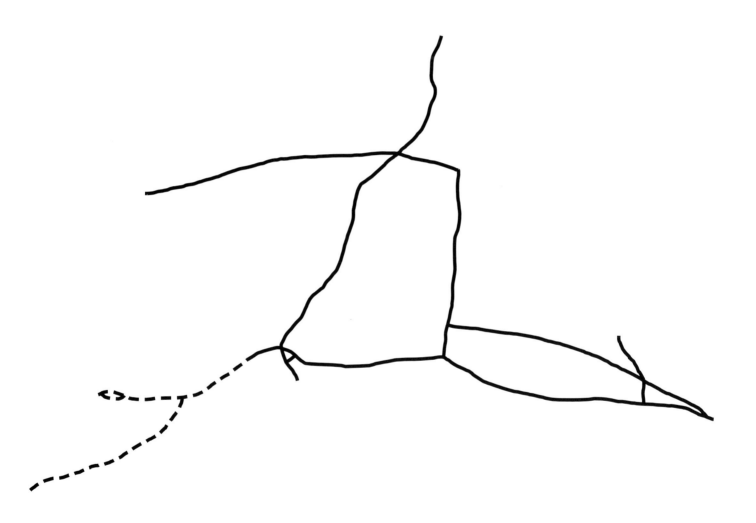

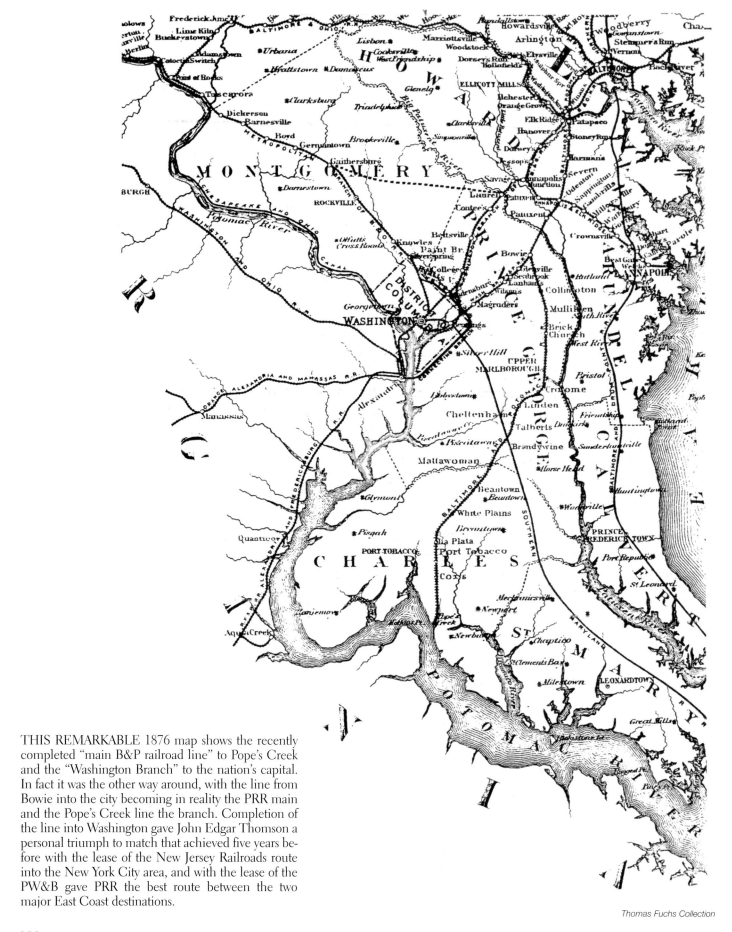

THIS REMARKABLE 1876 map shows the recently completed "main B&P railroad line" to Pope's Creek and the "Washington Branch" to the nation's capital. In fact it was the other way around, with the line from Bowie into the city becoming in reality the PRR main and the Pope's Creek line the branch. Completion of the line into Washington gave John Edgar Thomson a personal triumph to match that achieved five years before with the lease of the New Jersey Railroads route into the New York City area, and with the lease of the PW&B gave PRR the best route between the two major East Coast destinations.

The Baltimore & Potomac RR had its beginnings in the desire of Southern Maryland planters and merchants to conquer two centuries of poor roads and slow water transport and form a railroad linking Baltimore with the Potomac River – and that would provide them with a reliable, all-weather system of transportation capable of moving local produce and passengers to major East Coast cities. In 1853 Colonel William D. Bowie and other members of the prominent Bowie family of Prince George's County secured a charter from the Maryland Legislature for the new road, with Owen Bowie, William's son, elected as President.

The road was initially planned to run from Baltimore south to Upper Marlboro and then to Port Tobacco in Charles County, ending on the Potomac between Liverpool Point and the outlet of the St. Mary's River. Little progress was made between 1853 and 1859 because of the difficulty of raising capital in the largely rural area. Preliminary surveys were begun in 1859 but further work was discontinued with the onset of the Civil War.

At the close of the war Bowie went to John Garrett for funds and was summarily turned down. At about this time, PW&B officials became aware of Bowie's dilemma and referred him to Thomson. As we have discussed in Chapter 6, Thomson was intrigued by the provision of the B&P's charter allowing construction of "branches" not exceeding 20 miles in length – by beginning such a branch at Huntington (later Bowie) Thomson could legally outmaneuver Garrett and establish a line to the District of Columbia, effectively breaking B&O's monopoly into the city. With Bowie's assistance Congress duly authorized such an extension on 5 February 1867.

And thus it came to pass on 4 September of that year that the PRR Board passed the following critical resolution:

> "Resolved, That the President be and he is hereby authorized to accept the proposition of Messrs. Cass, Potts and others for the assignment of a contract dated August 7, 1866, for the construction of the Baltimore and Potomac Railroad to J. Edgar Thomson, J. Donald Cameron, Trustees, in consideration of the sum of four hundred thousand dollars."

It was all very neat and clean – and seemingly innocuous – for the triumphant invasion that it represented.

Now that resources were available, construction began in earnest the following year with 35 miles of right of way grading completed, but it again bogged down because of lawsuits filed by recalcitrant property owners and the usual opposition from both the City of Baltimore and in Congress – most notably the Maryland delegation – for a road that they knew would obviously undermine the B&O's sacred monopoly. The opposition was fairly quickly overcome, however, and late in 1868 Charles County purchased $175 thousand of the road's shares, providing not only a financial boost but also an indication of local support.

On 18 March 1869 Congress passed a supplementary Act authorizing a tunnel under Virginia Avenue through the southeast portion of the city. With completion of this critical objective assured, this in turn allowed the B&P to secure the financial resources it needed from PRR to complete the "main B&P Railroad line" from Bowie to Pope's Creek, the new destination. This would allow freight to be transported (under the original scheme for this road) by ferry across the river to connect with the RF&P at Aquia Creek.

PRR had other plans, however. On 21 June 1870 Congress authorized the branch to extend along Maryland Avenue to the "Long Bridge" at 14th Street and to establish the critical connection with the RF&P main to Richmond at the southern end. The line into Washington was opened on 2 July 1872 and double tracked in 1883.

Completion of the line to Pope's Creek was approved on 5 July 1870, and construction proceeded quickly. The road was completed and opened on 1 January 1873 at an overall cost of nearly $10 million, largely because of the difficult and complex Baltimore tunnels.

The remaining history of the B&P is essentially the history of the stations in the nation's capital. The B&P was justifiably proud of its ornate Victorian terminal and train shed at 6th and B Streets, but as traffic grew complaints arose because of trains operating on the approach tracks blocking the increasingly congested city streets. A similar problem existed with B&O trains in and out of their terminal.

In response to the growing clamor PRR presented a plan in 1899 to elevate the B&P right of way through the city, thus eliminating the grade crossings, as well as constructing an entirely new terminal and rebuilding the Long Bridge because of the heavy tonnage it was sustaining. This proposal, and others, were debated at great lengths in the halls of Congress for many months until on 12 February 1901 two Acts were passed, supposedly providing the "final solution" to the rancorous problem. One provided $1.5 million reimbursement to the B&P (later PB&W) for the elimination of grade crossings, construction of an expanded terminal facility at 6th Street and rebuilding of the Long Bridge. A similar Act also provided $1.5 million to the B&O for elimination of grade crossings, construction of a new station at C Street and

Delaware Avenue, nearer to the Capitol, and specifically authorized formation of a Terminal Company "to locate, construct and operate new terminals and new lines of railroad to accommodate traffic of the B&O in Washington."

The Washington Terminal Company was incorporated on 6 December 1901, but shortly after the original enabling legislation was passed it became apparent to the newly-established Park Commission that the new station plan was unacceptable. The location of the B&P terminal and tracks obstructed the concept of a grand Mall from the Capitol to the Washington Monument. The proposed B&O station and trainshed on Delaware Avenue at C Street was worse because of its proximity to the Capitol itself.

The Park Commission (a distinguished body chaired by architect Daniel Burnham and including Charles F. McKim, Augustus St. Gaudens and Frederick Law Olmstead, Jr.) met with Presidents Cassatt of PRR and L. F. Loree of the B&O and both agreed to support the construction of a new union terminal at Delaware and Massachusetts Avenues that satisfied all considerations of both utility and esthetics.

Thus on 28 February 1903 Congress passed new legislation repealing the provisions of the previous Acts that called for separate terminals and authorized the Washington Terminal Company (with PRR and the B&O now providing joint support) to construct a new station "monumental in character," at a cost "not less than 4 million dollars." The PB&W was directed to build a connecting line (that became known as the Magruder Branch) from Landover to the new facility and a line between the south portal of a new 1st Street Tunnel and the existing line at Virginia Avenue, and to remove the connection to the 6th Street station. PB&W and the B&O jointly were to construct two double-track passenger lines, coach yards, engine terminal, shops and power house to serve the complex. The Act stipulated that the work was to be completed within five years and upon opening of the new terminal PB&W would turn over its station at 6th and B Streets to the federal government.

Work began almost immediately on all fronts – construction of the new terminal on a 200-acre site bordering "Swampoodle" (a notorious shantytown on the remnants of Timber Creek), building the 1st Street Tunnel and extending the Virginia Avenue cut, elevation of the right of way in other areas and rebuilding the Long Bridge. The new bridge was completed in 1904 and then raised 8 ft. to match the track elevation, which was finished in 1906. In early 1907 a temporary passenger station was built at 8th Street and Maryland Avenue.

On 27 October 1907 a magnificent new Washington Union Terminal opened to a dazzled public. It fulfilled its charter of being truly monumental – the white granite edifice was characterized as one of the finest examples of Beaux-Arts style that on the one hand echoed the best of Burnham's achievements at the Chicago World's Fair and at the same time set the stage for decades of classic architecture in the nation's capital.

The cost of the project was monumental as well – $20 million for the station itself and an additional $105 million for the yards, tunnels and approach trackage work. In fulfillment of the terms of the 1903 legislation, the keys to the old station were officially conveyed to a representative of the Federal government at 2:15 p.m. on 4 March 1908.

Although Cassatt did not live to see either of his grand terminals brought to fruition, this one in particular brought both elegance and functionality to the city it served – at one time upwards of 5000 people operated an elegant restaurant, Turkish baths, hotel and such lesser amenities as a bowling alley, butcher shop, bakery, liquor store, nursery, police station and even a mortuary.

It was specifically designed to cater to the needs of the U. S. Presidents, the diplomatic corps and their guests. For years the Presidential Suite was used to officially welcome many dignitaries and members of royalty. The station served the nation's capital and the nation as a whole through the traffic surges and crises of two world wars. It witnessed many historic events, including gala Inaugural Balls and society receptions – and even assassinations and presidential funeral trains.

There were disasters as well – on 15 January 1953 the *Federal Express* crashed into the main concourse of the station, demolishing a newsstand and collapsing the floor under the locomotive, but miraculously no one was killed. Four days later a special train for guests attending the inauguration of President Eisenhower rolled into the terminal – on the same track – without incident.

However, as long-distance passenger travel by rail began to decline in the 1950s, the grand terminal began to fall into disuse and the financially-strapped railroads cut down on maintenance. As part of a bold program to dramatize the overall plight of U. S. railroads, PRR President James Symes in January 1958 offered to sell the $23 million facility to the U. S. government for $1 as a tax-saving measure. The government refused, but the program began a lengthy dialogue and debate on the terminal's future, with multiple proposals put forth from various groups. In 1967 it was decided to convert the station into a National Visitors Center for the upcoming Bicentennial. The Center opened with appropriate fanfare on 4 July

1976, but it proved unpopular and closed in 1978.

While Congress deliberated the terminal's fate, rain damage took its toll – portions of the roof caved in and unsightly mold grew on the walls, resulting in the building being closed in 1981. With talk of demolishing the historic structure rampant, Congress finally passed the landmark Union Station Redevelopment Act of 1981, which directed the Transportation Secretary to promulgate a plan for the commercial development of the facility with the objective of making it a financially self-sustaining, multi-use transportation center, connected to Amtrak, the Washington Metro and vehicular access.

After three years of intense effort – and an expenditure of $160 million – the gloriously restored station was reopened on 29 September 1988. It has subsequently become the most visited site in the nation's capital – a thriving transportation, commercial, cultural and exhibition center once again celebrated by U. S. Presidents.

THE PRR MAIN emerges from the east-west B&P Tunnel and turns sharply south at Fulton Junction, crosses Gwynns Falls and then continues southward, crossing the historic B&O main and then the West Branch of the Patapsco River. This was the route of the B&P's "branch" to the nation's capital, shown here in a 1904 USGS map. Note the Catonsville Branch.

WE WILL BEGIN our journey from Baltimore to Washington DC at Fulton Junction (MP. 14.1 from Bengies). Fulton was briefly the northern terminus for the B&P. Passengers were transferred between the first Union, Calvert and President Street Stations by a special stagecoach service. This was an interim arrangement that was discontinued when the B&P Tunnel was completed.

This view looks northward at FULTON Tower and the junction with the Western Maryland running behind the tower to the left – the southern entrance to the tunnel is out of the picture to the right. The date of the photo is 9 October 1935.

J. W. Wolf/ F. A. Wrabel Collection

FULTON Interlocking controlled the junction with the WM at the southern end of the B&P Tunnel and the entrance to Lafayette Yard as well as the beginning of four-track territory.

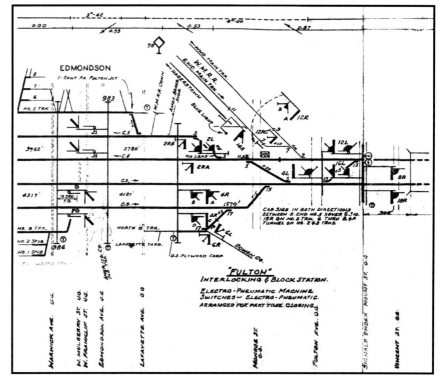

LAFAYETTE was the site of the small yard shown here in a ca. 1915 view, with the passenger station in the distance. We're not sure quite how the individual at the right proposes to unload the upright boiler by himself – or for that matter if the vehicle can handle it.

LAFAYETTE Station was located at Lafayette Avenue crossing, protected by gates and a watchman assigned to an even smaller shanty.

PRIMITIVE GATES protect the crossing at Gwynns Run station (MP. 15.6) as a train approaches ca. 1915. The frame station is surrounded by a neatly-trimmed hedge and shrubs.

VN Tower was located at the south end of Gwynns Run Yard, shown here in a superb 1917 photo.

F. A. Wrabel

GWYNNS RUN Tower is shown here looking north-ward in 1933. Beyond the tower are the railings for the viaduct over the Falls. The name of the tower was short-ened to GWYNN ca. 1949, and the cast iron signs were scrapped and replaced with keystone-shaped sheet steel ones. After the Penn Central merger the keystones were duly cut off, the signs sanded and then painted in PC green and white. Whither progress!

J. W. Wolf / F. A. Wrabel Collection

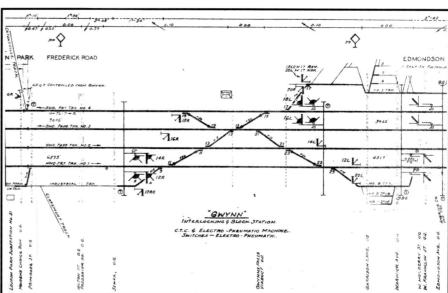

GWYNN controlled the complete set of crossovers on the main, the entrances to Gwynns Run Yard and the end of four-track territory at WINANS farther southward. The interlocking is shown here as of March 1962.

The new (1931-2) tower forecast the future of rail operation because it was the most extensive use of the "remote" concept at that time on the Baltimore Division. The new interlocking placed VN (Calverton Yard), LOUDON PARK and WINANS under the control of one operator.

Note the "Catonsville track" at upper left.

MASSIVE but graceful, the four-track concrete arch structure over Gwynns Falls was opened in December 1915 replacing a double-track deck plate girder bridge. This view is dated 1920. The track running under the viaduct (seemingly in the weeds) is the WM Tidewater Extension to their pier facilities at Port Covington.

F. A. Wrabel

J. W. Wolf / F. A. Wrabel Collection

THIS VIEW looks northward at the Frederick Road area ca. 1915. At right are the team tracks, with the freight station obscured by a structure advertising Bull Durham Smokeless Tobacco. The passenger station is in the distance at the road overpass.

The multi-story industrial building under the water tower at upper right is a brush manufacturing firm. Mother recalls that a female relative worked there for several years on the production line, we worked on the advertising account when the firm was a subsidiary of Pittsburgh Plate Glass and, in recent years, an ex-fiancé was chairwoman of the Board as the Maryland Brush Company.

HERE'S a closer look at the Frederick Road station (MP. 16.2). A bottle of Coca-Cola was still 5¢ in 1915.

IMPROVEMENTS – The station has now been demolished to make way for widening of the right of way to four tracks in a 1931 view. The inevitable gathering of sidewalk supervisors (all wearing hats, of course) checks on the progress of the construction as a streetcar (upper left) moves along Frederick Road. The southbound shelter at the left was originally built in 1901. That streetcar, by the way, was on the locally famous Number 8 line from Catonsville to Towson via the downtown Viaduct. This was the last Baltimore streetcar line converted to buses.

J. W. Wolf/F. A. Wrabel Collection

SA Cabin is shown here in a northward view ca. 1915, with a trim Loudon Park station (MP. 16.5) and shelter behind it.

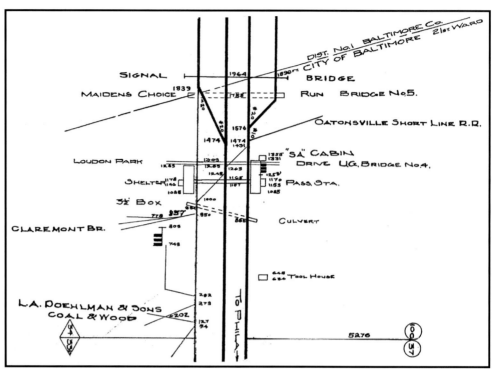

SA controlled the signals at the beginning of a section of four-track territory on the line between the City of Baltimore and Baltimore County, south at the top. This track chart shows the setting in 1914. Note the Catonsville Short Line and Maiden Choice Run as well as the Claremont Branch.

F. A. Wrabel Collection

F. A. Wrabel Collection

A SOUTHBOUND train roars past the tower, re-named LOUDON PARK, in a 1931 view. The train, which has run from Harrisburg to Baltimore down the Northern Central, has its consist reversed i.e. the Pullmans are behind the tender and the combine brings up the rear.

THE Claremont stockyards were located on the short branch of the same name. They are depicted here jammed with cattle cars (but no visible livestock) ca. 1915. This branch reached into the Union Stockyards and associated meatpacking facilities known locally as Pigtown. And it was a true "Union," operated co-operatively by PRR and B&O, thus showing that it was possible for the two rivals to work together. It is all gone now, the victim of "boxed beef" trucked-in from midwestern feedlots and local farmers.

Catonsville Railroad Still Going Strong

—*All drawings by Herbert Klinger.*

Perhaps "Old Trusty" looked like this as she blasted her way around the bend under Bloomsbury avenue.

By Charles Roberts

Local eyes recently turned toward the Mellor avenue "yards" of the Caton and Loudon Railway as a proposal for construction of a loading platform loomed. The petition of nearby residents against such a move on the part of the railway company gained the support of the Zoning Commissioner and subsequent sustainment by the Board of Zoning Appeals, thus defeating the plan. But if local eyes were to stay in that general area for a few seconds, sight of what was, in bygone days, a combination freight and passenger station would come into focus.

Closer inspection of this yellow building, just behind a Frederick avenue tavern in the heart of the business section, would disclose that it had burned recently, although it is structurally intact. Upon entering the building, any doubts as to its history are dispelled. Harry J. Schaub is there ready to tell of the days when gowned ladies and plump capitalists passed through this station of an up-and-coming railroad.

Even today, in the loft above the station, there is a piece of an old carriage, probably unclaimed freight. The waiting room and a section of what was a ticket office are evident, despite storage of cases of beer and liquors belonging to the adjoining tavern.

Delving into the history of the "Golden Era" Catonsville, one finds that this station is a landmark pointing to an age when Catonsville was a center of interest in the railroad construction fever which gripped the nation during the last half of the nineteenth and first of the twentieth centuries.

Few local people know that a great volume of freight entered this town through that medium. It is truly rare to find a person who knows that the old Catonsville "Argus" was originally published with the hope of promoting, through insistent editorials, the construction of a rapid transit system to Catonsville.

For instance, an article in the June 8, 1881, issue of the *Meteor*, forerunner of the old *Argus*, which newspaper was combined into the current HERALD ARGUS, bewails the fact that, probably because of transportation difficulties, no European noblemen were coming here to capture local beauties as wives, as in the days of the three Caton sisters.

The real motive behind this advocacy of a rapid transit system is believed to have been real estate promotion, rather than a matrimonial move. Primarily an old, rich family town, Catonsville's vast properties were being offered for sale as members of the old fraternity died. Residents were wanted for these newly opened properties, but lack of decent transportation to Baltimore city curtailed any mass development.

Finally, on February 25, 1882, the Catonsville Short Line was incorporated under the laws of Maryland. Construction was started and on November 10, 1884, the road was open for traffic. The cost was $105,000, $60,000 of which was raised in stock and $45,000 in bonds.

The Baltimore and Potomac railroad company, at that time controlled by the Pennsylvania railroad, took a 99-year lease on the line.

Business, as expected, was good. According to the *Argus*, over 15,000 tons of freight were carried into Catonsville every year. Train time to downtown Baltimore was only half an hour, and revenue from this department of the line must have been good, to judge by the schedule which announced departure of trains 12 times a day from Catonsville.

The main recipients of goods here were the old Cochran and Oler Ice and Coal company, which stood on the corner of Frederick and Mellor avenues, and the John S. Wilson Lumber company. Whole freight trains entered the ice company, say oldtimers here.

The route of the Short Line was in the form of a rough "L." With its terminal at the station house in Catonsville, the tracks ran due south for about a half mile, then easterly on a serpentine course, never more than three-quarters of a mile from Frederick avenue, to Loudon Park, where a connection was made with the main line of the Baltimore and Potomac. From there to Calvert station in Baltimore, the trains followed B. & P. rails.

The total length of the Short Line from Catonsville to Loudon Park was 3.8 miles.

Rolling stock on the road was probably that of the B. & P. In his "Tales of Old Catonsville," Walter Brinkmann says that "each bondholder had his own private station, named for his country estate, such as Loudon, Kenwood or Paradise. It (the Short Line) was probably the only railroad in the United States which gave its owners such service." Passenger equipment consisted of a baggage car, smoking car and a day coach on each train, says Brinkmann, drawn by "Old Trusty," a wheezy locomotive.

A prosperous railroad serving a growing community. But there was a fly in the soup. That intruding bug was electricity and the threatening tentacles of the rate-slashing City and Suburban Electric company.

Proven in other eastern cities,

the economy and speed of this mode of transportation were being endorsed on short lines everywhere.

Along with this prospect of competition came another proposition. An interurban electric railway between Washington, D. C., and Baltimore was being contemplated by several capitalists. In October of 1892, the decision was made to form the Maryland and Columbia electric railway company, also to be known as the Baltimore-Washington Boulevard electric railway.

This line was to be double tracked with rock ballast, capable of carrying trains at 60 mph.

To supplement this idea came the Edmondson avenue, Catonsville and Ellicott City electric railway. This company was endeavoring to construct a line following about the same route of the present No. 9-14 line of the Baltimore Transit company.

The Maryland and Columbia obtained franchise rights over the Edmondson avenue line, and then began to bargain with the Short Line for possible purchase.

The plan of the M. & C. was to finish the Baltimore-Ellicott City line, then to buy the Short Line, electrify it, and form a loop around Catonsville back into Baltimore City. They also hoped to build out from Washington to meet the line from Baltimore at Ellicott City.

The project was a clever one, but an important phase of it depended on the attitude of the PRR to release claims on the Short Line. "The prospects of the Short Line as a money-earner in recent years have brightened," said a PRR official in a statement to the *Argus*.

A small notice in the *Argus* of June 8, 1895, showed that eight "capitalists," as they were frequently dubbed in those days, as in these, visited Bernard N. Baker, a director for the Edmondson avenue line, at his "Ingleside" mansion on Old Frederick road. A few days later the Short Line was sold to the Edmondson avenue line, which, in effect, meant the M. & C. They obviously didn't waste much time in business deals during those days.

The plan, on paper, was favorable. Surveyors started to lay out a track bed across Egges Lane to join the Short Line with the Edmondson avenue line. At Loudon Park, the plan demanded connection with the Wilkens avenue branch of the City and Suburban line.

An elaborate description of the electric cars to be used for passenger service on the Short Line appeared in the *Argus*. The cars, powered by "heavy electric motors," were to seat 100. They were to be electrically lighted, a novel thing in those days.

The M. & C. estimated that the line to Washington, D. C., would be completed in 18 months. It was never finished.

In the Curtis Bay sector of Baltimore, electric cars of the City and Suburban had filed steam traffic down to almost nothing. The directors of the Short Line probably took that into consideration as they voted to team up with the M. & C. Although they moaned that steam could deliver patrons in the city in 30 minutes in lieu of electric's 40 minutes, they probably realized that steam suburban lines were becoming obsolete and the only alternative was to "go electric."

The Short Line mistake was that they chose the wrong electric line.

The Maryland and Columbia took off to a grand start. On the Washington end, track was laid to Hyattsville. Here, rail eventually reached Ellicott City. But the link between Hyattsville and the Patapsco never materialized.

Nor did the half mile of track to unite Edmondson avenue with the Catonsville station of the Short Line ever come to life. Property owners whose land would be partitioned screamed bloody murder to the county commissioners, who gave a sympathetic reply.

The last shot into the carcass of the M. & C. came when the Catonsville Construction company and a Baltimore firm, affiliated builders of the Edmondson avenue line, went into receivership.

The last material move on the part of the M. & C. was to place an order with an Ohio rolling mill for 13,000 tons of 85 lb. rail. The price was listed as $24 a ton. (The weight of rail is expressed in pounds per yard. The average streetcar rail weighs 95 lbs. a yard; standard railroad rail, about 130 lbs.)

The sad ending came in 1897 when the finally completed Frederick avenue line of the City and Suburban took over the majority of business formerly carried by the Short Line. The M. & C. could not operate the Short Line, as they themselves were up to their necks with the receivership of the two construction companies. The only

alternative from shutting down the line entirely was to ask the PRR for another lease. The PRR refused.

To this the merchants of Catonsville set up a loud cry. To have freight carted out from Baltimore meant double the existing rate. Many of them also had investments in the Short Line, and they stood to lose heavily.

The wheel that squeaks loudest gets the grease.

On June 24, 1905, the *Argus* carried a little item in which it was stated that the annual board of directors meeting of the Short Line was held. One Frank Callaway then owned it, with a lease agreement with the PRR. There were no passenger trains — the Frederick avenue electric line had canceled any hope of resumption of that source of revenue.

From then on, the Short Line passed from owner to owner. Then it lapsed into receivership, where it stayed until 1945, when a Baltimore realty company acquired title to the right of way from receiver Michael Paul Smith. It was renamed the Caton and Loudon railway company and continued to be operated under lease to the PRR.

Steam remained the power on the Short Line, as it is still called, until recently, when Mellor avenue residents petitioned the railroad to change to Diesel.

But the old line is not dead, by any means. The PRR, in 1946, carried 360 carloads of freight over it, about 160 cars of which went to the Spring Grove State Hospital. About $45,000 gross revenue was realized from the line last year, says the PRR. Coal, lumber, sugar, flour, bricks and feed enter Catonsville each week on three trains which originate, for the most part, in the Gwynn Run yards of the PRR. During times when the county or State is indulging in road work, great quantities of sand, gravel and cement are shipped in.

Now there are four switches in the yard to aid in car shifting.

Perhaps this is a comeback for Catonsville's own little railroad. It has met with good and hard times, but has managed to survive any talk of dismantling.

In any event, it's still there. Gaze at the station and the rusty rails for a few moments and imagine. See there, the courtly ladies. And the gay steamers with carloads of freight.

Hurry, the 7:50 is pulling out!

AND NOW we come to the Catonsville Short Line, a tiny branch that figures in railroad, personal, national and, indeed, international history out of all proportion to its size and significance.

The preceding article reproduced here was written by us and published in the 25 July 1947 issue of the *Herald Argus*, one of a chain of weekly Maryland newspapers. At the time we had been a reporter for this newspaper for several years and, indeed, our first article submitted as a free lancer was published by them ca. 1945 and resulted in a job offer swiftly accepted by us. We had been writing for our high school newspaper in 1944-45, hence our claim that we have been writing for publication since age fourteen.

First, the CSL and personal history. The line ran through Loudon Park Cemetery. Father and Grandmother Mabel Simpson Roberts are buried near the line. The rails are still in place, covered by weeds. U.S. Grant's mother was a Simpson, as was Grandmother, hence the tie to this giant in American history.

The CSL then followed along Maiden Choice Run to Maiden Choice Lane, the site of a Catholic Seminary and the wry local reference to the seminarians forced to endure constant reminders that they were prohibited from choosing local maidens, a restriction as we shall see did not stop others from delving into such delights.

The seminary is now a vast retirement community and the chapel (an impressive structure in and of itself) is still active. Indeed, a daughter married there, three granddaughters have been christened in its halls and an ex-fiancé married her first husband at its altar, or so she claimed.

CSL then reached Spring Grove State Hospital, a mental institution with a power house that burned coal and was a steady source of revenue for the railroad until converted to oil some years ago, a death knell for the line.

The line then terminated in, of all places, Catonsville just behind the Catonsville High School where we spent too much time watching the PRR steam switcher doing its thing and letting geometry slide.

Now to the drawing of the Catonsville "yards." The Ice House, located to the left of this scene, was the site of our first fist-fight much to the delight of the onlooking workers. We won, by the way.

The Fire Station is extant. Father remembers the Railroad Hotel. As a boy he watched farmers trundle into Baltimore with their produce and, on the return trip, visit the bar to spend some of their proceeds before returning to their wives. The barkeep would put the well-lubricated farmers in the back of their wagons, slap the horse and let the latter loyally wander home. No risk of DWI in those days.

Second, railroad history. The CSL was a quintessential short line/branch typical of thousands of such lines that fed the trunklines. The rise of the truck and changing traffic patterns put paid to most of them. The history of CSL is the history of all of them.

Third, national history. Now the story gets really interesting.

We have met Charles Carroll of Carrollton, a Founding Father of the Republic, the last surviving (and only Catholic) signer of the Declaration of Independence and the richest man in the colonies in that era. He had a lot to lose if the Revolution did not go well and his signature convinced a lot of waverers to take the plunge. And a plunge from the scaffold would have been

Looking North from the heart of the "yards" of the Caton and Loudon Railway, the Fire and Police Buildings, where the old Railroad Hotel once stood, and, on the right, the station of the Short Line come into view. The spur off to the right leads to the John S. Wilson lumber company.

the end game if the revolt had failed.

Charles Carroll's daughter, a beauty who even attracted the eye of George Washington, married a rich Baltimore merchant named Richard Caton. The Catons built a mansion named Castle Thunder in, naturally, Catonsville on high ground where the Catonsville Library now stands.

And now the International implications. The Catons gave issue to three daughters (the Three Sisters in the article), by name Marianne, Louisa and Elizabeth. All inherited their mother's beauty.

Marianne married Robert Patterson, another wealthy Baltimore merchant whose sister Elizabeth married Napoleon's youngest brother Jerome in 1803. They had a son, Jerome Bonaparte-Patterson. Big Nappy did not approve of this union and had it annulled.

In 1814 Marianne and Robert Patterson visited Europe, taking along Marianne's two sisters Louisa and Elizabeth. They made a hit in London society, a bit surprising since Baltimore was the scene in that year of a savage defeat of British arms as we have reported.

And in 1815 it seems that Marianne became a mistress of none other than the Duke of Wellington, we assume as another reward for his stunning victory at Waterloo.

Sister Louisa married a Colonel Felton Harvey, one of Wellington's aide-de-camps, in 1817. Harvey died in 1819 and Louisa married a marquess in 1828.

In 1820 Marianne and Robert Patterson returned to America,

(continued from previous page)

where Robert died in 1822. Marianne and still unmarried sister Elizabeth returned to England and, lo and behold, she married Wellington's rake brother Richard Wellesley. Richard immediately became unfaithful and Elizabeth went to the Duke "and found consolation," whatever that means. As few years later she married another peer.

One cannot say that the sheets grew cold in Merrie Olde England.

Actually, Charles Carroll's three granddaughters began a long tradition of joining American money with British nobility, a process that produced, by the way, Sir Winston Churchill.

An then, of course, Baltimore's Wallis Simpson (no relation!) nailed a King a century later. *She* did it without money! Small State though it is, Maryland sure has produced a lot of fascinating history.

No one is free of scandal, of course, so we wish to make a small point. The reader knows we have dedicated this book to Thomas Swann and our middle name is Swann. Why, then, did we use just "Charles Roberts" as a byline for this article? Another *distant* descendant of Thomas with the last name of Swann had a distressing tendency to get caught having affairs with underage girls and, worse, getting into the newspapers. So the family urged us to drop our middle name until things cooled down.

THE Halethorpe station (MP. 19.3) is looking a bit under the weather in this undated (but post-electrification) photo.

F. A. Wrabel Collection

POWER – Three GG1s in the stealth Conrail livery easily roll a southbound mixed freight through Halethorpe on 15 January 1978. We reside in the complex on the hilltop to the right of the far bridge. The location of Grandfather Stewart's home was just south of this scene as reported. Mother was picking strawberries in the garden near the tracks while a young girl when a locomotive derailed and rolled into the garden. PRR certainly got *her* attention.

Fred W. Schneider, III

THIS stone and brick arch carries the four-track B&O main over the PRR east of St. Denis at Halethorpe. It was constructed in 1873 when the B&P line to Washington was built. The historic arch is shown here in 1917. It was widened later for four tracks.

National Archives

THE LINE then crossed the West Branch of the Patapsco River over a double-track, eight-span deck plate girder bridge erected in 1898. This view looks northward in 1917.

National Archives

TRACK TANKS and water stations are better known on the more mountainous east-west PRR main, but here's a combination of the two on the tangent approach to Stony Run shown in a 1928 view looking northward. Note that the left-hand overhead pipe can be turned to serve either Track 2 or 3.

F. A. Wrabel Collection

NO FOOLING – or stopping for that matter. Today that stretch is the site of this functional station constructed to serve Baltimore-Washington International Airport (BWI). Here the engineer of Amtrak AEM-7 934 gets a wave as the train barrels through on April Fools Day 1983.

Fred W. Schneider, III

ALL WAS QUIET at the passenger shelter at Stony Run (MP. 23.2) this day in 1920. Beyond the platform area is the broad curve just north of town.

F. A. Wrabel

F. A. Wrabel

THIS PHOTO has it all – classic SV Tower at Severn, a section house, the station (far right – MP. 26.4) and last but certainly not least, a Washington-Harrisburg train speeding northward with reverse consist. A long-gone image to savor from pre-electrification days in 1920.

LOCATION CHART
P. R. R.
MARYLAND DIV.
PROPOSED
THIRD TRACK
ODENTON, MD. TO SEVERN, MD.
AND
SEABROOK, MD. TO BOWIE, MD.
OFFICE OF CHIEF ENGINEER
PHILA., PA. NOV. 25, 1942.　　SCALE-1"=4 MILES

Hagley Museum & Library

PRR had proposed several times to complete the three-track system between Baltimore and Washington – in 1919 and again in 1931 in conjunction with the Baltimore Improvements. Finally with the surge of World War II traffic – freights hauling coal and war materiel and passenger trains carrying military personnel – the two remaining sections of double track seriously restricted the free movement of tonnage to and from Potomac Yard.

There were several alternate proposals for this project, but the final one consisted of an additional electrified track (No. 1) for 3-1/2 miles from Severn to Odenton and four miles from Bowie to Seabrook, finally completing the three-track system. The $1.1 million project was approved on 14 October 1942 and construction began shortly thereafter.

F. A. Wrabel

THIS strange structure allowed the Washington, Baltimore & Annapolis interurban line to cross the electrified PRR main. In this 1935 photo the catenary is aligned for cross-traffic. Not to be overlooked are Z (later ODENTON) Tower, a Victorian gem in superb condition, and in the distance another classic PRR tool shed.

BY RAISING and rotating the trolley bar in the catenary "turntable" as demonstrated here a mainline PRR train could pass through unobstructed. Afternoon shadows are lengthening as a modified P5a in the original striping moves a southbound train through the crossing in the same year. Both of these photos were taken from the Odenton station platform, which was just south of the crossing.

PRR went to great expense to design and construct this crossing mechanism, but it was only used for a short while before the traction line went out of business at the end of 1935.

James P. Shannon/Fred W. Schneider, III Collection

The local power company took it over in an attempt to create a "power monopoly" to the detriment of the interurban line, and probably to the relief of PRR since it was trying to fill its own commuter trains and eliminate the competition.

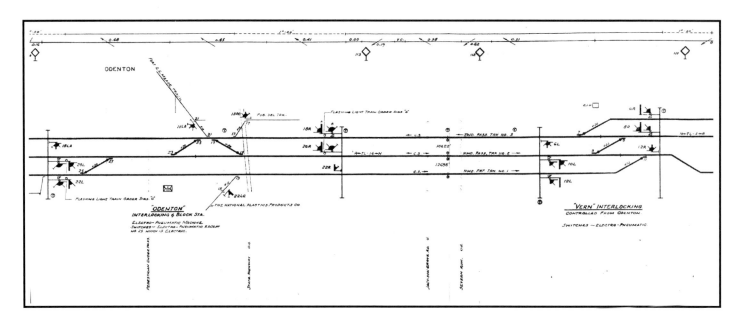

BY 1962 the WB&A was gone and ODENTON Tower had taken over VN (later VERN) interlocking. Note the branch to Fort Meade.

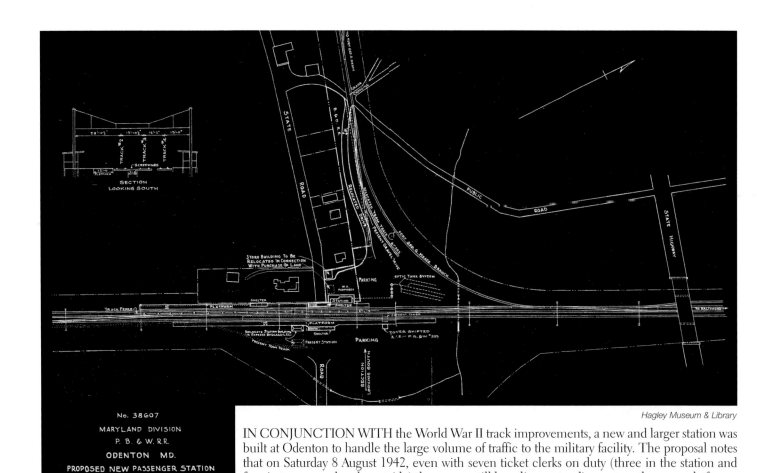

No. 38607

MARYLAND DIVISION

P. B. & W. R.R.

ODENTON MD.

PROPOSED NEW PASSENGER STATION

SCALE 1"=100'

OFFICE OF CHIEF ENGINEER
EASTERN REGION · P.R.R.

NOVEMBER 3·1942

IN CONJUNCTION WITH the World War II track improvements, a new and larger station was built at Odenton to handle the large volume of traffic to the military facility. The proposal notes that on Saturday 8 August 1942, even with seven ticket clerks on duty (three in the station and four in temporary booths outside) there were still long lines extending out on the open platforms. The project consisted of a new 24 X 56-ft. one-story station, a 50-ft. long southbound shelter and an 80-ft. long northbound shelter. It was finally built in late 1943.

THE NEW STATION was another functional but attractive design by Raymond Loewy Associates, shown here in May of 1993.

Thomas Fuchs

IN NOVEMBER 1975 Fall rains have swollen the Patuxent River, giving us a nice reflection of a south-bound Amtrak train – freshly relettered GG1 912 commands a set of Heritage equipment.

Thomas Buckingham/Fred W. Schneider, III Collection

THE MOTORIST at the crossing would do well to obey the gates and flashing lights as a southbound Metroliner speeds past the shelter at Jericho Park (MP. 35.8) on 10 May 1969. The year-old Metroliners have recently had their PRR key-stones removed and the Penn Central logo applied in their place.

Fred W. Schneider, III

NO PROBLEM – Doing what it was designed to do, GG1 4915 hustles Penn Central Train No. 351 southbound up the grade north of Bowie in February 1971. Even in PC black their beauty and power are compelling.

Fred W. Schneider, III

WE NOW COME to Bowie (MP. 36.9). At the left in this northward view taken in 1935 we have the southbound passenger shelter and across the tracks the old block station, the newly-constructed BOWIE Tower (obscured by a photographic blotch) and the picturesque Victorian station.

F. A. Wrabel

FOURTEEN YEARS have passed, and the old station has been demolished, replaced by this trim structure. The Popes Creek Branch is just visible behind the tower.

F. A. Wrabel

BOWIE IN THE EARLY 20th Century looking south with the Popes Creek line at left and the mainline to Washington DC at right. The Railroad Hotel on the left and the tower burned down ca. 1910.

David Goldsmith Collection

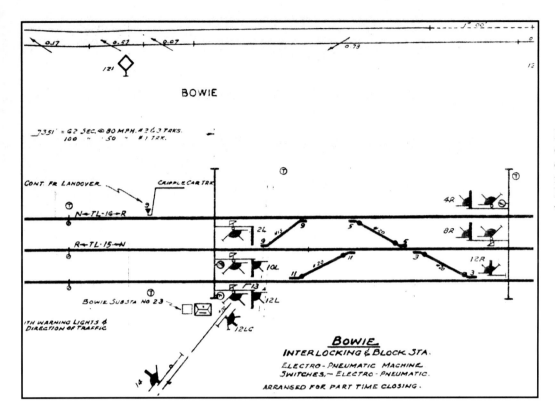

BOWIE interlocking is depicted here in a 1962 diagram. It controlled the crossovers on the main and the junction with the Popes Creek Branch, which we'll look at briefly.

MOVING DOWN the Popes Creek line we come to Collington (MP 3.1 from Bowie). This view looking northward at the station on 11 May 1928 appears to have been taken from a train. But we can't figure out what the individual tipping up the large crate intends to do with it – whatever it was we trust he was successful.

F. A. Wrabel

Charles Kilborne/David Goldsmith Collection

HERE WE SEE the freight station at Marlboro in the late 1960s, a sleepy Southern Maryland town in tobacco country. Perhaps the origin of the famous cigarettte brand.

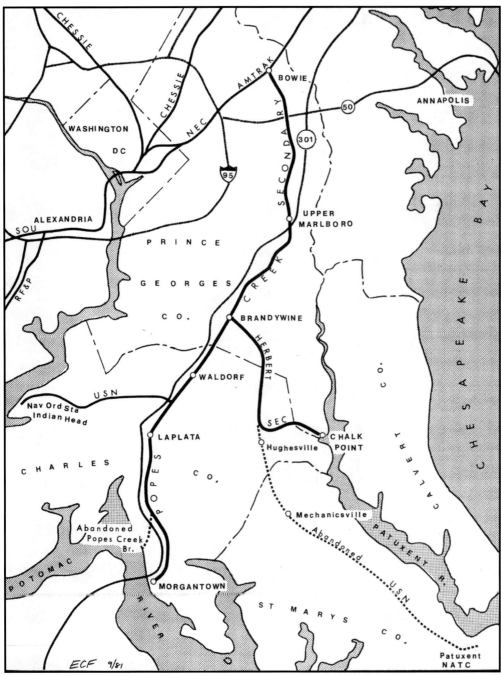

THE Popes Creek line would probably have fallen into oblivion if it hadn't been for the construction by Potomac Electric Power Company (PEPCO) of two coal-fired power plants, one at Morgantown and the other at Chalk Point. The branch to Chalk Point utilized part of the old Southern Maryland RR, which joined the B&P at Brandywine and ran as far as Hughesville by 1893. Changing ownership several times, this road reached Mechanicsville in the 1920s. At the onset of World War II the line was extended by the U. S. Navy to its Patuxent Naval Air Test Center at Cedar Point. PRR leased the section of the SMRR from Brandywine to Herbert (just north of Hughesville) to access the Chalk Point plant, and the remainder of the line was abandoned in 1970. This map shows the Popes Creek Secondary in 1981.

Rails Northeast/Tim Garner Collection

THE STATION at Waldorf (MP.31.1) looks more like a logging camp than a rail facility, particularly with the piles of logs in the background of this 1928 view.

F. A. Wrabel

ALL IS QUIET at the station at Brandywine (MP.25.0) in 1928.

F. A. Wrabel

THE FREIGHT STATION at Indian-head Junction in the 1960s where the Navy line to their ordnance facility on the Potomac River left the Popes Creek line.

Charles Kilborne/David Goldsmith Collection

AT LA PLATA (MP.38.8) a worker is trying to shove a trunk behind the bagage wagon located on the platform in a 1928 view.

F. A. Wrabel

HAPPILY the station at LaPlata was acquired by the town, restored and moved across the tracks in 2001. The caboose in a nearby spur is a U.S. Navy cab used on their line from Indian Head Junction. Unhappily, an F5 tornado (winds 261-318 mph) struck LaPlata on 28 April 2002, devastating the town and killing three people. The station itself suffered only light damage. In 1926 an F4 tornado savaged the town and a school-house where 14 children were killed. Mother Nature at her worst.

David Goldsmith

END OF THE LINE – The terminal (such as it was) at Popes Creek (MP.48.7) looked rather lonely on this day in 1928. The pier into the Potomac River is at bottom and the passenger "station" at right.

F. A. Wrabel

THE POPES CREEK line was awash in pivotal railroad history, but ended awash in junk. The pier ca. 1969.

Charles Kilborne/David Goldsmith Collection

THERE WAS A HAPPIER TIME, although the date of this photo is uncertain. Looking toward the river, the 39 will not have to strain with a one-car consist. This section of the line was abandoned as reported earlier, but continued to Morgantown farther down the river. Now back to Bowie.

Herbert H. Harwood, Jr.

PASSAGE of the Northeast Rail Service Act (NERSA) in 1981 allowed Amtrak to assume complete ownership and control of its lines – including the Northeast Corridor – and state-subsidized and regional commuter authorities such as Maryland Area Rail Commuter (MARC) to take over local passenger operations. MARC, a unit of the Maryland Transportation Authority, was formed ca. 1980 to take over local commuter service on former PRR/PC lines between Baltimore and Washington and Baltimore to Perryville, plus B&O/Chessie System routes Baltimore-Washington and Washington-Brunswick, Harper's Ferry and Martinsburg.

Here a MARC local, headed by its own version of Amtrak's AEM-7 4903 and equipped with matching Bombardier coaches, performs its daily chores as it hustles past the Bowie substation in the summer of 1988.

William D. Middleton/Fred W. Schneider, III Collection

THOTSG – No, that's not a typo – it's the acronym our (DWM) high-school English teacher used as a convenient term for Nathaniel Hawthorne's classic novel, *The House of the Seven Gables*. The interesting frame station at Landover (MP. 45.1), shown here in a 1915 photo, reminds us of that structure. Landover is at the junction of the old B&P line (now the freight route, which we'll look at shortly) to Potomac Yard and the Magruder Branch to Washington Terminal.

National Archives

ACCOMMODATION? – Penn Central certainly didn't do anything to encourage commuters, forcing them to walk across the freight tracks at Landover in April 1971.

Thomas Buckingham/Fred W. Schneider, III Collection

Fred W. Schneider, III

A SIX-CAR Penn Central Metroliner set outruns the camera shutter as it races northward
past LANDOVER Tower on 10 May 1969. The overpass is Landover Road (Route 202).

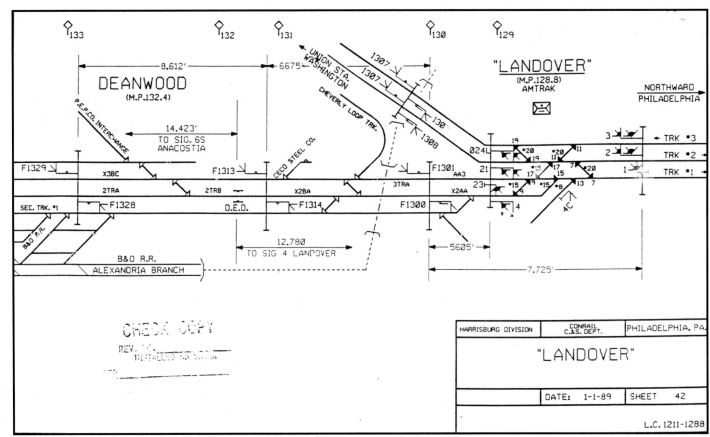

David Goldsmith

AT LANDOVER the railroad gets interesting and confusing. Study this 1989 track chart and find the Magruder Branch diverging to Union Station in Washington DC. Then follow the three-track main through Deanwood – this is the line to Potomac Yard in Virginia. Both of these lines cross the Anacostia River as we shall see. Also note the B&O Alexandria Branch, passing under this complex to reach B&O rails nearby. Now let us follow the line to Union Station.

DISASTROUS ENCOUNTER – In September 1933 the Southern RR's crack New York-New Orleans *Crescent Limited* found a damaged bridge across the Anacostia River, swollen by hurricane rains, with savage results. Recovery operations were underway when this aerial photo was taken, with a crew of onlookers already gathered. Thank God there were no catenary poles.

F. A. Wrabel

F. A. Wrabel

ONE of the Southern's classy Virginia green and gold PS4 heavy Pacifics left the railroad and toppled over, ploughing a deep furrow into the rain-soaked embankment.

MEANWHILE heavyweight Pullman *John T. Morgan* teeters precariously off the edge of the bridge. The train had been completely re-equipped just four years before with these matching two-tone green cars. Note the heavily damaged pier underneath, apparently the cause of the problem.

F. A. Wrabel

PLEASE REFER to the overview map of the Washington DC area on the front endpaper. This USGS map shows the immediate Union Station area in 1982. The Amtrak main enters from the right, heading toward the terminal, with the B&O lines above that. The Conrail freight line swings across the bottom with the 1st Street Tunnel line diverging at lower left.

THIS 1953 aerial photo gives us a good overview of the Ivy City Engine Terminal and yards in the waning days of steam. The view looks east (railroad northward). At the right are the PRR and B&O mains – first the PRR (PB&W) Magruder Branch and then the B&O Washington Branch. To the right of that are the PRR team tracks along New York Avenue. The large building is the Hecht's department store warehouse.

In the foreground at left is the coach repair and storage yards, in the center are the ash pits and 1200-ton coaling station and at right are several GG1s, one lone steamer and is a group of diesels from the C&O, RF&P and Southern RRs. Behind that are the shop buildings and the west (l.) and east (r.) engine houses, each with its own turntable. A fascinating complex designed specifically to serve the unique needs of Washington Union Terminal!

MOVING farther west – the engine terminal is in the distance at the upper right and the PRR and B&O mains are at the far right. We find the coach yards jammed with an amazing variety of equipment from several roads. From left to right are Yards A, E, F, G and H. The power house is in the center background and behind it the connector between the B&O Washington and Metropolitan Branches.

THIS VIEW looks south. At the left are the coach yards and in the center is the B&O Metropolitan Branch. At the right are the B&O freight yards. The two road overpasses are T Street in the foreground and New York Avenue in the background. Union Station is visible in the distance.

Jim Shaughnessy

VETERAN photographer Jim Shaughnessy is well known for capturing the magic of railroading – especially the haunts of engine terminals – at night, and this shot of the diverse power stored at Ivy City is no exception. Here E-units from the Southern, B&O and C&O await assignment on the ready tracks, reflecting the true diversity of Washington Union Station.

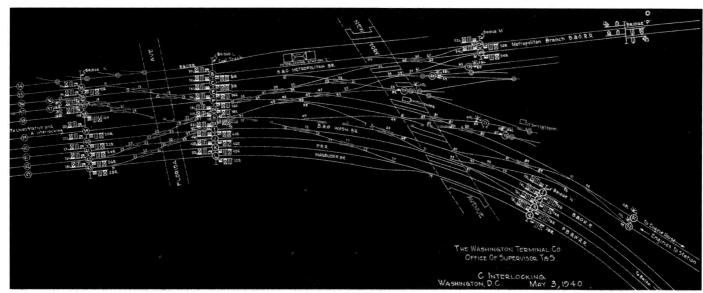

Hagley Museum & Library

C Tower controlled the complex junction of the PB&W and B&O lines from Baltimore with the B&O Metropolitan Branch. It was located at the terminal throat and was operated by the Terminal Company.

THE NATION'S capital did not always have a union station. The B&P extended its tracks across the city and constructed this imposing terminal at 6th and B Streets. It was accessed from the south by the "Long Bridge" over the Potomac, which figured prominently in Thomson's southern strategy.

Railroad Museum of Pennsylvania (PHMC)

THIS LATE 19TH CENTURY photo shows a more congested scene in front of the terminal, with street cars and carriages – note that there are no clocks in the tower as depicted in the preceding drawing. As it turned out, both the B&P and B&O were not ideally situated, with portions of the approach trackage running in the streets and others crossing at grade. As vehicular traffic began to increase, public agitation grew to eliminate the grade crossings and replace both stations. Discussions continued for several years and a plan was put forth in 1899 to eliminate the grade crossings by elevation of the tracks and construct a new terminal.

Finally, responding to public pressure to do *something*, the U.

Ted Xaras Collection

S. Congress in its collective wisdom passed two similar bills on 12 February 1901, one for the B&P (later PB&W) and the other for the B&O. The B&P bill provided $1.5 million in reimbursement funds for elimination of the grade crossings, reconstruction of the Long Bridge and a new, larger terminal on the Mall. The B&O bill, which also provided reimbursement of $1.5 million, authorized elimination of grade crossings and construction of a station at a new location at C Street and Delaware Avenue, closer to the Capitol. Interestingly, this bill also included a provision for formation of a Terminal Company to build and operated the new facilities in the city.

The Washington Terminal Company was incorporated on 6 December 1901, but it soon became apparent that Congress had created a two-headed monster by retaining duplicate rail facilities in the city. And so, after more deliberations Congress passed new legislation repealing the provisions of the 1901 Acts requiring separate terminals and stipulating that a Union Passenger Station be constructed at the intersection of Massachusetts and Delaware Avenues. The new terminal was to be "monumental in character" and cost "not less than $4 million."

In a new display of cooperation (remember, this was Washington, not Baltimore) PB&W purchased a 50 per cent interest in the Washington Terminal Company and undertook joint construction of the station and associated yards. PB&W constructed the Magruder Branch (which became the passenger main), eliminated the grade crossings on the original line (which became freight only) and rebuilt the Long Bridge. PB&W jointly built – and then leased to the Terminal Company – a $3.4 million coach yard at the junction of the two passenger mains and the B&O Metropolitan Branch.

AND THUS on 17 November 1907 the monumental new $6 million Union Station opened to the public, and the old B&P passenger station was abandoned shortly thereafter. A temporary passenger facility built at 8th Street and Maryland Avenue was closed the following year.

This stunning aerial view shows the impressive front façade ca. 1930. The main terminal building was designed in Roman classical style to complement the Capitol and other government buildings by noted Chicago architect Daniel H. Burnham. It was built of gleaming white Vermont marble, 632 ft. long, 210 ft. deep and 120 ft. high over the main waiting room.

The three 50-ft. high entrance arches lead to a vaulted open-air vestibule and then into the main waiting room. The 40-ft. arches at the end pavilions were designed as carriage entrances, with the eastern one leading to a suite of apartments for the President of the U. S., government officials and foreign dignitaries. The central vestibule and the end pavilions are connected by a covered portico running along the front of the building, which faces a semicircular plaza featuring balustrades and fountains. Railroad offices were located on the second story.

Ted Xaras Collection

THE PASSENGER CONCOURSE, shown here shortly after opening, was designed to handle large crowds. It measured 130 ft. wide, and 760 ft. long, covered by a single-span arched ceiling decorated with inset panels and two long rows of glass, giving a light and airy feeling throughout. The space to the left of the train gates is 35-ft. wide for arriving passengers and the one at right is 85 ft. wide for departing patrons. The concourse opens into the high-arched waiting room of similar design by means of 15 doors, as well as the carriage portico and plaza.

Ted Xaras Collection

THE STATION was constructed without a large train shed so as not to detract from the appearance of the Capitol a short distance away. As built the station had 29 tracks, of which 18 terminated at the concourse level. The remaining 11 tracks descended a ramp to 20 ft. below the waiting room, coming together into six that continue under the building into the 1st Street Tunnel under Capitol Hill, allowing a connection for passenger trains to and from the South.

This late 1940s view looks south toward the Capitol and shows the mail facilities added to the original configuration. In front of these are the East Yard and the Express Building, 420 ft. long and 60 ft. wide, and across the throat are the West Yard, turntable and Power House. K Tower is located in the center foreground.

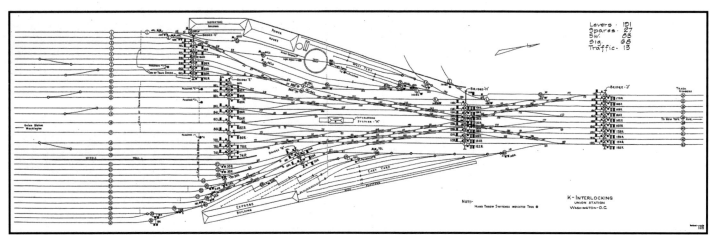

Hagley Museum & Library

THIS DIAGRAM shows K interlocking, which had the enormous task of controlling the terminal throat. The configuration is shown as of 1931 prior to addition of Tracks 34-36 for the new mail facility. The functional beauty of the track layout is compelling.

K TOWER on an unknown date but busy as ever.

David Goldsmith Collection

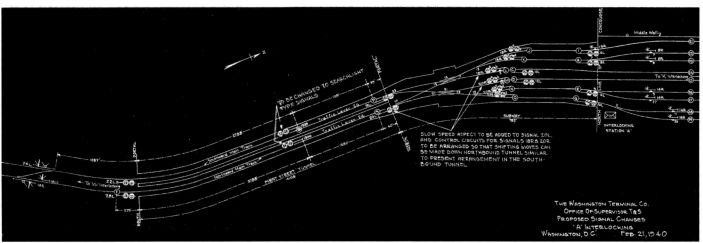

Hagley Museum & Library

TRACKS 21-29 continue under the terminal concourse to the 1st Street Tunnel, tapering down to two main tracks. This transition under the station is controlled by A interlocking, shown here in a 21 February 1940 diagram. The proposed changes noted were implemented in October of that year.

THE 1st Street Tunnel was constructed in 1903-6 to allow passenger trains from southern railroads to enter Union Terminal without obstructing city streets. It became the subject of extended lawsuits with the city and the Washington Terminal Railway regarding alleged above-ground damage.

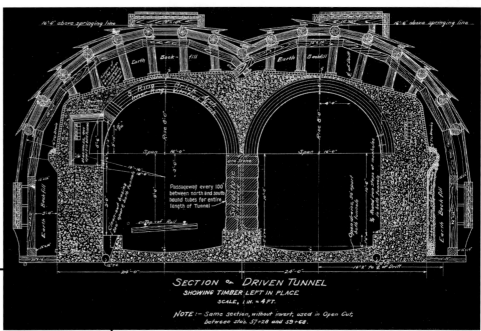

SECTION on DRIVEN TUNNEL
SHOWING TIMBER LEFT IN PLACE
SCALE, 1 IN. = 4 FT.
NOTE:— Same section, without invert, used in Open Cut, between stas. 57+28 and 59+68.

Hagley Museum & Library

THE TRACKS EMERGE from the tunnel and join with the freight line at VIRGINIA AVENUE Tower near 2nd Street, as shown here. Grade crossings were eliminated on all of the streets shown here as part of the 1904-1908 track elevation project.

William J. Coxey

THE southward end of the 1st Street Tunnel is shown here in October 1971. Construction of this tunnel was difficult under the city streets and the subject of considerable legal interaction between PRR and city officials and the Washington Railway and Electric Company – before, during and after completion – mostly over responsibility for restoration of the streets and trolley right of way, and the resultant settling.

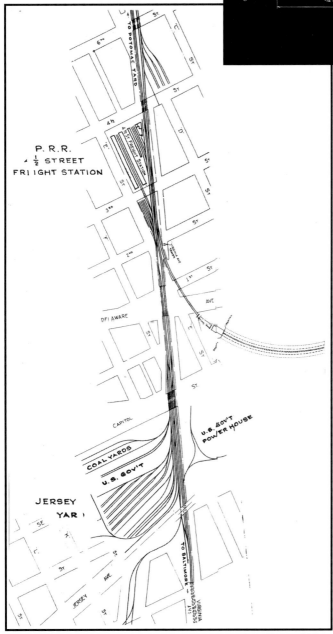

Hagley Museum & Library

VIRGINIA TOWER as it appeared in March 2002.

David Goldsmith

VIRGINIA IN 1987. The line runs south (left) to 14th STREET interlocking, remotely controlled from VIRGINIA for many years. CP-14th ST condensed three tracks to two to cross Long Bridge and enter Potomac Yard at RO Interlocking, which by 1989 was controlled by RF&P from Richmond. We will visit the bridge and Pot Yard later in this chapter. On the right see the line from Landover to which we will now return.

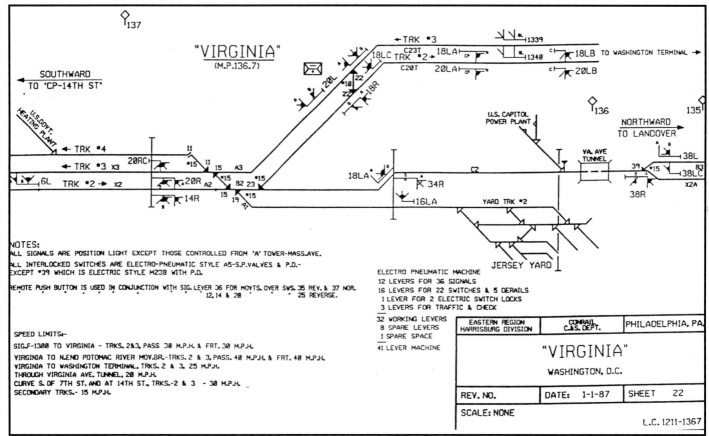

David Goldsmith

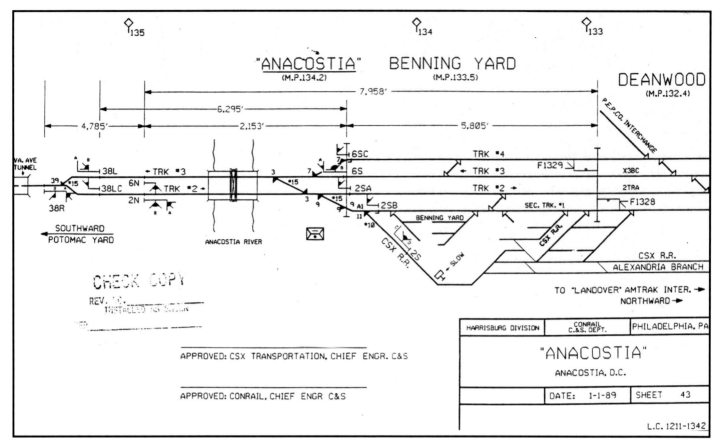

David Goldsmith

THE "POT YARD" line leaves Landover, passes Benning Yard, crosses the Anacostia River and enters Virginia Avenue tunnel under downtown Washington DC, the latter another infamous bottleneck on the Corridor. The B&O (CSX) Alexandria Branch joins PRR trackage as shown. The year is 1989.

David Goldsmith

ANACOSTIA TOWER, a little worse for wear, is seen here in March 2007

MOVING to the river, we find Penn Central freight B4A as it rumbles across the Anacostia draw toward Potomac Yard on 9 May 1970.

Fred W. Schneider, III

CAPITOL SCENE – The catenary frames both the Capitol and Penn Central freight MD117 as it approaches L'Enfant Square on 9 April 1970. B&O, of course, captured the Dome as its trademark. A nice victory.

Fred W. Schneider, III

THE TRACK ELEVATION project carried out in 1905-6 involved a series of one-half through plate girder bridges over several city streets, including 3rd, Water, South Capitol and the 3rd Street freight yard, plus a deck plate structure at 2nd Street. An additional group was constructed over 4-1/2, 6th, 7th and 9th Streets in 1908. This 1917 photo shows typical construction.

National Archives

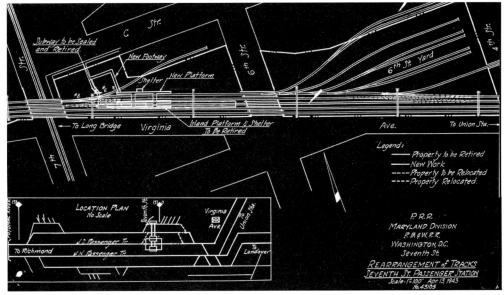

EVEN AFTER ELEVATION of the right of way the southward main tracks at 7th Street had a 20 mph speed restriction. This was because of sharp reverse curves at both ends of the station to accommodate the station platforms between the tracks. In 1943, because of a reduction in use of the station as a result of the relocation of government offices and businesses from the area, PRR proposed this plan to eliminate the island platform, shelter shed and umbrella shelter, steps and subway entrance – and realign the tracks to a tangent configuration.

Hagley Museum & Library

Jeremy Taylor

THE ORIGINAL "Long Bridge" over the Potomac was an 1811-ft., 14-span Pratt Truss structure. After extended discussions a new plate girder bridge on the elevated grade and revised alignment was finally completed in 1906 and the old bridge abandoned and removed the following year. The bridge was in turn rebuilt in 1943 for heavy wartime traffic to and from Potomac Yard – that structure is shown here on 18 April 1990 with Conrail freight WHWA 01 crossing northbound to Benning Yard with Norfolk Southern interchange traffic.

SOUTH OF THE BORDER – The 4761 rolls a southbound freight past RO Tower having crossed the Long Bridge in 1947 and prepares to enter Pot Yard. And "tower" is correct. No way a Southern railroad would call this a "cabin" as it might remind them of Lincoln's birthplace. This tower marked the border between PRR and RF&P. Just as the Potomac River marks the true boundary between North and South. *Not* the Mason-Dixon Line, as true Marylanders are always eager to emphasize. Maryland was *blue*, not *gray*. Both Maryland and Virginia were Cavalier but alike in this regard only.

Herbert H. Harwood, Jr.

F. A. Wrabel

POTOMAC YARD stretched some 2.5 miles along the river, providing the primary traffic interchange between PRR and the South. Its 157 tracks had a capacity of over 6700 cars. It was owned and operated by the RF&P, which served a vital connecting role via Richmond. The engine terminal was located in the center of the yard.

This 1927 view looks northward from the hump tower at the vast Northbound Classification Yard. This yard was the largest component of the facility, with 46 tracks holding over 2000 cars. Note the light-duty steam crane and standpipe for returning locomotives.

PERISHABLE PRODUCE was a major – albeit seasonal – traffic element through the yard, requiring reicing facilities. This 1927 view from the overhead bridge looks south at the icing platforms (with several classic "watermelon cars") and refrigerator cars jamming the West Storage Yard at right.

F. A. Wrabel

CLOSE TO their Alexandria VA shops, thousands of Fruit Growers Express reefers passed through Potomac Yard annually. This view looks northward from the same bridge at a group of FGEX reefers in the Heavy Repair Yard, with the Advance Yard beyond. At the left are the through passenger tracks and the Washington and Alexandria Turnpike. The coaling tower is just visible in the distance.

F. A. Wrabel

ALTHOUGH perishable shipments by rail had dropped drastically and other traffic had declined as well, the yard was still busy in this October 1971 view.

William J. Coxey

THE END IS NEAR: Further declines and changing traffic patterns resulted in an empty Potomac Yard, except for stored RF&P boxcars, by the summer of 1990.

Thomas Fuchs

Insights, Hindsights, Oversights and Foresights

History Club was one of the delights of our High School career, along with journalism and history courses, and we still look back with warm regard to the vigorous discussions and debates which were the hallmark of academics in that school.

A compatriot, apparently irritated by one of our positions, stated that we were born in the wrong century. References to buccaneering were made, an apparent reference to a well-known pirate with the surname of Roberts. As we recall, there was unanimous agreement and it was not meant as a compliment.

The 19th Century was the subject. Now that we have studied and written about that century we will have to confess that it would have been the greatest of times to have been alive, even as an observer.

It was the age of Napoleon, Wellington, Nelson, Bismarck, Victoria and Albert, Gladstone, Disraeli, Washington, Jefferson, Jackson, Hamilton, Lincoln and Grant. The century of the industrial and agricultural revolutions, the *Pax Britannica*, the creation of the railroad and a bevy of attendant giants, the rise of steam power for railroad, ship and industrial uses, the soaring use of coal as an energy source, stunning advances in metallurgy, wire communication, electricity, internal combustion and divers fields of science.

The arts flourished, the visual arts broadened by photography. Slavery was abolished and Unions were formed to protect the working man. The seeds of universal suffrage were blossoming on the principle of one man/one vote and the vote would ultimately be given to women, of all things!

Advances in health care and public health were astonishing. Mass production was instituted, originally in the field of railroad equipment and then other industrial avenues. Interchangeability of parts, little remarked but fundamental to the revolution, became a reality requiring minute tolerances.

Sadly, so did the evolution of total war and modern weapons.

We have already related the astonishing rise of the United States to Superpower status without, by the way, the acquisition of an overseas empire.

And the financial markets. In 1895 the United States loaned more money to the rest of the world than it owed, reversing a flow of some four centuries. The wise money knows, of course, that this game is fixed but it was exciting nonetheless. Millionaires grew on trees and exported daughters to Great Britain.

If Jimmy the Greek had been alive, we wonder what odds he would have granted in 1800 that the fledgling Republic would attain such heights or, for that matter, still be in existence a century later. After all, even George Washington doubted that the new Republic and its Constitution would last more than twenty years.

Yes, it was a heady century and, yes, it would have been a great time to be alive even as a buccaneer.

The 19th Century was succeeded by the 20th, about which a writer observed that if one likes an exciting life the 20th would be the choice. Since we were born in 1930, we will attest to the merit of his comment.

The 20th began well, as Barbara Tuchman (the heroine of all historians along with hero Will Durant, including this lowly writer) reported in her seminal work *The Proud Tower*. In 1914 it all started down the tubes.

It was the Century of Churchill, Thatcher, Adenauer, the two Roosevelts, Eisenhower and Reagan but also the beasts of history, Hitler, Stalin and Lenin.

The 20th Century produced *two* World War convulsions with staggering casualties, a Holocaust and experiments in genocide, the Great Depression, fascism, communism, Marxism and socialism, the dissolution of all the Empires, a Cold War, the stain of rampant chemical, biological and radiological warfare and other fruits of mankind's sadistic streak.

The demise of the Empires, whatever their faults and they were manifest, resulted in a Balkanization of nations almost beyond count and, usually, corrupt beyond measure.

There was no *Pax Americana*.

The 20th Century also saw the rise of the airplane,

wireless communication, automobiles and trucks, oil as the primary energy source, the nuclear age, the exploration of space and the computer. And the creation of a totally new art form, audio/visual communication. Yes, it was exciting.

The 21st Century is young, but rich with serious problems. A new "ism" dramatically appeared on 9/11, by name, Terrorism. What a mindless, self-defeating obscenity. It is based solely on murder of the innocent and mayhem with no rational goal whatsoever. Even the communists had a vision of a better life, flawed though it was. One thing is apparent. Reason is out of the question. They must be exterminated.

And the 21st Century starts with economic and financial distress, the perils of unleased global capitalism, another war, pollution, environmental problems and the abandonment of regulation, the purpose of which has always been "protection of the public." Worse, the United States is now a creditor nation with a threat of deflation. This century, too, will be exciting.

We have always been a short-term pessimist and but remain a long-term optimist. This is a versatile, diverse, energetic, well-meaning Republic with a free press and the most precious gift of all – an unabated thirst for freedom and liberty. We will triumph. The best days of this Republic lie in front of us.

And now back to railroading.

OF GODS – In this and other books, we have had much fun in needling our British cousins and hope to continue in the future.

It is important to remember, however, that we Americans needed British help to push out the French and French help to push out the British. The Indians and Spanish we took care of on our own.

Whether or not God is an Englishman remains in question, but there is no question that the most fundamental Right of all is the Right of Conquest. PRR conquered, as did the British in their time.

Both Britain and PRR may or may not be Godly, but they certainly did act that way. We submit that the whole World owes them a great debt regardless of their state of divinity.

OF CROSSES AND THORNS – We have posited that PRR's New York Division (Triumph V) was a cross too heavy to bear and Maryland Division (Triumph VI) a crown of thorns.

Both divisions were predominantly passenger railroads. Other than possibly the early years in the mid-19th Century, railroad passenger business has always been a bottomless pit of capital investment and operating losses. There is no way any railroad can make money out of passenger business, whether long haul, medium haul or commuter.

Amtrak took over long and medium haul business in 1971 and local and State governments acquired commuter business in the same time frame. Governments simply took the capital investment, have no tax burden or cost of capital whatsoever and yet still lose money in prodigious quantities. So, by the way, do airlines. On a cumulative basis, the airlines have lost money as an industry since Wilbur and Orville got off the ground.

One can make an interesting argument that society needs rail passenger service for a host of reasons, many quite convincing, but it must be regarded as a public service and subsidized accordingly. We repeat – there is no way it is going to pay.

PRR, being number one, suffered the most from this curse. B&O, merely a minor player, proved that sometimes it pays to be lowly. B&O, as a corporate entity, lasted until 1987 and did not go broke. PRR did.

Now for a few minor anecdotes. In the early 1950s we worked for a large Baltimore Advertising agency that had a telephone number similar to that of PRR's Penn Station and every day we received many wrong numbers.

One evening we were working late and Buck Cooke answered the phone. The conversation went as follows:

"When does the next train leave for New York?"
"I don't know."
"Well, can you find out?"
"Well, I guess so but it would be a lot of trouble."
"Take the trouble!" (Gurgling rage)
"Well, there might be a timetable around here somewhere. Charley, do you have one?"

"No." (Gurgling laughter)

"Here's one. How do you read this thing?"

"What is your name, by God!"

"Buck Cooke."

"Well, when I am finished you will no longer be working for the railroad!" (Slamming phone)

It was not a good night to be a ticket agent at Penn Station. Those poor devils were dying out there.

The B&O/PRR conflict was not always so acerbic, however. At lower levels, most relations were pleasant and polite. For example, during the War Father took Mother, Sister and Self on a trip on the Ma and Pa to York, returning on the Northern Central. All on B&O passes, of course.

The train was crowded. Father flashed his passes and the PRR conductor pointed out that these passes were not good on that train that day.

Tense moment since Father did not have enough money to pay for tickets. The conductor shrugged and said he would collect them the next day. The railroad fraternity was a strong one.

OF KEYSTONES AND REALITY – The State of Pennsylvania, or Commonwealth as they prefer, regard themselves as the Keystone of the nation. That title is accurate and apt.

Consider that Pennsylvania was a cornucopia of coal, ores, timber and oil in an area almost the same size as England, the Mother of the Industrial Revolution.

Pennsylvania was surrounded on three sides by New York State, New Jersey, and Maryland *none of which* had significant raw material assets of any consequence.

PRR ran right through the middle of this Garden of Eden.

Pennsylvania would have to work at it to blow this catbird seat and for many years they did just that, a fascinating story told in *Triumph I*. If you want to screwup something, get the Government to do it.

But along came PRR, late to the show but determined to become the Keystone railroad and literally the "Standard Railroad of the World." What a show it was!

No contest would be interesting without vigorous competition and PRR had just that. They had New York Central to the north reaching into their patch, B&O on the south, Erie in the upper corner and Reading to the east. Plus a bevy of other minor but nonetheless irritating railroads.

The most serious threat was NYC and indeed in the end that railroad became the number two trunkline railroad albeit a distant second.

Erie, a very real threat in the early years, finally choked on their insane route over the mountains from somewhere to nowhere and financial manipulations that still attract the eye.

Reading never did become a trunkline in spite of several interesting attempts as we have reported in a number of books. Their route from New York to Harrisburg was the best then and *now* but they could never get west of Harrisburg.

And then there is B&O. We, of course, are deep students of this railroad and have written and published many books on it. Curiously, the founders of B&O never did suffer under any illusion that they would be number one. They *knew* that they could not compete with their northerly rivals and were prepared to be satisfied with a share of the bonanza.

With a railroad that was "uphill in all directions," B&O ended up in third place. As we have reported in *Sand Patch*, they had a chance to be number two but that went awry with the Garrett administration and the PRR invasion of Maryland which is, of course, the subject of this book. Poor B&O couldn't win for losing.

It has been said that Love, Lust, Loathing and Lucre (the four Ls) speak to the human condition. This story is replete with all of them.

In the end, it can be said that PRR was Loathed and they didn't care.

Love is the most difficult emotion to define, but it has been said that you know it if you step in it. B&O, the brave, dashing, cavalier underdog, came out of history being Loved. They had more fun.

OF FANTASIES AND TIDBITS – In April 2003 Amtrak announced plans to replace the B&P Tunnels. They are requesting $4 million for design and engineering and estimate the new tunnel will cost "hundreds of millions of dollars" (a nice, vague round sum) and be done in 2008 *if* the money can be found.

Sources tell us that the Federal government is studying another grand scheme to wit tunneling the inner harbor for use both by CSX and Amtrak. And a Maglev demonstration proposal is afoot between Baltimore and Washington DC on an elevated track.

We can also report the demise of Rye Whiskey in Maryland, a development long overdue as this liquid is a synonym for poison. Apparently our planners have sequestered the remaining supply.

Rye, however, was still popular in 1940 when Congress considered replacing the Long Bridge with *two* tunnels (one for rail and one for trucks) and an automobile bridge over the tunnels at a cost of $15 million. The bill died in committee and the old bridge was rebuilt instead.

Another ghost bypass surfaced ca. 1900 – the Patapsco and Susquehanna Railroad. It was to leave the B&O Old Main Line at Gorsuch just east of Sykesville and run for 36 miles north of Baltimore generally along the route of the present Baltimore Beltway and rejoin B&O at Van Bibber. This plan bounced around with various permutations for many years before being laid to rest. We owe Harry C. Eck and Herbert H. Harwood, Jr., for bringing this little pearl to light. Actually, this project would have made some sense but it was not to be.

Garrett Island came into the news in early 2003. It seems that various interests wish to make the island a wildlife refuge and preserve it for its archaeological significance. There is evidence of Indian presence from 3000 to 1000 BC, which is a long time ago. The island also sits atop an ancient volcano. Let us hope that it keeps its cool.

John Snow, a figure in modern railroading and referenced in many of our books has become Secretary of the Treasury. His reign as the head of CSX has been something less than positive, to say the least, but now he has "risen to the top of the tree." If we may borrow again from *HMS Pinafore* via paraphrasing, he "never, ever, ever went to sea" and "polished up the handle on the big front door and now he is ruler of the Trea-sur-ee." Quite a Snow job.

Now let us return to Heroes. First, Will Durant. He saw history "not as a dreary scene of politics and car-

nage, but as a struggle of man through genius . . . to understand, control, and remake himself and the world." He suggests that we should "warm ourselves at the fire that consumes them." Not bad at all.

B&O, first in so many ways, also produced the first true railroad history book. "History and Description of the Baltimore and Ohio Rail Road" was written by William Prescott Smith and published in Baltimore by John Murphy & Company in 1853. Smith is buried, by the way, in Greenmount Cemetery in Baltimore a few yards from the grave of Thomas Swann. He makes reference to Charles Carroll's "if second to that" comment and describes it as an aside to a friend after the service rather than a segment of his speech. Since Carroll was "over ninety" in 1828, we will have to say that his vision was unimpaired. Smith's book was published 25 years after the event, so the reader may come to his own conclusions. For our part, we hope it is true.

It is definitely true that the 1829 ceremony was honored by a "Song for the Day." The refrain was "We're all crazy here in Baltimore." Crazy likes foxes.

ON THANKS AND APPRECIATION – Major books have heroes, too, often unsung. Christopher Baer, assistant curator of the Hagley Museum and

Library, has made so many contributions to so many books from so many publishers that he deserves the appellation "Giant" of railroad history. Unlike many of his peers, he treats all comers with an even hand and unrestrained cooperation. He is not burdened with ego and regards his mission with true professionalism. DuPont certainly can be proud of their servant, as are we.

With each succeeding volume in the monumental *Triumph* Series there emerges a few individuals who have provided support above and beyond. For this volume those deserving of special recognition are as follows: Bill Coxey, who as in previous volumes provided not only a substantial number of photos but also extensive historical and operations information to go with them, as well as answering numerous questions. Veteran photographer, author and historian Frank Wrabel generously provided photos from his large collection of early 20th Century photos and responded graciously to endless questions. Ted Xaras, also a noted historian and lecturer, again made available numerous vintage photos from his vast collection and also answered many questions, especially on the PW&B.

Others deserving mention are the following: Kurt Bell, for his assistance in plumbing the Railroad Museum of Pennsylvania archives; Jim Cassatt, who provided photos and other information from his collection on the C&PD; Lila Fourhman-Shaull, for her expertise in making available material from the archives of the York County PA Heritage Trust; Barbara Hall, for her gracious assistance with the Hagley Museum & Library photo collection; Dave Pfeiffer, for his guidance in accessing the ICC Valuation records at the National Archives and Mike Sherbon, for his assistance at the Pennsylvania State Archives.

For all of these and the many other photographers and collectors listed in the credits, our sincere appreciation for their efforts in support of this ongoing project to document the history and triumphs of the mighty PRR.

Color Tour

WE BEGIN our color journey over the Maryland Division with a farewell run – a special consist of red MP54s, still with PRR Keystones, on the West Chester Branch at Cheyney PA on 11 March 1978.

Robert L. Davis, Jr.

BLACK AND WHITE – A freshly painted Penn Central GG1 kicks up the snow as it races southward through Edgemoor DE on 19 February 1972. Superb shot, Bob!

Robert L. Davis, Jr.

377

Andrew M. Wilson

OLD AND NEW – A southbound *Acela* train flashes past the Old Swedes Cemetery
just east (railroad north) of downtown Wilmington on a sunny March day in 2002.

Andrew M. Wilson

RESTORED inside and out, the station at Wilmington shows off its granite foundation and
red terra cotta trim in April 2000. The building at right was originally the Division offices.

WE AGAIN pay tribute to the leadership and legacy of long-time PRR Chief Engineer W. H. "Stone" Brown, known for his strong advocacy of enduring masonry bridgework. This stone is located at the Wilmington station. The 1902 date reflects the beginning of the track elevation project through the city on stone piers and arches.

Andrew M. Wilson

A TRIO of new Conrail EMD SD40-2s roars past the 1878 brick station built by the PW&B at Newark DE on 10 July 1984.

John F. Born

TEN YEARS LATER a pair of AEM-7s hustles a string of Amfleet cars though Newark in January 1987.

Thomas Fuchs

BOB DAVIS captures virtually the entire length of the Susquehanna Bridge as a pair of GG1s in the stealth Conrail scheme rolls WM-4 with 64 cars northward toward Perryville on 12 June 1977.

Robert L. Davis, Jr.

PENN CENTRAL GG1 4825 rolls 75 empty hoppers northward at Milepost 14 on the C&PD Branch on a pleasant day in November 1975.

James B. Kerr

THIS VIEW of our favorite location on the C&PD shows the Safe Harbor dam and power station at the left, the Port Road right of way on the lower level and the Low Grade Line on the high trestle.

Robert L. Davis, Jr.

THE SETTING SUN and the low camera angle combine to make a dramatic shot of two Penn Central (ex-New Haven) E33s as they roll B-6 with 103 cars through Safe Harbor on 19 October 1976.

Robert L. Davis, Jr.

TWO Conrail GG1s have things well in hand as they move TH-3 with 62 cars along the frozen Susquehanna just north of Safe Harbor on a cold day in January 1977.

William J. Coxey

RETURNING to the main, Amtrak Train 176 glides through the draw span of the Susquehanna Bridge just north of Havre de Grace in November 1977.

Thomas Fuchs

RESTORED to its full glory, the waiting room of Baltimore's Penn Station glows in the winter sunlight in January 1998. Holiday lights add to the warmth of the Pentellic marble walls.

MTA light rail trains now ply the right of way where the legendary Parkton Locals once trod on the Northern Central, shown here at Jones Falls MD on 19 March 2002.

LEMO (formerly J) Tower stands sentinel at the crossing of the Cumberland Valley Branch (left to right) and the Northern Central/Low Grade Line right of way on 17 May 1972. The tower was later carefully dismantled and reassembled at the Strasburg RR in 1984.

AGAIN returning to the main, we find Amtrak B60 952 emerging from the gloom of the infamous B&P Tunnel as it approaches Penn Station in Baltimore in May 1977.

Fred W. Schneider, III

AT THE OTHER END of the tunnel there is light – a southbound Metroliner set emerges into the sunlight at Fulton in May 1977.

Fred W. Schneider, III

A SOUTHBOUND PRR GG1 is nicely framed as it approaches seldom-photographed Edmondson Station, Baltimore, on 14 October 1963.

AEM7 942 rolls a mixed consist of Heritage and Amfleet equipment through the modern BWI Station on 5 May 1984.

THE LIGHTS of an approaching Amtrak train are reflected in the windows of the Raymond Loewy-designed station at Odenton MD in May 1993.

Thomas Fuchs

AEM 913 rolls a string of Amfleet equipment through the "tunnel" of overhead and past the substation and shelter at Bowie on 5 May 1984.

Fred W. Schneider, III

HERE A MARC push-pull train of bi-level commuter coaches rolls through Seabrook in October 2001.

Thomas Fuchs

Fred W. Schneider, III

FRAMED by a PRR-era signal bridge, AEM-7 916 rolls past
another substation, this time at Landover on 5 May 1984.

Thomas Fuchs

WITH PERHAPS a touch of irony, a CSX intermodal train passes L'Enfant Plaza
as it follows the original B&P/PB&W route through Washington DC in April 2000.

William J. Coxey

BILL COXEY caught southbound Penn Central MB 117 as it passed VIRGINIA Tower on its way to Potomac Yard in October 1971. The passenger line to Union Station through the 1st Street Tunnel curves to the left.

ADAPTIVELY RESTORED to its former glory, Union Station is resplendent in the sunshine in August 1971, concluding our tour of the Maryland Division.

Dedicated to . . .

Good Taste in Design

Relevance in Philosophy

Quality in Reproduction

Consideration in Pricing

Eagerness in Service

When this House was born 30 years ago, we advertised the above Statement of Commitment as a promise to those we serve. This volume happens to be the 30th book published by us in the field of railroad history. We hope you feel that we are fulfilling our duty.

BARNARD, ROBERTS & CO., INC.
Publishers

Bibliography

BOOKS AND REPORTS

Abdill, George B., *Civil War Railroads*, Indiana University Press, Indianapolis, 1999

Alexander, Edwin P., *The Iron Horse*, Bonanza Books, New York, 1950.

Alexander, Edwin P., *The Pennsylvania Railroad – A Pictorial History*, Bonanza Books, New York, 1967.

Alexander, Edwin P., *On the Main Line – The Pennsylvania Railroad in the 19th Century*, Bramhall House, New York, 1971.

Baer, Christopher T., *Canals and Railroads of the Middle Division-Atlantic States, 1800-1860*, Regional Economic History Research Center, Eleutherian Mills-Hagley Foundation, 1981.

Bain, David H., *Empire Express – Building the First Transcontinental Railroad*, Viking Penguin, New York, 1999.

Ball, Don Jr., *The Pennsylvania Railroad – 1940s-1950s*, Elm Tree Books, Chester, VT, 1986.

Brands, H. W., *The First American*, Doubleday, New York, 2000.

Catton, Bruce, *The American Heritage New History of the Civil War*, Viking Penguin, New York, 1996.

Comstock, Henry B., *The Iron Horse*, Galahad Books, New York, 1971.

Cupper, Dan (Editor), *The Pennsylvania Railroad – Its Place in History, 1846-1996*, Philadelphia Chapter, PRRT&HS, Wayne, PA, 1996.

DeGraw, Ronald, *The Red Arrow Lines*, Haverford Press, Haverford, PA, 1972.

Dredge, James, *The Pennsylvania Railroad – Its Origin, Construction and Management*, John Wiley & Sons, London and New York, 1879.

Dubin, Arthur D., *Some Classic Trains*, Kalmbach Publishing Co., Milwaukee, 1964.

Durant, Will, *Heros of History*, Simon and Schuster, New York, 2001.

Ellis, Joseph J., *Founding Brothers – the Revolutionary Generation*, Alfred A. Knopf, New York, 2001.

Farrell, Michael W., *Who Made Our Streetcars Go*, Baltimore Chapter, NRHS, 1973.

Gamst, Frederick C., *Early American Railroads*, translation of Franz Anton Ritter von Gerstner's Die innern Communicationen (1842-1843), Stanford University Press, Stanford, California, 1997.

Garner, Timothy A., *Intergovernmental Interaction on the Reinstatement of Railroad Passenger Service to Harford County, Maryland*, Unpublished Manuscript, April 27, 1976.

Garner, Timothy A., *Amtrak's Perryville Tower*, Unpublished Manuscript, May 6, 1978.

Gay, Edward F., *Report on the Proposed Direct Rail-Road from West Chester to Philadelphia*, WC&P Acting Committee, Philadelphia, 1848.

Goodrich, Carter, *Canals and American Economic Development*, Columbia University Press, New York, 1961.

Gunnarsson, Robert L., *The Story of the Northern Central Railway*, Greenberg Publishing Company, Sykesville, MD, 1991.

Harwood, Herbert H. Jr., *Impossible Challenge II*, Barnard, Roberts & Co., Baltimore 1994.

Harwood, Herbert H. Jr., *The Royal Blue Line*, Greenburg Publishing Co., Sykesville, MD, 1990.

Jacobs, Timothy, *The History of The Pennsylvania Railroad*, Bonanza Books, Greenwich, CT, 1988.

Kelso, Fred, *Port Deposit Collections: Trade and Commerce*, Granite City Press, Port Deposit, Maryland, 1997.

Lane, Wheaton, J., *From Indian Trails to Iron Horse*, Princeton University Press.

Livingood, James W., *The Philadelphia-Baltimore Trade Rivalry 1780-1860*, Pennsylvania Historical and Museum Commission, Harrisburg, 1947.

McPherson, James M., *Battle Cry of Freedom – the Civil War Era*, Oxford University Press, New York, 1988.

Messer, David W., *Triumph II – Philadelphia to Harrisburg 1828-1998*, Barnard, Roberts & Co., Baltimore, 1999.

Messer, David W., *Triumph III – Philadelphia Terminal 1838-2000*, Barnard, Roberts & Co., Baltimore, 2000.

Messer, David W., *Triumph IV – Harrisburg to Altoona 1846-2001*, Barnard, Roberts & Co., Baltimore, 2001.

Messer, David W., and Roberts, Charles S., *Triumph V – Philadelphia to New York 1830-2002*, Baltimore, 2002.

Middleton, William D., *Landmarks on the Iron Road – Two Centuries of North American Railroad Engineering*, Indiana University Press, Bloomington, IN, 1999.

Moore, Charles (editor), *Federal and Local Legislation Relating to Canals and Steam Railroads in the District of Columbia 1802-3*, GPO, Washington, DC, 1903.

Morgan, Ted, *Wilderness at Dawn – The Settling of the North American Continent*, Simon & Schuster, New York, 1993.

Phillips, Kevin, *The Cousins' Wars – Religion, Politics and the Triumph of Anglo-America*, Basic Books, New York, 1999.

Phillips, Kevin, *Wealth and Democracy – A Political History of the American Rich*, Broadway Books, New York, 2002.

Potter, Jack C., *The Philadelphia, Wilmington and Baltimore Railroad, 1831-1840 – A Study in Early Railroad Transportation*, University of Maryland Master's Thesis, June 1960.

Righter, H. S., *Elevating Tracks of the Philadelphia, Baltimore & Washington Railroad through Wilmington, Del.*, Paper read before the Engineers' Club of Philadelphia, June 6, 1908.

Roberts, Andrew, *Napoleon and Wellington*, Simon and Schuster, New York, 2001.

Roberts, Charles S., *Sand Patch – Clash of Titans*, Barnard, Roberts & Co., Baltimore, 1993.

Roberts, Charles S., *Triumph I – Altoona to Pitcairn 1846-1997*, Barnard, Roberts & Co., Baltimore, 1997.

Roberts, Charles S., *PRR Great Photos* (Series), Book I (Milton A. Davis) 1977; Book 2 (E. L. Roberts Jr.) 1978; Book 3, (H. H. Harwood, Jr.) 1978, Book 4 (Bob Lorenz) 1979. Barnard, Roberts & Co., Baltimore MD

Schlerf, Gary W., *History of the Canton Railroad Company – Artery of Baltimore's Industrial Heartland*, The Canton Railroad Company, Baltimore, 1996.

Schotter, H.W., *The Growth and Development of The Pennsylvania Railroad Company*, Allen, Lane & Scott, Philadelphia, 1927.

Sharrer, George Terry, *Flour Milling and the Growth of Baltimore 1783-1830*, University of Maryland Doctoral Thesis, 1975.

Smith, William Prescott, *History and Description of the Baltimore and Ohio Rail Road*, John Murphy & Co., Baltimore MD, 1853.

Staufer, Alvin F., *Pennsy Power I* (1962), *II* (1968), *III* (1993), Medina, OH.

Strouse, Jean, *Morgan – American Financier*, Random House, New York, 1999.

Symonds, Craig L., *American Heritage History of the Battle of Gettysburg*, HarperCollins Publishers, New York, 2001.

Taylor, Alan, *American Colonies*, Viking Penguin, New York, 2001.

Ward, James A., *J. Edgar Thomson – Master of the Pennsylvania*, Greenwood Press, Westport, CT, 1980.

Wearmouth, John M., *Baltimore and Potomac Railroad – The Pope's Creek Branch*, Baltimore Chapter and Washington D.C. Chapter, NRHS, 1986.

Weber, Thomas, *The Northern Railroads in the Civil War, 1861-1865*, King's Crown Press, New York, 1952.

Weigley, Russell F. (Ed.), *Philadelphia – A 300-Year History*. W. W. Norton & Co., New York, 1982.

Westhaeffer, Paul J., *History of the Cumberland Valley Railroad 1835-1919*, Washington, D.C. Chapter, NRHS, 1979.

Wilson, William B., *From the Hudson to the Ohio*, Kensington Press, Philadelphia, 1902.

Wilson, William B., *History of the Pennsylvania Railroad Company*, 2 volumes, Henry T. Coates & Co., Philadelphia, 1899.

PW&B/PB&W/PRR/PC/CONRAIL PUBLICATIONS AND RECORDS

A *Minute Description of the Philadelphia, Wilmington and Baltimore Railroad*, by the railroad, Baltimore, 1850.

Annual Reports, 1856-1968.

Association of the Freight Traffic Officers of the Pennsylvania System, Vol. 11, No. 4, April, 1904.

Burgess, George H. and Kennedy, Miles C. of Coverdale & Colpitts, Consulting Engineers, *Centennial History of the Pennsylvania Railroad Company, 1846-1946*, by the railroad, Philadelphia, 1949.

Coverdale & Colpitts, Consulting Engineers, *The Pennsylvania Railroad Company*, by the railroad and press of Allen, Lane and Scott, Philadelphia, ca. 1947.

Guide Book to the West Chester and Philadelphia Railroad, by the railroad, Philadelphia, 1869.

Guide Book to the West Chester and Philadelphia Railroad, by the railroad, Philadelphia, 1876.

Guide Book and Industrial Journal of the Philadelphia, Wilmington and Baltimore Railroad, Andrew S. Brown, West Chester, PA, 1877.

Pennsylvania Railroad System – A Description of Its Main Lines and Branches with Notes of the Historical Events Which Have Taken Place in the Territory Contiguous, by the Railroad, Philadelphia, 1916.

Philadelphia, Wilmington & Baltimore Rail-Road Guide, by the railroad, Philadelphia, 1856.

Sipes, William B., *The Pennsylvania Railroad: Its Origin, Construction, Conditions and Connections*, by the railroad, Philadelphia, 1875.

Suburban Homes on the Lines of the Pennsylvania Railroad within a Radius of Thirty Miles around Philadelphia, with Useful Information for Summer-Home Seekers, by the railroad, Philadelphia, 1890.

Temple, E. B., *Pennsylvania Railroad – Philadelphia Suburban Electrification*, Paper Presented to the Washington Society of Engineers, November 1, 1927.

Watkins, John Elfreth, *History of the Pennsylvania Railroad Company 1846-1896*, 3 volumes, unpublished, ca. 1896.

Various correspondence files, reports and memos (primarily PRR Engineering Dept.), as well as CT 1000, employee timetables and other operating publications.

PERIODICALS

Delaware History: Gray, Ralph D., *The Early History of the Chesapeake and Delaware Canal*, Part 1, *Early Plans and Frustrations*, March 1959; Part 2, *Delay, Debate and Relocation*, September 1959; Part 3, *Completion of the Canal*.

The High Line, Philadelphia Chapter, PRRT&HS, various issues and especially the following:

Brubaker, Robert D., *The Station at Ridley Park*, Winter 1993.

Brubaker, Robert D., *Wawa*, Part 1, Summer 1992, Part 2, Autumn, 1992.

Giannantonio, Al, *The Philadelphia Electric Coal Train*, Spring, 2002.

Hall, Richard E., *The Elkton & Middletown Railroad Co. of Cecil County*, Autumn 2002.

Klaus, Philip W. Jr. et al, *The Newtown Square Branch*, Part I, Winter 1986-7; Part II, Summer 1987 (Reprinted Winter 1991-2).

Lynch, James J. D., Jr., *The West Chester Branch*, Winter-Spring 1988.

Moore, Paul, *The Origin of the West Chester Railroad Company (1830-31)*, Spring, 2002.

Ormsby, George D., *The Chester Creek Railroad*, August 1999.

Russell, William W., *Operations on the Chester Creek Branch*, August 1999.

Small, Melvyn, E., *The Pomeroy and Newark Railroad, "The Pumpsie Doodle,"* Autumn-Winter 1990.

Whitley, Louis S., *Octoraro Odyssey*, Vol. 6, Nos. 3 and 4, Vol. 7, No. 1.

Journal of the Franklin Institute: Strickland, William, *Address upon a proposed Rail-Road from Wilmington to the Susquehanna, together with a Report of Survey made by William Strickland, Esq., Architect and Engineer*, April 1835.

The Keystone, PRRT&HS, various issues and especially the following:

Denney, John D., Jr., *Columbia on the Pennsy*, Autumn, 1994.

Frantz, Ivan E. Jr., *The PRR's Frederick Branch*, Spring 2000.

Pitz, George L., *The Baltimore Division, Revisited*, Summer 1998.

Wrabel, Frank A., *Remembering the Parkton Local*, Winter 2001.

Wrabel, Frank A., *Terminals, Tunnels and Turmoil – The History of Pennsylvania Station, Baltimore*, Spring 1995

Milepost, Friends of the Railroad Museum of Pennsylvania, various issues and especially the following:

Denney, John. D., Jr., *The Bridge . . . We Burned It*, October 1999.

Denney, John D., Jr., *A Glimpse of the Olden Days on the Philadelphia & Columbia*, December 2001.

The Mutual Magazine, various issues and especially the following:

Dubois, Howard B., *Reminiscences of the Susquehanna River Bridge*, February 1927.

Bulletin of the National Railway Historical Society, various issues and especially the following:

The Railroad Gazette, various issues and especially the following:

    Electric Interlocking at Wilmington, Vol. XXXV, No. 10, June 6, 1903.

    The Washington Union Station, Vol. XXXV, No. 49, December 4, 1903.

    Track Plan for the Washington Union Station, Vol. XXXVI, No. 8, January 15, 1904.

    New Shops of the P., B. & W. at Wilmington, Vol. XXXVI, No. 11, March 11, 1904.

    The Fairview Yard, Northern Central and PRR, Vol. XXXVI, No. 16, April 15, 1904.

    Progress on the Washington Terminal, Vol. XXXVI, No. 23, June 3, 1904.

    Improvements on the Philadelphia, Baltimore & Washington Railroad, Vol. XXXVII, No. 17, October 7, 1904.

    New Yards and Terminal Approaches at Washington, D. C., Vol. XXXVII, No. 22, November 11, 1904.

    Opening of the Washington Union Station, Vol. XLIII, No. 45, November 1, 1907.

Railway Age/Gazette, various issues and especially the following:

    Wilmington Passenger Station, Vol. XLV, No. 8, July 24, 1908.

    Pennsylvania Station at Baltimore, Vol. XLVIII, No.14, April 8, 1910.

    Bush Train Shed at Baltimore, Vol. 50, No. 2, January 13, 1911.

    New Susquehanna River Bridge at Harrisburg, Vol. 60, No. 11, March 17, 1916.

    An Improved Grain Elevator for Export Service, Vol. 69, No. 1, July 2, 1920.

    Station Named after Dean of Conductors, Vol. 77, No. 18, November 1, 1924.

    Heavy Work Features Line Relocation on the Pennsylvania, Vol. 84, No. 21, May 26, 1928.

    Pennsylvania Builds Large Modern Marine Pier at Baltimore, Vol. 97, No. 25, December 22, 1934.

    Pennsylvania Builds Large Double-Track Tunnel at Baltimore, Vol. 98, No. 15, April 13, 1935.

    Pennsylvania Completes Many Improvements at Baltimore, Vol. 98, No. 18, May 4, 1935.

Railroad & Locomotive Historical Society Bulletin, various issues and especially the following:

    Fisher, Charles, E., *The Philadelphia, Wilmington & Baltimore Railroad Company*, No. 21, March 1930.

    Parker, George A., *The Susquehanna Bridge on the Philadelphia, Wilmington, and Baltimore Railroad*, No. 134, Spring 1976.

Railway Maintenance Engineer, various issues and especially the following:

    Enlarging a Busy Tunnel Under Traffic, May, 1917.

Rails Northeast, various issues and especially the following:

    Frevert, Edward, *The Pope's Creek Secondary*, March, 1982.

    Van Horn, Martin K., *The Northern Central Railway*, March 1979.

    Walton, Al, *Bottleneck in Baltimore – The History and Operation of the B&P and Union Tunnels*, August 1978.

Amtrak Northeast Corridor – 1981 Division Control (Track Diagrams), March 1981.

    Northeast Corridor (Track Diagrams), Part I, January 1978, Part II, February 1978, Part III, March 1978, Part IV, April 1978, Part V, May 1978.

    Pennsylvania Railroad Profile – New York to Washington, September 1979.

Railway Review, various issues and especially the following:

    A Great Bridge at Havre de Grace, Md., Vol. XXIII, November 24, 1883.

Railway Signaling, various issues and especially the following:

    Coded Track-Circuit Signaling on the Pennsylvania, May 1935.

    Pennsylvania C.T.C. Installation, December 1937.

Signal Engineer, various issues and especially the following:

    Toft, Guy, *Signaling the Union R. R. of Baltimore*, Vol. 8, No. 7, July 1915.

    New Signaling at Washington, D. C., Vol. 4, No. 7, July 1911.

    Union Station Interlocking at Baltimore, Vol. 6, No. 5, May 1913.

Time Magazine, *The Pennsy's Predicament*, March 1948.

Trains Magazine, various issues and especially the following:

    Moedinger, William Jr., *Blueprint Railroad*, June 1943

    Westing, Frederick: *GG1*, March, 1964.

MISCELLANEOUS

Hydroelectric Power Development of the Susquehanna Valley, Pennsylvania Water & Power Company, Holtwood, PA, 1948.

Ice and Floods – Holtwood and Safe Harbor, March 1936, Pennsylvania Water & Power Company/Safe Harbor Water Power Corporation, Baltimore, 1936.

New Locust Point Grain Elevator, Baltimore, MD., Baltimore and Ohio Railroad Company, Engineering Department, Office of Chief Engineer, Baltimore, Md., May 24, 1926.

Report on the Sparrows Point Branch, Baltimore and Ohio Railroad Company, Operating Department, Office of General Manager, Baltimore, Md., July 19, 1911.

The Pennsylvania Railroad Electrification, Westinghouse Electric & Manufacturing Co. East Pittsburgh, PA.

Credit for certain material such as maps, track diagrams, photographs and specific sources are given throughout the volume.

Index _____

Jim Shaughnessy

We get a close look at two magnificent GG1s at Ivy City Engine Terminal – 4874 in
classic pinstripes and 4905 in the later single-stripe scheme. The date is 18 June 1960.

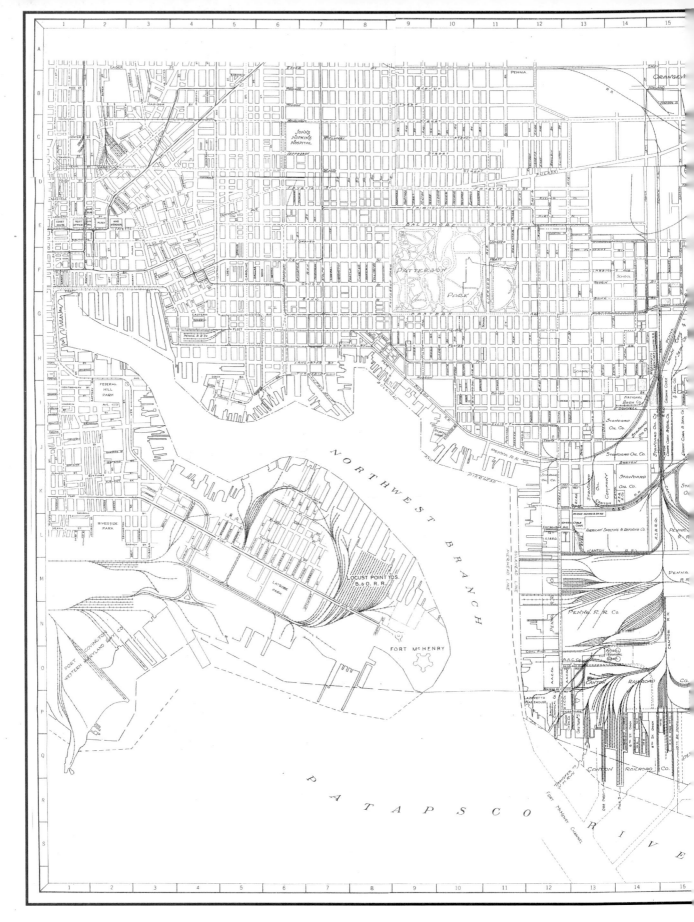

THIS SUPERB MAP – the best we have found for its clarity in depicting the Baltimore harbor area –
was published in 1948 by the Canton Company to show the pier and rail facilities serving the Canton
(PRR, B&O, Canton Co.), Locust Point (B&O) and Port Covington (WM) marine terminal areas.
This period represents the culmination of the extensive development of the grain and coal loading
facilities that was initiated during the 1920s and prior to the rebuilding of the ore piers, yards and other